D0931333

The Social Psychology of
Bargaining and Negotiation

The Social Psychology of Bargaining and Negotiation

Jeffrey Z. Rubin

Department of Psychology
Tufts University
Medford, Massachusetts

Bert R. Brown

Department of Psychology
Rutgers University
New Brunswick, New Jersey

With a Foreword by Morton Deutsch

ACADEMIC PRESS
A SUBSIDIARY OF HARCOURT BRACE JOVANOVICH, PUBLISHERS
New York   London   Toronto   Sydney   San Francisco

The following is a list of pages incorporating excerpted material reprinted from the Journal of Conflict Resolution by permission of the publisher, Sage Publications, Inc.:

p. 114: from V. Edwin Bixenstine *et al.*, Collaboration among six persons in a prisoner's dilemma game, *Journal of Conflict Resolution*, Dec. 1966, x (No. 4) 488-496.

p. 7, 28, 46, 47, 59, 60, 94, 110, 132, from Morton Deutsch and Robert M. Krauss, Studies of interpersonal bargaining, *Journal of Conflict Resolution*, March 1962, 6 (No. 1), 52-76.

p. 49: from Robert B. McKersie *et al.*, Intraorganizational bargaining in labor negotiations, *Journal of Conflict Resolution*, Dec., 1965, 9 (No. 4), 463-481.

ACADEMIC PRESS, INC.
111 Fifth Avenue, New York, New York 10003

United Kingdom Edition published by
ACADEMIC PRESS, INC. (LONDON) LTD.
24/28 Oval Road, London NW1

Library of Congress Cataloging in Publication Data

Rubin, Jeffrey Z
    The social psychology of bargaining and negotia-
tion.

        Bibliography: p.
        Includes index.
        1.   Negotiation.   I.   Brown, Bert R., joint au-
thor.   II.   Title.
BF637.N4R76   301.6'4   74-30810
ISBN 0-12-601250-4

PRINTED IN THE UNITED STATES OF AMERICA
    82   9 8 7 6 5

Contents

Preface

Late in the fall of 1968, after a hiatus of several years, we chanced to meet one evening in a local Manhattan haunt renowned for its oriental cuisine. Over shrimp roll, dumplings, and a magnificent poached fish, the dinner conversation turned to the world of work, and it soon emerged that each of us had been separately contemplating the prospect of writing a monograph on the social psychology of bargaining. Out of this exotic first encounter, and the "bargaining" between us that ensued, this book has come. The order of authorship we have chosen is in no way meant to indicate anything about the quality of our respective contributions to this enterprise. We seriously doubt that either of us would have undertaken the task of writing this book had it not been for the inspiration, prodding, and continued support of the other.

The world is teeming with real and eventful illustrations of bargaining. During the year of 1974 alone, when the manuscript was completed, a host of events—ranging in scope from the wars in Cyprus and the Middle East, to the impeachment and resignation of the President, to the increasing number of divorce proceedings and the countless small- and large-scale disputes between labor and management—probably took the particular course they did partially because of the ubiquitous process known as bargaining.

Despite the omnipresence and importance of bargaining in the lives of all of us, there have been surprisingly few attempts to summarize and interpret the state of the art. Of course, recent years have seen an increasing number of books and articles that have reviewed important segments of the bargaining literature. Particularly noteworthy in this regard are the review articles by Apfelbaum (1974), Hamner (1974), Oskamp (1971), Rapoport (1968), and Terhune (1970), as well as books by Deutsch (1973), Krivohlavý (1974), and Wrightsman, O'Connor, and Baker (1972). These fine contributions notwithstanding, this book represents perhaps the first attempt to present an extensive overview and analysis of the research in this area.

That researchers and theoreticians have found the area of bargaining important and worthy of their attention is attested to by the fact that more than 1000 different articles and books have been devoted to the subject since 1960 alone! Indeed, the very immensity of the bargaining literature has necessitated some decision on our part with respect to the inclusion or omission of material. To this end, our review is based primarily on the findings of the social psychological laboratory studies that have been reported in approximately 40 journals from 1960 through the spring of 1974. In addition to these papers, more than 500 of which are discussed throughout the book, numerous other articles and books have been cited in the bibliography, yielding what we believe is a fairly comprehensive (1000 entry) listing of the bargaining literature.

We have written this book with an eye and ear toward a variety of audiences, ranging from practitioners and professionals to researchers like ourselves. While the vantage point from which we have approached the material is that of the experimental social psychologist, we believe that students and professionals in other such diverse disciplines as economics, law, business administration, management, and sociology will find our presentation interesting and germane as well.

The many ideas over which we have labored so long in preparing this volume would never have reached fruition were it not for the support, insight, and generosity of a great many people. Foremost among these is Morton Deutsch, our mentor, colleague, and friend, who has been a source of both confidence and wisdom. We are also indebted to John W. Thibaut, without whose early encouragement this project might never have begun.

A great many of our colleagues have agreed to read and critically comment upon earlier drafts of the manuscript, and in so doing have provided us with invaluable intellectual assistance. We therefore extend our sincere thanks to Norman Berkowitz, Yakov Epstein, Lorenz Finison, Roy Lewicki, Robert McKersie, Steven Schiavo, Leonard Solomon, and Walter Swap. We also wish to acknowledge Carolyn Arbetter, Donnah Decker, M. Robin DiMatteo, and Martin Greller for their help in abstracting the voluminous literature.

Finally, To Carol, David, and Joslin, our parents, as well as those few others who are near to our hearts and affection, we lovingly dedicate this book.

Foreword

The world is entering into a difficult era in which growing demands and diminishing resources will increase the frequency and intensity of conflicts between individuals, groups, and nations. Yet it is evident from the many tragic episodes in this century of deadly quarrels, violent racial and tribal strife, and destructive civil and international wars that we know little about how to cope with conflict constructively. It is urgent that we develop more systematic knowledge about the processes of dealing with conflict, including those of bargaining and negotiation. The development of such knowledge will not only need original thought and research by many scholars in different disciplines, it will also require creative efforts to bring together and integrate into a coherent pattern the diverse bits of knowledge emerging from the investigations of individual scholars.

The present book is an integrative survey of the work that has been done in social psychology on the processes of bargaining and negotiation, one of the social science disciplines that has been most active in conducting research in this problem area. Such an integrative survey is sorely needed. There has been a proliferation of research by many different investigators, employing diverse approaches and concepts. Even those who have been active researchers in this area have found it difficult to keep up with the work being done by others.

I am delighted and proud to have learned a good deal from reading this book written by two of my former students. Although it will be apparent to any reader that the book has been influenced by my theoretical and research studies, it will also be evident that the authors have developed their own integrative framework which is responsive to the scholarship of many other social psychologists working in the area of bargaining and negotiation. It is a book that will be useful not only to scholars in social psychology but also to those in other social science disciplines who seek a good overview of the work in social psychology on bargaining and negotiation. And, personally, I shall be delighted to use it in the courses I teach on conflict resolution as a text to supplement my own recent book (Deutsch, 1973) dealing with my work in this area. It will give me special pleasure to have my present and future students learn from the work of my former students.

Morton Deutsch

The Social Psychology of Bargaining and Negotiation

1

Introduction

Bargaining and *negotiation* are words that appear with considerable frequency in our daily lives. We informally describe those stores or parts of stores in which goods may be purchased at unexpectedly low prices as "bargain basements." We read about "bargaining tables," "plea bargaining," "negotiated treaties," and "negotiated settlements." Indeed, the mass media daily report the proceedings of so many diverse bargaining and negotiation episodes that the mere enumeration and categorization of these episodes appears extraordinarily difficult.

This difficulty is perhaps indicative of the gradual emergence of bargaining and negotiation as major mechanisms of conflict resolution in our society. Students bargain with university administrators, husbands with wives, clients with attorneys, attorneys with judges, unions with management, nations with one another. This is not to say, of course, that conflicts are resolved exclusively through bargaining and negotiation. Numerous other techniques have been employed, including a variety of legal procedures, joint problem-solving efforts, the creation of third party roles, and of course violence. It is nevertheless clear that bargaining and negotiation have been, are, and will no doubt continue to be employed in an increasing number and range of conflict situations.

What then is meant by these two terms, which comprise the framework for our inquiry? The following dictionary definitions are of some help:

> **to bargain:** to negotiate over the terms of a purchase, agreement, or
>   contract . . . to establish an agreement between parties settling

> what each shall give and take or perform and receive in a transaction
> between them.
>
> **to negotiate:** to deal or bargain with another or others . . . to confer
> with another so as to arrive at the settlement of some matter.

It can be seen that the two terms are defined in nearly equivalent fashion. Whether one is engaged in bargaining or in negotiation, at least one other party must be involved; the parties must be engaged in some form of transaction or interaction; and the purpose of this transaction must be to arrive at the settlement of some matter or issue. Given these defined similarities, we propose to treat the terms *bargaining* and *negotiation* as synonymous throughout the book. This is in spite of the fact that we occasionally make a distinction between them when using the terms in our daily lives.

In general usage, the term *bargaining* often seems to refer to the interaction between individuals over some sale or purchase. *Negotiation,* on the other hand, seems to be used primarily in connection with interaction involving complex social units (e.g., unions, nations, etc.) and, usually, multiple issues. We talk about bargaining when we describe the proceedings at a used car lot, flea market, or fruit stand—while negotiation seems to be more often reserved for a description of attempts at merger among industrial giants, attempts at the resolution of labor–management disputes, or the establishment of international peace talks and treaties. Despite these and other differences in everyday usage, we will treat the terms as interchangeable. This is consonant with the positions taken in various authoritative treatises on collective bargaining (Chamberlain, 1965; Cullen, 1965) and international negotiation (Iklé, 1964; Schelling, 1960). Furthermore, since most of the experimental work in this area has been referred to as bargaining research, we will make almost exclusive use of the term *bargaining* throughout the book.

In keeping with dictionary definitions, we may now define *bargaining* as *the process whereby two or more parties attempt to settle what each shall give and take, or perform and receive, in a transaction between them.* We recognize that this definition, like many definitions, is so general as to be of limited usefulness. It states what bargaining is but not what it is about. A more informative characterization of the bargaining relationship is presented in the next chapter.

But why, after all, devote a book to an examination of the social psychology of bargaining? First of all, we see a need for a review and integration of the increasingly massive research literature in this area. Over the course of the last decade, hundreds of experimental studies of bargaining have appeared in journals of psychology and related disciplines. The analysis and integration of this work seems a necessary if not sufficient step in pointing the way to further experimentation and theory development.

Second, and perhaps in partial explanation of the enormous popularity of bargaining research, we consider bargaining to be of direct relevance to the world of everyday events. As husbands, wives, citizens, consumers, employers and employees, as the occupants of an enormous range and variety of roles, interdependent with others in numerous and complex ways, we are often engaged in some form of bargaining. An acquaintance with the dynamics of this complex process may, we believe, facilitate a more systematic understanding of people's many, highly varied day-to-day activities.

Finally, and perhaps most important, an examination of the bargaining process may provide a useful lens through which to analyze a wide variety of complex social relationships. Bargaining is a cardinal illustration of social interaction. It is no more possible or sensible to discuss the psychology of a single bargainer in the absence of his partner than it is to attempt a description of the sound of one-handed clapping. Bargainers need each other. They do things to and with each other. Neither can hope to satisfy his individual needs and interests without in some way taking account of the fact that his relationship with the other is one of mutuality and interdependence. Agreement cannot be reached without the consent and active involvement of both sides. The bargaining relationship is thus a microcosm within which many of the causes and consequences of social interaction and interdependence may be fruitfully examined.

Most generally we view bargaining as a subset of those social relationships concerned with the resolution of conflict. Conflict is a state that exists whenever incompatible activities occur. Depending on whether those activities originate within or between individuals, groups, or nations, they may be described as intrapersonal, interpersonal, intragroup, intergroup, intranational, or international conflicts (Deutsch, 1973). It is our contention that regardless of origin, the resolution of conflict at each of these levels may be described in terms of bargaining processes. Most of the bargaining research within the last decade or so has focused on the resolution of interpersonal, especially dyadic, conflict, and to a lesser extent on intragroup and intergroup conflicts. In keeping with this research emphasis, the analysis presented in this book is primarily concerned with bargaining at each of these three levels.

We have attempted to plan the structure and flow of the book to fit with our rationale for writing it. Chapter 2 informally describes some of the general characteristics of bargaining relationships, citing examples of intergroup, intragroup, and interpersonal conflict as illustrations of the range and complexity of the processes under analysis. These illustrations are considered in terms of a number of structural and social psychological features which we believe are common to all true bargaining relationships.

Chapter 3 provides an introductory overview of social psychological approaches to the study of bargaining. Several of the major research paradigms used to examine the bargaining process are briefly described, as are the dependent and independent variables typically employed in these paradigms.

Chapters 4 through 9 represent the core of the book. It is here that the task of reviewing and integrating the massive bargaining literature has been undertaken. In these five chapters we attempt to develop several important theoretical issues, to use them as guides for an extensive review and integration of the relevant research literature, and to examine illustrative examples and applications, whenever appropriate. The "real world" abounds with accounts of bargaining and negotiation processes. We believe that reference to such accounts serves the important function of continually reminding the reader of the inextricable relatedness of the worlds of research and reality.

Finally, in the last chapter of the book, Chapter 10, we present a few afterthoughts: some questions suggestive of future research in bargaining, as well as brief consideration of several experimental and theoretical issues of a more general nature.

2

The Bargaining Relationship

Consider the following situations:

Situation (A)

A struggling, young, upwardly mobile fellow (let's refer to him as Mike) decides the time has come to part with his battered old car in favor of a more sophisticated and impressive vehicle. While not impoverished, Mike has limited assets and (like each of us) is concerned with securing a product which is optimally efficient, attractive, and reliable at the lowest possible price. After due consideration of the various courses of action open to him, Mike decides to trade in his car for a newer and better model. With his checkbook in his pocket, and a grimace on his face, he sets off for his friendly neighborhood used car lot.

Situation (B)

A family is planning a two-week August vacation and is trying to decide where to go. The boy would like very much to spend the entire time in Cooperstown, New York, paying homage to his favorite baseball idols. His sister would like to visit grandmother, who lives in another part of the country and makes nifty tollhouse cookies. Mom dreams of the boutiques and soirees of "gay Paree," while Dad would like nothing better than to stay at home, sleep, watch television, and play golf. Having somehow managed in the course of their busy lives to avoid discussing their individual trip preferences, the family convenes one evening for what turns out to be a rather strenuous exercise in joint vacation planning (a family council).

Situation (C)

The teachers union of a large city has asked the local board of education for certain across-the-board increases in pay and fringe benefits. The board has refused to meet these (what it considers) excessive demands, and has made an offer which the union leadership considers unacceptable. Having failed to come to some agreement by midnight of the day before school is to open, the union votes to go on strike, and to remain on strike until a satisfactory agreement is reached.

These three situations, diverse as they may appear to be, share a number of important features. Each illustrates a different level of conflict—(A) being interpersonal, (B) intragroup, and (C) intergroup. Despite these differences, all three situations have the distinctive markings of a bargaining relationship—a relationship which may be informally described in terms of a number of prominent features.

STRUCTURAL AND SOCIAL PSYCHOLOGICAL CHARACTERISTICS OF BARGAINING RELATIONSHIPS

1. At least two parties are involved. They may be individuals, as in situations (A) and (B); small groups, as, for example, in a game of bridge; or larger, more complex social units, as in situation (C) and as in international diplomacy.

2. The parties have a conflict of interest with respect to one or more different issues. Where a single issue is at stake, the parties may be expected to have conflicting preferences for the different agreements that are within reach. Where several issues are at stake, the conflict of interest will be represented as a difference in the order of importance given by the parties to the issues involved.

(A) In Mike's case, the primary issue he and the used car salesman must confront is the value to each of a final "deal." A trade that Mike might view as being in his best interest would most probably be seen by the salesman as exploitative, unfair, outrageous, etc. And conversely, of course, a profitable deal for the salesman might spell financial hardship for Mike. What we have here is a classical bargaining problem, discussed by Siegel and Fouraker (1960) in their description of buyer–seller relationships, in which "one man's meat is another man's poison." This is true, of course, only to the extent that Mike and the salesman view their conflict of interest as lying along a single dimension of "final value." They might, however, choose to treat their transaction as concerned with *two* related but independent issues: first the value of Mike's jalopy and second, the value of the car acquired from the salesman.

(**B**) Now consider the family. Their conflict of interest is, on the surface, rather straightforward. It focuses on the issue of vacation preference, about which there is clear disagreement. Given that the four individual trip preferences are the only ones possible, and given that only one of the four trips can be made within the limited time available, the situation confronting these bargainers is much like that of our buyer and seller: a "win" for one party represents a "loss" for each of the other three. On the other hand, to the extent that more than one trip is seen as possible, and to the extent that new compromise proposals are viable, the nature of the bargaining problem is changed accordingly.

(**C**) Finally, consider the teachers union–board of education dispute. The conflict of interest may be initially focused about a single primary issue (such as the teacher's pay), but almost certainly there are several additional issues over which bargaining must develop (such as retirement benefits, sick leave, increase in the number of teachers, etc.). In a situation as complex as this, we might well expect the teachers union and the board of education to have different importance orderings for the several issues at stake. Thus, the union might attach particular significance to the issue of sick leave, viewing the issue of number of teachers with relative indifference. The board, on the other hand, might take a relatively intransigent position with respect to the second issue, while being willing to make certain concessions over the first.

3. *Regardless of the existence of prior experience or acquaintance with one another, the parties are at least temporarily joined together in a special kind of voluntary relationship.* The most important word in the above statement is the word *voluntary*. For bargaining to exist, the parties must believe they are participants by choice rather than by compulsion. Each is thus confronted with *two* important and related kinds of choices.

At a first, most basic level, each bargainer must choose whether or not to enter into and remain in this special relationship with the other. In making this choice, each must decide whether he expects to gain more by bargaining than would be possible in its absence. Deutsch and Krauss (1962) describe this feature as follows: "Both parties perceive that there is the possibility of reaching an agreement in which each party would be better off, or no worse off, than if no agreement is reached [p. 52]." Each party, to borrow one of Thibaut and Kelley's (1959) important theoretical constructs, must believe he is above his "comparison level for alternatives" (CL_{alt})—where CL_{alt} is defined as "the standard the member uses in deciding whether to remain in or to leave the relationship . . . the lowest level of outcomes a member will accept in the light of available alternative opportunities [p. 21]." Thus, in order for bargaining to occur, the parties must believe that there is more to lose than to gain by *not* interacting with the other.

At a second level, not only must each party be able to choose when to enter and for how long to remain in a relationship with the other, but each must be able to choose which of several possible agreements to ask for and which (if any) ultimately to accept. In bargaining relationships, more than one agreement can be reached. It is the push for one agreement rather than another that represents the second kind of critical choice available to each party. Each must believe that somewhere among the array of possible alternative solutions to the conflict of interest there exists at least one with which he will be satisfied (one which is of optimal "utility"). Each party—to borrow another of Thibaut and Kelley's (1959) notions—must expect to be above his "comparison level" (CL), where CL is defined as "a neutral point on a scale of satisfaction–dissatisfaction [p. 81]." It is "the standard against which the member evaluates the 'attractiveness' of the relationship or how satisfactory it is [p. 21]." Thus, to say that bargaining parties expect to be above their CL is to say that each enters the proceedings expecting to reach an agreement with which he will be at least minimally satisfied. Of course, the final agreement reached may well turn out to be less satisfactory than either or both of the parties had originally expected; we would nevertheless argue that for bargaining to exist, the parties must enter the relationship believing that they have more to gain than to lose in interaction with the other.

(A) Consider Mike's situation. We may assume he enters the used car lot expecting to reach an agreement with the salesman with which he will be satisfied. Related to this first point is the assumption that Mike would not have come to trade in his car at this particular lot if he really believed he could get a better deal elsewhere. In the course of the proceedings, Mike may be expected to push for one agreement rather than another. If, in response, the salesman proposes a settlement that Mike considers unsatisfactory, Mike can either (a) leave the relationship and bargain elsewhere or (b) threaten to do so (e.g., "If you don't give me a better deal, I'll leave and peddle my wares someplace else"). The latter option represents a not unimportant bargaining strategy Mike might elect to employ. It is a strategy that makes sense, particularly if Mike and the salesman are strangers to each other—that is, to the extent that the salesman has little or no knowledge of how likely Mike is to carry out his threat. Prior experience or acquaintance with each other would surely mitigate the effectiveness of a threat strategy, and indeed it would dramatically alter the form the bargaining relationship might take.

(B) The choices available to the family are somewhat different. Inasmuch as they are members of a group that will continue to function after their trip is planned and taken, they cannot (or will not) withdraw from their ongoing relationship. Furthermore, any such threat (e.g., "I'll sue for divorce unless you go where I choose" or "I'll run away unless we go to Grandmother's house") would probably be seen by the other family members as noncredible or inappropriate. Nevertheless, to the extent that each views the alternatives to bargaining as sufficiently unattractive (e.g., "You didn't take part in the decision-making process, therefore you have no say in where we go"), we may consider participation in the "council" proceedings to be voluntary. Each party is thus above his CL_{alt}. In addition, while permanent departure from the relationship is improbable or impossible, each can choose whether or not to leave temporarily. Thus, the son, upon seeing that the bargaining is developing in such a way as to make a trip to Cooperstown highly unlikely, could threaten to "have a tantrum and run screaming from the room" unless the negotiations take a more favorable turn. While such a choice lacks the decisive, definitive quality it has in other, less constrained relationships (such as that of Mike and the salesman), we would argue that it must, at least in principle, be available to each party if their relationship is to be viewed as a bargaining one.

At a second level, it is clear that more than one agreement can be reached by our family. There are, in fact, at least four agreements possible, corresponding to each family member's trip preference. In addition, there exists the more complex possibility of tradeoff agreements (e.g., "We'll go to Paris this year, but we'll take a weekend trip to Cooperstown when we get back"). In any case, we may expect each of the four members to enter the family council hoping (if not completely expecting) to take the special trip he or she has in mind. If it turned out that the daughter, for example, really believed that a trip to Grandmothers's was out of the question, she would either (a) refuse to attend the council (an unlikely but possible alternative), (b) attend and have nothing to say, or (c) form some kind of alliance with one of the other three family members. Thus, we argue that for bargaining to occur each party must enter the proceedings expecting to reach an agreement with which he will be satisfied—or, at the least, believing he is capable of preventing the other parties from fully achieving their goals.

(C) Finally, consider the teacher dispute. We may expect poststrike negotiations to begin and to continue only to the extent that representatives of the teachers union and the board of education believe that they are better off interacting across a bargaining table than they would be otherwise. The example we have cited in this third situation is, of course, of considerable complexity, and in this analysis we propose to do little more than highlight certain of its prominent features. The complexity inherent in this situation may be illustrated by pointing to the two rather different levels at which bargaining choices occur. We may describe the bargaining relationship as having begun at the point when the teachers union demanded across-the-board increases in pay for their membership. The board refused to meet these demands, and the union leadership was then confronted with its first choice—whether to accept the board's counterproposals or to leave the relationship. They chose the latter and elected to strike. Thus, bargaining occurred even before the strike materialized. The second choice in the bargaining relationship is represented by the point at which the parties decide whether or not to resume and remain in negotiation with each other. Implicit in the resumption of negotiations is each party's expectation that a satisfactory agreement can be reached. It may, of course, turn out that the final settlement is not completely satisfactory (even unsatisfactory) to both the teachers union and the board of education. However, to the extent that each believes there is more to lose than to gain by not coming to an agreement, the conflict(s) of interest can be resolved.

The above analysis of the bargaining relationship as a voluntary one can perhaps be described more generally by stating that the parties have *mixed motives* toward one another. While their interests are partly in conflict, *there must exist some degree of commonality of interest for bargaining to occur.* As Kelley and Thibaut (1969) write: "If the interests are totally congruent, there is nothing to bargain for; and if they are totally opposed, there is no basis for bargaining [p. 44]." Thus, the parties' interests must be sufficiently divergent to warrant interaction, and, at the same time, sufficiently convergent to permit it. If each party's interests and those the other is perceived to have do not fall within this spectrum, bargaining cannot take place.

4. *Activity in the relationship concerns (a) the division or exchange of one or more specific resources and/or (b) the resolution of one or more intangible issues among the parties or among those whom they represent.* The upshot of bargaining activity is that each party receives some outcome. And it is a critical characteristic of bargaining activity that these outcomes be interdependent. Thus, each party must, at least in part, be dependent on the other for the quality of the outcomes which he, himself, receives. Their relationship, as Thibaut and Kelley (1959) express this characteristic, must be one of "outcome dependence." We may further describe this aspect of the parties' interdependence by stating that, for bargaining to occur, the outcomes each party can receive (be they a portion of allocated resources or concessions on some intangible issue) must be partially noncorrespondent with those of the other. Consider the extreme cases: Were the parties' outcomes completely correspondent (as would be the case when whatever benefited A invariably benefited B as well), bargaining would be unnecessary. On the other hand, were outcomes completely noncorrespondent (as would be the case when a gain for A invariably resulted in a loss for B), bargaining would be impossible. Thus, bargaining occurs when outcomes are partially noncorrespondent (or partially correspondent, if you prefer); when interaction is both necessary and possible; when, at least initially, a gain for one party is equivalent to a loss for the other.

As a consequence of their outcome dependence, the parties are confronted with what Kelley (1966) has referred to as the "dilemma of goals." Each would like to reach an agreement which places him above his own CL. In pushing for such an agreement, he must chart a course between two risks: On the one hand, in driving too hard for an agreement which maximizes his own gain (in being too "tough"), he may provide the other party with so unsatisfactory an outcome that the other refuses to settle or leaves the relationship (i.e., falls below his CL_{alt}). On the other hand, in not driving hard enough for a preferred agreement (in being too "soft"), each may end up providing the other with too good an outcome, thereby settling for less than necessary. In resolving this dilemma, each party must decide on a reasonable settlement—one which will yield the most for him while, at the same time, having a good chance of being acceptable to the other side. Thus, each party must seek a solution to the bargaining problem (the "minimax solution") that represents the best he can obtain in the face of the other's opposition.

(A) The activity in Mike's relationship with the used car salesman concerns the exchange of one resource (Mike's car) for another (the "new" used car). Outcome dependence in this relationship is reflected in the fact that each party needs the cooperation of the other in order to do well. Furthermore, since a good deal (a win) for one party is generally equivalent to a loss for the other (i.e., since outcomes are partially noncorrespondent), each must carefully strategize a settlement which is maximally satisfactory to himself while at the same time being at least minimally satisfactory to the other. The salesman, for example, needs to propose a settlement to Mike which is sufficiently attractive to "close the deal," while at the same time maximizing his own profits in the transaction. Stated somewhat differently, the salesman runs two risks in proposing any single agreement: first by pushing Mike too hard, he may drive him away, thereby losing the very business he seeks; on the other hand, by not pushing hard enough, he may give Mike too good a deal, thereby settling for less than he could really get.

(B) The bargaining activity in the family council is likely to be somewhat more complex than that described in Mike's relationship. At one level, a rather tangible issue is being discussed: namely, where to go. The decision reached represents an allocation of resources (the time and money set aside for vacation) based on the initial trip preferences of the four parties. There is a second level, however, at which we might expect activity to occur. This concerns the resolution of such intangible issues as the locus of power within the relationship ("who wears the pants in the family"), the saving or loss of "face," and so forth. It appears to be generally characteristic of most bargaining relationships that, even when the division of tangible resources is the primary focus of activity, intangibles such as self-esteem, honor, or principle become intimately involved. We merely cite the illustration of the family (a relationship which is both ongoing and replete with potential power struggles) as a highlighted, sharply etched case of a more general phenomenon. Consider, for example, the conflict of interest as seen from the son's vantage point. At one level, the goal of his bargaining activity is the trip to Cooperstown, a trip he no doubt believes would be enjoyable. At a second level, however, we might suppose that his efforts are more subtly focused on his ability to influence his parents and his sister in the direction he chooses. The son might well view the very bargaining activity itself as constituting one in a series of ongoing tests, a test of his power in relation to the other members of the family; perhaps even a test of his parents' love for him. Thus, he is interested not only in the outcome of the family council, but also in the process by which a decision is reached. It is not at all unlikely that he (as well as each of the other family members) views the process and outcomes of the bargaining activity as having considerable symbolic significance, the council being an arena in which subtle alliances are formed and broken, in which battles are waged, won, and lost, in which true feelings cannot help but emerge.

As described above, each member of this family is dependent on the behavior of the other three for the quality of both the tangible and intangible outcomes he or she receives. In a situation as complex as this, we may expect each party to view the "dilemma of goals" as both very difficult and very important to resolve. There are, after all, *two* kinds of goals inherent in this relationship: first, to win the preferred agreement (going where one wants); and second, to feel that one is viewed by the others as powerful as well as lovable (i.e., as important).

(C) The teacher–board of education dispute presents an even more complex situation. Once again, as in the family, we have an example of a relationship in which the parties occupy roles within a larger, continuously ongoing system. Implicit in this continuity is the fact that not only tangible issues (such as pay) but also intangibles (such as the maintenance or loss of face) have to be resolved in the course of the activity. The issue of face, or image, maintenance (as brilliantly described and annotated by Goffman, 1959) is important in all bargaining relationships, but it is of special relevance and importance in situations such as this one, in which each bargaining party has a constituency whom it represents. The teachers union, after all, is ultimately responsible and accountable to its membership—a membership which is probably concerned not only with the attractiveness of any agreement reached but with the attractiveness of its spokesmen as they push for such an agreement. "Is the leadership making a good showing for itself and us?" "Are the leaders showing the other side that we mean business?" "Are our spokesmen going to sell out?" These are each questions that are at least implicitly asked by any group of its leadership. Even more important for the purposes of this discussion, they are questions of which the bargainers are very much aware.

In developing a bargaining strategy in this situation, the parties must each resolve a rather complex dilemma. Consider, for example, the problem confronting the union leadership. By being tough, they stand to receive the necessary and desired support of their constituency ("Those guys are really in there fighting for us"). At the same time, however, they run the risk of driving the other side away from the bargaining table, in which case they may well lose the very membership support they initially had. On the other hand, in pushing for an agreement that has a good chance of being acceptable to the board, they run the risks of settling for less than necessary, as well as of losing the confidence and support of the union membership ("Those guys are a bunch of lily-livered sellouts"). Thus each party must, in effect, bargain not only with the other side but with his own constituency as well.

In situations as complex as our Situation C, in which multilateral bargaining is required, we might expect to find the spokesmen engaged in various attempts to establish norms (implicit rules) that stabilize their relationship. One such norm, examined by Gouldner (1960) among others, is that of "reciprocity." This norm acts to regulate the relationship by legitimizing an "eye for eye, tooth for tooth" bargaining posture, inducing bargainers to return, in kind, the benefit or harm incurred by the other party. A second norm, that of "equity," has been described by Adams (1965) as existing when one party perceives that the ratio of his outcomes to inputs is equal to that of the other. This norm (closely akin to Homans' (1961) notion of "exchange") may act to stabilize the bargaining relationship by specifying the rule by which parties allocate or divide their resources. Each of these norms, as well as others, may be thought of as a mechanism that heightens the staying power or endurance of the bargaining relationship. Each is a "contractual" norm (Thibaut & Faucheux, 1965), a commonly understood and agreed-upon prescription for acceptable behavior, which may be either explicit or tacit in any given bargaining relationship and specifies the rules to be observed as well as the sanctions that may be applied for their violation.

We note in passing that the very complexity of our illustration of intergroup conflict, a complexity that may necessitate the formation of various contractual norms, in some sense provides the bargaining parties with a special kind of freedom of movement within their relationship. Thus, the spokesmen can attempt to take advantage of the fact that they must bargain not only with each other but with their own constituencies as well by "playing off" one party against the other. If, on the one hand, the spokesmen feel they are being subjected to unreasonable and unwarranted pressure at the hands of their respective constituencies, they may attempt to form a tacit alliance with each other, seeking an agreement that will *appear* satisfactory to their constituencies. Here, each party takes advantage of his middle-man status to form an "alliance of adversaries." On the other hand, in attempting to extract agreement from the other side, each party may exploit the fact that he is "caught in the middle" by developing a strategy of powerlessness. Thus, in pushing for some preferred agreement, each side can confront the other with its own helplessness, arguing that it is being tough not because it wants to, but because it "has to." It is the "I can't help myself," They're pushing me from behind," "I just work here" gambit with which we are all familiar.

5. *The activity usually involves the presentation of demands or proposals by one party, evaluation of these by the other, followed by concessions and counterproposals. The activity is thus sequential rather than simultaneous.* Implicit in this fact is the notion that one party's push for some preferred agreement at Time 2 must, at least in part, take into account the other party's behavior at Time 1. At the outset of their interaction, each party knows only about his own preferences for agreement (how far above his CL he would like to be) and his own CL_{alt}. In order to bargain effectively, each must acquire information about the other's preferences and the other's CL_{alt}. This is information, however, which only the other can provide. Each party is thus dependent on the other not only for the outcomes he receives but for information that will allow him to structure his own preferences and corresponding bargaining posture accordingly. This characteristic of the bargaining relationship is what Kelley and Thibaut (1969) have referred to as "information dependence."

Whenever one of the parties directs some demand or proposal at the other, he of necessity provides the other with information about his own preferences, which the other party can use in fashioning a counterproposal. The other is thus given an advantage in negotiation. To the extent that the other party knows both what the first wants as well as the least that he will accept, he (the other) will be able to develop a more effective, more precise bargaining position than would be possible in the absence of this information. Ideally, then, each party would like to obtain maximal information about the other's preferences, while at the same time disclosing minimal (or misleading) information about his own position. In his brilliant essay on classroom negotiations, Kelley (1966) speaks to exactly this point: "How information is exchanged in these negotiations and why this exchange takes the complex and tortured form it does is explained by the shared conflict between the need for information and restraints against providing it [p. 58]." Kelley goes on to articulate these needs and restraints in terms of two related dilemmas that bargainers must resolve.

First of all, in satisfying their need for information about the other's position, each party must resolve the "dilemma of trust." Kelley (1966) writes: "To believe everything the other person says is to place one's fate in his hands and to jeopardize full satisfaction of one's own interests. . . . On the other hand, to believe nothing the other says is to eliminate the possibility of accepting any arrangement with him [p. 60]." At some point in their relationship, each party is confronted with the critical problem of having to infer the other's true intentions, interests, and preferences from his behavior. Where the relationship is predominantly governed by mutual trust, the other's behavior can be taken as a true indication of his underlying disposition. In relationships ruled by mutual suspicion, on the other hand, the parties must each develop a "translation" scheme which permits them to decipher what the other really means (e.g., "When he demands X, he expects Y"; "When he asks for Y, he will settle for Z," etc.). In either case, in deciding which agreement to push for and which to accept, each party must learn to make attributions about the other's true intentions in which he can have some minimal degree of confidence.

At a second level, in their reluctance to provide the other party with the accurate information he needs and seeks, each must resolve what Kelley has described as the "dilemma of honesty and openness." Inasmuch as information must at least appear to be exchanged in order that bargaining activity remain viable, each party is confronted with the problem of deciding how frank or deceitful to be. Being completely frank may commit one to a position from which it is difficult to move at a later time. Moreover, to be frank in the face of a deceptive or exploitative other is to risk exploitation by him. There are thus real advantages to be gained by concealing information that could be turned against oneself at a later time. As Kelley (1966) writes: "Playing things close to one's vest permits later flexibility and allows a delay in deciding whether to attempt deceit or not [p. 60]." On the other hand, each party must be able to convince the other that he is being honest and open about his position. Kelley (1966) points out: "A satisfactory agreement can be reached only if each negotiator can be finally convinced that the other will not go any further [p. 60]." To sustain the bargaining relationship, each party must select a middle course between the extremes of complete openness toward, and total deception of, the other. Each must be able to convince the other of his integrity while not at the same time endangering his bargaining position.

(A) In attempting to resolve their conflict of interest and bargain effectively, Mike and the salesman must each come to grips with their mutual information dependence. At the outset, each knows only the range of values that constitute what he wants and what he will settle for, but not the equivalent values for the other party. Mike and the salesman would each probably like to know what the other will settle for, while divulging as little as possible about his own position. A not uncommon script in a situation such as this might be as follows:

MIKE (presenting jalopy):   *What will you give me for this fine old car?*

SALESMAN (kicking tires):   *How much (or what) do you want for it?*

MIKE: *Oh, I don't know. How much do you think it's worth?*

SALESMAN: *What do you think?*

On and on it might continue, each party doing his best to peek at the other's card holdings while keeping his own cards clutched to his bosom. When offers are finally initiated, we might well find Mike asking for more money (or a better trade-in) than he expects to get and the salesman offering less than he expects to settle for. Round and round the proceedings would go, demands and proposals being shunted back and forth, as each party attempted to increase the precision in his calibration of the other's true position. When each of them has reached the point of believing he knows the other's true intentions, we might expect offers to be made and a tentative agreement (if any) to be reached.

(**B**) The situation confronting the family members is somewhat different than that of the first illustration, and far more complex. This increased complexity can perhaps be traced primarily to the structural fact that there are now four rather than two parties sending proposals and counterproposals back and forth. Each party must now receive and evaluate information from not one but three other sources. In turn, any information that each either implicitly or explicitly transmits is now received (and most likely differently evaluated) by each of the three others. As a consequence, we might expect the family members to encounter considerable difficulty in resolving the conflict between information needs and information restraints. It is clear, on the one hand, that each needs to know what the others really want and what they will really settle for. Without such information, how can he possibly hope to fashion a bargaining strategy that can successfully accommodate the preferences of the three others? Yet consider the complexity of the task each faces. In attempting to extract the true position of his father, for example, the son must attempt to correct for the fact that his father's stated position has been altered not only by the son's own presence, but by the presence of the mother and sister as well. Thus, each party must attempt to take into account the fact that the information he receives has been transmitted in a complex social context and has probably been shaped by the transmitter's awareness that this information is being received and processed not by one but by three others.

Each party is, of course, not only a receiver of information but a transmitter as well. The information he elects to disclose (and he must reveal some information about his preferences if bargaining is to occur) must ideally be fashioned to allay the needs and suspicions of three others. To be effective, each must win at least the partial support of the other parties to the relationship. Yet, how difficult a task this is, in light of the fact that what may be seen as "integrity" by one of the parties may look like "deception" to the second, and "foolishness" to the third. Thus, in stating her preference for a trip to Paris, the wife may be seen as "outrageously honest" by her husband, "dishonest and deserting" by her daughter, and "foolish" by her son.

We might perhaps add that the resolution of the conflict between providing and withholding information in this complex relationship may be further complicated by the presence of certain implicit expectations of trust, honesty, and openness. Children, for example, are often brought up to "tell the truth," and parents seem well versed in the virtues of the "close and happy family." It is in a context such as this, a setting in which trust and trustworthiness may well be the golden rule by which family members believe their interaction should be conducted, that bargaining activity may occur in our illustration. As we pointed out earlier, however, in order to bargain effectively, each party may want to conceal some aspect of his position, at least initially. The problem, then, of appearing completely open and honest while, at the same time being secretive enough about one's holdings to permit effective bargaining, is one which all bargainers—especially those in such enduring relationships as our family—must resolve. It is a problem akin to the matter of learning how to play simultaneously a single game with two sets of rules.

(C) Finally, consider the teacher–board of education dispute. In deciding how much and what kind of information to communicate, each of the bargaining parties must consider not only how it will be interpreted by the other side, but also how it will be interpreted by his own constituency. On the other hand, as the receiver of proposals set forth by the other side, each of the two parties must attempt to systematically account for the fact that these proposals are not meant for his ears alone. Thus, we might expect to find the union leadership and the spokesman for the board of education embroiled in the exceptionally complex task of trying to appear open and honest both to his constituency and to the other side, while at the same time trying to decode correctly the true position of another (the other side) who is in very much the same bind.

We might expect the exchange of information in this situation to follow fairly structured lines: the parties initially sounding each other out, testing the potential and actual power of the other side, and checking the support of their constituencies; then a series of proposals, counterproposals, demands, and influence attempts (such as threats and promises); and, finally, a firm statement by each of his position, with a binding agreement (if any) the end result.

CONCLUDING COMMENT

In this chapter we have attempted to describe briefly some of the prominent characteristics of bargaining relationships. To summarize, this special kind of relationship has the following features:

1. At least two parties are involved.
2. The parties have a conflict of interest with respect to one or more different issues.
3. Regardless of the existence of prior experience or acquaintance with one another, the parties are at least temporarily joined together in a special kind of voluntary relationship.
4. Activity in the relationship concerns: (a) the division or exchange of one or more specific resources and/or (b) the resolution of one or more intangible issues among the parties or among those whom they represent.
5. The activity usually involves the presentation of demands or proposals by one party, evaluation of these by the other, followed by concessions and counterproposals. The activity is thus sequential rather than simultaneous.

In describing the range and complexity of psychological processes and behaviors that we consider to be bargaining, we have chosen to present and informally analyze some of the features of three illustrative situations. By searching through the reservoir of his own everyday experience, the reader will no doubt emerge with numerous additional examples of relationships with these same distinct and interesting characteristics.

3

An Overview of Social Psychological Approaches to the Study of Bargaining

The major task we have set ourselves in this book is to review, and at least partially integrate, the rather voluminous bargaining research that has emerged since about 1960. Before turning to this task, however, it may be useful to obtain a more general picture of social psychological approaches to the study of bargaining. What, for example, are some of the major research paradigms developed and used by social psychologists in order to analyze the bargaining process? To what extent do these paradigms contain the prominent characteristics of bargaining relationships, described in Chapter 2? How have social psychologists typically assessed bargaining effectiveness? Or, to put it another way, what kinds of dependent variables have bargaining researchers typically employed? Finally, what factors (independent variables) have typically been studied with respect to their effects on bargaining effectiveness? It is to the end of answering these questions, and thereby laying the groundwork for a closer analysis of the bargaining literature, that the present chapter is directed.

SOME MAJOR BARGAINING RESEARCH PARADIGMS

At first glance it would appear that almost as many different methodological paradigms have been devised for the study of bargaining as there are researchers themselves. Each experimenter begins with his own set of constraints, assumptions, and interests; each is curious about the effects and effectiveness of a particular constellation of variables; and each carries with him into the research enterprise a particular methodological uniqueness and creativity. Closer inspection of the vast experimental literature, however, reveals that there has been far more convergence on the use of a relatively small range of research paradigms than one might initially expect. The Prisoner's Dilemma game, alone, has accounted (incredibly) for more than 300 of the bargaining studies done within the last 10 years or so. Research using the Parcheesi Coalition game has accounted for approximately 40 studies, while about 25 studies have been conducted using the Acme-Bolt Trucking game, and a similar number using the Bilateral Monopoly game. In the sections that follow we will look briefly at each of these paradigms and discuss them in relation to our previous characterization of the bargaining relationship.

The Prisoner's Dilemma Game

The Prisoner's Dilemma, attributed to a mathematician, A.W. Tucker, was first popularly described by Luce and Raiffa (1957):

> Two suspects are taken into custody and separated. The district attorney is certain that they are guilty of a specific crime, but he does not have adequate evidence to convict them at a trial. He points out to each prisoner that each has two alternatives: to confess to the crime the police are sure they have done, or not to confess. If they both do not confess, then the district attorney states he will book them on some very minor trumped-up charge such as petty larceny and illegal possession of a weapon, and they will both receive minor punishment; if they both confess they will be prosecuted, but he will recommend less than the most severe sentence; but if one confesses and the other does not, then the confessor will receive lenient treatment for turning state's evidence whereas the latter will get "the book" slapped at him. In terms of years in a penitentiary, the strategic problem might reduce to:

		Prisoner 2	
Prisoner 1:		Not confess	Confess
Not confess:	1 year each		10 years for 1 and 3 months for 2
Confess:	3 months for 1 and 10 years for 2		8 years each

Excerpted from Luce and Raiffa, 1957, p. 95.

Consider the situation confronting Prisoner 1, which is identical, of course, to that facing Prisoner 2. Assuming he wishes to minimize his stay in prison (3 months), Prisoner 1 should confess and hope that Prisoner 2 chooses not to confess. If, however, Prisoner 2 reasons the same way, and also chooses to confess, each will end up with an 8-year term, whereas, by both confessing, each could have received only a 1-year sentence. A "not confess" decision in this situation may be seen as a cooperative choice, since it results in a minimal sentence for the other prisoner (either 3 months or 1 year) and may result in the most favorable joint outcome for the two prisoners—1 year each. A "confess" choice, on the other hand, may be seen as competitive, inasmuch as it results in a maximal sentence for the other prisoner (8 or 10 years) and may result in exploitation (if the other prisoner chooses not to confess).

It is precisely because the Prisoner's Dilemma represents a mixed-motive situation, in which there is incentive both to cooperate and to compete, and because these motives are contrasted so elegantly, that this paradigm has become the object of such overwhelming interest to bargaining researchers. A more general model of the Prisoner's Dilemma (PD) game may be represented in matrix form, as shown in Figure 3-1.

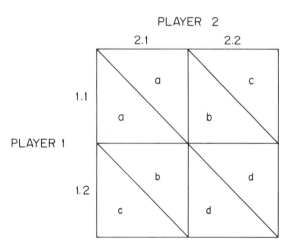

Figure 3-1 *General Matrix Representation of the Prisoner's Dilemma Game.* The letters in the lower left-hand corner of each cell denote Player 1's potential outcomes; those in the upper right-hand corner of each cell represent Player 2's potential outcomes.

To satisfy the mathematical requirements of the PD paradigm, the matrix entries must meet four conditions (Rapoport & Orwant, 1962): (1) $2a > b + c > 2d$; (2) $c > a$; (3) $c > b$; (4) $d > b$. Note that the Luce and Raiffa (1957) description satisfies all four conditions.

Another version of the PD game also satisfying the above conditions and used with considerable frequency by bargaining researchers is presented in matrix form in Figure 3-2. In a not atypical PD experiment employing this matrix, two naive subjects are brought into the laboratory, are seated in separate rooms, and are not permitted to communicate with each other in any way. In front of each subject are two buttons, one *black* and the other *red*. The subjects' task is simply to push *one* of these buttons. Depending on the choices made simultaneously by the two of them, each wins or loses points. If both indicate black, each wins 1 point; if both push the red button, each loses 1 point; and if one indicates red while the other indicates black, the player pushing the red button wins 2 points and the person pushing black loses 2 points. The subjects are told, finally, that there will be only one trial, and that they should go out of their way to make as many points as possible for themselves.

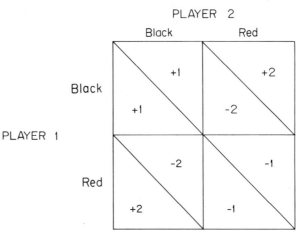

Figure 3–2 *A Typical Example of a Prisoner's Dilemma Matrix Used in Bargaining Research.* The matrix entries may denote points, money, or imaginary money, and correspond to the outcomes received by Player 1 (lower left-hand cell entries) and Player 2 (upper right-hand cell entries), respectively.

Beginning with this simple experimental situation, researchers have typically introduced a great many variables. Keeping in mind that the following list is by no means exhaustive, these variables have included:

1. *Number of Trials.* Many PD studies have consisted of only one trial, while others have consisted of more than one and up to several hundred trials.

2. *Availability of Posttrial Feedback about the Other's Previous Choice.* Most studies have provided the subject(s) with such feedback, but others have not.

3. *Presence of a Real Other Player.* While considerable research has been done using two real, naive subjects, at least as many studies have had a single subject play against either a confederate of the experimenter or an experimental strategy.

4. *Availability of Communication between Subjects.* Although most PD experiments have been run with the subjects kept incommunicado (except with regard to feedback, typically provided by the experimenter, about the other player's previous choice), there are a number of studies in which direct

communication (orally or via written messages of various types) has been made available or required.

5. *Structure of the Matrix.* An enormous amount of PD game research has involved manipulation of this variable. Some researchers have simply varied the outcome values in each cell, while continuing to meet the four defining mathematical requirements of the PD game. Others have more drastically restructured the matrix values, creating such related paradigms as the Maximizing Difference game (devised by McClintock and McNeel), the game of Chicken (Rapoport), the Decomposed Prisoner's Dilemma game (Pruitt), and so on.

6. *Incentives.* Yet another variable of major interest to researchers has been the nature and magnitude of the incentives at stake in the game. Subjects have been asked to play the game for points, for imaginary money, and for real money.

7. *Simultaneity of Choice.* While most PD studies have required the two players to make their choices simultaneously, others have permitted or required sequential behavior, in which one player makes a choice and this choice is communicated to the second player, who then makes his decision.

8. *Motivational Orientation.* In a number of studies subjects have been given either a cooperative orientation ("Try to maximize your joint earnings"), a competitive orientation ("Try to do better than the other player"), or an individualistic one ("Try to make as much for yourself as you can").

Notice that our simple black–red version of the PD game can be considered in relation to all of the above variables: It is a one-trial game with posttrial feedback; two real subjects are involved and communication between them is not permitted; the matrix (see Figure 3-2) is of standard form and the game is played for points; finally, choices are to be made simultaneously and subjects are given an individualistic motivational orientation. Given this simple, prototypical situation, let us consider the dilemma confronting each of the two players.

Each may perhaps reason more or less as follows: "In order to decide whether to push red or black, I need to know what the other person is likely to do. But I don't know anything about him, and I can't communicate with him, so how can I guess what he is going to do? I know. First, I'll figure out what I would do if he were to choose black, then I'll consider what I would do if he were to choose red, and finally I'll try to combine these calculations in some sort of effective, winning strategy. If he pushes his black button, I can *make more* by choosing red (+2 points) than by choosing black (+1 point)—so in this case I should push my red button. If, on the other hand, he chooses red, I can *lose less* with a red choice (−1 point) than a black one (−2 points)—so here's yet another reason for pushing my red button. So, I should choose red regardless of what the other player does, since I stand to make the most and lose the least." Given this "convincing" chain of reasoning, the dilemma then arises from the possibility that the other player may have reasoned in exactly the same way—in which case both will choose red and lose, when both could have chosen black and won. It makes sense to choose black (to cooperate), however, only to the extent that the other is expected (can be trusted) to choose black also.

Given this brief characterization of a prototypical version of the PD game and the dilemma it poses for its participants, let us now consider, finally, the extent to which the PD paradigm satisfies each of the characteristics of a true bargaining relationship.

It is obvious that at least two parties are involved, even where there is only a single subject playing against a confederate or experimental strategy. The parties, moreover, have a clear conflict of interest. The combination of choices (black–red or red–black) resulting in the most favorable outcome for one party provides the least favorable outcome for the other. A win for one represents, at least in part, a loss for the other—outcomes, that is, sum to zero. Note, however, that this "zero sum," purely competitive aspect of the paradigm is offset by the presence of choice combinations that result in both losing (red–red) or both winning (black–black). Outcomes in these two choice situations do not sum to zero—hence the overall characterization of the PD paradigm as a two-person, nonzero sum game.

While the PD paradigm satisfies the first two of our characteristics of a true bargaining relationship, it only partially satisfies the third. We have argued that for bargaining to exist, the parties must be joined together in a relationship that is voluntary in two respects. First, each party must be able to choose from among several possible outcomes. Strictly speaking, such choice is indeed possible in the PD paradigm: by choosing red or black, each player can attempt to obtain or avoid any one of four outcomes. Second, each party must be able to choose when to enter, and how long to remain in, a relationship with the other. This latter choice is clearly not available to participants in the PD paradigm. The players are provided with no formal mechanism for opting out of their relationship (or threatening to do so). It is in this sense that one may question whether true bargaining can occur in the PD game.

The fourth characteristic of bargaining relationships, that activity is focused on the resolution of one or more tangible or intangible issues, is present in the PD paradigm. The tangible issue is represented by the resource at stake (points, money, imaginary money) and its potential distribution among the players. Each player, moreover, is dependent on the other for the quality of the outcomes he, himself, receives; the parties are thus outcome dependent. While intangible issues are not automatically present in the PD paradigm, largely because the players are usually incommunicado, they may nevertheless arise—as, for example, when information is conveyed to a player about the nature or intentions of his adversary, his trustworthiness, and so forth.

A fifth characteristic of bargaining, we have suggested, is that the activity involves the exchange of offers and counteroffers and is sequential rather than simultaneous. When run as a 1-trial game, the PD game clearly fails to meet this requirement. Choices are made simultaneously, and there is no opportunity for one player to affect the other's behavior on subsequent trials. However, when the PD game is played iteratively (over a repeated series of trials), this requirement of sequentiality may indeed be satisfied. Even though moves are made simultaneously, and even though moves and countermoves are not strictly equivalent to verbal or written offers and counteroffers, it becomes possible to view behavior over a series of trials as sequential: Each player's move on trial $n + 1$ is likely to be affected by the other's move on trial n, and is likely to affect both players' behavior on trial $n + 2$, and so forth. Note, however, that while PD game behavior may be analyzed and interpreted in this way (and indeed has been, using Bayesian statistics), most bargaining researchers have failed to do this. Instead, they have treated a PD game with multiple trials as a situation composed of a series of separate, independent moves.

In summary, the PD paradigm contains many, but by no means all, of the characteristics of a true bargaining relationship. In light of this fact, it is interesting that so much research has been conducted using this relatively simple, if elegant, game, and that so much reliance has been placed on the findings to emerge. Much of the PD research is obviously interesting and important. In interpreting this work, however, its limitations as a bargaining paradigm should be kept in mind, and PD results—whenever possible—should be interpreted in relation to findings that have emerged using other, "truer" bargaining paradigms. We will, of course, attempt to follow this exhortation through the subsequent chapters of this volume.

The Parcheesi Coalition Game

This board game was designed by Vinacke and Arkoff (1957) to study the circumstances under which three or more people tend to align themselves into coalitions of various kinds. The game typically involves three players, seated face to face around a Parcheesi board numbered from 1 to 67. Each player is given a marker and is told that his task is to move this marker around the board from start (1) to finish (67). Each marker is assigned a numerical weight that, when multiplied by the results of a die toss by the experimenter, determines the number of spaces that its owner can move. For example, if the die comes up "6," a player with a weight of "2" gets to move 12 spaces, while another with a weight of "5" moves 30 spaces. Players draw their markers at random at the beginning of the game, and move simultaneously after each toss of the die by the experimenter. The player or players finishing first receive a prize of 100 points and win the game. The experiment typically consists of 18 games.

Superimposed upon the structure of this simple board game is the option to form alliances with the other players. Players who form an alliance (coalition) move only one marker, at a rate equal to the sum of their combined weights, times the value of the die toss. (For example, if the die comes up "6," and the players with the weights of "2" and "5" agree to form a coalition, they would move a single marker a distance of 42 spaces.) It is at this point of forming alliances that bargaining occurs in the paradigm, since establishment of a coalition also requires the players involved to reach agreement (beforehand), through a series of verbal offers and counteroffers, about how they will divide the 100-point reward. Any player may form an alliance with any other player at any point in the game, but, once formed, this alliance cannot be broken for the remainder of that game. Any player can, moreover, concede defeat if he views his position as hopeless—an option that is obviously most likely to be chosen by the player who is excluded from a coalition.

Using this paradigm, Vinacke and Arkoff (1957), and their colleagues, have examined the bargaining process that emerges in the formation of coalitions, as well as the circumstances under which particular coalitions are likely to form. The Parcheesi Coalition game obviously has many of the characteristics of a true bargaining relationship. Three parties are involved, whose conflict of interest revolves around their motivation each to be the winner of the game. As in the case of the PD paradigm, moreover, motives are mixed: the competitive motivation to win the game is offset by the realization that an alliance (cooperation) with one or both others may be necessary in order to accomplish this objective.

With respect to the volitional characteristic of true bargaining relationships, it is apparent that the Parcheesi Coalition paradigm contains the two necessary components. Each player, in the process of forming alliances, can choose which of several possible agreements to ask for and which, if any, to accept; at a second level, the players are free to decide both whether to bargain with one another at all and whether to opt out of the game by conceding defeat. The players are thus bargaining participants by choice rather than by compulsion.

Activity in the Parcheesi Coalition paradigm obviously concerns the division of a specific tangible resource (the prize of 100 points awarded to the winner[s] of each game); furthermore, the activity is also likely to concern the resolution of intangible issues, such as face or self-esteem, that are likely to arise in a situation where the participants are seated face-to-face and are permitted to communicate freely. The bargaining activity, finally, is likely to entail the exchange of offers and counteroffers and is therefore sequential rather than simultaneous. The issue remains, of course, of how to treat the 18 games typically run in a single coalition experiment. Are these games independent events, each representing a bargaining experience unto itself? Or are these 18 games, taken together, a single bargaining encounter in which the moves and outcomes in one game are likely to shape subsequent behavior? We would argue that the latter perspective is necessary if the Parcheesi Coalition paradigm is truly to satisfy the requirement of sequentiality. Yet it is not clear that researchers employing this paradigm have consistently chosen to adopt this perspective.

The Acme–Bolt Trucking Game

This game, devised by Deutsch and Krauss (1960), consists of two players, each of whom is asked to imagine that he is in charge of one of two trucking outfits—one named the Acme, the other the Bolt Trucking Company. A player's task is to move his truckload of merchandise from start to destination in as little time as possible—pay being based on the time taken to complete the trip. Each player can take one of two roads to his destination: the *main* or the *alternate* route. The main route is the shorter of the two pathways, but it contains a section that is only one lane wide. This means that the two trucks, which are heading in opposite directions, cannot pass each other on this one-lane section. The alternate route, on the other hand, is considerably longer than the main route, but the players' paths do not cross at any point along the way.

In a not atypical version of the Acme–Bolt Trucking game, both players, in addition to having a choice of two routes to their destination, have control over a device known as a *gate*. Each player's gate is located on the main route, at the end of the one-lane section closest to his own starting position. By closing their respective gates, the players can prevent each other from successfully traversing the one-lane section and reaching their destination via the main route. Each player can, however, move back and forth through his own closed gate at will.

In a typical Acme–Bolt Trucking experiment, two naive subjects are brought into the experimental laboratory and are seated at separate consoles, facing each other but separated by a dividing barrier. The subjects thus cannot see each other and are instructed not to communicate with each other at any time during the experiment. The subjects listen to taped instructions that explain the rules of the game, how to read the road map each subject is given (see Figure 3-3), and the use of the consoles. Each control console consists of: a switch, which can be engaged in forward, reverse, or stop positions; a counter, indicating the subject's position on the main or alternate route; a gate button, which can close or open the gate a subject controls; a light, which comes on whenever the other subject has closed the gate he controls; and a sign panel, which lights up whenever the two trucks collide on the one-lane section of road ("Trucks head-on—one-lane section blocked").

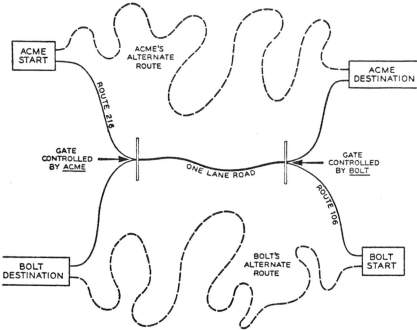

Figure 3-3 *Subject's Road Map in the Acme–Bolt Trucking Game* (reprinted from Deutsch and Krauss, 1962, p. 55).

Before beginning the game, subjects are typically run through a series of practice trials to ensure understanding of the rules and options available to them. The experiment is then typically run for 20 trials, at the end of each of which the experimenter announces the time taken and money made (or lost) by each subject, and returns the subjects' trucks to the "start" position for the beginning of the next trial.

Given this cursory description of the game, let us now consider the extent to which the Acme–Bolt paradigm contains each of the five characteristics of a true bargaining relationship. The conflict of interest between the two parties concerns the issue of right of way along the one-lane road. Only one player at a time can completely traverse the one-lane section: If Acme goes first, Bolt must wait (thereby losing money) before proceeding to his destination via the main route. Thus, on any given trial, one party's gains are equivalent to the other's losses. Note, however, that in the long run it is also possible for both to win (by alternating the right of way on consecutive trials) or both to lose (by remaining in deadlock on the one-lane road). The paradigm is thus nonzero sum in nature.

The relationship between Acme and Bolt is a voluntary one in both necessary respects. On the one hand, each player can decide how demanding or lenient to be with respect to the issue of right of way. By varying the position of his truck and the amount of time spent in deadlock on the one-lane road, he can choose which agreements to (nonverbally) ask for and which to accept. On the other hand, each player can also choose, if he wishes, to opt out of his relationship with the other by taking the alternate route to his destination on any trial. And if in addition to taking the alternate route a player also closes the gate he controls, he can prevent the other from proceeding unencumbered along the main route.

The specific resource to be divided by players in the Acme–Bolt Trucking game is the total amount of money which can be jointly won or lost in the experiment, where this is based on the amount of time taken to go from start to destination. While activity in the relationship between Acme and Bolt may also focus on the resolution of one or more intangible issues, it is important to keep in mind that the players are typically kept incommunicado (except with respect to information about the other's gate). Hence, one might expect intangible issues to be less important than they are in a paradigm like the Parcheesi Coalition game, in which face-to-face contact and open communication are possible. Note also, however, that the conflict of interest in the Acme–Bolt Trucking game is highly graphic. Deadlocking on the main route (accompanied as it is by the flashing sign, "Trucks head-on—one-lane section blocked") may well give rise to perceptions of the other as a person who is exceptionally stubborn, selfish, or greedy, in which case intangible issues may develop despite the lack of visual or oral contact.

Finally, with respect to the manner in which demands or proposals are exchanged, we have already noted that communication is usually (although by no means always) prohibited, which means the exchange of offers and counteroffers must occur entirely at a nonverbal level. This limitation makes the process of analyzing the bargaining activity in sequential fashion rather difficult, but nevertheless possible, if the experimenter, as in the case of the PD paradigm, considers the 20 trials as a single, interdependent event rather than as a series of separate, unrelated "games."

The Bilateral Monopoly Game

While several of the paradigms we have already examined contain many or all of the characteristics of a true bargaining relationship, they tend to bear relatively little resemblance to more familiar bargaining encounters. It is for this reason that Siegel and Fouraker's (1960) Bilateral Monopoly game is particularly interesting and important. This paradigm not only has most of the characterisitcs of a true bargaining relationship, but considerable face validity as well. The game consists of two players, the lone *buyer* and the lone *seller* of imaginary merchandise, each of whom attempts to maximize his profits by negotiating the particular price and quantity at which this merchandise will be bought or sold. Negotiations are conducted through a written series of offers and counteroffers and are based on a profit table which specifies the amounts (in cents) than can be made for each possible transaction between the two players. Samples of buyer and seller profit tables are reproduced in Table 3-1, and it can be seen that the potential outcomes to the players are negatively (although not perfectly) correlated: the higher the price, the greater the seller's profit and the less the buyer's; the greater the quantity, the less the seller's profit and the greater the buyer's. The seller thus wishes to negotiate a sale of small quantity at high price, while the buyer seeks the reverse.

Table 3–1

Profit Tables Used by Players in the Bilateral Monopoly Game (in Cents)

| | BUYER'S PROFIT TABLE | | | | | SELLER'S PROFIT TABLE | | | |
| | Quantity | | | | | Quantity | | | |
Price	*7*	*8*	*9*	*10*	*Price*	*7*	*8*	*9*	*10*
240					240	1190	1280	1350	1400
230					230	1120	1200	1260	1300
220					220	1050	1120	1170	1200
210	50	24	0		210	980	1040	1080	1100
200	120	104	90	70	200	910	960	990	1000
190	190	184	180	170	190	840	880	900	900
180	260	264	270	270	180	770	800	810	800
170	330	344	360	370	170	700	720	720	700
160	400	424	450	470	160	630	640	630	600
150	470	504	540	570	150	560	560	540	500
140	540	584	630	670	140	490	480	450	400
130	610	664	720	770	130	420	400	360	300
120	680	744	810	870	120	350	320	270	200
110	750	824	900	970	110	280	240	180	100
100	820	904	990	1070	100	210	160	90	0

Adapted from Siegel and Fouraker, 1960, pp. 114-115.

In a not atypical version of the Bilateral Monopoly game, two naive subjects are brought into the laboratory, are seated in separate rooms, and are randomly assigned to the roles of buyer and seller. Subjects are given an individualistic orientation ("It is in your interest to get the largest share possible, since that is the amount you will take home") and are instructed in the use of the profit tables. (Whether a subject is given only his own profit table, or both tables, is a variable commonly manipulated at this point.) At the beginning of the bargaining session, which is permitted to last no more than 2 hr, one player is selected to begin the negotiations by making a written bid (offer) in terms of both merchandise quantity and price (e.g., "8 @ $1.90"). This written offer is then brought by the experimenter to the other player, who can either accept the offer or write a counteroffer which is then conveyed back to the first player. Offers and counteroffers are transmitted back and forth in this fashion until agreement is reached or until the session ends. Once the players have come to agreement, they are paid in accordance with the terms of their transaction and the experiment ends.

The conflict of interest between the buyer and seller obviously concerns the division of profits, since outcomes are negatively correspondent. Note, however, as in the preceding paradigms, that it is also possible for both to do well or both to do poorly.

The buyer and seller obviously each have a great deal of choice with respect to the agreements it is possible to seek or accept, and the bargaining relationship is voluntary in this important respect. On the other hand, in many (although by no means all) versions of the Bilateral Monopoly paradigm, the players cannot choose to opt out of the relationship if they wish; they are constrained to continue negotiating until agreement is reached or until time runs out. This limitation of the paradigm has been overcome in more recent research through the introduction of an option that permits one or both players simply to terminate negotiations at any point.

With respect to the bargaining activity itself, it is clear that the tangible resource at stake (profits) is divided through a series of offers and counteroffers. Activity is thus sequential rather than simultaneous, and it may be neatly analyzed through the series of bids and counterbids subjects make in the course of the game. Intangible issues may arise, of course, although the lack of face-to-face contact, coupled with the condition of limited communication (via written bids only), may reduce the likelihood of such an occurrence.

Bargaining Paradigms: Summary

Although a great many paradigms have been developed in order to study the bargaining process, four have received particular attention in the literature, especially the PD game and its variants. Our cursory review of these four paradigms has indicated that each contains several, if not all, of the characteristics of a true bargaining relationship. We have summarized these characteristics and the extent of their presence in each paradigm in Table 3-2. Other paradigms, some of which are at least as interesting as the four discussed here (although less frequently employed), will be described subsequently in the context of the particular set of experimental findings to which they pertain.

Table 3-2

Four of the More Commonly Used Bargaining Paradigms and the Extent to which They Contain Each of the Characteristics Found in True Bargaining Relationships

Bargaining characteristics	PD	Parcheesi Coalition	Acme-Bolt	Bilateral Monopoly
Two or more parties	Yes	Yes	Yes	Yes
Parties have a conflict of interest with respect to one or more issues	Yes	Yes	Yes	Yes
Parties are joined together in a voluntary relationship and are:				
able to push for several possible agreements	Yes	Yes	Yes	Yes
able to choose to leave the relationship	No	Yes	Yes	No
Activity focuses on the resolution of one or more tangible or intangible issues	Yes	Yes	Yes	Yes
Activity involves the sequential exchange of offers and counteroffers	No[a]	Yes	No[a]	Yes

[a]Unless repeated trials are considered as dependent, interconnected events.

DEPENDENT VARIABLES: CRITERIA OF BARGAINING EFFECTIVENESS

The single question that is perhaps most likely to arise after having either observed or participated in bargaining is: Did it work? Did bargaining, in other words, permit the opposing parties to resolve their differences without excessive cost or damage to themselves or others? Did the parties bargain effectively?

Bargaining effectiveness is most commonly evaluated against criteria involving the relative gains and costs to the bargainers and, in the case of representational bargaining, those whom they represent. It would be a far easier task to evaluate the effectiveness of bargaining if the gains and costs were limited only to those outcomes that are tangible and of immediate consequence to the parties involved. This, however, is not generally the case, since bargaining frequently involves intangible issues as well as tangible ones (as in the case of the family described in Chapter 2), and because agreements often have long-term or future consequences (as in the case of the teachers-union–school-board dispute). Thus, the determination of bargaining effectiveness becomes a complex task: The gain or loss of honor, prestige, or reputation cannot easily be assigned a dollars and cents value; moreover, the effect of highhandedness—even if "successful"—on a future bargaining relationship is equally difficult to assess. Nevertheless, social psychologists do attempt to make appraisals of how effective bargainers have been, and it is necessary that they do so. These appraisals often grow out of the questions that tend to be asked when any bargaining relationship is examined, regardless of whether bargaining focuses on labor–management, international, or interpersonal issues.

Among the most frequently raised questions about bargaining effectiveness are: Was agreement reached on all or only some of the issues involved? How long did it take before agreement was reached? In what manner were the available outcomes distributed among the parties? If unequally, which side made the largest (or smallest) concessions? How much of what was initially sought by each party was ultimately obtained? How satisfied were the parties with the outcomes obtained? What types of threats and promises, if any, were used and with what frequency? Was the general tone or quality of the bargaining cooperative or competitive? Under what kinds of rules and norms did the bargaining proceed? To what extent were these observed or violated, and what constraints did they impose on the bargainers?

Bargaining effectiveness has also been assessed by raising questions related to the structural context in which bargaining occurs. For example: Did the parties make effective use of the communication options available to them? How did their communication affect the outcomes they received? Did communication increase the outcomes for both sides or did it serve less cooperative ends? How did the presence or absence of audiences or the use of third parties affect the outcomes?

As suggested by the broad range of questions outlined above, bargaining effectiveness may be gauged from a variety of different perspectives. How, then, have bargaining researchers dealt with the problem of distinguishing among these perspectives? In more empirical terms: What dependent measures have researchers traditionally settled upon as being reliable and valid indicators of effective bargaining? It appears that experimental studies of bargaining have generally focused on such dependent variables as: the number or percentage of cooperative or competitive choices made; the outcomes obtained by the bargainers (separately or jointly); the difference in outcomes between the bargainers or the "symmetry" with which the outcomes are divided; the time taken to reach agreement; the frequency with which such signals as threats or warnings are used, when these are available; and the frequency and severity of punitiveness, if mechanisms for its expression are available. Since many of the experimental bargaining studies conducted to date have been iterative, investigators have also examined "trends over trials" as a supplementary indicator of changes in bargaining effectiveness. Capitalizing on the value of such iterative bargaining paradigms, investigators have introduced variations in the structural features of the bargaining tasks they have employed. Inspection procedures, opportunities to communicate with the other side after the completion of a certain number of trials, and shifts in the strategy of the other party are typical of such variations.

While the range of dependent variables chosen for analysis has been wide, the two most frequently selected measures of effectiveness have been *(1) the number of cooperative or competitive choices made throughout the total number of trials* and *(2) the magnitude of the outcomes obtained by the bargainers.* In many cases, focus on these dependent measures has been dictated by the characteristics of the specific bargaining task being used, a fact sometimes acknowledged by researchers as leaving unanswered or open to speculation important questions about the underlying reasons for a bargainer's behavior. On the other hand, an advantage inherent in the use of such dependent measures is that they permit systematic analysis along a few specified dimensions.

An implicit assumption often made in experimental bargaining studies is that the dependent measure will reflect (in operational terms, at least) the essential character of the events that occurred during bargaining. For instance, when the joint payoffs of the bargainers are relatively low in comparison with the potential outcomes they could have earned, the assumption may be correctly made that *something* occurred during the process that limited the bargainers' ability to maximize their outcomes. Such reductions in joint outcomes may be due to a variety of factors; these range from faulty or incomplete understanding of the particular bargaining task, at one extreme, to fully informed but mutually destructive or competitive behavior at the other. In instances where the former is true, there is always the danger of making erroneous interpretations about the reasons for reduced outcomes. Most experimental investigators, however, have taken pains to reduce the likelihood of such errors by providing prior practice sessions, making instructions to subjects as clear as possible, and administering informal quizzes followed by corrective feedback to assure satisfactory understanding of the bargaining task.

Another example of the difficulties inherent in inferring the quality of a bargaining relationship from outcome measures can be seen in situations where there has been an asymmetrical allocation of a reward that was, at least potentially, equally divisible among the bargainers. In this case it may be inferred that the party who obtained the lion's share behaved exploitatively. While this has generally proven to be true, there are cases in which the inequality of a particular division may not be so easily explained. Thus, for a variety of reasons, one party may be interested in seeing that the other side gets more than himself in a particular bargaining situation or with respect to a particular issue. These reasons range from a clearly altruistic orientation toward the other to a more machiavellian concern with causing the other to become indebted so that he may be called on at a later time to repay the advantage afforded him earlier. Clearly the strategy of making concessions on relatively unimportant issues so that "credits" may be accumulated toward maximizing gains on more important ones is an example of such utilitarian concern.

In summary, then, in their attempt to understand the nature of the bargaining process, social psychologists have generated and assessed a vast array of dependent variables, each of which ultimately concerns itself with the issue of bargaining effectiveness. The reliance on two dependent measures in particular, the frequency of cooperation and the magnitude of outcomes obtained, has provided a useful common "metric" by which to evaluate the effects of different, independent variables manipulated in a variety of paradigms. This same emphasis, however, has also given rise to problems concerning the interpretation and validity of experimental findings and has resulted in a tendency to generate additional measures. In order to overcome some of the difficulties inherent in relying too heavily upon outcomes as measures of bargaining effectiveness, for example, investigators have generally attempted to test the accuracy of their interpretations by performing supplementary data analyses, in the hope that these will clarify the obtained results. Usually these analyses focus on bargainers' perceptions of one another, the intentions each attributes to the other, and their reactions to the other's apparent strategy.

INDEPENDENT VARIABLES: FACTORS AFFECTING
BARGAINING EFFECTIVENESS

Our major purpose in this concluding section is to provide an overview of the factors most commonly studied with respect to their effects on bargaining effectiveness. Given the several hundred bargaining studies conducted within the last 10 years or so, manipulating at least as many independent variables, the question arises: How may these variables be organized so as to present a clear and integrated picture of the findings to emerge? Any organizational scheme, of course, contains an inherent danger: Even as it systematically sharpens the clarity of certain issues, it removes or obscures others from the investigator's (and the reader's) view. In light of the massive bargaining literature, however, an organizational plan for the presentation of experimental findings is clearly necessary. The plan we have elected to adopt (in Chapters 4–9) is based on the types of independent variables that researchers have commonly measured or manipulated, and it considers these variables in the context of four underlying dimensions: (a) the structural context within which bargaining occurs; (b) the behavioral predispositions of the parties involved; (c) the nature and underlying characteristics of the bargainers' interdependence; and (d) the use of social influence and influence strategies in bargaining. Let us now turn to these dimensions, and consider some of the independent variables that may be subsumed under each, as well as the ways in which these variables have been manipulated or assessed.

The Structural Context of Bargaining

Experimental games serve the function in bargaining research of providing a standardized context within which bargaining can be observed. Beyond this, however, they also provide the opportunity for systematic variation of the conditions in which effective bargaining is likely to develop. A variety of factors relating to the structure of these games, for example, may be varied for the purpose of studying their effects on the behavior of the parties involved. An investigator interested in the effects of unlimited (as opposed to restricted) communication upon bargaining effectiveness might create these conditions by developing two sets of instructions, or rules, which vary in this respect but are exactly the same in all others. He might then examine bargaining effectiveness in terms of the time required to reach agreement or the amount of cooperation or competition among the parties. He would certainly want to compare bargaining effectiveness in each of the two communication conditions, to determine whether or not there are differences and, if so, whether or not these can be attributed to the availability of communication. A similar approach might be taken by an investigator concerned with the question of whether or not the availability of threat has any noticeable effect on bargaining effectiveness. In this case the experimenter might provide one or both of the participants with a threat mechanism in one condition, without providing such an option in a second. He might then make a comparison of bargaining effectiveness (as indicated by the outcomes obtained by bargainers in each condition) and try to determine whether or not the introduction of threat produces differences in effectiveness. Or an experiment might be undertaken to determine whether or not differences in the type of available outcomes produce differences in bargaining behavior. Here the investigator might provide the parties with instructions which are identical in every respect except that in one condition the subjects bargain over points or imaginary money while in another they bargain over the division of a real monetary reward. A comparison of bargaining effectiveness (such as joint outcomes or differences in outcomes earned by the parties) would then shed light on the question of whether or not the magnitude and nature of the incentives has any effect on the bargainers' behavior.

The structural variables described above represent only a limited sample of those that have been examined in experimental studies of bargaining behavior. In their attempts to understand more fully the structural determinants of effective bargaining, experimental researchers have also studied the effects of: the presence or absence of audiences; the availability and role of third parties; the number of parties involved in the bargaining exchange; coalitions; the location of the bargaining site; physical arrangements at the site itself; variations in the types of threat and communication options available, both verbal and nonverbal; time limitations and the duration of bargaining sessions; incentive magnitude and reward structure; and the number of issues at stake, as well as their presentation, format, and the prominence of alternative solutions.

The research related to these and other structural factors found to influence bargaining effectiveness will be reviewed systematically in Chapters 4–6. Chapter 4 deals with the work done on social structure, Chapter 5 with physical and temporal structure, and Chapter 6 with issue structure.

The Behavioral Predispositions of Bargainers

There is little doubt that personality variables, as well as other individual characteristics, are important determinants of bargaining behavior. Social psychologists have followed two basic approaches in their attempts to discover relationships among personality variables and behavior in experimental games. The first involves the measurement of relevant personality dimensions (using standardized personality assessment techniques) and the subsequent comparison of bargaining effectiveness between groups that differ along such dimensions. On another level, some investigators have designed experiments to determine the extent to which personality differences interact with other variables (structural or strategic variables, for example) and thereby produce systematic differences in bargaining behavior.

A second major approach involves varying the information given to bargainers about the personal characteristics of the other party. Such information is typically provided either through a meeting between the parties before the experiment begins or through the exchange of subject questionnaires. For example, the parties might each be provided with a personality profile of the other that (unknown to the parties) has been substituted by the investigator for one completed earlier. The nature of this substitute information is, of course, carefully controlled by the investigator, facilitating comparison among the conditions thereby created.

Using either or both of these two approaches to the study of individual differences, bargaining researchers have attempted to assess the effects of background and personality variables such as the following: age; intelligence; religion; social status; sex; risk-taking propensity; cognitive complexity; intolerance of ambiguity; generalized trust and cooperativeness; authoritarianism; internationalism; flexible ethicality; machiavellianism. The research related to these and other individual difference factors will be reviewed and integrated in Chapter 7.

The Interdependence of Bargainers

In addition to being concerned with the effects of structural and individual difference factors on bargaining behavior, social psychologists have also focused on the effects of different types of interpersonal relationships or interdependence bonds. While a number of techniques have been used to assess the effects of varying patterns of interdependence between bargainers, these generally involve superimposing variations upon the task in which they are engaged. On the simplest level, participants in bargaining studies may or may not be acquainted with one another; they may or may not be given an opportunity to have informal, prenegotiation contact with each other; they may or may not expect to have future interaction with the other party.

A second type of relational variation which has been studied concerns the bargainers' motivational orientation toward one another. In this regard a number of studies have been conducted in which the bargainers receive instructions that are variously of a "cooperative," "competitive," or "individualistic" nature. The investigators then explore differences in bargaining effectiveness as a function of these induced motivational postures.

Still another type of variation focuses on the power and dependency relations among bargainers. In this case one member of each bargaining pair might be given the power to affect directly the other party's outcome through the introduction of particular rules and constraints. Conditions of this type are generally created to determine the effects of certain types of dependency relationships on bargaining behavior.

Again, the types of variations mentioned above represent only a few of the relational controls that experimental researchers have superimposed upon specific bargaining tasks. This research will be considered in Chapter 8.

The Use of Social Influence Strategies

Another major interest of bargaining researchers has concerned the effects of different influence strategies upon bargaining behavior. Two general approaches to this and related problems have been typically followed. In the first of these, pairs of bargainers have been allowed to bargain freely (within the context of a standardized task), and the pattern of responses of each to the other has been observed. It is generally hoped that, over a given number of such pairs, consistent patterns of relevant behavior (e.g., behavior that is conciliatory, yielding, resistant, reciprocatory, retaliatory, threatening, or punitive) will emerge. Researchers have found this approach somewhat unsatisfactory because of the extreme difficulty in maintaining control over the behavior of the bargainers and the subtle, uninterpretable variations in behavior that may occur.

The second approach, which has been used more frequently and with greater confidence, involves only one real bargainer who (unknown to him) is confronted by a programmed adversary. This approach provides increased opportunities for control and enables researchers to answer questions such as the following with greater confidence: How do bargainers respond to a (cooperative, competitive, deterrent, punitive, or other) strategy? How do they respond to a specified level of cooperativeness or competitiveness? At what specific points do their responses reflect changes in attitude, such as diminished or increased resistance? Studies that typify this general approach have relied upon the creation of operationally definable strategies, such as "reformed sinner" (initial competitiveness followed by cooperation), "lapsed saint" (cooperation followed by competition), "turn the other cheek" (altruistic response to threat or attack), "nonpunitiveness" (self-protection, rather than counterthreat, in the face of threat), and "deterrence" (a threatening response to noncooperation, and counterattack in the face of attack).

Using either of these two major approaches to the study of bargaining influence strategies, researchers have attempted to assess the effects of variables such as: the pattern of initial offers and counteroffers; the overall cooperativeness of the other party; the rate and degree of concessions; the magnitude of promises and threats and the language in which these are expressed; the credibility of promisors and threateners. The research concerned with these and other variables dealing with the strategic determinants of effective bargaining will be examined in Chapter 9.

CONCLUDING COMMENT

In this chapter we have briefly considered several of the major research paradigms employed in the study of bargaining. In addition, we have taken a look at several of the more important dependent variables by means of which bargaining effectiveness has been assessed. Finally, we have presented four underlying dimensions in terms of which the plethora of independent variables in bargaining research may be considered. It is to the task of reviewing the experimental literature in light of these dimensions that we now turn.

4

Social Components Of
Bargaining Structure

In this and the following two chapters, we shall attempt to identify some of the structural components of bargaining situations and to describe the consequences of these components for the bargaining process. By structural components, we refer to the social, physical, and issue characteristics of the bargaining situation—those that are either present at the outset of bargaining or that the parties introduce as the exchange unfolds. As we shall see, variables related to each of these components are likely to have considerable impact on bargaining behavior.

Before moving toward our task, however, it may be useful to state explicitly several basic assumptions. First, although we shall be talking about the effects of a variety of structural components, we do not wish to imply that such components are rigid or fixed, that they cannot be altered by the bargainers during the course of their exchange. On the contrary, it is our belief that structural components may be appropriately manipulated in order to make bargaining a more effective instrument of conflict resolution. At the same time, however, we are aware that bargainers frequently seek to manipulate these very components for their own personal gain, often at considerable expense to the opposing party. This latter strategy, we believe, reflects a misuse of bargaining as a conflict resolution tool, since bargainers can increase their long-term gains to a greater extent by manipulating structural components for common rather than personal gain.

Second, the approach we have adopted may be interpreted by some as implying that bargaining behavior tends to be determined, in large part, by factors that are external to the participants in such relationships. We wish to dispel this argument, for it will become increasingly clear in this and sub-sequent chapters that, although bargainers are indeed highly susceptible to externally imposed pressures, they are by no means passively engaged in the pursuit of desired outcomes. Instead, it is clear that bargainers exert control over various elements of the psychological setting in which they function. This control is a manifestation of a bargainer's personality—his internally generated needs and characteristic behavioral orientations—and, as we shall see in Chapter 7, personality seems to play a large part in shaping a bar-gainer's responses to the situation at hand.

Finally, we make the assumption that since any bargaining relationship (by definition) consists of at least two parties, occurs in a physical and tempo-ral context, and involves at least one issue, there will always be structural components that affect the behavior of the participants. We assume, there-fore, that it is primarily by identifying and assessing such components that participants as well as observers can deepen their understanding of the events that occur in bargaining and thereby perhaps increase their ability to promote more satisfying outcomes.

The social structure of any bargaining situation may be seen as ranging from "simple" to "elaborated." In the former case, bargaining is likely to occur in the context of limited external social components; in the latter it is likely to be embedded in a highly differentiated context. Consider the ex-ample of a husband and wife who, in the privacy of their home, bargain about sharing the family car, versus an instance of multilateral international negotiation that receives widespread mass media coverage. If we assume that our married couple is childless, that neither in-laws nor neighbors are likely to be concerned with the outcomes or involved in the exchange, and that the parties represent their own personal interests exclusively, we may safely conclude that the external social structural constraints in this situation are relatively limited. In contrast, if we assume that our international negotiators represent large and diverse constituencies who will be directly affected by the outcomes, that the mass media publicly report events as they occur during the proceedings, that "neutrals" become involved as third parties, and that the various constituencies subsequently press their repre-sentatives to obtain their preferred outcomes, then we would be inclined to view the external social structural constraints in this latter situation as elabo-rated to a far greater extent.

As suggested by the above examples, three social structural components that are particularly likely to be of importance in bargaining are: the pres-ence of audiences, the availability of third parties, and the number of partic-ipants involved in the exchange. We turn now to an examination of the effects of each.

THE PRESENCE OF AUDIENCES

Although there has been little controlled research directly concerned with the effects of audiences on bargaining, it is nevertheless clear that audiences play an important part in shaping a bargainer's behavior. Evidence to support this view comes from a variety of sources, including bargainers' verbal reports, news analyses, case histories of collective bargaining and international negotiation proceedings, and many of the prominent textbooks in this area (including Iklé, 1964; Schelling, 1960; Stevens, 1963). However, despite the rather widespread agreement among such sources that audiences do influence bargainers, there are only vague indications of the mechanisms through which this occurs. The goals of this section, therefore, are twofold: (1) to examine several investigations that shed light on the effects of audiences on bargainers and (2) to integrate the findings of these investigations by outlining what we believe to be the most important underlying mechanisms.

At the outset, however, it is necessary to clarify exactly what we mean by the term *audiences,* for although they may be present in a variety of bargaining situations, audiences may have strikingly different effects as a function of their specific attributes. For instance, an audience may be either physically present or absent from the site of a bargaining encounter (although, in the latter case, still psychologically present in the mind(s) of one or both of the bargainers). Psychological presence pertains when it is supposed by a bargainer that, even though the proceedings may not actually be witnessed, the events that transpire and the performance of the bargainers will eventually become known to an audience.

An audience, moreover, may be either dependent or nondependent on a bargainer for its outcomes, and dependency may apply either to tangible outcomes (such as the amount of a wage settlement) or intangible ones (such as the winning of moral support for a favored position). Both kinds of outcome dependence are typically found in labor–management and other forms of bargaining, in which the opposing parties each send representatives to bargain for tangible outcomes but where intangible issues may also be at stake.

Audiences that are to any extent dependent on a bargainer for representation of their interests may be appropriately termed "constituencies," although such groups provide variable amounts of solidarity and support to their representatives. Nondependent audiences appear in bargaining when individuals or groups function as observers but have no vested interest in the outcomes. The press often (although not always) functions in such a role. Nondependent audiences may also become quite salient to a bargainer, especially if he believes that they are purposefully evaluating his perform-ance rather than serving merely as casual or transient observers.

Aside from their presence or absence and dependency or nondependency, audiences may affect bargainers differently as a result of their: identity, composition, and size; relationship to the bargainer; specific role in the situation; style and content of communication with the bargainer; and appar-ent readiness to make demands or impose sanctions upon him if their prefer-ences are not pursued to their satisfaction. Such audiences may consist of peers or nonpeers, acquaintances or strangers, persons expected to be criti-cal or accepting, individuals with clearly known or vague preferences, and so forth, and they may be homogeneous or heterogeneous with respect to any of these characteristics.

Audiences transmit evaluations by providing feedback. Such feedback may take a variety of forms, ranging from nonverbal facial expressions and gestures to more highly structured written messages. Feedback may be given in response to positions that a bargainer has taken, concessions that he has made, agreements that he has reached, or his personal bargaining style. In formal bargaining situations, messages containing instructions or advice, received by a bargainer from his audience, may subtly inform him of its satisfaction or dissatisfaction with his performance. In a meeting with a constituency, or in a private caucus with other members of a bargaining team, feedback may be transmitted in the nuances of the verbal exchange that occurs.

The Need for Positive Evaluation

Clearly, any or all of the variables we have mentioned may operate to a greater or lesser degree in different bargaining situations. Several general propositions nevertheless appear plausible, the first of which is as follows: *The mere presence of an audience (including psychological presence) moti-vates bargainers to seek positive, and avoid negative, evaluation—especially when the audience is salient to the bargainers.*

In one of the few studies directly concerned with audiences in bargaining, Brown (1968) examined the effects of different types of audience feedback on retaliation in a competitively structured version of the Acme–Bolt Trucking game. In addition, the effects of informing the opposing party of the subject's costs for retaliation were also examined. The major hypothesis was that, following publicly visible exploitation, a bargainer would be likely to seek increasingly severe retaliation against his exploiter—at increasingly high costs to himself—as a direct result of the impression he thought he had created in the eyes of an observing audience. It was also predicted that costly retaliation would be curtailed when a subject believed that his costs for engaging in such behavior would be revealed to the other party.

Throughout the first 10 trials of the experiment, 60 bargainers were systematically exploited by a preprogrammed opponent. They then received evaluative feedback from an audience of peers informing them either that they looked foolish and weak as a result of their exploitation or that they looked good—even though exploited—because they "played fair." A group of control subjects, similarly exploited, received no audience feedback. In a second round of 10 trials, all subjects were given a choice between using graduated retaliation at increasing costs to self or disregarding their prior exploitation and substantially increasing their monetary outcome. Before the second series of trials began, half of the subjects were led to believe that their costs for retaliation would be made known to the other bargainer, while the remainder were assured that their costs would remain unknown to him. The results were striking: Publicly humiliated subjects—those who received the derogatory feedback—were far more likely to retaliate, and with greater severity and self-sacrifice, than subjects who received the more favorable feedback. And subjects who were assured of nondisclosure of their costs retaliated more frequently and severely than those who received the opposite information. Of special interest is the fact that when asked why they chose severe retaliation, 75% of the subjects who did so reported that they didn't want to look foolish and weak as a result of having been exploited, and that they retaliated in order to reassert their capability and strength.

The basic assumption borne out by the results of Brown's study is that saving face, defined as choosing to retaliate rather than maximize tangible outcomes, can be induced by the feedback that a bargainer receives from an audience, as well as by his concern with how he looks in the eyes of the opposing party. These results converge with research by Friedell (1968) and McDaniel, O'Neal, and Fox (1971), indicating that there is a general tendency for retaliation to follow exploitation. They also reveal that such behavior is likely to be exacerbated by feedback from others indicating to a bargainer that his public image has been damaged and by his being given assurances that the costliness to himself of such acts will remain unannounced.

There are several intriguing implications of Brown's (1968) results. First, since the audience members were neither identified by name nor outcome dependent, there is the suggestion that even when the relationship between a bargainer and an audience is rather vague, the audience may nevertheless exert considerable influence over the bargainer's behavior. Moreover, as the results suggest, accountability to an audience may occur even if its members are neither visible nor identifiable, so long as it is known that the audience functions in an evaluative role. Second, since the severity of retaliation differed as a result of the subject's beliefs about whether the opposing party had been informed of the costs for retaliation, it becomes quite clear that the opposing party, too, was seen as an audience. Apparently subjects feared looking even more foolish to the other by retaliating when they knew that he would be informed of their monetary sacrifices. Finally, since subjects who received the more favorable feedback engaged in less retaliation than those who received the derogatory feedback or none at all, there is the suggestion that audience feedback may either heighten or mitigate face saving and other forms of behavior. In a sense the supportive feedback ameliorated the need of subjects to retaliate, freeing them instead to seek greater monetary outcomes.

The results of Brown's investigation thus support the proposition that the presence of salient others drives bargainers toward actions designed to elicit positive performance evaluations from them. This need for positive evaluation may arise in the presence of dependent as well as nondependent audiences. In general though, is puts the bargainer on notice that his behavior is being, or will be, scrutinized, and that the esteem in which he is held is contingent upon the appropriateness of his performance, as this is defined by the particular audience.

It is thus apparent that the need for positive evaluation carries a great potential for influencing bargaining behavior. But why? What is it about this need that renders bargainers so susceptible to the influence of others? To answer this question, it is necessary to deal with a much broader question, concerning the general extent to which individuals throughout our society are susceptible to such pressures. Brown (1968, 1970), Goffman (1959), Heider (1958), White (1966), and, more recently, Brown and Garland (1971), Frey and Adams (1972), and Kogan, Lamm, and Trommsdorff (1972), have pointed out that there are strong culturally defined pressures on individuals in our society toward projecting an image of competency, strength, and effectiveness to others, regardless of the particular context in which social interaction occurs. And correspondingly, there are strong pressures toward avoiding or repairing those situations that threaten public exposure of deficiency or ineptitude.

Although these pressures are apparent on a general level throughout our society, there are two reasons for suspecting that they are particularly intense in the case of bargaining: First, bargainers often occupy a limelight position of public visibility; second, bargaining activity is essentially an aggressive form of social encounter, in which the participants are required to demonstrate sufficient strength and capability to protect themselves against exploitation. Deutsch and Krauss (1962) have portrayed the existence and operation of such pressures as follows:

> To allow oneself to be intimidated, particularly by someone who does not have the right to expect deferential behavior, is (when resistance is

not seen to be suicidal or useless) to suffer a loss of social face, and, hence, of self-esteem; and . . . the culturally defined way of maintaining self-esteem in the face of attempted intimidation is to engage in a contest for supremacy vis-à-vis the power to intimidate or, minimally, to resist intimidation [p. 54].

As Stevens (1963) points out in his handbook of collective bargaining, the basic dilemma facing bargainers is that, although concessions must be made in order to reach agreement, the act of concession-making is likely to be seen by the conceder, the opposing party, and others as a sign of weakness that may invite exploitation. Therefore, such acts are to be avoided or minimized.

Though scant, there is further empirical evidence attesting to the potency of positive evaluation pressures in bargaining. While these investigations have not been particularly concerned with the generation of such pressures by audiences external to the bargaining relationship, they are relevant because they provide insight into the effects of such pressures generated by the opposing party and by third parties—and such audiences are in fact prominent ones for most bargainers.

Pruitt and Johnson (1970), for example, conducted a study of the effects of mediation on the reduction of face saving in a simplified Bilateral Monopoly bargaining task. It was found that bargainers were less apprehensive that making concessions would be seen as a sign of weakness when they could make them at the suggestion of a mediator than when no mediator was involved. Although this study focused on the effects of third party interventions (and will therefore be discussed at greater length in a later section of this chapter), it bears on our contention that audiences (in this case the opposing party and the mediator) generate pressures toward positive evaluation, and that, in bargaining, such evaluation is often predicated on promoting an appearance of capability and strength. As Pruitt and Johnson point out, a conceding bargainer may blame his own concessions on the mediator in such circumstances and thereby salvage his public image. A related possibility is that a bargainer might want to avoid looking unwise by declining to heed the advice of an authoritative third party such as a mediator. In either case, however, a similar mechanism (concern with how one looks to others) would seem to be the motive behind the behavior.

Several additional findings are indicative of the potency of the motive to appear capable and strong. These are reported by Deutsch (1961b), who concluded that the use of threat, especially when it is available bilaterally, is likely to be grounded in such concerns; by Schlenker et al. (1970), who attributed increased retaliation in the PD game to this motive; and by Johnson (1971), who found that deterrent threats (see Schelling, 1960), which normally produce a high level of compliance, were likely to be far less effective in this respect when the threatened party had an increased need for positive evaluation.

Accountability

We have argued that salient audiences generate pressure toward positive evaluation and that this pressure meshes with bargainers' needs to receive such evaluations. Through what mechanisms, however, do positive evaluation pressures derive their strength to induce or limit specific types of behavior?

In order to understand the deeper effects of the need of bargainers for positive evaluation, we must first examine the nature of the relationship between an audience, which is in a position to provide such evaluation, and the bargainer who seeks it. In more general terms, this profile resembles that of a power relationship in which one party may control the outcome of another. In the audience–bargainer relationship, the former has power to determine whether the latter shall receive a positive or negative evaluation. And it is in this respect, at least, that an audience has the potential for controlling a bargainer's behavior.

Hence a second general proposition: *If a bargainer is accountable to an audience for whatever it is that will bring positive evaluation, then his accountability is the mechanism by which he may be controlled.* To obtain a positive evaluation a bargainer must at some point permit his actions to be scrutinized by an audience, and he must behave in a manner that is acceptable to it. Thus, if the presence of a salient audience arouses the need for positive evaluation, then accountability to an audience is the minimum buying price for satisfaction of this need.

That positive evaluation and accountability pressures are likely to be particularly intense when a bargainer represents others who are dependent on him for their outcomes is demonstrated in a study by McKersie, Perry, and Walton (1965). This investigation analyzed the effects of conflicting role pressures experienced by bargainers in a live (labor–management) negotiation, and provides an excellent opportunity to bring the dynamics of accountability into sharper focus. The investigators observed the 1961 Auto Workers–International Harvester contract negotiations and interviewed members of each bargaining team. They found that a negotiator's failure to bargain in accord with his constituency's preferences had serious implications for his continuation as a member of the bargaining team; moreover, defensive maneuvers were employed by each side's representatives to protect their image and reputation in the eyes of their own constituents. According to the investigators, accountability pressures were quite strong and were used by each constituency to promote advocacy of its position. Regarding the pressure generated by the Union constituency, McKersie, Perry, and Walton (1965) report:

> The rank and file can best be characterized by high aspirations backed by strong emotions. . . . Commensurate with the strength and level of rank-and-file aspirations are strong expectations about appropriate behavior for their elected representative [p. 471].

Management negotiators faced similar pressures:

> Similarly, the Company negotiator was the target of conflicting expectations. Top managment and other line managers expected settlements which did not increase labor costs excessively or reduce management flexibility. . . . At the same time they expected him to avoid a stoppage in production. The behavioral implications of such objectives were clear—hard defensive bargaining. . . . Failure to cope adequately . . . could lead either to a deterioration in interorganizational relations or to a weakening of his position within his organization [p. 465–466].

In the case of the Union representatives, failure to comply with the accountability pressures had the following kinds of implications:

> The rank and file, through their delegate on the committee, expected the chief negotiator to accept their demands and to bargain aggressively for all of them. The negotiator was not expected to differentiate among issues or to be afraid to use power in an attempt to secure a favorable settlement. The fact that the Union had frequently resorted to strike action in support of its demands and that some locals had engaged in wildcat strikes during previous negotiations . . . acted as a reminder of the behavior which was considered appropriate [p. 465].

As a result,

> A good number of delegates perceived high costs in failing to advocate their constituent's demands. Many of the delegates faced serious challenges to their leadership from organized factions within the membership and could be said to have chosen their orientation in response to implicit political sanctions [p. 465].

The results of this investigation suggest that labor and management constituencies, and dependent audiences in general, often have the power to apply sanctions to their representatives when the latter fail to satisfy accountability requirements. In collective bargaining, such sanctions include removal of the negotiator from his role (summarily or by defeat in a subsequent election), reduced constituency support (through wildcat strikes, the emergence of uncontrollable factions, or other signs of discontent), and damage to the bargainer's reputation. A common element in all of these sanctions, however, is negative evaluation, with its attendant implications of incompetency, inadequacy, and weakness. It follows, then, that the degree to which a bargainer seeks favorable evaluation from a constituency is likely to determine his accountability to that constituency and is thereby likely to shape his behavior in the bargaining exchange.

Empirical evidence about the effects of accountability is also provided by Gruder (1969), who conducted a study of two-person bargaining in which a subject bargained against a standard preprogrammed other on behalf of a bogus partner and himself. Subjects were led to believe that they had been arbitrarily chosen to represent their dyad in the negotiation and that the other team member would serve as a constituent. The experimenter varied the extent to which each subject felt accountable to his bogus constituent by informing him that he either would or would not meet with him following the negotiation. The hypothesis that accountability would lead to more "demandingness" was borne out: Bargainers who were accountable tended to make smaller first concessions than those who were not. (This finding has been replicated in a more recent study by Gruder, 1971, who employed a similar technique to create accountability pressures.)

Gruder's results are intriguing for several reasons. (1) They suggest that accountability pressures may be generated by audiences that are newly formed and with which a bargainer has had no prior relationship as well as by long-established constituencies. (2) They suggest that a bargainer's responsiveness to accountability pressures may be increased by the mere expectation of a forthcoming meeting with his constituency as well as by an explicit set of sanctions. (3) The finding that increased accountability led to more demandingness provides a clue about the manner in which accountability affects bargaining behavior. As McKersie, Perry, and Walton (1965) have observed, bargainers are induced by accountability to exhibit greater advocacy of their constituency's positions. Let us now consider this latter implication in greater depth.

Loyalty, Commitment and Advocacy

Although the empirical evidence on which our positive evaluation and accountability arguments rest is somewhat sketchy, this is less the case with respect to a third general proposition: namely, that *audiences, especially dependent ones, generate pressures toward loyalty, commitment, and ad-*

vocacy of their preferred positions. The results of several investigations may be viewed as tests of this proposition.

Blake and Mouton (1961b), for example, required each of 62 groups of subjects (46 groups of executives and supervisors and 16 groups of college students) to determine the best solution to an open-ended problem. Prior to receiving their problem, each group spent between 10 and 12 hrs (privately) in a human relations training program. Upon receiving the problem, each group spent a period of time discussing it and preparing a written statement of the group's preferred solution. The group solutions were then exchanged, and representatives of pairs of groups met in public negotiations to choose the best one. The investigators hypothesized that loyalty would win out over logic. In situations such as the one created—where conflict could only be resolved by choosing one position rather than another—loyalty to one's own group's position would be more frequent than capitulation, even when the other group's position was rated as superior by impartial judges.

The results were striking. Only two out of 62 group representatives capitulated, while the remainder stood firmly behind their group's position. These results suggest that at least in situations involving all-or-none (zero sum) disputes, representatives may be easily induced to become advocates of their own group's positions, even when the superiority of opposing points of view may be perfectly obvious to those who are less involved.

One contributing factor to the strength of the advocacy pressures which apparently were operating in the Blake and Mouton (1961b) study is the likelihood that the procedures (public negotiation following intense ingroup activity) functioned to heighten the concern with winning both of the teams and of their representatives. This concern was probably strengthened by having instructed the opposing teams that the solution judged to be the best one would win the contest. It is noteworthy that, although no tangible outcomes were at stake, the intangible gains to be derived from winning (reinforced by ingroup–outgroup distinctions and public negotiation) obviously became quite important. This suggests that, in general, when a constituency is highly dependent on a representative—whether for a tangible outcome (such as money) or an intangible one (such as winning)—it may be expected to generate pressures toward loyalty, commitment, and advocacy of its positions. Furthermore, the results suggest that a representative of a group, having a strong commitment to the group's position, may not merely be handicapped in accepting an opposing position, but, on a more fundamental level, may be impeded from being able to even recognize superior elements in that opposing position. Moreover, the sheer number of representatives who exhibited loyalty rather than logic—although they presumably differed considerably in personality characteristics—suggests that the strength of the pressures toward loyalty, commitment, and advocacy may in some cases be so great as to override differences in personality. The former implication is acknowledged by Blake and Mouton (1961a) in their contention that group identification makes it difficult, if not impossible, for an individual to accurately perceive and comprehend the position of the opposing side, thereby making resolution of the conflict all the more difficult.

Another perspective on the results of this study may be gained by taking a closer look at the nature of commitment, particularly in terms of the limitations that it may impose on an individual's ability to creatively mainpulate his environment. Roby (1960) has proposed that while commitment may have beneficial effects, it may also function to limit one's awareness of alternatives and one's latitude to make alternate choices. Roby implies that in a sense excessive commitment leads to "insulation" from information, a proposition similar to that advanced by Schelling (1960) who speaks of the "binding" qualities of commitment. It is thus possible to view the study by Blake and Mouton as one in which the structure of the situation—characterized as it was by exclusive ingroup activities prior to negotiation, a focus on issues that were zero sum in nature, and public exposure while bargaining—probably intensified the strength of the loyalty, commitment, and advocacy pressures and thereby limited the ability of group representatives to recognize and accept solutions that were more efficacious than their own.

A study by Shure, Meeker, and Hansford (1965), although not directly concerned with loyalty, commitment, and advocacy, provides striking evidence for both their existence and strength. These investigators, interested primarily in studying the responses of bargainers to a pacifist strategy, placed each of 143 subjects in three-person teams which in actuality contained two confederates. Subjects were assigned the role of negotiator and were led to believe that, during a bargaining session with a similar team, their teammates would be performing other "essential tasks" and would be dependent on them for their outcomes. After being initially exposed to the behavior of a "pacifist" on the opposing team (and a statement of his intentions as well) subjects completed a questionnaire indicating how they expected to treat him during the remainder of the bargaining session. Somewhat more than half of the subjects (75) reported that they would employ a dominating strategy, while slightly less than half (68) said that they would bargain equitably. Following several exchanges, an opportunity was provided for the teammates to send messages to the subject indicating how they expected him to behave during the remainder of the session. The messages exerted considerable pressure on the subject to exploit the pacifist. Subjects were free, however, to accede to this pressure or to disregard it. Of the 68 subjects who initially reported an intention to cooperate, 54 (more than 80%) shifted to a strategy of domination!

Lamm and Kogan (1970) gave pairs of triads (threesomes) a set of decision-making tasks and asked each to elect a representative and an alternate to negotiate agreement on those items on which the two teams differed. It was found that representatives held to their group's position for a longer time, while nonrepresentatives and alternates moved more rapidly toward convergence with one another. The authors concluded that the role of negotiator may in fact tend to make negotiation more difficult.

This general position is supported by evidence obtained by Vidmar (1971), who found that the same issue, when given to discussion as compared to negotiation groups, was more effectively resolved by the former than the latter. He also found that members of negotiation groups perceived themselves and their opponents as more committed to their own positions, had less esteem for members of opposing groups, and saw the atmosphere as more antagonistic and disagreeable than members of discussion groups.

In a study concerned with the effects of a negotiator's ties to his group, Hornstein and Johnson (1966) confirmed the hypothesis that a negotiator having a strong sense of identificatfion with his group and its proposals will be more competitive than a negotiator who identifies less with his group. These investigators also found that more highly committed negotiators encountered greater difficulty in negotiation and were more firmly committed to the superiority of their own group's proposals. These results corroborate earlier findings obtained by Campbell (1961), who observed a reduction in bargaining effectiveness when each of two opposing parties was attitudinally similar to his reference group than when only one of them was similar. These results, in addition to those obtained by Hornstein and Johnson (1966) and Lamm and Kogan (1970), suggest that the best negotiators may not be those who, as representatives, are highly committed to their reference group's positions.

An interesting perspective on the findings outlined above can be seen in a series of studies by Druckman (1967). He found that representatives of opposing teams which met prior to bargaining in a "bilateral" discussion session (in which they were instructed to spend the period discussing the issues together but without taking specific positions on any of them) resolved a greater number of issues in a shorter period of time than teams which spent a comparable period of time, prior to negotiating, in a "unilateral" team discussion (in which the members committed themselves to positions on each of the issues involved). An interesting implication of these results is that certain types of prenegotiation activity apparently increase pressures toward loyalty, commitment, and advocacy while others decrease such pressures. Perhaps such activities serve to substitute pressures toward ingroup commitment with pressures toward joint effort.

To summarize: The evidence presented above suggests that salient dependent audiences are likely to generate pressures of considerable strength toward loyalty, commitment, and advocacy of their preferred positions. There is also evidence which suggests that as a negotiator's commitment to his constituency's position becomes more pronounced (regardless of whether the issues at stake are tangible or intangible), his ability to perceive alternatives posed by an opposing party and to act affirmatively on them (if necessary) may be curtailed. This general pattern of results lends support to Deutsch's (1969) hypothesis that a "narrowing of vision" often parallels conflict intensification, and to other conceptualizations of the binding effects of commitment.

Thus the picture which emerges is that bargainers who have needs for positive evaluation may be controlled by audiences which can provide or withhold such rewards. The satisfaction of such needs depends on the extent to which a bargainer satisfies an audience's accountability requirements, and this normally requires a demonstration of loyalty and commitment as well as advocacy of its positions. Curiously enough, however, excessive commitment and advocacy may be in neither the bargainer's nor his constituency's best interests.

THE AVAILABILITY OF THIRD PARTIES

A second, social structural component that may markedly affect bargaining behavior is reflected in the availability or presence of third parties. Such individuals may function in a variety of formal or informal conflict resolution roles. Whether formal or informal, however, the interventions made by third parties may be either apparent to the casual observer or nonapparent, and they may range from the structuring of physical space, to the establishment and reinforcement of norms, to the diagnosis and satisfaction of a bargainer's personal needs.

Examples of formal third party roles include those of conciliator, mediator, arbitrator, and fact finder; examples of the informal type include those of intermediary and special envoy. There are considerable differences between the formal and the informal. For instance, formal third party roles are often defined legally or on the basis of prior formal agreement between the participants. In many instances some form of licensure, such as certification by an appropriate outside agency attesting to the third party's competency and impartiality, may be required. Also, formal third parties, such as mediators, are normally equally accessible to each of the opposing parties.

From the perspective of the participants in a dispute, when there is formal third party involvement the opposing sides are normally bound to recognize at least the legitimacy of such an individual's involvement, although they are not necessarily compelled to abide by his recommendations. While formal third parties may indeed have the authority to make interventions affecting both sides, this in itself is no guarantee that a given intervention will be heeded or seen as impartial. The effectiveness of formal third parties rests to a large extent on their personal characteristics, on their demonstrated and reputed impartiality and authoritativeness and on situational constraints.

In the case of informal third party roles, there are frequently no mutually agreed upon prior specifications—legal or otherwise—as to such an individual's authority or legitimate range of activity. Instead an informal third party may be enlisted unilaterally to perform a specific function (e.g., an intermediary who is asked to transmit a message) without necessary implication that his role will be seen as legitimate or that he will be used in any capacity by the other side. Informal third parties are often viewed as representatives of the sender's interests and are thus regarded with suspicion (unless there is demonstrable evidence of nonpartisanship). For these reasons, informal third parties such as intermediaries and special envoys are likely to be called on by one of the participants to serve relatively short-lived, narrowly defined functions, such as that of a one-way communication channel.

Formal third parties, especially when they are seen as impartial and authoritative, generate pressures toward agreement through the reduction of differences. This is true not only in bargaining situations per se but seems to occur in a variety of other kinds of conflict situations as well. For example, the ombudsman whose function it is to resolve differences between individuals and institutions, the judge who resolves differences between claimants and defendants, and the marital counselor concerned with resolving differences between husbands and wives are all instances in which pressures toward the reduction of differences may be generated by third parties having formally vested authority to serve in this capacity. It is also interesting to note that in bargaining—as perhaps in each of the instances mentioned above—these pressures can be seen to operate prior to, as well as following, third party intervention.

In other words, the mere availability of a third party may itself generate pressures toward agreement. The mere knowledge, for example, that a declaration of impasse will bring a mediator into a negotiation, may push bargainers toward creating an impasse so that they may then make concessions—ostensibly at the mediator's suggestion rather than on their own initiative. This kind of motive has been noted by Johnson and Tullar (1972), Kerr (1954), Pruitt (1971), Walton (1969), Walton and McKersie (1965), and others. The mediator's suggestion in this case permits a concession that, if proffered by the bargainer himself, could be seen as a sign of weakness by the opposing party or even by his own constituency. A concession made on the advice of a mediator may reduce a bargainer's accountability for having made that concession and may thereby ameliorate negative evaluations of him. On the other hand, third party interventions may also serve to illuminate alternatives that are not readily apparent to bargainers because of their commitment to their own or to their constituency's positions.

In general, then, *the pressures toward agreement generated by third parties may emanate from the mere knowledge of their presence and/or future involvement, from their specific attributes (such as personality and reputation), and most directly from the interventions which they initiate.* In large part these pressures push bargainers in two primary directions: toward deference to norms of fairness, social responsibility, reciprocity, and equity of exchange; and toward the search for alternatives to their preferred positions.

Several important questions must be raised about third-party interventions in bargaining. First and foremost, are such interventions effective? Second, if they are effective, why? (In other words, what functions do third parties serve?) Finally, what are the psychological mechanisms that make bargainers receptive to such interventions? Raising such questions makes it immediately clear that psychological research directly concerned with third parties has been scant. However, several studies have been conducted that provide insight into these questions and into the pressures generated by third party interventions.

In addition, an extremely interesting, though perhaps more speculative, perspective on some of these questions is provided by a class of investigations which have not specifically sought to control elements of third party involvement but are instead concerned with other variables. We are referring here to investigations in which the experimenter intervenes directly (personally) into a bargaining relationship for the purpose of creating the experimental variations. We consider such interventions to be roughly analogous to formal third party interventions in several important respects. First, an experimenter is in fact an authoritative third party, much like a mediator in collective bargaining. Second, an experimenter is likely to be seen as responsible for structuring the experimental situation, just as third parties such as mediators are often seen as providing similar functions. Third, the experimenter's role may itself impart a sense of commitment to norms of fairness, responsibility, reciprocity, and equity, just as formal third parties reinforce such norms in live bargaining situations. Finally, a common concern among research subjects is with looking good in the eyes of the experimenter—to behave as is thought appropriate. Though this motive generally proves to be a contentious problem in much psychological research, it may actually approximate the reality of some bargaining situations in which third parties are involved because bargainers may become highly motivated to be favorably regarded by such individuals.

Although many of the general conditions of third party interventions tend to be created when experimenters intervene personally between opposing bargainers, we would caution against overgeneralization from such experiments, since most often such investigations are not primarily concerned with factors related to the delivery of an intervention but rather with its effects. Moreover, the experimenter in such situations is neither treated nor studied as a third party but tends to be viewed as an integral part of the context in which the bargaining takes place. We look to such studies for their suggestive implications rather than for definitive conclusions about third party roles.

The Effectiveness of Third Parties

Perusal of any major daily newspaper informs us that formal third parties become involved in a suprising number of community disputes, labor–management negotiations, and international conflicts. Also widely publicized are numerous accounts of smaller scale conflicts (e.g., divorce and child possession proceedings, grievances by individuals against institutions, etc.) in which neutral third parties are introduced in order to ease conflict resolution between the protagonists. The overall impression gained from these accounts is that third parties, although they may fall far short of optimal effectiveness, are generally useful in helping to bring about more rapid and effective conflict resolution.

Psychological research in bargaining and conflict resolution provides support for this impression. For example, Pruitt and Johnson (1970) conducted a version of the Bilateral Monopoly game in which male college students participated in a negotiation task as buyers, each paired with a programmed seller. Subjects were to agree on a price for a resource held ostensibly by the seller. Bids were exchanged within each pair, but the programmed seller never made or accepted an offer allowing the buyer to purchase the resource at a profit. One half of the subjects received a "mediator intervention" after either 5 or 20 exchanges (these variations were introduced to create differing time pressures). The intervention was made by a person identified as a "recorder" (rather than the experimenter), whose job it was to merely record offers and counteroffers after each exchange. Subjects were informed that the recorder could, on his own initiative, send a note to either bargainer indicating what he thought would be a fair offer. The standard intervention was in the form of a brief written message sent to the subject (buyer), which said, "On the basis of my predictions, I suggest that you agree on a price of _____ . A copy of this note has also been sent to your opponent." The suggested price was always midway between the subject's and the program's last offer.

Briefly, the results showed that bargainers who received the mediator's intervention subsequently made larger and more frequent concessions than subjects who received no intervention. Interestingly, data obtained from postexperimental questionnaires revealed that concession making was seen as a sign of personal weakness more among bargainers in the no-mediation condition than among those who received the mediator's intervention. The investigators interpreted their results as supporting the view that an intervention by a mediator may enable bargainers to make concessions without viewing themselves as weak for having done so. As stated by Pruitt and Johnson (1970): "Mediation provides the negotiator with a face-saving device whereby he can retreat without feeling that he has capitulated. Presumably, this face-saving results from throwing the blame for one's own concessions onto the mediator [p. 246]."

Pruitt and Johnson's results are intriguing because concessions were increased by a rather limited intervention, originating from a source never explicitly identified as a mediator or third party in the traditional sense. Yet greater concession making was induced as an effect of even this rather minimally defined third party role and this rather "skeletal" intervention.

In an experiment conducted by Podell and Knapp (1969), business students participated in a simulated labor–management wage negotiation against a preprogrammed management negotiator. The program followed a predetermined sequence of responses to subjects' offers. Subjects negotiated in either a mediation or nonmediation condition, with the experimenter serving as the mediator in the former. The investigators found that subjects saw the programmed other as more willing to make concessions when these concessions were preceded by an intervention from the mediator than when this did not occur—although the actual concessions made by the program were identical. The investigators concluded that self-initiated concessions give more of an impression of weakness than similar concessions initiated by a mediator.

The results of the Podell and Knapp study coincide with those obtained by Pruitt and Johnson and suggest that interventions made by neutral third parties—even if rather vaguely defined—generate pressures toward the reduction of differences between opposing positions. These pressures seem to operate by reducing the constraints on bargainers to promote an outward appearance of toughness and by increasing pressures toward the observance of fairness or equity norms.

This conclusion is consistent with the results of several other investigations. For example, the previously discussed study by Vidmar (1971) revealed that although discussion groups were more effective than negotiation groups in reaching agreement, performance among the latter increased in effectiveness when a mediator was present. This finding is especially interesting because the persons who served as mediators in this study were actually peers of the negotiators and thus enjoyed no distinctive status advantages, other than being identified arbitrarily as neutral third parties.

In a study conducted by Meeker and Shure (1969) subjects played a modified version of the Acme–Bolt Trucking game in the presence or absence of an older, neutral observer, who monitored the bargainers' behavior and interviewed them after the bargaining session. It was striking that the amount of cooperation in the third party condition—especially at the outset of the session—was more than twice as great as that found in the no third party condition. Here, as in previously discussed studies, the bargainers had very little information about the third party who, in fact, made no intervention; yet his mere presence, coupled with the sparse information provided, apparently increased cooperation significantly. The interpretation advanced by the investigators was that the presence of the neutral third party probably pushed bargainers to behave ethically, a notion not unlike our argument that neutral third parties generate pressures toward the observance of fairness or equity norms.

A similar finding was obtained in a study by Krauss and Deutsch (1966) which, although primarily concerned with the availability of communication as a device for ameliorating conflict, has extremely important third party implications. These investigators had found in an earlier study (Deutsch & Krauss, 1962) that when threat was available to both players in the Acme–Bolt Trucking game, conflict tended to intensify, resulting in extremely poor bargaining outcomes; and communication channels, although available, were not used for conflict resolution. The later experiment employed the same procedure, with the exception that the experimenter intervened directly in one-half of the bargaining pairs and tutored subjects in more effective use of the communication channel available to them. The experimenter instructed the players: "Make a proposal which you think is reasonable and acceptable both to yourself and to the other person. Try to make a proposal which is both fair to yourself and which you would be willing to accept, if you were in her shoes [p. 574]."

On the basis of the foregoing discussion, it should not be surprising that tutored subjects bargained more effectively (obtained higher outcomes) than those who were deprived of the experimenter's intervention. The question remains, however, whether the difference was due to the tutoring per se, or to the implications of the experimenter's intervention having to do with fairness, reasonableness, and mutuality of interest. As Krauss and Deutsch concluded:

It is clear that the incentive to make fair proposals derived from the instructions of the experimenter. . . . When the experimenter, a figure not without prestige and authority for the subjects, instructs them to use the communication channel to exchange fair proposals, he is doing more than simply suggesting the content of communication. He is, in effect, establishing a social norm of "fairness" or "equity" as a part of the context of the experiment [pp. 576-577].

Here again we are presented with evidence which suggests that if a third party, invested with authority and presumably neutrality, reinforces norms of fairness and equity, he will be likely to generate pressures toward agreement. Taken by itself, this is not a surprising revelation. However, the studies we have examined also suggest that it may not take a great deal of active involvement by third parties to generate such pressures. These pressures may be activated even when third party interventions are rather limited and their roles rather minimally defined, as long as there are no indications of partiality or unfairness evident in their behavior.

The Functions Served by Third Parties

The evidence we have examined so far seems to suggest that, when neither impartiality nor authoritativeness are in question, formal third parties are likely to generate pressures that drive bargainers toward agreement. However, having reached an affirmative answer to the question of whether or not third parties are effective, we must now confront the broader problem of determining the reasons for their effectiveness. To gain a toehold on this question, it may be useful to examine the range of functions which third parties provide in bargaining. Since we know of no empirical investigations of the effects of differing third party roles, we shall borrow heavily from conceptual analyses in this area.

In a discussion of the resolution of industrial conflict, Kerr (1954) points out that a mediator may provide any of the following forms of assistance:

1. *Reducing irrationality,* by providing the parties with ". . . an opportunity to vent their feelings to him, by keeping personal recriminations out of joint discussions, and by drawing the attention of the parties to the objective issues in dispute and to the consequences of aggressive conflict [pp. 236–237]."

2. *Reducing nonrationality,* by making interventions that enable the parties to clarify their intentions and their expected gains and costs;

3. *Exploring alternative solutions,* by recasting issues on which positions may be solidified in terms that evoke less rigidity;

4. *Providing opportunities for graceful retreat or face saving,* in the eyes of one's adversary, one's constituency, the public, etc., (a) by removing concession making from face-to-face or public exposure, (b) by controlling

the pace of retreat, and (c) by taking responsibility for concessions made.

5. *Facilitating (constructive) communication between opposing parties,* by acting as a go-between or providing opportunities for informal communication;

6. *Regulating the costs of conflict,* ". . . by bringing or threatening to bring public wrath down on [the bargainers'] heads, by persuading their allies to withdraw their support, by threatening retribution (or reward) from government or customers or some other source . . . [pp. 238–239]"|;

7. *Regulating public intervention or interference;*

8. *Identifying and promoting the use of additional resources not initially apparent to the parties; and*

9. *Establishing and reinforcing norms and rules of procedure.*

In a slightly more general vein, Walton (1969) has examined the kinds of interventions that third parties may make to bring about "constructive confrontation." Walton's formulation is intended to be applicable to a broad range of conflicts, ranging from those that are primarily interpersonal to more structured bargaining situations. He thus argues that:

> The third party can facilitate a productive confrontation by assessing and managing the following ingredients in the interaction setting: motivation, situational power, timing, pacing, tension level, communicative signs, and the group norms, process skills, and support relevant to openness [p. 115].

Specifically, Walton points out that third parties may exert influence over: *the structure of the confrontation,* including the neutrality of the site, the formality of the setting, the time constraints, and the composition of the meeting with respect to others who are present; and over *the dialogue process,* including refereeing the interaction, initiating agenda, restating issues and views, eliciting reactions, offering observations, and diagnosing aspects of the conflict.

Psychological Mechanisms Determining the Effectiveness of Third-Party Interventions

Although it is clear that formal third parties such as mediators may perform a variety of functions (and may even perform several of these simultaneously), it is equally clear that to do so effectively there must be sufficient trust in their integrity and confidence in their ability for them to execute this role. The importance of these factors as necessary conditions for third party effectiveness has been studied intensively by Kressel (1971), who conducted in-depth interviews with 13 prominent labor mediators. Kressel found that "the respondents were in general agreement that [gaining the trust and confidence of the parties] was the first and most important task of the mediator [p. 41]."

As reported by Kressel's respondents, the trust factor seems to embody at least two different dimensions: the safeguarding of privileged information and the commitment to being "a servant of the parties and of nobody else [p. 41]." It was also reported that trust in a mediator generally required a demonstrable concern on his part with the particular dispute, and an empathic, nonjudgmental understanding of each side's position. With respect to the ability factor, the interviewees indicated that among the main criteria often employed in assessing a mediator's competency are manifest signs that he understands the intricacies of the bargaining process, the real issues at stake, and the relationship between the parties.

We view "trust in integrity" and "confidence in ability" as major factors that mediate responsiveness to third party interventions. We therefore hypothesize that *other things being equal, the greater the trust and confidence in a third party, the more effective his interventions are likely to be.* Stated somewhat differently, the strength of the pressures toward agreement generated by third parties will be a function of the amount of trust and confidence placed in them by bargainers.

But what are the reasons for the importance of these factors? Why, in short, should trust and confidence be necessary elements in determining third party effectiveness? A somewhat deeper probe into both the nature of the third party's role and into one of the fundamental dilemmas of bargaining provides several answers to this query.

First, if we assume that successful bargaining normally requires a continual downward adjustment of preferences (rather than adherence to a fixed position) then, as Podell and Knapp (1969) point out, bargainers continually face the dilemma of making concessions while appearing to be unyielding. Any concession made by a bargainer carries the potential for what Pruitt (1971) identifies as "position loss" and "image loss." Since such losses may either be increased or decreased by making a concession at the recommendation of a third party, a conceder in such circumstances must believe that the third party's recommendation is sound, fair, and in *his* best interests before acceding to it. In a sense, a bargainer places a portion of his fate (and his "face") in the hands of a third party when making a concession recommended by the latter. Unless there are other reasons for doing so, bargainers are not likely to give control over their outcomes to another who is not trusted to safeguard their interests—in this case by protection against excessive position and image loss. Hence the paradox: While it is necessary to make concessions if bargaining is to occur, there are pronounced pressures against such behavior. Mediators and other formal third parties can reduce the strength of these pressures—in some cases perhaps even cause their reversal—if they can promote in bargainers the belief that their interventions are sufficiently sound and free of partiality that position or image loss or both may be reduced.

A factor pointing to the necessity of trust and confidence may be extracted from the often stated view that the task of a mediator consists largely of "trying to persuade each party to accept the largest concession which the other is willing to make [Pruitt, 1971, p. 230]." If, as implied by Pruitt's use of the word "persuade," we view third parties as influence agents, then it becomes possible—and interesting—to think of such individuals as themselves functioning in a bargaining role. Viewed in these terms, a mediator is merely another party to a bargaining relationship—one whose primary interests lie in the area of promoting agreement between the principal opponents rather than in competing for the specific outcomes which they seek.

Toward this end the mediator has a variety of devices at his disposal for promoting agreement. He may: attempt to heighten the salience of norms having to do with reciprocity, fairness, equity, social responsibility, etc; act to protect the parties against excessive position and image loss; exercise power over the participants, as this may be derived from his legitimacy, expertise, or reputation as well as his ability to reward or punish them; and reveal alternatives that the opposing parties may have been unable to perceive by themselves. However, in order to do any of these effectively, he must have the trust and confidence of the disputants.

To summarize briefly: Effective third party interventions generally create pressures toward agreement. These pressures drive bargainers to make concessions and narrow the differences between them, or at least to demonstrate that they have given serious consideration to alternatives to their initially preferred positions. Authoritativeness and impartiality, as these affect confidence and trust in a third party, seem to be the foundations of effective intervention. Pressures toward agreement may be strengthened by structuring the situation (physically or normatively or both) to protect against excessive position or image loss to the conceding party. This may involve the subtle provision of rewards by the third party when a desirable concession is made (such as the obtaining of a reciprocal concession from the opposing party or the giving of public praise to the conceder), or subtle threats of increased position or image loss for failure to make an appropriate concession. A third party's reward–punishment potential may be grounded in his personal prestige (e.g., his prior reputation for promoting equitable agreements), his institutional role (e.g., his status as a representative of "the people," national interests, etc.), and the opportunity he provides for bargainers to attribute their concessions to him.

THE NUMBER OF PARTIES INVOLVED IN THE BARGAINING EXCHANGE

A third major component of the social structure of bargaining concerns the number of parties involved in the exchange. As we pointed out in our definition of bargaining (Chapter 1), the simplest form of this type of relationship occurs when two parties have conflicting interests with respect to a single issue. However, as the number of issues increases, the number of external audiences proliferates, or the number of parties directly involved in the exchange expands, bargaining becomes far more complex.

Bargaining relationships frequently involve more than two principal parties. Clear examples of multiparty, multilateral bargaining include the European Common Market negotiations, negotiations between the Uniformed Civil Service Workers (policemen, firemen, sanitation workers, etc.) and the City of New York, and a spate of recent community disputes involving opposed racial, political, and economic interest groups. Multiparty bargaining of a different sort also occurs in conjoint marital therapy, where entire families—including parents, children, and perhaps in-laws or other relatives—may, in an attempt to reconcile disagreements among them, meet with one or more counselors over a period of time.

In general, expansion of the number of parties directly involved in a bargaining relationship increases the difficulty of coordination and introduces a variety of problems, stemming primarily from the conflicting interests and interdependencies among the parties involved. Marwell and Schmitt (1972), for example, have found that triads have significantly greater difficulty establishing a pattern of cooperation in a PD-type game than do dyads. Typical of the problems that arise when more than two parties are involved in a bargaining exchange are the need for increased time to reach agreements, an increase in the number of both tangible and intangible issues that may arise, accountability to a greater number of salient audiences, and tendencies to form coalitions.

Reasons for the Formation of Coalitions

The word *coalition* may be defined as the unification of the power or resources (or both) of two or more parties so that they stand a better chance of obtaining a desired outcome or of controlling others not included in the coalition. If we make the assumptions that there are likely to be differences in power and resources (real or imagined) among the participants in a multiparty bargaining relationship, and that it is normally to one's advantage to use such resources to obtain a desired outcome, then (unless it is futile to do so) we would expect coalitions or alliances to be formed as a mechanism for offsetting weakness in such circumstances. We therefore view tendencies toward the formation of coalitions as a primary characteristic of multiparty bargaining.

We have seen that in two-party bargaining there are typically pressures that drive the participants to seek positive evaluation, in order to demonstrate their capability and strength, lest they be seen as weak and therefore vulnerable to exploitation. *In multiparty bargaining, pressures toward coalescence are generated when self-perceptions of weakness, disadvantage, or insufficiency of resources needed to obtain an outcome drive at least two bargainers to join forces in order to maintain or increase their individual strength, so that they are neither viewed nor treated as weak by others who are also involved in the exchange.*

Psychological theory and research concerning the formation of coalitions provides insight into several basic questions, which we shall explore subsequently. These questions are: Under what conditions are coalitions likely to form? What factors tend to prevent their formation? What are some of the factors that affect another's desirability as a coalition mate? And, finally, how are outcomes obtained as a result of coalescence likely to be divided among the members of such groups? These questions suggest not that coalitions will always form in multiparty bargaining but that they are more likely to form under some conditions than others. And, as we shall see, there is a general tendency for such alliances to occur in competitive multiparty bargaining, except where it is useless to do so or where one or more of the parties actively attempts to prevent their formation.

Much of the theory and research that has been undertaken to answer the questions outlined above has focused on coalitions in three-person groups (triads). Although some attention has been given to larger groups, the complexity of the problem and the difficulty of extending existing theory have restricted inquiry into these questions in groups of larger size. Accordingly, we intend to focus our own examination on the formation of coalitions in triads, although we will briefly discuss several investigations concerned with alliances in larger groups.

Preceded by the pioneering work of Georg Simmel at the turn of the century, it was Caplow (1956) who first became concerned, in a predictive sense, with the determination of which parties would be likely to enter into coalitions. He viewed the relative power of the parties as a primary determinant of coalition formation and derived several predicitions about how coalitions would be likely to form as a result of the distribution of power within such groups. Caplow's predictions are summarized in Table 4–1.

Caplow based his predictions on several assumptions: *(1)* that power differences in competitive triadic encounters motivate individuals to seek alliances in order to gain control over others or at least to prevent the latter from gaining control over them; *(2)* that weaker parties in such circum-

Table 4–1

Caplovian Coalition Predictions [a]

Index of relative power for each member			Type of power relationship	Predicted coalition	Character of alliance
A	B	C			
1	1	1	All equal ($A = B = C$)	Any pair	Two parties pair to to outweigh the third
3	2	2	One stronger ($A > B; B = C; A < B + C$)	BC	Two weaker parties pair to outweigh the stronger
1	2	2	One weaker ($A < B; B = C$)	AB or AC	Each stronger party seeks the weaker to outweigh other strong party
3	1	1	One all-powerful ($A > B + C; B = C$)	None	Coalition useless— weaker parties cannot outweigh stronger
4	3	2	All different ($A > B > C; A < B + C$)	AB or AC	Any coalition of two outweighs the third
4	2	1	All different ($A > B > C; A > B + C$)	None	Coalition useless— weaker parties cannot outweigh stronger

[a] Adapted from Caplow, 1956.

stances will normally be inclined to form coalitions against the stronger; and (3) that processes of coalition formation in the triad are generalizable to larger social groups. In connection with the second assumption, Caplow pointed out that coalitions will generally tend to favor the weaker parties over the stronger, for it is the former who stand to gain as a result of their alliances while the latter, who are disinclined to share their advantage, are likely to be excluded or isolated and thereby become functionally weakened. As can be seen in Table 4–1, Caplow's predictions suggest that, in general, coalitions are likely to occur in competitive multiparty interactions except where it may be useless for them to do so.

On the basis of an extensive review of the literature, Gamson (1964) has distinguished among several different theories that attempt to account for the formation of coalitions:

1. *Minimum resource theory* holds that coalitions will be formed on the basis of the resources that each prospective member can contribute, the

determining criterion of coalescence being the accumulation of resources minimally sufficient to control outsiders. This theory holds that outcomes obtained by coalitions will be divided in proportion to the resources contributed initially by each party.

2. *Minimum power theory* holds that power is not derived from initial resources, but from an individual's attractiveness as a partner. Attractiveness refers to the number of alliances that such an individual might enter into and, by his entry, cause to become winning coalitions. This theory holds that, since it will be recognized by coalition members that as individuals they have insufficient power to gain control over the outcomes, these outcomes will tend to be divided equally among them.

3. *Anticompetitive theory* stresses the likelihood that rather than coalitions being formed along the lines described above, there is in some instances a tendency for parties to unite against a common target, in order to maximize their joint outcomes while maintaining the solidarity of the group. A theory such as this seems to rest on two assumptions: (a) that the disruption of group solidarity is negatively valued and hence will normally be avoided and (b) that superordinate goals tend to provide a basis for unification, regardless of differences in initial power or resource contribution.

4. *Confusion theory* rests on the assumption that the situation surrounding the formation of coalitions is so complex that, when alliances are formed, they will occur largely as a result of nonsystematic or random factors.

Considerable research has been conducted that provides a basis for judging the soundness of the above theories and for gaining insight into the questions raised earlier. Let us now examine some of this evidence.

The Conditions under which Coalitions Are Likely to Form

In general, we wish to argue, *coalitions are especially likely to form in competitive, multiparty bargaining relationships when power (or other resources necessary for obtaining an outcome) is distributed, or perceived to be distributed, in such a way that one or more of the parties views himself as disadvantaged with respect to obtaining some outcome and does not consider it fruitless to join forces with another in pursuit of the outcome he seeks.*

Vinacke and Arkoff (1957) designed the Parcheesi Coalition game for the purpose of testing several of the coalition predictions made by Caplow (1956). Six conditions were created, in which power was distributed in the following ways: (1,1,1; 3,2,2; 1,2,2; 3,1,1; 4,3,2; and 4,2,1). The investigators recorded the coalitions formed and the manner in which the reward was divided in each triad. It was found that in the equal power condition (1,1,1) there were no consistent tendencies for any subject to choose either of the others as a partner. However, in approximately 90% of the 90 triads in this condition, two-person coalitions were formed. This pattern of results thus corroborates Caplow's prediction for the equal power case, and provides evidence in favor of the minimum power and resource theories, but it offers little support for the anticompetitive and confusion theories. The fact that 90% of the triads formed coalitions supports our own contention that in a competitive situation such as this one, forces toward coalition formation press bargainers to seek to increase the resources needed to obtain a desired outcome.

In the second condition (3,2,2), coalitions among the weaker parties (2,2) occurred in about 70% of the 90 triads. Only 1 of the 90 triads failed to form a coalition. These results also support Caplow's prediction for this case and again favor the minimum power and resource theories over the others. The fact that alliances were formed in all but 1 of the 90 triads offers impressive evidence in support of our proposition. In conditions four (3,1,1) and six (4,2,1), where coalitions among the weaker parties could not offset the weight of the stronger, approximately two-thirds of the 90 triads in each condition failed to form them, again in support of Caplow's predictions. In the 1,2,2 condition, approximately 70% of the coalitions that formed (64 out of 79) consisted of alliances between the weaker party and one of the stronger members. Corroborating Caplow again, it was in only 10% of the triads that no coalitions formed. Caplow's reasoning was also borne out in the 4,3,2 condition, where about two-thirds of the 88 coalitions that formed included both weaker parties. Again, no coalitions were formed in only 2 of the 90 triads.

The high overall incidence of coalitions (given that it was useful to form them) found in the Vinacke and Arkoff (1957) study has generally been replicated in subsequent investigations. For example Bond and Vinacke (1961), Uesugi and Vinacke (1963), and Vinacke (1959), although primarily concerned with sex differences, all report pronounced tendencies for coalitions to occur, although all found that women seem to establish different kinds of coalitions than men. Similarly, all the following observed clear tendencies toward the formation of coalitions in multiparty bargaining exchanges: Lieberman (1964), using a different type of three-person game to investigate the stability of coalitions; Shears (1967), studying coalitions in four-person bargaining groups; Gamson (1962), who conducted an historical analysis of coalitions formed in political conventions; and Kelley and Arrowood (1960), using a modification of the Vinacke and Arkoff (1957) game.

In general, the results of the studies mentioned above are not only indicative of the strength of the forces toward coalescence, but also provide evidence for the power-inversion or "strength is weakness" effect described by Caplow (1956), and later verified experimentally by Cole and Phillips

(1967) and Cole (1969). The consistency with which this effect has been noted also carries the clear implication that perceived weakness or vulnerability is probably an underlying motive in coalition formation.

Kelley and Arrowood (1960) took issue both with the Vinacke–Arkoff (1957) procdures for creating power differences and with Caplow's (1956) prediction that AB and AC coalitions should occur most frequently in the 4,3,2 power condition. Specifically, they argued that power was illusory rather than real in Vinacke and Arkoff's 4,3,2 condition because *any* combination of two players had sufficient strength to be a winning coalition. Thus they reasoned that the Vinacke–Arkoff results for the 4,3,2 condition (65% of their triads formed the weaker coalition) probably occurred as a result of subjects' failure to recognize that any two-person coalition would win, and that this was brought about by the complexity of the task and poor understanding of the instructions. They reasoned that had subjects understood the problem sufficiently, no particular coalition would have occurred more often than any other. They also contended, in opposition to Caplow (1956), that when power is real rather than illusory, subjects would be most likely to form the BC coalition against the stronger party.

Kelley and Arrowood conducted two experiments to test their contentions. The hypothesis of the first was that since subjects would realize (with the help of clarified instructions and simplified procedures) that the assigned weights did not represent real power in this situation, the high power party should be excluded from coalitions no more than might occur as a result of chance, and that the high power party should not receive, on the average, more than 50% of the outcome. Thirty triads played the Parcheesi Coalition game under the 4,3,2 power distribution for an extended number of trials. The results revealed that "4" was excluded from coalitions with slightly greater than chance frequency. This failed to replicate the findings obtained by Vinacke and Arkoff (1957), in which "4" was excluded far in excess of chance expectancy. Moreover, it was found that the likelihood of "4" being included increased over trials and his percentage of the outcome decreased—suggesting that increased understanding caused a reduction in the perception of "4" as powerful. This was corroborated by questionnaire data which revealed that, while at the outset 85% of the subjects perceived "4" as having the greatest power, the figure declined to 25% by the end of the experiment.

Kelley and Arrowood's (1960) second experiment was designed to test the hypothesis that power differences perceived as real should lead to the formation of weak against strong alliances. Fifteen male triads participated in a simple 20-trial "business" game. Members were assigned weights of 4, 2, and 0, representing the number of points that could be won if each played alone, but they were also free to form coalitions if they wished. As in the Vinacke and Arkoff experiment, subjects who sought coalition membership had to agree on how to divide a 10-point payoff. They knew that if no division was agreed upon, they would have to settle for the equivalent of their assigned weight. The results of this experiment revealed that "4" was excluded from alliances far more often than were other members, and that 0,2 coalitions occurred most frequently. Neither the frequent exclusion of "4," nor the frequency of 0,2 coalitions, supported Caplow's predictions.

If weight alone was the basis of alliance formation, then the 0,2 coalition (which was decidedly a losing one) should not have formed with such great frequency. The fact that it did suggests that something other than the assigned weights accounted for its occurrence and that (in opposition to Caplow), even in the face of adverse conditions, weaker parties may combine whatever strength they do possess in order to counter a more powerful other more effectively. Anderson's (1967) analysis of the effects of status on the attractiveness of coalition partners, and the results of an experiment by Hoffman, Festinger, and Lawrence (1954) suggest that factors other than those represented by the assignment of power weights (factors such as skill, ability, and other external status characteristics) may also play a part in the formation of alliances. We shall examine the results of these experiments in greater detail in our discussion of factors which affect another's desirability as a coalition-mate.

Several conditions other than the distribution of power per se also seem to affect coalition formation. For example, the experiments by Vinacke and his associates concerning sex differences (see Chapter 7) suggest that if an external object or party is identified as a common enemy and if there is an initial proclivity toward cooperation, then unification among the partners against the "oppressor" is likely to develop. Studies by Deutsch (1958) and by Radinsky and Myers (1968), which introduced a third party who would gain by noncollaboration between players in the PD game, also reveal that coalitions are likely to form against this type of common enemy. Mazur (1968) found that in certain situations, two parties who are in conflict with one another and are intruded upon by an outsider are likely to form a coalition against him. Finally, Chacko (1961), who analyzed a multiplant, multiproduct manufacturing company's negotiations with two of its distributors, proposed that "concomitant coalitions" are likely to occur in such complex situations. Concomitant coalitions are simultaneously entered into by the same parties, who band together, for and against the same party at the same time, in order to achieve joint outcome maximization in nonzero sum situations.

The Conditions under which Coalitions
Are Unlikely to Form

There are at least three general conditions in which coalition formation in multiparty bargaining is likely to be inhibited: (1) when the combined initial weights or resources of the weaker parties are simply seen by them as insufficient to offset those of the more powerful parties (we shall refer to this condition as one of perceived futility or uselessness), (2) when a more powerful party effectively blocks the formation of alliances among weaker parties; and (3) when sources of external contention or conflict among would-be partners are of sufficient intensity that seemingly advantageous coalitions are avoided.

Futility of Coalition

The most frequent inhibitor of coalitions reported in the experimental literature seems to be an initial distribution of power or resources which results in it being unequivocally useless for the weaker parties to form an alliance against the stronger (Caplow, 1956; Michener & Lyons, 1972; Vinacke & Arkoff, 1957). However, as Kelley and Arrowood (1960) observed, futility may not be perceived in absolute terms by the weaker parties in a multiparty exchange—especially if the outcome may be distributed in a nonzero sum manner. Instead it may be seen as worth the effort by the weaker parties to attempt to increase their outcome as much as possible, even though the stronger may obtain a larger share.

The results of studies by Kelley and Arrowood (1960), Hoffman, Festinger, and Lawrence (1954), and Psathas and Stryker (1965) suggest that weak or disadvantaged parties may search for sources of strength in potential allies along dimensions other than those directly relevant to the exchange in which they are involved. Power equalization strategies of this sort have become increasingly apparent in community disputes where weaker parties having extremely limited resources enter into coalitions with others who are similarly limited, in order to mobilize public support and protest against an all-powerful political machine.

In general, then, when the outcomes at stake are zero sum, and when the resources necessary for obtaining them are strictly defined (such that the weaker parties believe that coalescence is not likely to increase their lot), alliances are unlikely to form.

Active Prevention of Coalitions

It is often the case that the power and resources of the stronger parties in multiparty bargaining are not limited to determining outcome distribution but may also be used to prevent coalitions from forming among others. Although the research evidence on this is scant, an experiment by Amidjaja and Vinacke (1965), concerned primarily with the effects of sex and personality differences on coalition formation, provides insight into how such groupings may be prevented in competitive situations. These investigators found that although few coalitions were formed by either males or females in the "all powerful" power distribution, males who held the high power position and also had high needs for achievement were less likely to allow coalitions to form among weaker parties than females of a similar personality type, who encouraged the formation of triple alliances. Strategies of coalition prevention in such situations include the formation of countercoalitions (Willis, 1962), concomitant coalitions (Chacko, 1961), and the instigation of divisiveness or contention among the weaker parties.

Further evidence related to the prevention of coalitions can be found in Schwarz's (1970) study of tendencies toward labor coalitions in collective bargaining. Schwarz documents a noteworthy movement toward coalition bargaining in union negotiations with giant multiplant and multiproduct conglomerates. The major reason for this development seems to be that single labor unions view themselves as being at a severe power disadvantage because they cannot exert sufficient strength to offset the massive economic power of large corporations. This is particularly felt by unions because one of their major sources of power—their strike potential—becomes ineffective in the face of multiplant companies. As Schwarz (1970), points out: "Once a union cannot hurt a company by a strike, the balance of bargaining strength has disappeared.. . . Labor leaders universally recognize that separate unions leave themselves open for 'whipsawing' or the 'divide and conquer' tactic [p. 6]." For their part, Schwarz argues, conglomerate management is usually loath to bargain with labor coalitions because doing so is likely to reduce its strength. In order to avoid this, management typically attempts to counter the formation of such alliances by insisting on conducting contract negotiations with individual unions or by challenging the legality of such coalitions.

Contention among Potential Coalition Mates

The third inhibitor of coalitions arises out of the existence of salient external issues or conflicts among parties who might usefully form alliances with one another. Such differences may prevent the parties from recognizing their common interests with respect to the issues of immediate concern. Common examples occur in the political arena, when ideological differences prevent splinter groups from forming coalitions against dominant factions; in labor–management disputes, when internal discord prevents a union from striking; and in community disputes, when economically disadvantaged groups fail to form alliances as a result of philosophical or strategic differences concerning the level of militancy to be exercised against a government agency.

Unfortunately there is no experimental evidence that reflects directly on the extent to which contention among weaker parties prevents them from forming advantageous alliances. However, several investigations shed indirect light on this question. For example, Stryker and Psathas (1960) and Psathas and Stryker (1965) created contention among two of the members of triads by informing them that they could not enter into a coalition with one another because they were "enemies of long-standing." These investigators were not concerned with whether coalitions would form when contention existed (they actually disallowed coalitions between contending parties) but instead examined the division of outcomes among the noncontending parties. However, indirect evidence about the general effects of contention can be inferred from the findings of these studies, which revealed that when there was contention between two parties the third received a larger share of the outcome than when no contention existed.

In a similar vein, Gamson's (1962) historical analysis of coalition formation at presidential nominating conventions suggests that ideological differences that exist between subgroups of political parties may cause such groups to form nonutilitarian coalitions. Finally, Mills (1953) studied the internal stability of coalitions formed in three-person work groups and discovered that contention was likely to have adverse effects on the activity rate and supportiveness of the members and was likely to produce heightened conflict, thereby decreasing the group's stability.

In short, we may say that there is a general tendency for coalitions to occur in multiparty bargaining. However, in order to persist and to be effective, the pressures toward coalition arising out of self-perceived weakness or vulnerability must outweigh the opposing pressures stemming from perceived futility, attempts by stronger parties to prevent the formation of coalitions, and contention among the parties themselves.

Factors Affecting Another's Desirability as a Coalition Partner

A variety of factors appear to affect a party's attractiveness as a coalition partner. Foremost among these are his relative power, his status, ability, and skill, and his reputation for success and the honoring of prior coalition commitments.

Relative Power

In general, much of the research discussed so far indicates that *when coalitions are not seen as useless, weaker parties are likely to seek each other out and exclude decidedly stronger parties from their alliances.* This finding has emerged rather consistently in studies by Amidjaja and Vinacke (1965), Caldwell (1971), Chertkoff (1971), Cole (1969), Cole and Phillips (1967), Kelley and Arrowood (1960), Nitz and Phillips (1969), Phillips and Nitz (1968), Vinacke and Arkoff (1957), Vinacke, Crowell, Dien, and Young (1966), Vinacke and Gullickson (1964), and Walker (1973). The results of these studies also suggest several conclusions with respect to the effects of relative power: (1) Weaker parties are unlikely to seek out others having decidedly greater power or resources. (2) Weaker parties are likely to seek others having less power and resources than they do, but who can nevertheless provide a sufficient amount to make the coalition a winning one. (3) Stronger parties are likely to "sit" on their power or resource advantage or seek exploitative alliances with weaker parties to ensure the outcome they seek. (4) Weaker parties may in some circumstances form coalitions that are nonmaximizing in terms of the tangible issue at stake but which increase their intangible gains. For example, coalitions doomed to failure at the outset (in terms of the tangible issue at stake) may persist in order to gain moral support for a position or to discredit a more powerful party in the eyes of the public.

There is also evidence suggesting that coalitions formed on the basis of initial perceptions of power and resources may shift over time as a function of: changes in the perception of a party's power (Kelley & Arrowood, 1960; Psathas & Stryker, 1965); impressions of his integrity in not abandoning prior unsuccessful coalitions (Lieberman, 1964); and shifts in the apparent probability that one will be successful in obtaining the outcome he seeks (Chertkoff, 1966).

The results of most of the studies mentioned above are based on observations of coalitions in three-person groups, but two experiments conducted with four-member groups suggest a need for caution in extending those findings to groups of larger size. For example, Willis (1962) used Vinacke and Arkoff's Parcheesi Coalition game to test several Caplovian predictions in four-person groups. Willis examined coalitions in the 4,4,3,2 and 5,3,3,2 initial power distributions and found tendencies toward the exclusion of weak members and the formation of countercoalitions. One implication of these results is that the power-inversion effect discussed by Cole (1969) may not be as apparent when the number of bargainers exceeds three. Shears (1967) contrasted the 4,2,2,1 and 3,1,1,1 initial power distributions and found that, in the latter, weak triplets occurred more frequently than they would have by chance (although they did not predominate) and that most winning alliances were of the 3,1 variety. The 1,1,1 alliance was tried by most tetrads, but its inadequate "return" caused a decline in its use. Finally, there was a tendency in the 4,2,2,1 condition for "4" to remain passive while weak members initiated alliance offers; but in the 3,1,1,1 condition, "3" was more active in seeking alliances because of his more vulnerable position.

Status, Ability, and Skill

Anderson (1967) has voiced the criticism that coalitions formed on the basis of randomly distributed resources (or power weights), in groups of unacquainted and rather homogeneous research subjects, provide limited opportunities to determine the effects of other important criteria of partner selection, such as status, ability, and skill. He argued that since external indicators are largely eliminated in this case, due to subject similarity and limited acquaintance, players in coalition games will tend to make status distinctions on the basis of performance in the experimental situation itself. He further reasoned that if external status differences are minimal and subjects perceive themselves as peers or equals, then they should strive to reduce outcome inequities accumulated by others over repetitions of the coalition game. This, he pointed out, can be accomplished by forming alliances that minimize cumulative outcome differences among the players. Anderson thus hypothesized that under conditions of equal status and equal initial resource allocation, outcome equalization should be a major determinant of coalition formation.

Anderson (1967) tested his hypothesis by examining the results of several prior studies. For example, in examining Vinacke's (1964) results, he discovered that when there was an equal distribution of initial resources (1,1,1), more than 70% of the two-person coalitions which formed included the two subjects who were behind in cumulative score. Anderson also found that this pattern was present in a study by Shears (1967), concerning coalitions in tetrads. Here he discovered that in the equal resource condition (1,1,1,1), players who were ahead in cumulative score were nearly always excluded from coalitions. Emerson (1964), who used a (3,3,3) initial resource distribution in the Parcheesi Coalition game also reported a sharp tendency for lagging subjects to form two-person coalitions against the player who was ahead: Of 84 games in which two players were behind the third in cumulative score, 72 coalitions (about 85%) occurred between the two lagging players.

Anderson concluded that status may be gained by outcome accumulation itself, and that a party possessing such a lead—especially if he has no corresponding external status advantage—is likely to be countered by coalitions among players who are deprived as a result of his gains. Thus, we may say that when the status rankings of participants in a multiparty bargaining exchange are roughly equivalent, and one of them obtains excessive early gains relative to the others, his attractiveness as a coalition mate is likely to be reduced and he may even become the target of countercoalitions. Conversely, parties who view themselves as similarly disadvantaged by the gains of another will be likely to assume increased attractiveness as coalition partners. Anderson interpreted this tendency in terms of pressures toward status equalization caused by a discrepancy between the outcome obtained by a bargainer and the outcome that the others involved in the exchange deem appropriate or just for him to receive, relative to themselves.

Anderson's reasoning is based on an experiment by Hoffman, Festinger, and Lawrence (1954), which explored the nature of status equalization forces in multiparty bargaining. These investigators reasoned that in such situations bargainers tend to become highly concerned about their own status relative to others and are normally motivated to equal or surpass others on relevant performance dimensions. Hoffman *et al.* postulated that the goal-object (outcome) itself tends to become a symbolic status yardstick, for it is primarily through outcome accumulation that individuals may directly compare their own performance with that of others. This formulation is quite similar to our contention about the strength of positive evaluation forces in multiparty bargaining, because the motive to perform as well or better than others reflects an underlying concern with how one is seen, and therefore treated, by them. To perform poorly is to cause oneself to be seen as weak and incapable, and such an image is likely to invite further exploitation.

Hoffman *et al.* (1954) reasoned that bargainers tend to compare themselves to others whom they view as similar rather than dissimilar and that the pressures to "match up" or exceed another vary directly as a function of his similarity (in terms of ability) and the importance of the task at hand. Hoffman *et al.* thus predicted that bargainers would generally form coalitions against others whom they viewed as having gained an unjustified early advantage at their expense; this pattern would be pronounced when the task was of great importance to them and the advantaged other was viewed as similar rather than dissimilar to themselves.

To test these hypotheses, an experiment was designed in which members of triads took a written intelligence test and then participated in a three-person problem-solving task requiring the formation of coalitions and bargaining over the division of an outcome. One member of the triad was always a confederate. The problem-solving task was presented as a test of social intelligence, and the points that subjects obtained in it were to be added to their written intelligence test scores. The experimenters varied the information given to triad members about the written intelligence test performance of the accomplice and about the importance of the task that they would engage in. In one condition the accomplice was presented as having superior intelligence, while in a second condition his intellectual ability was described as equal to that of the other two members. Variations in the apparent importance of the task were produced by stressing the importance of the research or by belittling it. The procedures were designed so that the confederate always gained a large initial point advantage in the bargaining task.

The results of the Hoffman *et al.* (1954) experiment revealed that the accomplice was involved in significantly fewer coalitions than the other members and had to pay more to be included. This tendency was pronounced when the task was portrayed as important and when it was believed that the accomplice had equal ability. However, it was also found that, although coalition membership was generally less frequent for the accomplice than for the other triad members, he was sought after and included in coalitions significantly more often when he had high, as compared to equal, intellectual ability.

Of special relevance to the present discussion is the fact that although coalitions tended to form against the advantaged party, information about his external status (intellectual ability) produced significant differences in his desirability as a coalition partner—he was more often sought as a coalition mate when he was thought to have superior intelligence. This suggests that although countercoalitions are likely to form against a party whose gains deprive others of an equal share of the outcome, such a tendency may be counteracted when it is thought that the advantaged bargainer is a highly capable one with respect to the task at hand.

In more general terms, then, the results of the studies cited above suggest that *the attractiveness of a coalition mate is in large part situationally determined; alliances will tend to form among parties who see themselves as sharing a common disadvantage at the hands of another.* However, there is also evidence that certain external indicators of status, such as high intellectual ability and prestige or fame (Gamson, 1964) may increase the attractiveness of a potential coalition partner, even if they lead to coalitions that are nonmaximizing in terms of the tangible outcome at stake but provide a potential for increased intangible gains—such as being associated with a prestigious other.

Reputation for Success and the Honoring of Prior Coalition Commitments

Experiments by Chertkoff (1966) and Lieberman (1964) indicate that bargainers who are seen as having a high probability of successfully obtaining an outcome and who have a reputation for reliability are likely to be more attractive as coalition partners than those lacking in these characteristics. Chertkoff (1966) observed 96 triads in a coalition game that simulated a political nominating convention. A 40,30,20 distribution of votes was given to members of each triad. Triads were then randomly assigned to one of four conditions, in which the "probability of victory in a national election" was varied for the high power member (40) but was held constant for the other two players. The four probability of victory conditions were: 50%, 50%, 50%; 70%, 50%, 50%; 90%, 50%, 50%; and a control condition in which no information about probability of victory was provided. Each triad participated in a series of three "conventions." The candidate elected in each triad would gain the opportunity to dispense 100 "jobs," and subjects were encouraged to win as many jobs for themselves as possible.

Chertkoff observed the initial partner preferences and the coalitions that formed, as well as the manner in which the outcome was divided. The results revealed that, as the high power player's probability of success increased, he was more often sought as a coalition partner (although this tendency decreased from the first through the third convention). It was also found that when probability of victory was equal (50%, 50%, 50%), coalitions between players having low power were most frequent.

The finding that probability of success had a significant initial effect on the likelihood of weak against strong coalitions is an intriguing one. It suggests that when early impressions are being formed, *a high power party who also has an announced high probability of victory may be viewed as an attractive coalition partner, due to the enhanced status he enjoys.* However, over time, attractiveness based on status enhancement may diminish as a result of the emergence of a more realistic appraisal, namely, that in such circumstances (40,30,20), a union of any two parties is sufficient to produce a winning coalition, and that an effective alliance between the weaker parties might yield a larger share of the outcome than might be obtained by coalescence with the more powerful one. In a sense, an announced high probability of success may function as a status enhancer and thereby increase a high power party's initial attractiveness as a partner, but such information may yield to more outcome-oriented considerations as the bargaining proceeds.

Lieberman's (1964) study of "i-Trust" focused in part on the question of how defection from coalition commitments, in order to obtain short-term gains, affects a bargainer's desirability as a partner and hence his own long-term outcomes. Lieberman defined "i-Trust" as "the belief that the parties involved in an agreement will actually do what they have agreed to do; that they will fulfill their commitment not only when it is advantageous for them to do so, but even when it may be disadvantageous, when they must sacrifice some immediate gain [p. 279]."

Lieberman had 24 subjects play a three-person, zero sum, majority coalition game for 40 trials. On each trial subjects had the choice of forming an alliance with another or declining to do so. The procedures were arranged so that no more than one two-person alliance could form on any given trial. Any union of two resulted in a penalty for the excluded player. (A coalition between players 1 and 2 received 10¢ from 3; one between 1 and 3 received 8¢ from 2; and a coalition between 2 and 3 received 6¢ from 1.) Real money stakes were involved. If subjects formed a coalition, they had to agree on how they would divide the trial outcome. The results reflected an awareness among subjects that payoff maximization could best be achieved by forming a stable coalition with a player who could be trusted not to defect from a coalition for a more attractive offer. Apparently subjects came to realize that reputation for reliability was an important attribute to seek in a potential partner and for oneself to exhibit, in order to increase one's own attractiveness as a coalition member.

The Division of Outcomes in Coalitions

Our discussion of coalitions may now be concluded with two general observations about the manner in which coalition members are likely to divide the results of their efforts.

First, the results of a number of experiments seem to suggest that *equality of initial power or resources among coalition members is likely to result in an approximately equal division of outcomes, whereas differential power or resources is likely to result in an unequal distribution—with members possessing greater power or resources generally demanding a larger share of the outcomes* (Chertkoff, 1966; Kelley & Arrowood, 1960; Psathas & Stryker, 1965; Shears, 1967; Shears & Behrens, 1969; Stryker & Psathas, 1960; Uesugi & Vinacke, 1963; Vinacke & Arkoff, 1957; Willis, 1962). For example, the results of the Vinacke and Arkoff (1957) experiment show that a 50–50 outcome split occurred in about 60% of the two-person coalitions that formed in the equal power $(1,1,1)$ condition, and that a similar division was agreed to in about 70% of the weak alliances $(2,2)$ that formed in the $3,2,2$, condition. However, this pattern was reversed in the $4,2,1$ power condition, where the outcome was divided equally in only 23% of the coalitions that formed. A similar tendency was reported by Kelley and Arrowood (1960), although they also found that, over time (in the $4,3,2$ "illusory" power condition), as the perception of "4's" real power diminished, the percentage of the outcome obtained by "4" decreased. In their second experiment (using a $4,2,0$ "real" power distribution), Kelley and Arrowood found that high-weighted members of $4,0$ and $2,0$ coalitions obtained a greater percentage of the outcome than low weighted members, but that in $4,2$ coalitions there was only a nonsignificant tendency in this direction.

A second general pattern which emerges is that *differences in status ranking may also affect the distribution of outcomes in a coalition, with the greater percentage going to high status members.* For example, the results of Chertkoff's (1966) experiment suggest that an announcement made at the outset of bargaining about a bargainer's probabilty of victory may function as a form of status enhancement and thereby affect both his desirability as a partner and the proportion of the outcome that he feels entitled to. In this experiment subjects were sought as coalition mates (and demanded a greater proportion of the outcome) more frequently when their announced probability of victory was high (90%) than when it was considerably lower (50%). Other types of status distinctions among coalition members may similarly affect their division of the outcomes. For example, the results obtained by Hoffman *et al.* (1954) suggest that intellectual ability may be a source of status differentiation among bargainers and that this may lead to differential outcome distribution. On the other hand, Hoffman *et al.* (1954) and Anderson (1967) also point out that the prior outcome accumulated by a bargainer may in itself become a source of status and, if this is seen as excessive or unjustifiable, may limit the outcome that a bargainer receives from then on. Sex and age may similarly operate as status differentiators (Shears & Behrens, 1969; Vinacke & Gullickson, 1964), leading to increased competitiveness and presumably to demands for a greater share of the outcome.

CONCLUDING COMMENT

This chapter has explored several of the factors that comprise the social structure of bargaining situations. Three factors in particular—the presence of audiences, the availability of third parties, and the number of participants involved in the exchange—have been discussed at some length and their effects on bargaining behavior considered.

The effects of these three components have been traced to bargainers' underlying needs for positive evaluation. Bargainers, we have suggested, have pronounced needs to look good, capable, and strong—or at least not incapable, weak, and foolish—in the eyes of others. As a result, bargainers experience themselves as accountable to a variety of others—audiences, constituencies, adversaries, third parties—each of whom, if salient, can either satisfy or frustrate the need for positive evaluation. In the presence of an audience of salient others, this need may lead to loyalty and commitment, as well as to advocacy of the group's position. In the presence of an authoritative, neutral, and trusted third party, this same need may enable bargainers to make concessions—for such concessions may now be made with less risk of looking foolish in the eyes of one's adversary. The need for positive evaluation, finally, helps explain why coalitions tend to form in multiparty bargaining relationships and why it is the weaker members in particular who tend to form coalitions with one another against the stronger. What better way to transform one's own weakness into strength than by forming an alliance with another—preferably someone whose strength is comparable to one's own but also sufficient to offset that of the more powerful "oppressor."

5

Physical Components of Bargaining Structure

One need only scan a major newspaper, such as the *New York Times*, over the last 20 years or so to document the importance of the physical structural components in bargaining. Consider, for example, the protracted dispute over the movement of the Korean cease-fire negotiations from Kaesong to Panmunjom (*New York Times*, October 9, 1951); the negotiations concerning the arrangement of tables and chairs at the Paris Vietnam Peace Talks (*New York Times*, January 3 and 4, 1969); or the dispute over bargaining deadlines between the New York City Transport Workers Union and the Metropolitan Transit Authority (*New York Times*, January 1, 1970).

Given the prevalence and importance of physical components in bargaining situations, it is the purpose of this chapter to analyze these components and consider their effects on bargaining behavior. Our analysis proceeds from two assumptions. First, we assume that since any bargaining exchange occurs within a physical context, pressures generated by this context are likely to operate, though in varying degrees, in any instance of bargaining. Second, we assume that, although disputes over physical considerations may appear to be independent of the substantive issues at stake, they are important expressions of less tangible sources of contention—such as power and status struggles between the parties. In such cases, seemingly trivial issues (like the selection of the bargaining site, the arrangement of furniture, the use of flags, nameplates, etc.) may require the bargainers' preliminary attention. Moreover, if left unresolved or if resolved unsatisfactorily, such issues may recur throughout bargaining or may proliferate, thereby hampering agreement on more tangible issues.

Four physical structural components that are particularly likely to be of importance in bargaining are: the location and accessibility of the bargaining site, physical arrangements at the site, the availability and use of communication channels, and the presence of time limits. Let us now turn to an examination of the effects of each.

LOCATION OF THE BARGAINING: SITE NEUTRALITY AND OPENNESS

The issue of site selection is often important in bargaining because it has implications for the amount of control that each party may exercise over the physical arrangements at that site, as well as for the psychological climate in which the exchange takes place. More specifically, when negotiations are conducted on one's home territory, the host has a legitimate right to assume responsibility for arranging the physical space. Although such actions may be contested by the visiting party, the host nevertheless enjoys greater freedom to exercise control—often to his own advantage—than when bargaining is conducted on neutral ground, where physical arrangements are normally decided upon by mutual consent.

Obvious psychological advantages may thus be derived from negotiating on one's home territory. Often these are of an intangible nature, in that they are related to the implied status relationship between the bargainers. A bargainer who views himself as having higher status than his opponent may seek control over the bargaining site in order to arrange it in a manner that both affirms his superiority and is likely to induce deference from the other. Conversely, a bargainer having subordinate status may attempt to arrange the site in a way that offsets the status differential. Clearly, control over physical facilities is more readily gained and less open to dispute when an individual bargains on his home territory than when he is either a guest on the territory of an opposing party or on neutral ground.

Ball's (1972) insightful analysis of the 1972 summit meetings between the United States and the People's Republic of China is illustrative of another way in which bargaining on one's own territory may influence the psychological climate of negotiations:

> No doubt for many Chinese the President's visit—on White House initiative—stirs atavistic memories of the old tradition of the Middle Kingdom that peoples of other countries—including rulers and their envoys—were barbarians. Because it was considered an act of grace for the Emperors of China to grant any foreign visitors passage to Peking, it was understood that they came as suppliants bearing tribute. This traditional Chinese arrogance toward foreigners points up at least a theoreti-

cal risk in the President's trip: that the Chinese leadership might, either during the visit or beforehand, deliberately take some action to embarrass the United States. No doubt one should substantially discount this possibility because, in the context of its quarrel with the Soviet Union, China needs the appearance of an amicable relation with America. Yet conditions can rapidly change and one should not ignore the fact that the options are now all in the hands of the Chinese leaders. Since it was the President who solicited the trip, Mao Tse-Tung would lose no face if the United States should cancel; yet America would be embarrassed if the cancellation should come from Peking. It is this possibility that points up one of the costs of summitry, for during the period that a summit meeting is pending—in this case seven months—the President becomes, in effect, a hostage to the situation. To some extent, he loses full freedom of action, since, once such a meeting is announced, he is reluctant to do anything that would provide the host country an excuse for breaking off the visit [p. 53: ©1972 by The New York Times Company].

This analysis suggests that even at the highest levels of international negotiation the party on whose territory the bargaining occurs has an advantage, while the visiting party is, in this respect at least, at the mercy of its host. Although, as Ball suggests, protocol often prevents the exercise of power, one who bargains on another's territory rarely has a guarantee that the other will not act in such a manner. Hence a visitor's behavior prior to and perhaps during negotiation may be constrained by such concerns. In contrast, when negotiation occurs on neutral territory—as in the case of the Strategic Arms Limitations Talks (SALT) held at Helsinki, Finland—the fact that the site is controlled by neither party substantially reduces the existence of such fears and thereby alters the psychological climate of negotiation.

As we shall see, *the advantages gained from bargaining on one's own territory represent potential sources of strength that are likely to increase both the assertiveness of, and the outcomes obtained by, the site controller. In contrast, a bargainer who is a guest may come to view himself as occupying subordinate status and may thus be induced to behave less assertively or even deferentially toward his host.*

Research concerning the effects of site selection has been almost nil. Yet there is evidence in the results of a recent study by Martindale (1971) attesting to the importance of site neutrality on a bargainer's behavior. Subjects in Martindale's study were formed into 30 separate dyads and were asked to bargain over a single issue: the penalty to be given a guilty defendant in a fictional legal case. Subjects within each pair were assigned randomly to the role of "defense attorney" or "prosecuting attorney." Territorial dominance was varied by manipulating the location in which the negotiations took place: 15 pairs negotiated in the living quarters of the defense attorney, and 15 pairs negotiated in the residence of the prosecutor. The researcher was never present during the negotiations, but the proceedings were tape recorded and later analyzed by computer. It was hypothesized that subjects negotiating on their home territory would dominate the negotiations; they would speak and "win" more often than visitors, regardless of the role they had taken.

Three behavioral measures of dominance were obtained: the total speaking time of each dyad member, the average length of speaking time by each dyad member, and the decision reached within each pair. The latter variable was used to determine the winner, a win being assigned to the defense attorney if the penalty agreed upon was shorter than an independently obtained estimate, and to the prosecutor if it exceeded this amount. The results were clear: Subjects who negotiated on their home territory spoke significantly longer than visitors. Moreover, when defense attorneys negotiated on their home territory, the penalties were significantly shorter on the average than when prosecutors negotiated on their home territory. Martindale (1971) concluded that "the environmental context is an important factor influencing both the course and the outcome of a negotiation [p. 306]."

Martindale's results may be viewed from several perspectives. First, we may consider their implications for behavior elicited as a function of territorial dominance. As studies of animal behavior have revealed, animals fighting on their own territory tend to behave dominantly, while intruders tend to behave submissively; the home animal, moreover, generally emerges victorious in such encounters. Martindale's evidence, in conjunction with the results of several other studies, suggests that human interaction may be affected similarly. For example, Sommer (1967) observed that offensive displays were frequently involved in the establishment and maintenance of dominance among students attempting to stake out preferred study areas in a library. (This type of behavior may be viewed as similar, though on a much smaller scale, to that which often occurs in international territorial disputes, such as those between Israel and its surrounding Arab neighbors.) Strodtbeck (1951), who observed the behavior of husbands and wives bargaining over differences of opinion, also found that the outcomes were most often in accord with the position held by the "dominant" partner, although this investigator did not define dominance in terms of territoriality.

Looking at bargaining in terms of the pressures that may be generated by the issue of territoriality, we may speculate that, because bargaining is a competitive type of interchange, bargainers are driven to assertiveness when on their home territory but are likely to be constrained from such behavior on the territory of another. This view is supported by several additional findings from the Martindale (1971) study. Briefly, he found that his situational manipulation of territoriality accounted for approximately 50% of the variance in the total amount of talking done by his subjects, while a paper and pencil assessment of dominance (the Dominance Scale of the California Personality Inventory), obtained prior to the bargaining session, accounted for only 8% of such behavior. Similarly, site location accounted for 30% of the variance in outcomes, while assessed dominance accounted for only 1%. These results suggest that the territory on which bargainers find themselves is likely to have a far greater influence on their level of assertiveness than more stable personality characteristics, and that behavioral correlates of assertiveness are especially likely to be evident on one's home territory.

Martindale's results press for explanation. One possibility is that suffering a defeat on one's home terrain may have implications both for the maintenance of control over this territory as well as for one's self-image as a worthy competitor or defender. Certainly the latter implication is quite evident in sporting activities, where athletic teams are generally expected to win more frequently on their home territory than on that of their competitors. Perusal of any baseball or football record book, in fact, reveals that a far greater percentage of these events are won by teams when they play "home" than "away" games. It may be argued that this effect is produced more by familiarity than territoriality, but we would argue that the two are not distinct, since greater familiarity with a physical site probably increases the individual's ability to use it to his advantage, and this probably results in increased assertiveness. Conversely, a visitor to another's territory may recognize that he should not act with impunity in such a role, or he may be constrained from assertiveness by a need for caution in an unfamiliar environment.

The main thrust of this line of reasoning, speculative though it may be, is that in competitive interchanges such as bargaining, a person's level of assertiveness may be guided in part by differing expectations about how he is to behave in the role of host or visitor—expectations that are absent when the territory is neutral. It is the host who enjoys the legitimate right to manipulate his environment, while the visitor is normally deprived of like advantage. This right is often seen in a host's magnanimous attempts to make a visitor comfortable—behavior which is normally acceptable from a host but which nevertheless reflects the latter's dominance.

The results of Martindale's (1971) study provide a sense of the pressures that seem to be generated when a bargaining site is a nonneutral one. In such circumstances, the party on whose territory the bargaining occurs is likely to be driven toward increased assertiveness, often instrumental in obtaining a larger share of the outcome, while the visitor is subject to pressures that impose constraints on this type of behavior.

That bargainers are sensitive to the advantages and disadvantages to be derived from bargaining on a nonneutral site is evident in the frequency with which bargaining exchanges occur at neutral sites: Panmunjom, a tiny village straddling the 38th parallel between North and South Korea, the site of the Korean cease-fire negotiations; Paris, the site of the Vietnam negotiations; Helsinki, the site of the SALT negotiations; and the Americana Hotel in New York City, the site of countless collective bargaining exchanges. Each of these examples attests to the pressures toward bargaining on neutral ground.

Frequently pressures to bargain on neutral ground are brought to bear by third parties. Walton (1969), in his thoughtful analysis of third party functions, argues that effective third party intervention often requires the resolution of site selection problems. He states:

> The site for the confrontation affects the balance of situational power. . . . By choosing a neutral site, one can preserve symmetry in the situational power of participants. . . . If it is desirable to offset a power advantage of one party, one might do this by deliberately favoring the other in the selection of the confrontation site [pp. 117, 149, 118].

Walton's observations parallel our argument that the site of a bargaining exchange may affect the relative power of the participants. They also suggest that from the standpoint of third party interventions aimed at conflict resolution, power differences may be altered by the strategic selection of an appropriate bargaining site.

Finally, it should be noted that factors other than neutrality may also influence the selection of a bargaining site. Among these are: the appropriateness of the site, sometimes gauged by its lavishness or austerity; its distinctiveness, which may be defined in terms of certain prominent characteristics or traditions associated with its prior use; and its openness to public visibility. Often the selection of a bargaining site on the basis of these criteria involves anticipating the influence of the site's distinctive features on the climate of the proceedings, and hence the behavior of the bargainers. For example, Helsinki's tradition as a site of international cooperation, in conjunction with Finland's small size and extreme vulnerability to the dangers of uncontrolled atomic stockpiling, may have played a part in the selection of this city as the site of the SALT negotiations—on the assumption that these symbolic factors might increase the pressure on the parties to reach accord. Or consider the site of the 1972 summit meetings between the United States and mainland China. A substantial part of these negotiations took place in the massive though austere Hall of the People, an edifice viewed as symbolic of the potential strength and dominance of the People's Republic of China in Asian and world affairs. This site may have been chosen by China to offset, at least symbolically, the strength of the United States in its international negotiations.

Another factor that often enters into the selection of a bargaining site is its openness to or protection from public visibility. In some instances a site may be chosen precisely because it is inaccessible or may be easily defended against unwanted audiences. According to a news release which appeared in the *New York Times* on October 9, 1951, an important reason for moving the Korean cease-fire talks from Kaesong to Panmunjom was the inaccessibility of the latter site to members of the international press. Similarly, there is little doubt that some of the more "sensitive" sessions of the U.S. and mainland China summit meetings were conducted in the privacy of Chairman Mao Tse-Tung's home rather than at the more public Hall of the People in Peking. More recently, the secrecy surrounding the high level Vietnam Peace Talks between President Nixon's special envoy, Henry Kissinger, and Le Duc Tho, North Vietnam's chief negotiator, reflects a similar need to protect sensitive negotiations from premature leaks or unwanted publicity. On a somewhat different level, a procedural guidebook distributed by the National Education Association (1971) advises its public education negotiators to avoid conducting their negotiations in public view.

Although site openness is often undesirable, it may become desirable when a party wishes to use negotiation for "side effects," such as marshalling favorable public opinion for its position or enhancing its status or standing through association with a prestigious adversary. An example of the former can be seen in the case of a New York City chapter of the Hospital Workers Union, which has been known to conduct its negotiations before an assembly of its constituents. An illustration of how one's standing may be enhanced through association with a prestigious adversary is provided by Ball (1972), who notes the benefits gained by mainland China as a result of the 1972 summit talks:

> For the Chinese leadership, on the other hand, the spectacle and excitement clearly mean a Great Leap Forward in world politics. Already the announcement of the trip has served as a catalyst bringing them into the United Nations earlier than expected, and, in terms of their larger strategy, they can see their new relations with the United States as having a deterrent effect on a possible Soviet strike at their nuclear installations. Almost certainly they hope—and, unhappily, they may be right—that the trip will bring about some loosening in Japanese-American ties. Finally, the vividly demonstrated American interest in China is rapidly releasing other states from their inhibitions regarding Peking [p. 53: ©1972 by The New York Times Company].

Each of the illustrations presented above acknowledges the strategic uses to which either the openness or the inaccessibility of the site may be put. However, the evidence presented in Chapter 4 indicates that, while a site selected for its public visibility may have strategic advantages in the short run, there are also adverse effects of audience exposure, which may offset such gains in the long run.

PHYSICAL ARRANGEMENTS AT THE SITE

Just as the location of a bargaining site has important consequences for the quality and outcomes of bargaining, so too do the physical arrangements at the site proper. The mere arrangement of tables and chairs, for example (an issue of considerable importance during the Paris Vietnam Peace Talks), as well as other bits of bargaining "apparatus," may affect and reveal the nature of the relationship between the parties as well as the psychological climate of the exchange. Moreover, seating and other physical arrangements may have important strategic implications—as, for example, when they become vehicles for accentuating status and power differences.

Although journalistic accounts of the effects of physical arrangements are rather plentiful, more systematic investigations are rare. However, there is a growing body of research evidence in ecological psychology which indicates that such factors as seating arrangements are not only likely to affect the quality of social interaction occurring in a given physical space but may also reflect the character of the relationship between the interactants (Proshansky, Ittleson, & Rivlin, 1970). In this section we shall examine evidence from several investigations directly concerned with the effects of physical arrangements on bargaining behavior, as well as the results of several studies having a more general perspective, but which nevertheless have important implications for bargaining. We make the assumption that because evidence provided by ecological studies speaks to the general effects of physical arrangements in a variety of social interaction contexts, it is suggestive of the possibility that such effects may operate similarly in bargaining exchanges.

Physical Arrangements as Indicators of the Relationship between Bargainers and the Climate of the Exchange

Bargaining relationships may be characterized in terms of the amount of cooperation or competition between the parties and their attitudes toward one another—characteristics which may fluctuate from one time to another. However, a proposition that is amply supported by empirical research is that the physical arrangements that exist at a given time tend to be expressive of the relational bonds between the parties—assuming, of course, that these arrangements result from choice and are not arbitrarily imposed. Sommer

(1965), for example, conducted naturalistic observation and questionnaire studies of seating preferences in several different social contexts and found that people engaging in casual conversation normally prefer to sit at right angles to one another (if seated at square or rectangular tables), or beside one another (often with a vacant seat separating them) when seated at circular tables. Side-by-side seating, he found, was preferred in cooperative relationships, regardless of the shape of the table. However, the most preferred configuration in competitive relationships was found to be opposite (face-to-face) seating, with a moderate to distant space separating the parties. When individuals did not wish to interact with one another, they preferred to seat themselves as far apart as possible. Sommer also noted less conversation when people were seated far apart than when they were side by side or opposite one another.

Sommer interpreted his findings in terms of the functions of distance and visual contact in interpersonal relations. Prior research had indicated that in certain social encounters, particularly those which are either nonintimate or competitive, proximity and direct visual contact (eye contact) are stressful and hence avoided (Birdwhistell, 1952; Goffman, 1963; Hall, 1966; McBride, 1964). Briefly, Sommer argued that in casual conversation nonintimates choose to sit corner-to-corner because this permits sufficient closeness to sustain verbal communication but allows them to engage in as much or as little eye contact as they wish. However, following from the stress hypothesis, eye contact tends to be avoided in competitive relationships because it may be intimidating (Cook, 1970), dominating, or overly revealing of motives that one wishes to keep hidden. In this regard, Exline, Thibaut, Brannon, and Gumpert (1961) found that people have greater difficulty telling a convincing lie when they are being watched closely.

Sommer suggested that the preference for opposite seating typically found in competitive relationships probably reflects a desire to obtain information about one's competitor, rather than a wish to establish a friendly relationship with him—an interpretation that is supported by his finding that, although competitors looked toward one another periodically, they tended to avoid eye contact when their glances met. Sommer thus concluded that opposite seating stimulates competition in these types of social encounters. However, in cooperative situations, where it is often useful to share materials, side by side seating is most frequently sought. Here, Sommer pointed out, if direct visual contact is desired it is easily attained by such an arrangement.

Sommer's findings suggest that two factors, proximity and bodily orientation, influenced as they are by seating arrangements, play a large part in regulating visual contact, and such contact is likely to be characteristically sought or avoided in different types of social relationships. In this regard,

Argyle and Dean (1965) argued that increased eye contact and proximity are correlates of intimacy, and the relative positioning of persons engaged in social interaction may therefore be taken as an indicator of the relationship between them. This proposition was supported by Jourard (1966), who found that people often express intimacy by increased physical contact; by Cook (1970), who found that as intimacy and the strength of affiliative motives increase, the distance between interactants decreases; by Hall (1966), who determined that the average distance maintained by casual acquaintances is approximately 30-48 in., while that maintained by intimates is in the range of 0–18 in.; by Mehrabian (1969) and Sommer (1965), who reported that persons liking one another or seeing each other as similar are likely to sit closer together than persons disliking one another or viewing each other as dissimilar; by Little (1965), who found that strangers prefer to sit further apart than friends; and by Gardin, Kaplan, Firestone, and Cowan (1973), who found that cooperation in the PD game tended to be correlated with a proximal (side-by-side) seating arrangement.

Beyond the evidence indicating that physical arrangements are often expressive of the relationship between individuals, it appears that such arrangements may also influence what we would identify as the psychological climate of social interaction. With respect to interactions involving bargaining, in particular, there are at least three relevant indicators of climate: the degree of formality or informality of the proceedings; the amount of tension or relaxation aroused in the participants; and the level of conflict intensity in the exchange.

In addition to findings indicating that seating arrangements may affect the nature of informal social interaction, there is evidence indicating that other types of physical arrangements may have similar effects on the formality or informality of social interaction. For example, Mehrabian and Diamond (1971) and Sommer (1969) found that the presence of objects such as flower vases and pieces of abstract sculpture tend to facilitate informality and affiliative behavior, presumably because they invite commentary, whereas articles such as books and magazines tend to inhibit these processes. However, the former investigators found that, while different physical arrangements either encouraged or discouraged informal social interaction between persons who were generally sociable, neither effect was visible in less sociable pairs.

Sommer (1965) has suggested that round-shaped tables increase informality and feelings of closeness in comparison to square or rectangular tables. However, the newspaper descriptions of the procedural negotiations at the Paris Peace Talks (see the *New York Times*, January 3 and 4, 1969) provide little indication of such informality, even though the proposals were all for round tables. Such evidence, together with the Mehrabian and Diamond (1971) results indicating differential effects as a result of personality, suggests that, in instances where conflict intensity is heightened or where there is a clear potential for this, the effects of physical arrangements as a means of inducing informality may be limited.

Although the findings we have outlined are not taken from studies of bargaining per se, they have clear implications for this form of social interaction. They focus on variations in ecological arrangements resulting from such factors as cooperation, interpersonal evaluation, similarity, and liking—all of which have been shown by Deutsch (1949) to be correlates of bargaining behavior. Assuming that the ecological findings are applicable to bargaining, several tentative conclusions may now be drawn about the meaning of physical arrangements in this type of social interaction:

First, it appears that there are pressures toward physical and visual distancing that operate when bargainers do not wish to interact, when they dislike or perceive one another as quite dissimilar, and when there is no prior relationship between them. Such pressures seem to operate most noticeably in bargaining relationships that are competitive, although constraints against excessive distancing are imposed by the informational needs often present in such situations. These pressures seem to operate in the opposite direction in bargaining relationships that are cooperative or intimate.

Second, such pressures are likely to be expressed behaviorally, through the physical positions that bargainers assume relative to one another. As conflict intensifies, there is likely to be a corresponding increase in the pressure toward distancing, to the extent that the conflicted parties may prefer to avoid interaction with one another altogether. When this level of conflict intensity is exceeded, the constraints imposed on physical and visual distancing by informational needs may give way to pressures toward communicational isolation.

Finally, the research suggests that if the pressures toward distancing are interfered with by physical arrangements that inappropriately impose or require physical or visual contact, then tension, defensiveness, and conflict intensity are likely to increase. It is important to bear in mind, however, that physical arrangements are not immutable; they can often be altered by the bargainers or by a third party.

THE AVAILABILITY AND USE OF COMMUNICATION CHANNELS

Communication is surely a primary ingredient of bargaining. In his discussion of the dilemmas facing bargainers, Kelley (1966) indicates that each must decide how much information to communicate to an opposing party about his true motives and preferences. Kelley points out that such a decision is likely to be based not only on a bargainer's own standards but, perhaps equally, will be determined by the opposing party's behavior—particularly his apparent openness and honesty—prior to and during the exchange. Hence the effectiveness of bargaining depends in large part upon the exchange of sufficient credible information between the parties. When the information exchanged appears to be insufficient or distorted, bargainers have little or no basis on which to assume good or equitable intentions on the part of the other. Nor is there a sufficient basis for recognizing common interests. Behavior resulting from excessive caution and a perceived need to protect oneself in these circumstances may be misconstrued by the other party, thereby arousing defensiveness on his part that in turn may be seen as threatening by the first. This threat reinforces earlier suspicions, and so the spiral deepens. Thus *communicational isolation, whether it results from physical or psychological conditions, imposes constraints on the development of cooperation and is likely to promote mistrust and suspicion.*

A well-known adage concerning the value of communication in a broad range of conflict situations states that "If you can only get the parties to communicate with one another, their conflicts will resolve themselves." This maxim has a familiar ring in bargaining, too, being typical of the sort of curative that both naive observers and armchair diagnosticians readily prescribe for the amelioration of conflict. Yet if one puts such advice to empirical test, one is likely to find that its applicability is somewhat limited—for experimental research as well as day-to-day bargaining incidents make it quite clear the *the mere availability of communication channels provides no guarantee that they will be used or used effectively.* To the contrary, it appears that a variety of conditions, such as the intensity of conflict, the relationship between the bargainers, and the importance of the issues at stake, are likely to be just as important in determining the quality and quantity of communication as the mere fact that opportunities for it exist. This is particularly apparent in "conflict intensified" bargaining relationships, where the availability of communication channels may not only fail to generate pressures toward agreement but may instead function to further increase conflict intensity. However, when conflict neither is particularly intense nor has the potential for becoming so, it is better to have communication opportunities than not, for it is then that bargaining effectiveness may indeed be enhanced by communication.

Given the importance of communication in bargaining and the detrimental effects of communicational isolation, several questions arise, each of which we will attempt to answer in turn. (1) Why does the availability of communication fail to facilitate the resolution of conflict in intensely competitive bargaining relationships? (2) What are the effects of communication availability and use in "normal" bargaining relationships, i.e., those in which conflict is not intense? More specifically, what are the effects on bargaining effectiveness of communicating: verbally versus nonverbally; freely versus minimally or not at all? (3) How may the availability and use of communication channels be structured so as to increase bargaining effectiveness?

Conflict Intensification and the Deterioration of Communication

Newcomb's (1947) "autistic hostility" hypothesis suggests that as interpersonal conflict becomes exacerbated, communication between the involved parties is likely to deteriorate. Such a breakdown, says Newcomb, typically occurs in two ways: The amount of overt communication between the parties decreases, and the meaning of the communication that does occur tends to be distorted. When hostile impulses exist, arising as they may from one party's readiness to injure another or from one party's perception that another threatens injury to him, barriers to communication are likely to arise out of the need to protect oneself from unpredictable or ego-damaging events. As a result, an essential mechanism for the reduction of initial hostility—communication—is either avoided or distorted, and the conflict is thus likely to be maintained or nurtured rather than ameliorated.

Studies of bargaining behavior provide a useful context in which to test Newcomb's hypothesis, because conflicts of interest are typically central in this type of activity and because many of the variables that contribute to conflict are brought under experimental control. For example, in one series of studies concerned with the effects of threat and the availability of communication in bargaining, Deutsch and Krauss (1960, 1962) found that when threat was available to both parties playing the Acme-Bolt Trucking game rather than to just one or to neither, conflict became intensified and bargaining effectiveness (as measured by joint outcomes) was reduced substantially. Of particular relevance to the present discussion is the fact that the investigators also provided the bargainers with varied opportunities for communication, in order to test the hypothesis that favorable outcomes would be most likely to occur when resources were available to the bargainers that would enable them to communicate freely with one another. In one experiment conducted by these investigators, half of the subject pairs were merely instructed that they were free to talk with each other about anything they wished during the experimental trials (bilateral communication). In the remaining pairs only one party received such instructions (unilateral communication). These variations were superimposed upon the three threat conditions, to determine whether differential effects would emerge.

The results revealed no differences in bargaining effectiveness as a function of the availability of communication. Interestingly, it was found that regardless of which threat condition they were in, subjects generally tended to communicate infrequently with one another. However, there was a tendency for more frequent communication to occur in the no threat condition, and it is there that outcomes were also greatest. Deutsch and Krauss (1962) concluded that "the opportunity to communicate does not necessarily result in an amelioration of conflict. Indeed, . . . the opportunity to communicate does not necessarily result in communication at all [p. 64]." Deutsch and Krauss interpreted their results by arguing that the potential for bilateral threat increased the competitive orientations of the bargainers to the point that any ameliorating effects of communication were lost.

Deutsch and Krauss (1962) conducted two additional experiments using similar procedures and subjects. Subjects were now either required to talk to one another on each trial (compulsory communication) or merely given the freedom to do so if they wished (permissive communication). The results of these experiments revealed that bargaining was less effective in the bilateral threat conditions than in either the unilateral or no threat conditions. Moreover, there was no improvement in bargaining in the bilateral threat condition when communication was compulsory rather than permissive.

A more recent study by Krauss and Deutsch (1966), briefly described in Chapter 4, was conducted to determine, in part, whether tutoring bargainers to use communication more effectively might not make a difference. The investigators instructed half of their subjects to use their communication channel for the purpose of transmitting fair and equitable proposals that they themselves would be willing to accept (tutored communication condition). The remaining subjects received no such instruction but were also free to communicate in whatever way they pleased. Compulsory communication and bilateral threat were present in all conditions of the experiment. The subjects and procedures were similar to those used in the earlier Trucking experiments.

Krauss and Deutsch's results provide a clear indication that, in addition to merely creating the opportunity for communication, "the provision of a strong incentive to utilize the opportunity to communicate to engage in fair bargaining . . . is central to the economical resolution of conflict [p. 576]." Indeed, only in the tutored communication condition was the conflict substantially reduced. Although this study may have been confounded somewhat by the fact that the experimenter (who was undoubtedly seen as a prestigious and authoritative third party) provided the tutoring, it is nevertheless clear that when left to their own devices in conditions of heightened conflict, bargainers may indeed find it difficult to use communication constructively in order to increase their outcomes.

It is interesting that the bargainers' apparent inability to communicate effectively in both the permissive and the untutored compulsory conditions occurred even though they represented none other than themselves. Assuming that forces toward loyalty, commitment, and advocacy were thus rather minimal, we might speculate that, had the bargainers been representatives of highly committed opposing constituencies, their ability to use the communication channel effectively might have been impaired still further.

The results of the Deutsch and Krauss experiments raise obvious questions about the content of communication under heightened conflict. For example, what is the nature of communication in such circumstances? How, and for what purposes, is it used? Why does it generally fail to ameliorate conflict? Deutsch (1969) attempts to answer these questions as follows:

> Typically, a competitive process tends to produce the following effects: Communication between the conflicting parties is unreliable and impoverished. The available communication channels and opportunities are not utilized or they are used in an attempt to mislead or intimidate the other. Little confidence is placed in information that is obtained directly from the other; espionage and other circuitous means of obtaining information are relied upon. The poor communication enhances the possibility of error and misinformation of the sort which is likely to reinforce the pre-existing orientations and expectations toward the other [p. 12].

Deutsch's interpretation coincides with the previously discussed autistic hostility hypothesis (Newcomb, 1947) and with an insightful analysis of misperception and the failure of communication in the Vietnam War (White, 1966). Further empirical evidence in support of this view may be found in Kee's (1970) study of the effects of trust and suspicion in bargaining. This investigator analyzed the content of communication between subjects playing the PD game in a condition of either trust or suspicion. He found that suspicious bargainers communicated more lies, threats, and ultimata—but less information—than those in the trust condition. Interestingly, suspicious subjects more often refused to bargain than did subjects in the trust group.

A rather dramatic example of the nonuse of an existing communication channel, when there is heightened conflict, is illustrated in the news release on the Korean Truce meeting shown in Figure 5-1.

The account provides stark evidence in support of our proposition that in conflict-intensified bargaining exchanges the mere availability of communication channels is not in itself sufficient to produce pressures toward agreement, but may instead further increase conflict intensity.

The Effects of Communication in "Normal" Exchanges

Having posed the question of how communication operates, or, more appropriately, fails to operate in conflict-intensified bargaining, we may move to an examination of its general effects in a broader range of bargaining exchanges, particularly those in which conflict intensity is not excessive.

10   The Evening Bulletin

I   PHILADELPHIA, Friday, April 11, 1969

2 Sides Sit Silently 4½ Hours At Korean Truce Meeting

Panmunjom, Korea – (UPI) – The American general and the North Korean general glared at each other across the table and the only sound was the wind howling across the barren hills outside their hut.

Maj. Gen. James B. Knapp, negotiator for the United Nations Command (UNC), was waiting for Maj. Gen. Ri Choonsun of the Democratic People's Republic of North Korea to propose a recess.

They sat there, arms folded, for 4½ hours. Not a word. Finally, Gen. Ri got up, walked out and drove away.

It was the 289th meeting of the Korean Military Armistice Commission at the truce village of Panmunjom and set a record as the longest such meeting since the Korean War ended July 27, 1953.

The generals had been there 11 hours and 35 minutes. Neither ate or went to the toilet in all that time. Delegates to such meetings may leave the room only with a formal adjournment proposal.

Whichever side proposes a meeting usually proposes a recess. North Korea called yesterday's session. Ri never did propose a recess.

"In view of North Korea's rude and unwarranted conduct," Knapp said, "I consider this meeting to be terminated."

Before the 4½ hours of silence, Knapp called on North Korea to start a four-step de-escalation to ease tension along the Korean border. He promised reciprocation with a similar UNC program.

Knapp asked that North Korea:

– Remove from the North Korean part of the Demilitarized Zone all illegal weapons and unauthorized personnel.

– Immediately quit all attacks against South Korean and UNC forces.

– Reduce what Knapp said was the excessive size of North Korea's armed forces.

– Discontinue "polemic, bellicose, war-mongering public statements."

Figure 5–1 *Silent Hostility at Panmunjom* (reprinted from the *Evening Bulletin*, Philadelphia, April 11, 1969, p. 10. By permission of UPI, New York, N.Y.).

Communication through Verbal or Nonverbal Channels

The communication of information, which seems to be a necessary condition of effective bargaining, is obviously not restricted to the verbal mode. In fact a good deal of psychological research has shown that nonverbal communication may play an important role in influencing social interaction, and bargaining, we suspect, is no exception to this rule.

For an extensive analysis of the nonbargaining research concerning nonverbal behavior, the reader is referred to a recent survey of experimentation in this area edited by Hinde (1972), which makes it quite clear that both personal feelings and interpersonal attitudes are often communicated nonverbally, through such behavior as head nods, gestures, posture, facial expressions, and eye contact. For example, Argyle (in Hinde, 1972) reports that a superior attitude toward another may be telegraphed by erect posture, an unsmiling or haughty facial expression, and staring another down; feelings of anxiety may be communicated by a tense, rigid posture and wringing of the hands.

Several social psychologists have studied the effects of verbal and nonverbal communication on bargaining proper. One approach has involved controlling the extent to which subjects may see or hear one another while engaged in a bargaining task. This approach was taken by Wichman (1970), who varied physical arrangements and thereby created four availability conditions in the context of a 78-trial PD game. Subjects played in isolation, unable to see or hear one another; saw but could not hear one another; heard but could not see one another; or both saw and heard one another. Spoken communication was unrestricted in the latter two conditions.

The results revealed the greatest amount of cooperation (87%) between subjects who could both see and hear one another and the least cooperation (41%) between those who were isolated. In the see only and hear only conditions, the average amounts of cooperation were 48% and 72%, respectively. These results indicate that, although seeing is less important than hearing, cooperation is likely to be enhanced when physical arrangements make bargainers available for both forms of communication.

Vitz and Kite (1970) conducted an experiment incorporating variations in physical facilities that in effect regulated the kind and degree of nonverbal communication available between bargainers. Although this was of secondary interest to the investigators (they were primarily interested in the effects of the initial resources of the bargainers), informal observation was made of the amount and quality of communication occurring during the exchange. Subjects played a mixed-motive, nonzero sum game either face-to-face (unrestricted verbal and visual access), by telephone (unrestricted verbal but no visual access), or by sending typewritten messages (no visual or verbal access). In contrast to Wichman's findings, there were no observable differences in communication content or in negotiation style between the face-to-face and telephone conditions, indicating that visual access was relatively unimportant. In contrast, communication that was limited to the typewritten word tended to be more formal, rigid, and forceful, and subjects tended to refer more often to previous arguments in defense of their positions than in the other conditions. In brief, the excessive commitment to defending earlier positions, the use of formal and stilted language, and the increased time needed to prepare and read written messages suggest that, in comparison to spoken communication, this form may actually hamper bargaining effectiveness.

Kleinke and Pohlen (1971) investigated the effects of the availability of nonverbal communication by examining *responses* to various forms of behavior. They had subjects play a 50-trial PD game against a confederate whose strategy and gazing behavior were controlled so that he was either 100% cooperative, 90% cooperative, or 100% competitive. In each of these conditions the confederate either gazed constantly at the subject with a bland and emotionless facial expression or refrained completely from eye contact.

Kleinke and Pohlen were attempting to refute earlier findings by Ellsworth and Carlsmith (1968), Exline (1963), Kendon (1967) and Mehrabian (1968) indicating that in general gaze and eye contact contribute to the formation of favorable interpersonal attitudes. Instead, Kleinke and Pohlen reasoned that, while this may occur in a friendly atmosphere where gazing is often indicative of a desire for affiliation, the effect should not be evident in unfriendly or competitive relationships where gaze might easily be construed as a challenge or threat. Kleinke and Pohlen thus examined the effects of both factors (strategy and gaze) on subjects' evaluations, liking for and attraction to the confederate. It was hypothesized that cooperation by the confederate would lead to more favorable evaluations and greater liking than would competition, and that gazing would cause subjects to evaluate him less favorably and to dislike him more in the competitive than in the cooperative condition.

The first hypothesis was confirmed, but the anticipated effects of the confederate's gaze failed to emerge. Although these results indicate that the confederate's strategic behavior was more important than his gazing or avoidance of it, several considerations render the results of this experiment equivocal. In the first place, although subjects were seated face to face, with the confederate at rather close proximity, no verbal communication was permitted. Moreover, a constant gaze, with no changes in facial expression (such as the confederate displayed) may have been seen by subjects as unnatural and unnerving, thereby causing unfavorable evaluations of him in both the cooperative and the competitive conditions.

Taken together, the results obtained by Kleinke and Pohlen (1971), Vitz and Kite (1970), and Wichman (1970) present an incomplete picture. Yet these experiments do suggest that physical arrangements that curtail the possibilities for spoken communication between bargainers are likely to result in decreased bargaining effectiveness, at least as this is reflected in the outcomes that are obtained; moreover, physical arrangements that deny visibility also tend to result in somewhat reduced outcomes but to a less marked degree. In other words, the evidence implies that *other things being equal, bargaining effectiveness may be sustained at a satisfactory level if the parties cannot see one another; but if verbal (spoken) communication is eliminated or interfered with, effectiveness is likely to suffer.*

Minimal as Compared with Unrestricted Communication

The most elementary comparison made in bargaining studies concerned with the effects of communication is between its unrestricted presence and its total absence. The results of a number of these investigations indicate *a general tendency toward increased bargaining effectiveness when the opposing parties may communicate freely with one another.* Such findings have emerged in various investigations: (1) those using the PD game and its variants (Bixenstine & Douglas, 1967; Bixenstine, Levitt, & Wilson, 1966; Cole, 1972; Deutsch, 1958; Loomis, 1959; Martin, 1966; Swensson, 1967; Swingle & Santi, 1972; Terhune, 1968; Voissem & Sistrunk, 1971; Wichman, 1970; Wiley, 1969); (2) those involving the role-playing of labor-management negotiations (Bass, 1966; Druckman, 1967, 1968b); and (3) those employing a coalition paradigm (Kline, 1969).

Loomis (1959), for example, using a two-person, 5-trial PD game, found that trust and the frequency of cooperative choices increased significantly when subjects could communicate via predetermined written messages—compared to when communication was not possible. This effect emerged even when the messages contained only the briefest statement of the sender's expectation for the receiver's behavior, and it became more pronounced as the messages became more detailed. Terhune (1968) reported a similar pattern of results in a two-person, 30-trial PD game. Subjects who could communicate freely (in writing) prior to each trial cooperated significantly more than those who could not do so. Wichman (1970), who required subjects to play the PD game in isolation or with varying degrees of visual and auditory contact, also found that cooperation was least among isolated subjects and increased as communication became less restricted.

Bixenstine *et al.* (1966) and Bixenstine and Douglas (1967), using a six-person PD game, also reported that cooperation increased to a greater extent when subjects had the opportunity to communicate freely (verbally) with one another during a 10- to 15-min break than when they were given no such opportunity. Similarly, Martin (1966), who used the PD game in the context of opposing three-person groups and either allowed or disallowed periodic intrateam communication, found that cooperation was greater when communication was allowed.

This same pattern can be seen in studies by Druckman (1967, 1968b) and Kline (1969). The former investigator either provided or withheld an opportunity for joint prenegotiation discussion sessions between opposing labor and management role players. The results indicated that the prenegotiation discussions led to more efficient bargaining (i.e., a decrease in the average amount of time taken to reach agreement, the distance between the opposing teams' positions, and the number of issues remaining unresolved at the end of the negotiation period). Kline (1969) found a similar effect in an investigation requiring members of coalitions to divide a limited resource among themselves. More equitable divisions were made in triads that had had prenegotiation discussions than in those not having such sessions.

However all does not turn out as straightforwardly as these findings might suggest. Several of the studies cited above (notably Bixenstine and Douglas, 1967; Bixenstine et al., 1966; Deutsch, 1958; Terhune, 1968), as well as others that failed to find the expected difference (Scodel et al., 1959; Shure et al., 1965; Wandell, 1968), also suggest that the manner in which the opportunity for free communication is likely to be used will be influenced by a bargainer's motivational orientation and personality as well as by situational factors.

First let us consider the relationship between motivational orientation and communication. Deutsch (1958) instructed subjects playing 1-trial and 10-trial PD games to adopt either a cooperative motivational orientation (try to increase their mutual gains), a competitive orientation (do better than the other person), or an individualistic orientation (gain as much as possible for themselves without trying to beat the other). In addition, subjects were either allowed to communicate freely with one another (by written message) before each trial or prevented from doing so. The results revealed that individualistically oriented subjects who could not communicate cooperated significantly less than those who could. In contrast, differences due to the presence or absence of communication were minimized when subjects received either the cooperative or competitive instructions: Cooperation was most frequent in the former condition and least frequent in the latter, regardless of whether subjects could communicate or not. Deutsch interpreted these results by suggesting that in contrast to behavior resulting from either a cooperative or a competitive orientation, behavior that results from an individualistic motivational orientation is particularly sensitive to situational factors such as the availability of communication.

Deutsch (1958) found that although there were no restrictions on what the free communication subjects could say, many of them in the individualistic and competitive conditions either failed to use the opportunity or used it ineffectively. Moreover, after examining the messages that were sent, Deutsch conjectured that communication that is most likely to produce a stable cooperative system must include several elements: (1) statements which indicate that the bargainers' intentions and expectations are both complementary and mutually rewarding, (2) statements which inhibit the violation of such intentions and expectations, and (3) statements which have the capability of restoring complementarity if it is violated. In the absence of these elements, Deutsch contended, a self-perpetuating cycle of violation of expectations, distrust, and further violation is likely to occur. This formulation received clear support in Loomis' (1959) experiment concerning the effects of communication on the formation of trust and cooperation in the PD game.

It is also possible for situational factors to influence motivational orientation and, therefore, the use of communication. In this regard, Deutsch and Krauss (1962) found that highly competitive motivational orientations tended to develop when opposing bargainers possessed mechanisms for threatening one another, and when such motives were heightened, communication was infrequent and often failed to ameliorate conflict. In fact, if one studies the verbatim extracts of statements made by subjects in the bilateral condition, as compared to the unilateral or no threat conditions of the Acme–Bolt Trucking game, it becomes evident that communication was more frequently used in a threatening and intimidating manner in the former than in either of the latter conditions. This pattern is reminiscent of the results of Kee's (1970) experiment, in which trust and suspicion were manipulated situationally. Kee found that communication was considerably more deceptive and threatening when bargainers were induced to be suspicious rather than trusting.

A similar effect is evident in an experiment conducted by Wandell (1968). This investigator had subjects play a 20-trial PD game in which half of the subjects were allowed to communicate simultaneously (by written message) during the first 10 trials, while the remainder were prevented from doing so until the last 10 trials. Wandell found, contrary to expectation, that communication reduced cooperation, and that the sequence of its availability had a negligible effect. He concluded that his subjects were unable to use communication to their own advantage. However, in this experiment the PD game was presented to subjects as an "arms race"—a situational definition that may well have had the effect of elevating the level of conflict or of increasing the competitive motives of the subjects to a point where (just as in the bilateral threat condition of the Deutsch and Krauss (1962) experiment) communication could not provide the ameliorative effects often found in situations of moderate conflict intensity.

Scodel, Minas, Ratoosh, and Lipetz (1959) also failed to find a difference in cooperation in the PD game due to the availability of communication. However, the communication opportunity in this experiment consisted only of a

2-min free discussion period, introduced after the twenty-fifth trial of a 50-trial sequence. Although it has been argued that 2 min allowed for ample communication, we cannot agree, especially since the matrix employed by Scodel *et al.* was a rather competitive one—as evaluated by applying Rapoport and Chammah's (1965a) index of cooperation. Instead we suspect that the competitive matrix, coupled with an extremely short discussion period, may have heightened subjects' competitive motives and thereby suppressed the effects that communication might have had in the last 25 trials. Apparently, according to Scodel *et al.*, the subjects in the communication condition used this opportunity primarily to discover what the other person's strategy was going to be, a use that falls far short of the Deutsch (1958) and Loomis (1959) recommendations concerning the components of communication required to establish stable cooperation. Perhaps, and we can only speculate on this point, had subjects in the communication condition been allowed more time for discussion, or had they been given a less competitive matrix, or both, the availability of communication might have had the general effect of increasing cooperation in the last 25 trials.

In short, the results of the studies cited above indicate that *conditions which contribute to the definition of the bargaining situation, such as the availability or nonavailability of threat, the existence of conditions promotive of trust or suspicion and their correlates, and the manner in which the issues are defined or presented, may influence the motivational orientations of the bargainers and their use of existing communication channels.*

Personality is yet another factor that may affect what a subject communicates when he has the opportunity to do so. Terhune (1968) found less competitiveness and defensiveness among subjects who could communicate in writing before each trial of a 30-trial PD game than among subjects who could not do so. However, he also found evidence of an interaction between communication and personality, such that persons having high needs for power were more apt to communicate in an ambiguous manner and for exploitative purposes than those having high affiliative or achievement needs.

Further evidence concerning differences in communication due to personality is found in an experiment by Bixenstine and Douglas (1967). These investigators, using a 40-trial, two-choice, six-person PD game, created six-person squads composed homogeneously of either "pathology-free" (normal) or "pathology-indicated" subjects. These distinctions were determined by subjects' scores on the Minnesota Multiphasic Personality Inventory. Half of the squads within each category were given a 10-min communication break after the first 20 trials, while the remaining groups were allowed no communication. The investigators hypothesized that since psychopathology often involves impaired interpersonal communication and an inability to trust others, cooperation and communication would be less apparent in the pathology-indicated than in the normal groups.

Their results supported these general hypotheses. However, a significant interaction effect also revealed that normals who were allowed to communicate cooperated more in the second series of trials than pathology-indicated subjects having the same opportunity. On examining the content of communication in these conditions, it was discovered that normals spent more time during the communication break discussing matters directly related to the task and developing collaborative strategies than pathology-indicated subjects, whose mistrust prevented such behavior.

An indication of how the other party's "disposition" may influence the *reception* of communication may be culled from an experiment by Shure *et al.* (1965), briefly described in Chapter 4. These investigators designed a two-person, nonzero sum, 15-trial bargaining game that, like the Acme–Bolt Trucking game, required the sharing of a limited capacity conduit in order to maximize joint outcomes. Unknowingly, subjects bargained with a computer program designed to be "pacifistic," and were either given an opportunity to exchange messages with the other at several points during the exchange or prevented from doing so. Subjects were led to believe that they would be representing two constituents whom they had met at the outset. The constituents were actually confederates, who pressed the subject to exploit the pacifist in order to increase their own monetary gains. In addition, subjects were given a mechanism which they were informed would enable them to shock the other if they wished. In the communication condition, the pacifist sent messages to the subject indicating that he would permit him to use the conduit first, but that he expected to share it—with the implication that if the subject were unwilling to be fair, he (the pacifist) would not use the shock device himself but would force the subject to do so. In the noncommunication condition, the pacifist's behavior was the same, but no messages were sent.

The investigators focused on the number of subjects who either continued to dominate the pacifist or became more equitable toward him after receiving his messages. The results indicated a pattern quite similar to that found in several of the experiments discussed previously. No subjects in the noncommunication condition altered their domination of the pacifist, but a number did so in the communication condition (no statistics reported by the investigators). However, there were also a number of subjects in the communication condition who continued to dominate the pacifist (again no exact number reported). It is these subjects who are of greatest interest in the present analysis. Shure *et al.* (1965) report that these subjects "thought it more likely than those in the noncommunication condition that the pacifist was trying to make them feel guilty or embarrass them and that he was trying to trick or deceive them [pp. 113–114]." The investigators concluded that the opportunity for communication had the desired effect for some subjects but that many others maintained or increased the severity of their domination as a result of the messages they received.

We may view the level of conflict in the Shure *et al.* experiment as being quite intense: Subjects were caught between their teammates' strenuous demands to exploit the pacifist for monetary gain and the moral issue of victimizing a helpless other. It is in this context that the effects of introducing opportunities for communication must be considered, for it apparently functioned to intensify the conflict and, among those subjects inclined toward domination, reduced the constraints against this type of behavior by providing a basis for rationalizing it. In short, this experiment demonstrates that domination or exploitativeness may be situationally induced and may with a little social support cause communication to be misinterpreted and mistrusted in the service of enacting exploitative motives.

In summary, the general finding that restricted opportunities for communication may hamper bargaining effectiveness should come as no great surprise to students of bargaining behavior. After all, communication is an essential element of bargaining, and without it bargaining suffers. Yet the experimental results that we have examined make it rather clear that, in itself, the opportunity for communication is no panacea. Even when opportunities for communication are freely available, pressures toward communicational isolation and misuse may be generated by motivational, dispositional, or situational factors.

Increasing Bargaining Effectiveness through the Structuring of Communication Channels

The position that we developed in the previous sections raises the question of how communication may be structured to bring about its more favorable use and thereby increase bargaining effectiveness. Fortunately several answers to this query may be derived from investigations in which opportunities for communication are structured, either purposefully or incidentally, by an experimenter's instructions or by inherent features of the research procedures used.

Investigations that structure communication via the experimenter's instructions are generally of two distinguishable types: those in which the experimenter spells out the occasions, intervals, or amount of time available for communication; and those in which the experimenter makes direct and substantive interventions into the ongoing bargaining process and suggestions concerning the content of communication. Investigations that structure communication via inherent features of the research procedure include those in which subjects may communicate only by means of standard messages—usually predetermined with respect to their number, timing, content and direction of flow (i.e., unilateral or bilateral). Many of these investigations have focused on the effects of persuasive communication such as threats and promises. Typically these investigations utilize an opposing party (confederate), programmed to behave or communicate according to a specified plan.

In general, the structuring of communication may take a variety of forms. These include variations in the frequency, duration, and number of modes in which communication may occur and, perhaps most importantly, in the structuring of its content. We have been careful not to suggest that increased bargaining effectiveness through structuring may be attained by simply increasing the frequency or duration of communication periods or the number of modes in which it occurs. As suggested previously, there are circumstances in which it may be useful to decrease the amount of communication between the parties. Consider, for example, the case of a third party who, upon recognizing an intensification of conflict, wisely decides to separate the opposing sides and serve as a filter through which their heated communications must pass. (A federal mediator recently followed exactly this procedure in an attempt to "cool" a deadlock between the opposing sides in a strike of the Long Island Railroad. See the *New York Times,* December 9, 1972, p. 60.)

Any of the different types of structuring described above may be introduced directly, as when a third party (such as a mediator or, for that matter, the experimenter) imposes rules regulating the sequence in which the parties are to present their positions or the amount of time in which they may do so. Or communication structuring may occur indirectly, as when mutually accepted norms or rules of protocol develop that shape the formality of the language used by bargainers of different status or rank.

Structuring through Experimental Instructions

Every controlled study of bargaining behavior, concerned with the effects of explicit communication, structures such opportunities in some way. This frequently occurs as a result of researcher-provided instructions about the use of available opportunities for communication. However, such instructions may be differentiated in terms of the amount of pressure that they impose on subjects to communicate and the definition of the situation that they impart. Both of these factors, in turn, may be influenced by the frequency, timing, or duration of periods in which communication may occur (e.g., at one specified time, at specified intervals, prior to or during each trial, etc.) and by the content of the instructions themselves.

Communication is structured only minimally, for example, when subjects are given an unrestricted opportunity to communicate and are informed by the experimenter that they are free to decide for themselves whether, when, and how to do so. Somewhat greater structuring occurs when subjects are advised when, how, or what to communicate, but remain free to either heed or decline such advice. In this case the pressures to communicate are very likely to be increased, relative to the pressures that are generated when structuring is minimal, and the definition of the situation may be somewhat illuminated by the content of the instructions. Still greater structuring occurs when subjects are not only advised about when, how, or what to communicate, but are required to use the opportunities provided, although they may still be free to decide on the content of their communication. Here the pressure to use communication for the suggested purpose is probably increased further, and the definition of the situation may become even more apparent to subjects.

At the other extreme, of course, instructions designed to prevent communication (as these are given in "no communication" conditions) may be differentiated along similar dimensions. Thus the instructions of some experiments simply inform subjects that they may not talk to one another, while others additionally implore them not to make any audible noise (such as sighs or groans) during the experimental session. *Just as instructions that require communication and advise subjects about its best use may create corresponding pressures toward such use and prompt a definition of the situation as one in which cooperation is positively valued, so too may non-communication instructions that stress isolation and independence rather than interdependence create opposite pressures and induce subjects to define the situation as one in which competition is positively valued.*

As a result of the subtleties often contained in their instructions, researchers may create situations that either constrain or induce subjects to use existing opportunities for communication in particular ways. Moreover, these subtleties may either function to reinforce the intent of the instructions and the hypothesis being tested (as when they increase differences presumed to be a result of the presence or absence of communication), or they may actually work against the experimental hypothesis (as when instructions to communicate are not sufficiently strong to outweigh situational factors that induce competitive motivational orientations). Thus, differences due to the presence or absence of communication may be either heightened or dampened as a result of additional components contained within the experimental instructions that create pressures and provide cues as to the definition of the situation.

A basic assumption that we make is that in their search for cues that define the experimental situation, research subjects are likely to be sensitive to and influenced by such subtleties as are contained in the researcher's instructions. Evidence to support this assumption is found in an experiment by Gallo and Dale (1968), who discovered that subjects playing a PD game were highly sensitive to what may be viewed as tacit instructions from the experimenter. By introducing subtle variations in the experimenter's tone of voice and facial expression (when he gave subjects score feedback after each trial, the experimenter was programmed to display either support or non-support for cooperative behavior), sharp differences in cooperation were produced. Subjects reinforced for cooperation made twice as many cooperative choices as those not reinforced. Furthermore, when subjects were questioned at the end of the experimental session, those who had responded appropriately to the intonational differences seemed to be unaware of the experimenter's behavior and its effects on them. While Gallo and Dale's experiment is not directly related to the question of how opportunities for communication may be structured, it does provide dramatic evidence of how subtleties in instructions—in this case an experimenter's nonverbal instructions—may influence the behavior of subjects.

Our purpose in pursuing this line of reasoning is not to raise issues about the effects of experimenter bias and demand characteristics in bargaining studies, for although these problems often exist, to focus on them would overlook a considerably larger issue. Instead we wish to suggest that *a researcher's instructions to his subjects are in many respects similar to interventions made by an authoritative third party who wishes to promote effective communication, for example, between opposing labor and management negotiators.* From this perspective it is entirely possible that, much like the effects of third party interventions in bargaining outside the research laboratory, the effects of subtle and often unrecognized elements of instructions given to research subjects may place pressure on them, and may imply a definition of the situation that induces them to behave accordingly.

Perhaps the clearest example of a researcher's instructions having been employed to produce differential use of an available communication channel occurred in an experiment conducted by Krauss and Deutsch (1966). Recall that in this experiment subjects obtained larger outcomes when they were given explicit instructions to communicate fair and equitable proposals (tutored communication) than when no such guidance was provided (untutored communication). Recall too that bilateral threat was present in all conditions of the experiment (so that the potential for heightened competitive motives was high), and that all subjects were required to speak with one another before each trial (although what they actually said was left entirely to them). The instructions to subjects in the tutored and untutored conditions were as follows:

> Subjects in the [untutored] condition were told that they would be required to talk to each other before each trial. They were told that they could talk about anything they wanted to, but that it would be necessary that they say something to each other before every trial.
> Subjects in the [tutored] condition were also told that they must

communicate before each trial; however, their instructions specified the content of pretrial communication. They were told to use this opportunity to make a proposal to the other player about what they would do on the forthcoming trial. Moreover, they were instructed to try to make proposals which were fair, both to themselves and to the other player. ("Make a proposal which you think is reasonable and acceptable both to yourself and to the other person. Try to make a proposal which is both fair to yourself and which you would be willing to accept if you were in her shoes.") [p. 574]

Our general interpretation of the results of this experiment comes quite close to that advanced by the investigators, namely, that the instructions, coming as they did from an authoritative individual, probably created demands that pressed tutored subjects toward greater cooperation. However, one must dig deeper into the nature of these demands to understand more fully what happened. Thus, it seems to us that an important part of the pressure toward increased cooperation among the tutored subjects, as compared to the untutored ones, stemmed from the possibility that the instructions increased the pressure on the former to engage in a more active search for alternatives and to experiment more readily with alternatives—in other words, to define the situation as one in which experimenting with alternative (fair) proposals would be positively valued.

If one considers the instructions provided in the tutored condition, it appears that subjects were exhorted to do two things beyond merely being "fair": They were asked to view their own proposals from the other's perspective, and they were asked to make proposals in accord with what they themselves would accept if proffered by the opposing party. Such instructions, when delivered by a source as responsible and authoritative as the experimenter, may be seen as having a rather strong potential for inducing recipients to take the role of the other toward themselves, thereby promoting a perspective broader than that of personal gain. Perhaps fairness does indeed involve putting oneself in the shoes of another and a concern with mutual rather than private gain, but the fact remains that the untutored subjects received neither the instruction to act fairly nor the advice about how to do so, while the tutored subjects enjoyed the benefits of both. Thus, we conclude that the instructions not only generated pressures toward fairness, but may also have increased subjects' identification with each other and thereby promoted a concern with mutual rather than individual gain.

A somewhat similar pattern can be observed in the results of an early PD study reported by Deutsch (1958). Although this experiment was primarily concerned with the effects of different motivational orientations, several different kinds of communication options were also examined. Subjects played a one-trial game in one of several conditions. These included no communication, free written communication (prior to making their choices), and "reversibility." In the reversibility condition, no explicit communication was allowed, and the instructions to subjects informed them that:

> After both . . . had made their choices and they were announced, either one or both of them could change their choices. They were allowed to continue changing choices as long as they wanted to. They were told, however, that if no one changed his choice during a 30-second interval, this would be taken to indicate that neither one wanted to change his choice [p. 271].

The results revealed that mutual cooperation occurred more frequently when subjects were allowed to communicate freely than when they were prevented from doing so. However, the reversibility instructions produced even more cooperation than the free communication instructions, and this effect was most evident among subjects given an individualistic motivational orientation—an orientation which we have already seen is highly sensitive to situational factors.

Let us look more closely at the conditions that may have been created by the reversibility instructions. One possibility is that they may have imparted to subjects a sense of the definition of the situation which implied that choices *ought* to be changed until a cooperative agreement was reached. This possibility gains support from the fact that the frequency of cooperation was also increased by the reversibility instructions among subjects who received the competitive motivational orientation!

A related interpretation emerges from the apparently greater amount of involvement of the experimenter in the reversibility condition. On the basis of the published report of the Deutsch (1958) experiment, it seems that the experimenter intervened repeatedly in the reversibility condition (to announce the time, to announce choice changes, and to restart 30-sec intervals)—whereas he intervened no more than once in any of the other conditions. This suggests that the experimenter's repeated interventions may have functioned to increase the pressure on subjects to make choices that corresponded to the values presumably attributed to him (objectivity, rationality, fairness, etc.).

In short, we think it possible that the implicit message contained in the reversibility instructions, coupled with the greater amount of involvement on the part of the experimenter, may have created pressures that caused individualistically oriented subjects (as well as some of those who were competitively oriented) to redefine the situation as one in which mutually cooperative choices were desirable. If this reasoning is correct, then the obvious implication is that the guidance provided by the reversibility instructions and by the researcher's interventions in carrying them out had a greater effect on inducing cooperation than the instructions that simply provided subjects with free communication. Again the important question to be raised is whether cooperation was increased merely as a function of the presence of the reversibility option itself or whether this occurred as a result of tacit indications that cooperation was valued and that an acceptable way to achieve it was to change choices until this occurred.

Standing in sharp contrast to the pattern outlined above are the results of the experiment by Deutsch and Krauss (1962) in which subjects playing the Acme–Bolt Trucking game in a permissive (free) communication condition received the following instructions:

> In talking to the other player you may say anything you want; or if you don't want to talk you don't have to. You may talk about the game, about what you'd like to happen in the game, what you're going to do, what you'd like the other player to do, or anything else that comes to mind. What you talk about—or whether you decide to talk or not—is up to you [pp. 62–63].

The same instructions were given to subjects in bilateral threat, unilateral threat, and no threat conditions.

The instructions were given once, at the beginning of a 20-trial series. They pointed out the possibility of communication, indicated that it need not be used, and stressed the diversity of its possible uses, but provided no cues about any preferred use. As the results indicate, neither the resulting pressures to communicate nor the definition of the situation imparted by the instructions was sufficient to produce differences in bargaining outcomes, although it did increase the frequency of communication in the no threat condition.

In a subsequent experiment reported in the same paper, Deutsch and Krauss (1962) introduced a compulsory communication condition. Here subjects playing the Trucking game received instructions that were identical to those of the earlier experiment, except that they were also informed: "During the game, when your trucks are en route, you both will be required to communicate with each other. . . . Remember, you must say something to the other player on every trip [pp. 65–66]." In addition, the investigators note: "On trials where either S failed to talk, they were reminded by E at the conclusion of the trial of the requirement that they talk to the other player on every trial. In no group was it necessary to make this reminder on more than four trials [p. 66]." The effects of these instructions were compared with the permissive instructions of the earlier experiment and with the instructions given in a no communication condition. The results revealed that compulsory communication led to higher outcomes than either permissive or no communication and that this effect was pronounced in the unilateral threat condition.

If we look more closely at the compulsory communication instructions, several things emerge. First, the pressure to communicate was increased not only by the requirement stated in the instructions, but also by the experimenter's reminders when it failed to occur. Second, the experimenter's repeated interventions also had the effect of bringing him into the ongoing process, whereas this did not occur in the permissive and noncommunication conditions. The heightened presence of the experimenter in the compulsory condition, in conjunction with the initial instructions, may well have had the effect of imparting and reinforcing a norm of "staying in touch" with one another. The implications of such a norm may have induced in subjects a definition of the situation that placed positive value on using the opportunity for communication to increase cooperative coordination. This, of course, is probably an implicit component of the effect that Deutsch and Krauss sought to produce with the compulsory communication condition. Nevertheless, the question remains as to whether the improved outcomes resulted from the requirement to communicate, from the implications of the experimenter's actions in enforcing this requirement, or both.

Similar questions may be raised about several other investigations that have compared conditions in which, on the one hand, opportunities for communication are structured by the researcher's instructions and, on the other, no communication is allowed. However, the general point to be stressed is not that instructions given to subjects may contain confounding elements but that the components of such instructions and their delivery may provide valuable clues about how third party and situational interventions may be structured to improve communication and thereby enhance bargaining effectiveness.

Communication may also be structured by the experimenter through the use of instructions that suggest how prenegotiation contacts with an opposing party may be used. This type of procedure was followed in investigations by Bass (1966) and Druckman (1967, 1968b), who provided subjects with varied instructions about how to use 30- and 40-min prenegotiation planning sessions, prior to engaging in simulated (role playing) labor–management contract negotiations. The subjects in these experiments were graduate business students and college undergraduates, respectively. Each experiment involved multiple issues.

Bass' experiments were primarily concerned with testing the hypothesis that difficulties in reaching agreement are heightened by group commitments and loyalties. Bass either had opposing representatives meet or prevented them from meeting, prior to a 70-min negotiation session. This prenegotiation meeting, when it occurred, was for the purpose either of "studying the issues" or for "strategy formation." However, beyond the intended purpose of creating varying degrees of loyalty and commitment, the instructions also structured the opportunities for communication in the four conditions created by the above manipulations. In the "bilateral study" condition, both subjects received the following instructions:

> You should devote the 30 minutes discussion time to learning as much as you can about each others' positions. You should do no negotiating or bargaining during this time. The purpose of the study group is to promote understanding of the other point of view in comparison to your own, to see the areas of greater and lesser disagreement [p. 6].

Subjects in the "unilateral study" condition received similar instructions, but these stressed studying the issues privately, without the opportunity to meet with the opposing side. Subjects in the "unilateral strategy" condition also had no opportunity to meet with the opposing side and were told to use their prebargaining session to formulate their own strategy privately—to firm up their minimal concession points, determine the importance rankings of the issues for themselves, and so forth. A fourth condition, "bilateral strategy," was also examined, but this condition is not relevant to the present analysis.

The results revealed that on several dimensions (including the amount of time taken to reach agreement and concordance on the importance rankings of the issues) unilateral strategy planning sessions resulted in the poorest outcomes, while bilateral study sessions with the future adversary resulted in the best outcomes. Although Bass interpreted these results in terms of the amount of loyalty and commitment engendered by the different prebargaining experiences, they may also be looked at in terms of structured communication: The unilateral study and strategy conditions prevented communication between opposing sides, while the bilateral conditions allowed and encouraged it and also advised subjects about how to use this opportunity. Much like the tutored communication instructions of the Krauss and Deutsch (1966) experiment, Bass' bilateral study instructions advised subjects to use communication to learn each other's positions, to "promote understanding of the other's point of view," and to avoid early commitment ("You should do no negotiating or bargaining during this time"). In addition to merely providing varied opportunities for prenegotiation contact, the instructions in the bilateral study condition may well have induced subjects to define the situation as one in which mutual exploration, mutual understanding, and mutual avoidance of unilateral position-taking would be valued.

One important implication of Bass' results is the suggestion that *interventions designed to improve bargaining effectiveness by structuring prebargaining communication must be sufficiently compelling to induce bilaterally the willingness and ability to use such opportunities for purposes of mutual rather than individual gain.* Short of this, if intervention fails to produce sufficiently symmetrical concerns with mutual gain, then the structure that has been imposed may have limited effectiveness in inducing the desired behavior.

Bass' findings were essentially reproduced in an investigation by Druckman (1967), who used a similar role-playing situation. Druckman found that bargainers who were deprived of an opportunity for prebargaining contact, but were instead instructed to formulate their strategy unilaterally, took longer to reach agreement, remained further apart on the issues involved, and were less yielding than those who were given an opportunity for prebargaining bilateral discussion with opposing parties. The condition differences in this study were even more striking than those obtained by Bass, largely, we suspect, because Druckman strengthened the instructions originally given by Bass to subjects in the bilateral study condition. Druckman added the following to those instructions:

> Do not formulate or plan any strategies for bargaining from either position. Do not take a position and argue its merits against someone who might profess to the opposite position. Finally, do not form coalitions with other team members to bargain or debate from a position.
> *If at any point the discussion seems to break down into an interteam competition, the experimenter will stop it and remind participants of the goal.* You should act bipartisan with respect to the issues during the session. There is no need to use any form of propaganda. . . . The emphasis is on informality. . . . Understanding is the goal! [Druckman, 1967, p. 282; italics added.]

In contrast, the instructions in the unilateral strategy formulation condition were designed to induce bargainers to take definite positions and to develop arguments in defense of these positions, without communicating with the other side while doing so.

Here, as in the Bass (1966) and Krauss and Deutsch (1966) experiments, the "enriched" instructions (in the bilateral study condition) stressed bipartisanship, mutual understanding, and avoidance of early commitment; *and* these instructions were reinforced by the experimenter's periodic interventions. Once again we suspect that the combined effect of these elements was to increase the pressures on subjects to cooperate and to prompt a corresponding definition of the situation by them.

In fact Druckman recognized that the content of the instructions went beyond merely creating unilateral and bilateral conditions. In a subsequent experiment using the same bargaining problem, he (Druckman, 1968b) introduced two additional conditions: "unilateral discussion" and "no prenegotiation experience." The unilateral discussion condition, designed to separate unilateral experience from formal position preparation, instructed subjects to discuss the issues informally among themselves, without formulating a definite strategy. Subjects in the no prenegotiation experience (control) condition merely studied the issues by themselves, without discussion, before the bargaining began.

The results (in terms of speed of resolution, distance remaining between the opposing sides at the end of the session, and amount of yielding) revealed that bargaining effectiveness was low in the unilateral strategy formation condition (although no worse than in the control condition) and was highest in the bilateral study condition. Moreover, subjects in the unilateral discussion condition bargained more effectively than those in the unilateral strategy condition.

One important implication suggested by these results is that the structuring of *within*-team prebargaining discussion may be useful in some situations, especially if the third party's (or experimenter's) intervention emphasizes gaining familiarity with the issues in an informal manner and prevents any strategizing or commitment to a position at this early time. As suggested by Druckman's procedures, such interventions should be directed to each of the opposing sides and may require some form of surveillance.

The questions generated by our analysis of the content and delivery of instructions to subjects about the use of available communication channels may be applied to additional investigations as well. For example, in a 50-trial PD study conducted by Scodel *et al.* (1959), the experimenters report: "Pairs were stopped after the first 25 trials and instructed to come out from behind their partition. They were then told to discuss the game in any way that they pleased for a two-minute period [p. 116]." These rather minimally structured instructions yielded only a slight, nonsignificant increase in cooperation in the latter half of the experiment when compared to conditions in which communication was prevented.

In a study conducted by Bixenstine *et al.* (1966), the authors write:

> At the end of 20 trials the E announced a recess. For half . . . of the squads, E then threw the recording switch on a tape recorder and left the room for 15 minutes. . . . The remaining squads were instructed not to talk while the same tape recorder played [music] for 15 minutes [during which E did not leave the room]. After the recess elapsed, the game was resumed for 20 trials [p. 491].

Cooperation was significantly greater in the communication than in the non-communication condition. Although the communication instructions were vague at best, the noncommunication instructions were less so, and they were reinforced by the presence of the researcher. In a later experiment, Bixenstine and Douglas (1967) used exactly the same procedure and obtained similar results.

In summary, differences in bargaining behavior that arise as a result of or in conjunction with instructions given to subjects about their use of existing communication opportunities reveal much about how interventions by authoritative third parties may be used to structure communication to improve bargaining effectiveness. In general the research indicates that bargaining effectiveness is likely to be affected adversely by instructions that eliminate opportunities for communication between opposing parties.

This, of course, is not a very startling conclusion. However, it also appears that minimal instructions, which merely advise subjects of the availability of communication opportunities, are likely to have less impact on the induction of effective communication than instructions that both provide additional information about how communication may be used advantageously and create pressures to use it accordingly. One apparent reason for the difference is that minimal instructions make it easier for personality, motivational, and situational factors—each of which may be detrimental to effective conflict resolution—to influence the manner in which communication will be used.

If one assumes as we do that there is at least a modicum of correspondence between bargaining behavior in the research laboratory and that which occurs in more naturalistic contexts, then the foregoing analysis suggests that one of the primary functions of third party interventions may be to define the situation for the bargainers. By providing bargainers with cues about how to proceed, their motivational orientations may be altered, thereby generating pressures toward movement in an appropriate direction. Of course, in bargaining outside the experimental laboratory, other formidable constraints—such as ideological commitment, economic and political pressures, and policy considerations—may limit the impact of a third party's attempts to structure communication. Nevertheless, we suspect that within the limits imposed by such constraints, the more authoritative a third party and the less severe the external constraints, the more effective his interventions are likely to be.

Structuring through Inherent Features of the Research Paradigm

The phrase *inherent features* refers to procedures that definitely prescribe the manner in which communication is to occur during the course of a bargaining exchange. Such mechanisms are frequently integral parts of the research designs used to study bargaining behavior. Structuring of this type can be seen, for example, whenever procedures are introduced that specify the timing and the content of communication. The former type of structuring (timing) occurs in investigations that permit communication only at specific times (e.g., early, midway, or late in the bargaining sequence); the latter (content) occurs in studies in which only a limited number of prescribed written messages are made available to subjects, who are then free to send such messages on specified occasions.

These procedures for structuring communication are not unlike those found in bargaining outside the research laboratory. For example, it is often the case in international negotiation that the parties communicate with one another by means of prepared written statements, that a predetermined sequence of presentation is to be followed, or that rules pertaining to formality or protocol are to be observed. The type of structuring that occurs in research studies as a result of inherent features of the procedures used may thus provide insight into how opportunities for communication may be incorporated into the structure of nonlaboratory bargaining situations and as to how the content of specific statements or messages is likely to affect a bargainer's behavior. Our examination of several experiments is primarily concerned with detecting the pressures that seem to be generated as a result of structures imposed by such research procedures.

A clear example of the manner in which the content of communication may be structured appears in an early investigation by Loomis (1959) concerning the development of trust and cooperation in a five-trial PD game. Pairs of subjects were provided with one of five different messages, prepared in advance, in order to determine which might produce the greatest amount of trust and cooperation. The experiment was designed to test Deutsch's (1958) assumption that the stabilization of a cooperative relationship depends on the bargainers' ability to communicate expectation, intention, retaliation, and absolution. In one condition, subjects could send only a prepared note declaring their expectations for the other's behavior. In another they could only disclose their own intentions. In a third, a note announcing both intention and expectation was available. A fourth condition enabled subjects to send a message in which expectation, intention, and commitment to retaliation (in case the other behaved exploitatively) were announced. Subjects in a fifth condition could send a message that announced all of the above elements plus the promise of absolution if the other would refrain from exploitation. In a control condition, subjects were prevented from communicating with one another. Loomis predicted and found a linear relationship between message availability and both trust and cooperation. Subjects who could only announce their expectations cooperated least (but more than control subjects), while those using the more elaborate messages displayed greater trust and cooperation.

A closer analysis of the implicit meaning conveyed by the five messages in Loomis' study suggests the possibility that subjects who could send and receive the more complete messages may have been induced by them to view the interchange differently than those who could only send or receive the shorter messages. Those subjects who could only send or receive a statement of expectation or intention may have viewed the situation as more competitive than those who could send or receive a message containing both expectation and intention, plus the contingent statements, "If you do not choose as I want you to choose, then on the next trial I will choose Y" (retaliation), and "If you do choose as I would like you to choose after first not doing so, then I will choose X on the next trial" (absolution).

One reason for the differences reported by Loomis, we suspect, is that the more complete the available message was, the more likely a sender or receiver may have been to define the situation in terms of the persuasive appeal, contingencies, and completeness of information apparent in the message available to him. In contrast, senders and receivers of the more limited messages may have been constrained to view themselves and their situation as less open to persuasion and the exchange of information than to unilateral announcement. The abbreviated messages may thus have induced a rather competitive motivational orientation, while the more detailed messages may have induced a more cooperative one. Although all subjects were given an individualistic motivational orientation via the experimenter's instructions, the messages that were available may have produced variations in these motives. In light of Deutsch's (1958) finding that individualistically oriented subjects are rather susceptible to the influence of situational factors, this does not seem unlikely. Thus it may be that the different messages used in Loomis' study affected not only the quantity of communication that could occur, but, on quite a different level, they may have contributed to qualitatively different perceptions of the other party as well as different definitions of the situation.

A parallel effect is evident in a study by Radlow and Weidner (1966), which is quite similar, conceptually, to the Loomis (1959) experiment. Radlow and Weidner had subjects engage in a 98-trial PD game in one of two conditions. In one, no communication was allowed. In the other, subjects were furnished with five cards containing preprepared messages designed to convey different contingent commitments to their future choice behavior. Subjects in this condition exchanged the cards of their choice prior to beginning the sequence, thereby announcing their future plans to one another. The instructions were left deliberately vague as to whether these early commitments would be binding.

The messages were similar to those used by Loomis. Two were simple statements of intention, cooperative or competitive. Two indicated intentions, expectations for the other's behavior, and readiness for retaliation. The fifth message contained statements of conditionally cooperative intention and expectation, and a readiness for retaliation if necessary, as well as for absolution.

The results indicated that there was significantly more cooperation in the message condition than in the no communication one. But why exactly should this have been so? First of all, the data reported by Radlow and Weidner indicate that the message adopted most frequently by both players was the one that was most detailed, containing the elements of intention, expectation, retaliation, and absolution. Second, the average level of cooperation in pairs selecting this detailed message was close to 100% over the complete 98-trial sequence. Only two of the pairs selecting this message failed to make 100% joint cooperative choices throughout. This suggests that something about the content of this message induced in subjects who selected it, as well as in those who merely saw it, an unswerving doggedness in the pursuit of joint cooperative outcomes. Examination of this message reveals that, in addition to containing the four central elements, it also included a phrase alluding to the desirability of making joint cooperative choices. Thus it was probably not only message capability that produced the difference between the message and no communication conditions but also the *content* of the messages (particularly the prominently selected one). This message may have strengthened the definition of the situation as a cooperative one and may also have provided additional information to subjects indicating how they might proceed toward stable cooperative choices—information that was clearly absent in the noncommunication condition.

We recognize that the above interpretation implies that the content of *any* predetermined message may provide clues about the definition of the situation as well as additional information of various sorts. We are not arguing that such information be removed, however, for this would surely be impossible to do. Rather, the fact that the implicit meanings transmitted through preprepared messages tend to generate pressures that influence behavior should be suggestive of procedures by which communication may be structured usefully outside the research laboratory.

For example, one implication of both the Loomis (1959) and Radlow and Weidner (1966) experiments is that beyond the general suggestions that an authoritative third party might introduce to bring about more effective communication lie possibilities for predetermining, filtering, or at least encouraging particular types of early communication—communication that will both reinforce a situational definition of mutual gain and provide information enabling the parties to move in this direction. Certainly the results of the experiments by Bass (1966), Druckman (1967, 1968b), and Krauss and Deutsch (1966) discussed earlier suggest several types of intervention that might be used for such purposes. The practice often followed by professional mediators, of separating opposing labor and management negotiators, reflects this reasoning. So does the strategy of the marriage counselor who keeps the feuding husband and wife apart but coaches each separately in constructive uses of communication until he feels they can be brought together to attempt to resolve their difficulties.

If standard messages may create or reinforce a cooperative situational definition, they may also foster perceptions of the situation as a competitive one. This effect is apparent in investigations conducted by Cheney (1969), Gumpert (1967), and Hornstein (1965). Hornstein provided subjects engaging in a real estate bargaining task with standard messages, enabling them to threaten and aggress against one another as well as to communicate their offers and counteroffers. For eight trials, 48 pairs of subjects bargained over the price of imaginary land parcels. The main focus of the experiment was to determine the effects of different amounts and distributions of threat potential on bargaining behavior. (See Chapter 8 for a more detailed description of this study.)

Hornstein found that, although subjects were not compelled to use either the threat or the aggression messages at their disposal, close to 70% of the pairs used at least one of these messages during the first trial. Moreover, the likelihood of reaching later agreement after using either of these messages was significantly reduced in comparison to pairs in which neither message had been used. Related effects were also apparent. For example, the average number of threats initiated over all conditions during the eight trials was close to four, or 50%; the tendency to respond to threat with counterthreat (over all conditions) occurred on 56% of the trials in which threat was used; and aggression occurred, on the average, on more than half of the trials in which it could have occurred. It is possible, then, that the provision of these deleterious messages may have legitimized their use, thereby contributing to a competitive situational definition.

Similarly, subjects in Gumpert's (1967) Acme–Bolt Trucking game experiment were provided in several conditions with standard threat messages, and either precise (calibrated) or imprecise (noncalibrated) capability to penalize the other party for failing to share the use of the one-lane road. Gumpert's results revealed that threat messages were used frequently when they were available, but that they served different functions, depending on whether they were used in conjunction with precise or imprecise penalty. Apparently threat messages were used as an additional influence mechanism in conjunction with calibrated penalty capacity but as a punitive device when subjects' penalty capabilities were imprecise. This again suggests that standard messages may become incorporated into the definition of the situation and may influence behavior accordingly.

An experiment by Cheney (1969) demonstrates this point. Here, subjects engaging in the Acme–Bolt Trucking game were given four different communication options. In one condition these consisted of promises and rewards; in another they consisted of warnings and punishments; in a third condition subjects were given both types of options; and in a fourth condition no communication was allowed. The results indicated that the opportunity to communicate warnings and punishments did not facilitate cooperative behavior in comparison to the control condition. The opportunity to communicate promise and reward, however, did increase cooperative behavior relative to the control condition. Here, the more favorable messages probably promoted a more cooperative situational definition, while the availability of warning and punishment may have caused the exchange to be seen in more competitive terms.

The results of the Cheney (1969), Gumpert (1967), and Hornstein (1965) experiments suggest that, in contrast to the generally beneficial effects of cooperatively structured messages on the situational definition of a bargaining exchange, the availability of competitive messages, such as warnings, threats, or punishments, is likely to introduce elements that may reduce bargaining effectiveness. One practical implication is that if an authoritative source endorses or introduces warnings, threats, or punishments, his legitimation of this type of communication could well lend itself to a competitive situational definition. On the other hand, the endorsement or introduction of structured cooperative communication seems more likely to promote a cooperative situational definition, and may also provide information that is useful in establishing such a relationship.

THE PRESENCE OF TIME LIMITS

Few of us, even those least involved in bargaining activities, are unfamiliar with the "eleventh hour" effect widely publicized in mass media accounts of collective bargaining. Recent years have seen a spate of instances in which labor unions, for example, have either threatened to strike or have struck, walked off the job or slowed down, when their contracts were unrenewed or remained unsettled by a specified date and time. Instances of final hour collective bargaining, moreover, have occurred so frequently that in one leading textbook of collective bargaining (Dunlop & Healy, 1955) it has been suggested that this phenomenon may be caused by fundamental characteristics of the collective bargaining process. Among the more prominent examples of the eleventh hour effect are the contract negotiations in the steel and auto industries, collective bargaining between the New York City

Transport Workers Union and the Metropolitan Transit Authority, and a variety of disputes between teachers unions and boards of education in the area of public education.

As a result of the eleventh hour tendency it is not uncommon for collective bargaining to begin months or even years in advance of contract expiration dates, in order to stave off the widespread costs and inconvenience of work stoppages. It is instructive to note that, even in such cases as these, agreement often fails to be reached until the final hour anyway.

In addition to deadlines in collective bargaining, various other kinds of time constraints—either self-imposed or introduced by third parties—also occur frequently. For example, educational negotiators may devise time allocation plans in order to facilitate progress in their negotiations. Real estate bargainers may set deadlines beyond which options are lost or penalties accrue. International negotiators may rough out the sequence in which specific issues are to be considered. And in any of these arenas, bargainers may introduce "time out" periods or set aside intervals for "cooling off," informality, press conferences, and the like. Moreover, when bargaining becomes severely conflicted, a third party may become involved, and many of his interventions may be directed toward the more efficient use of time: the delineation of time periods, clarification of phases, pacing the exchange, or developing (as Walton, 1969, suggests) a future perspective.

Obviously time is of paramount importance in many instances of bargaining. Yet, interestingly, there are some situations in which it appears at first glance to be of little consequence. Consider, for example, the SALT negotiations. Because these talks are viewed as having such serious long-term implications, and because they are so sensitive to world political developments, they are not tightly bound to the sweep of the hands on the face of a clock. Nonetheless, here too agenda have been set and target dates heralded, delays due to the turn of international events have occurred, and pressures to move toward agreement have been in evidence—as a sense of urgency has compelled the world's two nuclear powers to slow the pace of an arms race fraught with potential future danger. Nor were the "secret" talks between the United States and mainland China, carried out in Warsaw over an entire decade, constrained by time in the conventional sense of the word. Here too, a long-term perspective prevailed and, although delays of up to several months occurred between many sessions, it became clear that the two nations were committed to an indefinite time perspective. Ultimately, of course, the Warsaw talks contributed to the willingness of these nations to participate in the 1972 summit meetings, from which more substantial agreements emerged.

Time limits in bargaining may be explicit or implicit, self-generated or imposed from without, flexible or rigid, and viewed in similar or dissimilar terms by the parties involved. The mere existence of time limits, however, is likely to have important effects. As Stevens (1963) states in his handbook of collective bargaining:

> An approaching deadline puts pressure on the parties to state their true positions and thus does much to squeeze elements of bluff out of the later steps of negotiation. However, an approaching deadline does much more. . . . It brings pressures to bear which actually change the least favorable terms upon which each party is willing to settle. Thus, it operates as a force tending to bring about conditions necessary for agreement [p. 100].

Empirical evidence bearing on Stevens' contention may be found in at least five separate studies. Pruitt and Drews (1969), for example, hypothesized that time pressure (defined as the mutual perception that negotiation will end, regardless of whether agreement is reached) and the passage of time will lead to a softening of demands, a reduction in aspirations and bluffing, and an increase in the magnitude of concessions. The assumptions underlying these hypotheses were: (1) that heightened time pressure increases the importance of reaching agreement; (2) that, since toughness requires increased time, it is likely to diminish as time pressures increase; and (3) that under heightened time pressure a softer strategy is less likely to be seen as a sign of weakness by the opposing party. Based on these assumptions, Pruitt and Drews further hypothesized that when time pressure exists, a bargainer's behavior will be a result of the strength of the pressure and the behavior of the opposing party. When time pressure is mild, a soft stance by one party will lead to increased toughness on the part of the other. But when acute time pressure exists, this same stance by the first will lead to decreased toughness on the part of the other.

Eighty subjects negotiated with a preprogrammed other in a variant of the Bilateral Monopoly paradigm. The experimental variables were time pressure (mild or acute) and the concession rate of the program (low or high). The results revealed that average demands, aspirations, and bluffing were greater under mild than under acute time pressure, and level of demand as well as bluffing declined as time expired. However, concession size failed to increase as time elapsed, and there were no appreciable effects of the other's concession rate. In terms of the subject's perceptions of the other, it was found that he was viewed as weak when his concessions were large—a finding that lends support to Stevens' contention that although making concessions is fundamental to reaching agreement, it is likely to be seen as a sign of weakness.

That time limits and deadlines are likely to soften bargaining positions is not only attested to by Pruitt and Drews' results but also by the findings of

Benton, Kelley, and Liebling (1972), Kelley (1966), Komorita and Barnes (1969), Komorita and Brenner (1968), and Pruitt and Johnson (1970). The results of the latter three investigations indicated that heightened time pressure, brought about either by varying the time allowed for bargaining or by varying the costs for failing to reach agreement within a specified time period, produced greater or more frequent concessions. Moreover, Komorita and Barnes (1969) found that concession rate and frequency of agreement increased as the bargainers' costs for not reaching agreement increased. Although Pruitt and Drews failed to find an increase in concession size as a function of elapsed time, the decline in level of demand noted in their study may be interpreted as a parallel effect. The research findings presented above lend support to the general proposition that *time pressures increase the likelihood of agreement and tend to be manifested in reductions in bargaining aspirations, demands, and the amount of bluffing that occurs.*

It would add considerably to our understanding of how time pressures operate if the underlying processes could be described. Thibaut and Kelley's (1959) notions of comparison level (CL) and comparison level for alternatives (CL_{alt}) are quite helpful in this regard. Recall, as discussed in Chapter 2, that CL represents what a bargainer expects to get, while CL_{alt} represents his minimally acceptable outcome, given the available alternatives.

It has been both acknowledged (Stevens, 1963) and demonstrated (Kelley, 1966; Rubin & DiMatteo, 1972) that a bargainer's initial demands are likely to be inflated with respect to his CL and CL_{alt} as a result of his need to feel the other party out and avoid settling for too little at the outset. Such needs, however, necessitate the avoidance of early commitment, which, says Kelley (1966), can be accomplished by making exploratory rather than firm offers, starting with high demands, and using the available time to obtain information about the other. Incidentally, Kelley's reasoning here offers an explanation of why, even when bargaining is begun far in advance of deadlines, these limits are likely to be approached anyway.

> Because the need for information will be met only slowly and grudgingly, and never completely, the reasons for avoiding early commitment continue to exist, though less compellingly, over time. In negotiations without deadlines, this will lead to extensively protracted interchanges. With a deadline, the negotiations should be carried on until the last minute [p. 65].

Thus, as bargaining progresses and the parties gain increasing information, CL and CL_{alt} are likely to decrease. This decrease is likely to be accompanied by greater concession making and decreased bluffing.

There are many instances, however, in which time pressures *fail* to operate as outlined above. These cases are known to all of us by the widespread inconvenience, costliness, and publicity resulting from strikes, disruptions in the delivery of services, production stoppages and, in some instances, by the public demonstrations that follow in their wake. Here the press of time fails to reduce CL and CL_{alt} sufficiently to produce convergence on mutually acceptable settlement points.

In general it appears that resistance to the lowering of a bargainer's CL and CL_{alt} over time occurs as a result of the existence of countervailing pressures operating simultaneously. These opposing pressures may arise from personality or from motivational or situational factors. Brown, Garland, and Freedman (1973), for example, have found that motives to appear strong—as these were induced by the presence of a noncommunicative, dependent constituency—caused bargainers to refuse a final offer from an exploitative other at the end of a bargaining session and to forfeit their own and their dependents' monetary outcome.

Beyond constituency pressures and the motives that are engendered by them, the resistance of CL and CL_{alt} to reduction may arise from a bargainer's ideological commitment to his position or to values related to justice, from his perceptions of the other party's behavior toward him, or from a variety of other factors. In general, though, it may be said that the amount of reduction in CL and CL_{alt} in response to time pressure is correlated with a bargainer's desire to reach agreement, where this desire is a function of the difference between the relative costliness of failing to reach agreement within a specified time period and the gains to be derived from doing so.

CONCLUDING COMMENT

The four physical components of bargaining structure we have discussed in this chapter—site location and neutrality, physical arrangements at the site, communication availability and use, and time limits—both reflect and exert a powerful influence on the nature and quality of the bargaining exchange. That each component has an important effect on bargaining should be obvious at this point. That each, through the issues it generates, reflects the quality of the bargaining relationship and allows us to diagnose this quality, is perhaps less obvious.

The location and accessibility of the bargaining site may inform us about the struggle for power and status among the parties and the way this struggle is resolved, if at all. Physical arrangements at the site (seating, the use of symbolic insignia of various kinds, the physical distance maintained, etc.) may provide valuable information about the degree of cooperativeness or competitiveness in the bargaining relationship. Similarly, the extent to which communication channels are made available and the manner in which they are used, reflect as well as dictate the climate of the exchange. Finally, the nature and extent of time limits imposed either by or upon bargainers may provide a useful estimate of the bargainers' chances of reaching agreement.

While our discussion of the literature concerning communication availability and use has been rather extensive, reflecting the considerable experimental attention given to these issues over the last decade, our discussion of the other physical components of bargaining structure has been more limited, reflecting the relative paucity of research in these areas. As a result, we have found it necessary to rely rather heavily on illustrative materials (case histories, journalistic accounts, etc.), which, while instructive, are no substitute for controlled research. We hope, therefore, that some of the more speculative ideas presented in this chapter will stimulate thoughtful consideration among both practitioners and theorists, and lead to more extensive research where little has gone before.

6

Issue Components of Bargaining Structure

Any bargaining exchange, in order to qualify as such, must involve at least one issue, namely, the manner in which (tangible) resources are to be exchanged or divided among the parties. Moreover, it is more often true than not that while bargainers are focusing on a given issue, intangibles may arise—as outgrowths either of the present conflict of interest or the prior relationship between the parties. In some instances intangibles may be of relatively minor importance, while in others they may become magnified to the point that they pose formidable barriers to reaching agreement over the tangible issues in dispute.

Issues vary not only in terms of their tangibility, of course, but in other ways as well. As we shall see, variables such as issue incentive magnitude, reward structure, number, format, presentation, and prominence are each likely to exert a profound influence on bargaining effectiveness.

Before beginning an exploration of the effects of each of the above factors, let us briefly consider a hypothetical bargaining episode in which the complex interplay among issue components may be illustrated.

AN ILLUSTRATIVE ASIDE

A prospective buyer is negotiating the price of an automobile with a newly trained used car salesman. The scene is the office on the used car lot. The customer makes a first offer, which corresponds to the minimum (but not the preferred) price that the salesman has been instructed by his boss to obtain. The neophyte salesman suspects that his boss, who is seated silently nearby, has been listening in on the exchange and evaluating his performance. Because he fears looking overly anxious to make a sale in the eyes of his employer, the salesman refuses the customer's offer. Instead, he makes a counteroffer which, being several hundred dollars higher than the customer's opening offer, is refused by the latter. The customer, having previously boasted of his bargaining acumen to his wife (who is also present), and wishing to be seen by her as a competent, effective bargainer, rejects the offer as ridiculous, tugs at his wife's arm, and together they walk out of the office. Later that day, the salesman realizes that he would have agreed to the customer's first offer, had his boss not been present. Similarly, while lying in bed that night, our customer admits to himself that the attractiveness of the car would have led him to make a compromise offer, had it not been for his boastful announcement to his wife that he would get it with his opening bid.

Although the vignette depicted above is a caricature, real life approximations probably occur every hour of every working day on used car lots across the country. Indeed, we believe that the central issue components found in this drama are not limited to bargaining over the price of a car but may also be detected in the countless other settings in which bargaining occurs. Let us look more closely at the issue structure of our little exchange.

There was only one tangible issue at stake—the overall selling price of the car. However, this became inextricably intertwined with equally present but less tangible issues, namely, the salesman's need to be favorably evaluated by his boss and the husband's need to live up to his prior boast in the presence of his wife. On the basis of the outcome of the exchange, it might be said that the tangible (dollars and cents) issue became subordinated to intangible issues related to image management. These concerns, moreover, both hindered the salesman from making a sale that was at least minimally acceptable and prevented the customer from obtaining the vehicle that he desired.

Notice that the overshadowing of the dollars and cents issue by the image issue prevented the parties from exploring a broader range of possible intermediary settlement points. Instead, the issue of selling price became compressed into all-or-nothing (zero sum) terms, at least for the customer. His essential position was, "If you don't take my first offer, no other offer will be tendered." The customer apparently felt that, after having boasted to his wife, he could not look like a good bargainer by purchasing the car for anything above his opening offer. Nor could the salesman easily accept the customer's first offer because, although it was minimally acceptable, he believed he had to exceed this amount in order to be evaluated favorably by his employer.

Although there was only one tangible issue at stake, additional tangible issues might have been introduced that would have affected the likelihood of agreement being reached. For example, issues related to auto accessories, the improvements or repairs to be made on the car, the length and amount of coverage to be provided in its service contract, the terms of its warranty, provisions for periodic inspection or other services, and a host of other negotiables might have been introduced by either party. From this perspective, the installation of a new radio, which might not have mattered much to the dealer (especially if he happened, by coincidence, to be in the process of liquidating an excess of radios at "cost") but might have made the overall price of the automobile sufficiently enticing to the customer to induce an offer beyond the initial one. Or the customer might have been willing to improve upon his opening offer on the condition that the dealer provide four new deluxe safety tires, or, possibly, two new studded snow tires. For his part, the dealer might have been agreeable to a reduced price, had the buyer indicated a willingness to waive the normally provided six-month full service contract in exchange for a more limited one. (The service contract might have been limited either in terms of its duration or its comprehensiveness of coverage, or both.) Such a concession might have been of considerable importance to the dealer (especially if his repair facility was operating at overload capacity) but of lesser importance to the customer (especially if his brother-in-law, a skilled auto mechanic, would service the car in his garage). And so on . . .

Although introducing such additional issues would probably have created a new series of problems, such as the order in which they would be discussed, their grouping or packaging, the possible tradeoffs among them, and their further fractionation (e.g., two new tires rather than four; provision of a new AM rather than AM/FM radio; provision of the radio at cost, but without installation), it might have become possible for the parties to reach a mutually satisfying agreement on the overall price of the car by taking several of these additional considerations into account. In short, the creative introduction of additional issues (assuming, of course, that they were not so numerous as to require excessive time or cause too much confusion, and assuming that they were sufficiently well defined) might have provided both the customer and the salesman with opportunities to agree on a compromise price. Thus, we might imagine our customer saying to his wife: "Well, honey, I paid a bit more, but from now on we ride on safe tires and have our choice of disc jockeys!" And we might imagine a triumphant salesman announcing to his employer: "Well, Mr. Whyte, I made our minimal price and threw in a cheap AM radio, but we're home free because I eliminated our future labor costs on warranty service to the car!"

Two important points are brought into sharp focus by our vignette and by the alternatives we have outlined. First, issues can often by manipulated— sized up or down, hooked together, broken apart, or stated in different language—in order to alter their initial importance rankings and thereby bring a wider range of alternatives into view. Although such techniques may introduce new problems into a bargaining exchange (such as increasing the amount of time needed to reach agreement), they may also provide mechanisms that enable the parties to reach agreements that might not otherwise be possible.

Second, intangible issues, such as concerns with the image one projects to others during the course of an exchange, may offset ("swamp") a bargainer's desire or capacity to reach agreement, even though this desire may have been the primary reason for entering into bargaining in the first place. We are all familiar with instances in which bargainers seem to throw away their chances for obtaining an economically satisfactory outcome in order to promote a favorable public image. In many of these cases, the loss is not considered a loss—as long as one loses less than the opposing party!

In short, to anticipate one of the central arguments in this chapter, we suspect that it is the creative manipulation of issues that often facilitates agreement on those tangible issues that are beclouded by intangibles; and such procedures may be used to increase the satisfaction derived by the parties from the outcomes they obtain.

Given this preliminary aside, let us turn now to a more systematic examination of the various issue components of bargaining structure and to a consideration of the consequences of each for bargaining effectiveness.

INTANGIBLE ISSUES IN BARGAINING

By now there is an impressive body of evidence indicating, in general, that factors which threaten bargainers with damage to their honor, self-esteem, face, reputation, status, or appearance of strength are likely to create intangible issues and, moreover, that such intangibles may become superimposed upon the tangibles that are at stake in the exchange. This evidence also suggests that when intangible issues exist, they are likely to arouse motives and induce behavior designed to prevent or repair such damage, even if heavy penalties are incurred for doing so.

Evidence attesting to the potency of intangible issues may be culled from conceptual discussions and descriptive accounts of a variety of different types of bargaining. On a general level, both Iklé (1964) and Schelling (1960), in their widely known treatises on international conflict and negotiation, discuss the importance of intangible issues such as honor, face, reputation, and status in the conduct of international affairs. Authoritative textbooks on collective bargaining in the labor–management sphere (see, for example, Douglas, 1962; Dunlop & Chamberlain, 1967; Peters, 1955; Stevens, 1963; Walton & McKersie, 1965) also attribute considerable importance to such issues.

Certainly, mass media accounts of both international and labor–management negotiations support the proposition that intangible issues may become as important as the tangible issues themselves in any given bargaining exchange. One need only look to the journalistic records of the Korean Armistice negotiations, to the accounts of various negotiations among the Arab states, to the Cuban missile crisis, and more recently to the Vietnam cease-fire negotiations, to become convinced of the crucial effects of intangible issues on the behavior of the principal negotiators. The evidence available in public records, moreover, is often substantiated by "insider" reports. To wit, there is Robert Kennedy's description of the closely guarded deliberations of the National Security Council during the days of the Cuban missile crisis (Kennedy, 1969); Halberstam's (1972) investigative account of the inner workings of the Kennedy and Johnson Administrations; and, of course, the "Pentagon Papers."

Still further indications of the importance of honor, public image and face saving appear in historical-psychological accounts of the events which led up to the alliance of nations prior to World Wars I (Tuchman, 1962) and II (Shirer, 1941). White (1966) and Frank (1967) also provide penetrating analyses of the profound psychological effects that issues of national honor, image, face, and self-esteem have had on American political and military decisions—concerning U.S. relations with the Soviet Union, the People's Republic of China, and both Vietnams. These analyses, supported by a variety of different kinds of evidence, make it quite clear that intangible issues are salient even at the highest governmental and military levels.

Factors Affecting the Emergence of Intangible Issues

Harsanyi (1962c) points out that bargainers' preferred outcomes and behavior are shaped by the mutual adjustments of expectation that normally occur during the bargaining process, as well as by the stereotyped expectations that each party has at the outset of the exchange. "Stereotyped utility functions," as Harsanyi defines them, are formed on the basis of each party's information about the other's sex, age, social standing, status, education, and other related factors. Harsanyi further suggests that the amount of influence that mutual adjustment processes exert on bargainers' expectations is often overestimated. In many instances, stereotyped utilities play an equal if not more important role in shaping bargainers' expectations and behavior toward one another.

Harsanyi's (1962c) conceptualization of stereotyped utilities leads not only to the common sense observation that bargainers will be likely to engage in a process of sizing each other up, through direct contact or indirect informational sources, but also suggests that status related stereotypes may have enduring effects on bargainers' determinations of how to treat (and what to expect from) one another throughout their exchange. In short, Harsanyi's position suggests that a bargainer will expect to receive concessions, compliance, and other forms of deferential behavior from another who is thought to be of clearly lesser status, and will have opposite expectations when positions are reversed. However, it is when status distinctions are unclear, contested, or are viewed by at least one party as illegitimate, that expectations for concessions, compliance, and deferential behavior will give rise to intangible issues. As Deutsch and Krauss (1962) have pointed out: "To allow oneself to be intimidated, particularly by someone who does not have the right to expect deferential behavior is (when resistance is not seen to be suicidal or useless) to suffer a loss of social face and, hence, of self-esteem [p. 54]." In a later theoretical paper, Harsanyi (1966a) gives further consideration to status struggles of the kind described by Deutsch. He points out that parties involved in such struggles often exhibit "demonstrative non-deference," and that this type of behavior is often apparent in the great lengths to which bargainers will go to avoid displaying deferential behavior to those whom they believe possess illegitimate power—even though such actions may result in heavy penalties to self.

One important implication of Harsanyi's reasoning is that a bargainer's formulation of his minimum necessary share and his break-even point (his CL_{alt} and CL) will, at least in part, be determined by what he believes he *deserves*, given his status relative to that of the opposing party. This analysis is consistent with Homans' (1961) formulation of the rule of "distributive justice," which postulates that rewards or outcomes received in an exchange relationship tend to be directly proportional to one's costs and investments, the latter being based (in part) on one's status relative to that of others. In terms similar to those used by Deutsch, Homans points out that when distributive justice fails, the party who has been inappropriately disadvantaged will seek to restore balance.

The following proposition may now be derived from the formulations of Deutsch, Harsanyi, and Homans, as these have been outlined above: *When a bargainer perceives a contending other to be unjustly demanding, resistant, or punishing (either as a result of excessive demands, insufficient concessions, or inhibiting movement toward what he considers to be his proper share of available outcomes), intangible issues related to the anticipated or actual loss of honor, public image, face, and self-esteem are likely to emerge.* These issues arise as a result of the (perceived) negative social implications of passively accepting insufficient returns on investments. They may become prepotent in circumstances that heighten the need to appear competent and strong and to avoid signs of incompetency and weakness—circumstances that are normally present in bargaining.

The results of a considerable number of experimental bargaining studies lend support to our proposition. Borah (1963), for example, had subjects engage in a modified version of the Acme–Bolt Trucking game in one of two status conditions. In one, each subject was told that the other belonged to a group that considered itself to be superior (i.e., to have higher status than the subject's own group), and that the other party agreed with this evaluation. In the second condition, the subjects were told that they were from the same group and were, therefore, of equal status. The results revealed that the average joint payoffs were significantly lower between pairs in which there was an (unacceptable) attitude of superiority on the part of the other bargainer.

Based on their research using the Acme–Bolt Trucking game, Deutsch and Krauss (1960, 1962) concluded that among the reasons for increased threat use is the likelihood that mutually available threat enhances the competitive aspects of the exchange and thereby increases the concern with self-esteem. Presumably, allowing himself to be threatened or acquiescing to another whose actions threaten to reduce one's outcomes heightens a bargainer's concerns with how he might look to the threatener, his future treatment by him, and his image in the eyes of significant others who may be viewing or may become informed about the exchange—in sum, it heightens the bargainer's concern with potential loss of self-esteem.

Among the more readily available ways to assert oneself—to express demonstrative nondeference—in the bilateral threat condition of the Trucking game are to use the barrier in response to its use by the other and to refuse to share the use of the one-lane path. In and of themselves, both actions have a clear potential for inducing the affront–offense–punitive spiral described by Siegel and Fouraker (1960). However, we suspect that the exacerbated use of threat observed by Deutsch and Krauss in their bilateral threat conditions may also have been a result of the possibility that subjects perceived each other as status equals. Even though they were prevented from seeing and learning one another's identities during the experiment, they saw and heard the other being treated similarly by the experimenter and may therefore have deduced that the other's participation had been solicited in a manner similar to their own. Moreover, in conditions where communication was allowed, subjects learned that the other's voice was similar to their own (female) and probably obtained further evidence about the other's status from the style and content of their communication.

As Homans (1961) points out, "Anything that can be perceived about a man may become a status indicator [p. 249]," and may be used in forming expectations about how others should behave. From the perspective of distributive justice, then, to the extent that Deutsch and Krauss' subjects supposed themselves to be of roughly equal status (but at the same time became targets of each other's threats), circumstances much like those created by Borah's (1963) "false sense of superiority" condition were probably approximated in the bilateral threat condition of the Deutsch and Krauss experiments as well. In short, we think it not unlikely that subjects in this condition increased their use of threat and resistance because, once they had been victimized (once they had felt unjustly threatened and penalized by the other party), they came under considerable pressure to either restore the balance or redress the insult, in order to avoid the anticipated implications of weakness in the other's eyes that might have arisen had they chosen not to assert themselves.

A similar effect was noted by Hornstein (1965), in a study briefly considered in Chapter 5. He found that subjects were apparently more sensitive to their status similarities than to the differences produced by the possession of differing threat potential. As a result, threat, counterthreat, and resistance were generally increased, irrespective of threat potential. Hornstein (1965) concluded:

> Bargainers who perceive their opponents to be of equal or lower status are less likely to show them deference than are bargainers who perceive their opponents to have higher status. Given that bargainers perceived each other as student-subjects, it is possible that they resisted yielding to the other who was perceived as an equal [p. 291].

As pointed out in Chapter 4, it was a similar motive (concern with not looking weak) that was found to cause subjects in Brown's (1968) Trucking game experiment to retaliate against an equal status other (at high costs to self), in response to being exploited by him and receiving derogatory audience feedback. In fact, many of the retaliatory subjects in this experiment actually reported afterward that their reason for doing so was to look strong, both to the exploitative other and to the audience.

Similar concerns have also been noted in the PD game. In this connection, Schlenker et al. (1970) linked increased retaliation toward a threatening same-sexed peer to face-saving motives. Berger and Tedeschi (1969) found differences in retaliatory behavior among several populations of preadolescents playing the PD game and suggested that these differences were due to increased needs to look tough and save face following humiliation. Bonoma, Schlenker, Smith, and Tedeschi (1970) found that, although an increase in a source's capacity to punish a target (the source was presumed to be a peer) led to increased compliance due to the high costs of noncompliance, targets refused to disclose their future intentions to the source and thereby found an alternate mechanism by which to assert themselves. Johnson (1971), who followed up on the Schlenker *et al.* (1970) experiment, observed that deterrent threats (found by Schlenker *et al.* to be rather effective in producing compliance) were met with increased resistance when the need to project an appearance of strength was heightened by the presence of an attractive female experimenter who functioned as scorekeeper.

Conceptual analyses of the PD game also speak to the importance of intangible issues. Thus Scodel *et al.* (1959) conjectured that one reason why competition often dominates collaboration in the PD game is because there are cultural norms that induce individuals to protect themselves against being tested by others. Such norms, they point out, make it necessary to avoid the ego-deflating experience that can result from nonreciprocated attempts at collaboration. Thus, the need to maintain self-esteem dominates the matrix values of the PD game to the extent that the major real choice is between doing as well or better than the other person or running the risk of doing worse. It is for this reason, argue Scodel *et al.*, that behavior in the PD game often reflects attempts to maximize differences, rather than attempts to maximize own outcomes. This point has also been made by Rapoport (1973), who suggested in a conceptual analysis of several variants of the PD game that one party may decline taking the initiative to reward another and may thereby forego the possibility of increased long term outcomes, in order to avoid the anticipated loss of face that could occur if his generosity went unheeded by the other party.

Shubik (1971b), moreover, has pointed out that two-person nonzero sum games (such as the PD) frequently become games of status in which the participants become more concerned with maximizing differences between themselves than maximizing their own outcomes. In such games, he says, it is winning that often becomes the most preferred outcome. Indeed, Tropper (1972) has found, using a dyadic auction paradigm, that subjects become so concerned with winning that they bid as high as $3.50 for a dollar bill, $11.15 for a pocket flashlight, and $1.15 for a felt tipped pen!

Related findings have emerged in experiments using Bilateral Monopoly-type bargaining tasks. Pruitt and Johnson (1970) and Podell and Knapp (1969) present results which clearly indicate that face-saving motives often function as regulators of the willingness to make concessions in this type of bargaining exhchange. In both of these investigations it was found that bargainers were likely to view concessions (their own or the other party's) as signs of weakness, and both investigations converge on the finding that third parties (such as mediators) may make it easier for bargainers to make concessions by reducing their fear of looking weak. The results of these investigations fully support Kerr's (1954) conclusion that one of the major functions of mediators in the resolution of industrial conflict is to enable bargainers to make a "graceful retreat"—to prevent the loss of face that normally occurs as a result of making concessions.

In summary, the evidence seems to indicate that intangible issues related to the maintenance or repair of face, public image, and self-esteem are often generated by needs to project an appearance of strength to the opposing party and to other salient audiences. Such needs appear to be grounded in the suppositions that one must look strong in order to obtain a satisfactory outcome, that one must avoid inappropriate deferential behavior toward another, and that, on a less conscious level, one must protect oneself against injuries to self-esteem that may arise from being evaluated negatively. Although these concerns seem to be present in many bargaining exchanges, we suspect that they may become heightened in certain circumstances. Thus, dispositional characteristics, such as low self-esteem, high need for power, and strong social acceptance and competency motives, may render some bargainers particularly susceptible to entanglement in intangible issues related to public image and face. And highly competitive motivational orientations (which may result from personality or situational factors or may be formed in response to another's behavior), with their implications for mistrust and misperception, may function in a similar manner.

ISSUE INCENTIVE MAGNITUDE AND REWARD STRUCTURE

Any bargaining exchange may be viewed from the perspective of the size of the issues at stake and the relative importance rankings assigned to these issues by the participants. Aside from any intangible payoffs that may be involved, a prime determinant of the importance ranking given to any issue is its scale of value (or "incentive magnitude"). Thus, issues involving millions of dollars are likely to be treated as more important than issues involving lesser amounts of money. In general, it may be said that the greater the magnitude of the tangible issues at stake the higher the importance ranking an issue is likely to be given.

However, there are instances in which the "magnitude rule" is not so easily applied, for, as discussed in the previous section, intangible payoffs may dramatically alter the importance rankings of issues having otherwise small scales of value. In his paper on "fractionating conflict" in international relations, Roger Fisher (1964) points out that concerns with principle, precedent, and national survival may increase the importance ranking of an issue far beyond that which it might have if only its concrete or tangible scale of value were considered.

Pursuing a similar line of reasoning, Gallo (1968) considered the relative effects of both tangible and symbolic outcomes on the determination of importance rankings. He argued that when tangible outcomes are of greater importance than symbolic ones conflict resolution is likely to be facilitated, but that when the reverse is true conflict is likely to become protracted. The reason for this, he proposed, is that, although tangible outcomes (such as those involving dollars and cents) can often be resolved in terms of a division or distribution of resources, symbolic payoffs such as those involving status and self-esteem are nondivisible. In effect, Gallo argued that conflicts over tangible payoffs are likely to be of a nonzero sum nature, while those involving symbolic payoffs are more likely to have a zero sum quality. Accordingly, Gallo suggested that an increase in the value of tangible payoffs relative to symbolic ones, should expedite conflict resolution, whereas a relative increase in the value of symbolic payoffs should have the opposite effect.

Gallo's (1968) reasoning leads directly to questions concerning the effects of increasing incentive magnitude. Is bargaining behavior likely to be affected differentially by variations in incentive magnitude? In and of themselves, are differences in incentives likely to generate differential pressures toward cooperative or competitive behavior? Conceptually, there seem to be two approaches to answering these questions. On the one hand, when incentives are increased we might expect bargainers to be more cooperative and to take fewer risks, in order to obtain a larger share of the outcome. On the other hand, it is also plausible that precisely because of the increased importance associated with large incentives, bargainers will become more oriented to their own self-interests, in order to obtain the lion's share of the outcome—or will at least protect themselves against the possibility that an opposing party may be so motivated.

Approximately 30 empirical investigations have been conducted to determine the effects of incentive magnitude on bargaining behavior. Among the investigators reporting no differences due to this factor, Axelrod and May (1968) found that the number of cooperative choices made by male subjects in a 60-trial PD game did not differ when the incentives were points, as compared to pennies, dimes, or quarters. Oskamp and Kleinke (1970) reported no differences in the number of cooperative choices made by male subjects engaging in a 30-trial PD game played for points, pennies, or dimes (per point). Friedland, Arnold, and Thibaut (1974) had subjects play a maximizing differences variant of the PD game for 4¢ or .20¢ per point. They found that absolute reward magnitude did not influence the frequency of cooperation.

Pate and Broughton (1970) had subjects engage in a 240-trial PD game for smaller incentives (paper clips, fake money, or pennies). They expected the paper clips and fake money incentives to increase the gamelike quality of the exchange, relative to the pennies condition. For although the latter incentive was small, the possibility remained that in this condition payoffs could accumulate over the 240 trials. The results of this experiment revealed no differences in the number of competitive choices among the three incentive conditions.

Evans (1964) contrasted the effects of a point incentive with that of an incentive that would allow subjects to improve their grades in a college course. The results of this six-trial PD experiment revealed that there were no differences in the amount of cooperation that occurred. Similar results were obtained by Evans and Crumbaugh (1966b), whose subjects engaged in a 100-trial PD game for either points or $1 per point.

Wrightsman (1966) conducted an experiment that provided a slightly different test of the effects of incentive magnitude in the PD game. He informed subjects either that they could keep their outcome (real money) or that they were playing for imaginary money or he gave them no information about monetary incentives. The real money condition involved dollars. The results again revealed that there were no differences in the extent to which subjects acted cooperatively or trusted one another.

Similar results have emerged in investigations using other tasks. For example, Shaw (1970) reported that there were no differences in subjects' expectations for an opposing party's outcome in a betting game as a result of real rather than imaginary money incentives. Cole and Phillips (1967), using a three-person Coalition game, found that real as compared to imaginary money payoffs had no noticeable effect on behavior. Summers (1968), whose subjects engaged in a task involving the negotiation of opposing points of view about the status of minority groups, found no differences arising out of the types of payoffs that subjects were to receive.

Although the results summarized so far seem to suggest that cooperation and competition may be unaffected by incentive magnitude, it would be inappropriate to reach a hasty conclusion on the matter. There are an even greater number of investigations whose results indicate that incentive magnitude may indeed produce differences in bargaining behavior. Thus, Alexander and Weil (1969), Gallo, Funk, and Levine (1969), and McClintock and McNeel (1966b, 1966c, 1967)—in three separate experiments utilizing a maximizing differences variant of the PD game—found that high incentives produced a significantly greater amount of cooperation than lower incentives. McClintock and McNeel found, moreover, that when incentives were low, subjects became more competitive over trials (1967); and when incentives were larger, a greater proportion of subjects locked into mutually cooperative choices (1966b). Similarly, Gallo and Sheposh (1971), Radlow (1965), and Radlow, Weidner, and Hurst (1968) found that large or real incentives increased cooperation in the PD game, while Knox and Douglas (1971) found that they tended to increase interdyad variance.

In a three-choice matrix version of the Acme–Bolt Trucking game, Gallo (1966) found that cooperation was roughly five times greater when incentives were real and relatively large (up to $16) than when they were imaginary. He also discovered that the barriers (gates) were used less frequently and outcomes were increased significantly when the incentives were real. Gallo concluded that the opportunity to obtain the large, real money reward may have become a superordinate goal for subjects, that this motive may have induced them to try to "beat the bank" rather than each other, and that the intense conflict stimulated by real monetary payoffs was thereby ameliorated.

Similar results have also been reported by investigators using different types of bargaining tasks. For example, Kelley, Shure, Deutsch, Faucheux, Lanzetta, Moscovici, Nuttin, Rabbie, and Thibaut (1970) used a task (the International Card game, described on pp. 142–144) in which subjects from several countries participated in a two-person, mixed-motive nonzero sum contract card game. On each of 30 trials, subjects had to negotiate the division of a resource without dividing it equally. Incentives were either real money or points. It was found that bargaining effectiveness (in terms of the favorableness of prenegotiation attitudes, outcomes, speed and dependability of reaching agreement) was enhanced when the stakes were real money rather than points. Kline (1969) reported that payoffs in a three-person Coalition game were distributed more evenly and coalitions were more stable when the incentive was $9 than when it was play money. Daniels (1967) found that outcomes were greater in a simple exchange type of bargaining task when the incentives were real rather than imaginary.

If there is one conclusion that can be drawn from the results summarized above, it is that, by itself, incentive magnitude is not a uniformly reliable predictor of bargaining behavior. Yet we have reviewed findings indicating that incentives may indeed influence bargaining systematically in some instances. How may this apparent contradiction be explained?

The results of four investigations provide a basis for a clearer understanding of the effects of incentive magnitude. The first, conducted by Hornstein and Deutsch (1967), utilized a two-person, nonzero sum "production" bargaining game, and was concerned with identifying the determinants of cooperative, competitive, and individualistic modes of behavior. Among the factors manipulated in this study were the presence of a cooperative alternative and incentive magnitude. Briefly, subjects could produce either individualistic or competitive products, and in several conditions they were also provided with the opportunity to produce cooperative ones. The magnitude of the incentives associated with products was systematically varied.

Subjects received 30¢ at the outset of a 20-min sequence (which was sub-divided into ten 2-min periods) and were instructed to earn as much as possible for themselves, regardless of how much the other earned. They were informed that they could keep their earnings at the end of the experiment.

Hornstein and Deutsch found that, although joint outcomes were highest when the cooperative option was available and incentives for using it were high, sharp decreases in joint outcomes occurred when an "attack" mechanism (available in all conditions) was used in cooperative–high incentive conditions. The investigators argued that this occurred because use of the attack mechanism represented a violation of the trust that had been situationally induced by the presence of the cooperative option and the high incentive. Hornstein and Deutsch thus concluded that the effects of economic incentives may be mediated by subjects' expectations of each other's behavior. In particular, when expectations are unclear, competitive behavior is likely to ensue.

The results of the Hornstein and Deutsch (1967) experiment are important because they suggest that, although the reward structure of a bargaining exchange may in fact be cooperative, other factors (such as a situationally available potential for exploitation and unclear expectations for the opposing party's behavior) may counteract the effects of reward structure—especially if the behavior of one of the parties confirms the other's suspicions about his motives. Pushing these results a bit further, if one acknowledges that the potential for exploitation and one's expectations for another's behavior may be influenced by a bargainer's motivational orientation and personality, as well as by situational realities, then it becomes apparent that even if the reward structure is conducive to cooperation it may nevertheless be misperceived.

A second experiment providing insight into how incentive magnitude may be mediated by situational and motivational factors was conducted by Gumpert, Deutsch, and Epstein (1969). In this simple but important experiment, subject pairs engaged in a 20-trial PD game in one of five incentive conditions. At the outset, subjects were variously informed that they would be paid in imaginary dollars, real dollars, or in 1¢, 5¢, or 10¢ multiples (for each point they accumulated over the entire sequence).

In the imaginary dollars (ID) condition of the Gumpert *et al.* (1969) study, subjects received $4 and were told that they "would keep this money regardless of the outcomes of the game [p. 68]." They were also given a "credit" of $10 in imaginary money and were instructed to "play as though you felt real money was at stake . . . that whether you win or lose the imaginary money is very important to you [p. 68]." In the real dollars (RD) condition, subjects received $10 in dollar bills and were asked to place this money in their pockets, and again "to attach great importance to winning or losing this money [p. 68]." Subjects in the 1¢, 5¢, and 10¢ multiple conditions were given $2 in real money and were also instructed to attach great importance to winning or losing.

The results revealed no differences in the number of cooperative choices per pair in the real money conditions. Competitive choices dominated in all conditions, and there was a general decrement in cooperation over the 20-trial sequence. However, contrary to almost all prior investigations that had examined the effects of incentive variations, subjects in the ID condition cooperated significantly more, on the average, than those in the RD condition (although there were similar decrements in the frequency of cooperation in both conditions as the sequence progressed).

Although the reasons for this reversal in the usual pattern of findings are not entirely clear, we believe that in addition to creating differences in incentive magnitude between the ID and RD conditions, the investigators may have also produced substantial differences in other aspects of the reward structure of these two conditions. Thus, in the ID condition, subjects were given $4 at the outset and had clear expectations of keeping this money—regardless of what happened. In contrast, subjects in the RD condition, although given $10 at the outset, were never informed that they could keep this money. Nor were they explicitly informed that deductions would be made from this sum, based on their outcomes. Hence, the reward structure of these conditions differed along a clarity–ambiguity dimension.

Another difference between the ID and RD reward structures is that in the ID condition the ($4) payment in advance, with no strings attached, might have been construed by subjects as a prepayment on a "contract" for work to be done, with the attending possibility that when one is paid in advance, especially at a rather generous rate, pressures to perform up to the standards of the "employer" are likely to increase. In the ID condition, cues as to the nature of these standards may have been provided by the instruction that subjects should "play as though you felt real money was at stake." This instruction (which of course was absent in the RD condition) may have suggested to these subjects that profit maximization was the desired standard. Coupled with the contract implications of receiving a guaranteed outcome in advance, this could well have increased the pressures toward cooperation in the ID condition.

In contrast, although RD subjects also received real currency at the outset ($10), this was identified as a "credit," and subjects were only instructed to "attach great importance to winning or losing this money"—a more open-ended instruction, which leaves considerably more room for the emergence of the competition that is endemic to the PD game. In short, there is reason to believe that the ID and RD conditions varied not only in terms of incentive magnitude, but also in terms of the reward structure suggested to subjects, with the result that differential pressures toward cooperation and competition may have been generated in each condition.

From our perspective, the most important implication of the Gumpert *et al.* findings is that the investigators succeeded in reversing a pattern of increased competition that is often observed in imaginary incentive conditions of the PD game. This reversal once again illustrates the mediating effects that situational and motivational factors associated with reward structure may have on incentive magnitude.

Earlier in this section we mentioned the results of Gallo's (1966) experiment on the effects of incentive magnitude. This investigation provides yet another view of how situational and motivational factors may influence the effects of incentive magnitude. In this experiment, subjects engaging in a version of the Acme–Bolt Trucking game for real money (they could earn up to $16) cooperated far more than those who played for imaginary money. Armed with these results, Gallo contested the findings of the earlier Deutsch and Krauss (1962) experiments, on the grounds that the incentives at stake in them were trivial and were therefore likely to increase competitiveness. Gallo suggested that as incentives increase, competitiveness becomes more costly, with the result that bargainers are likely to become more cooperative. However, we suspect that even in Gallo's (1966) experiment, the increased cooperation found in the real money condition was due not only to incentive differences but also to other procedures, which varied between these conditions and had differential effects on subjects' motivational orientations. Briefly, the instructions in the real money condition included showing subjects a letter from the "vice-chairman of the department," in which this official made himself "personally responsible" for the payment that the experimenter had promised. Nothing resembling this procedure appeared in the imaginary incentive condition. Instead, the instructions made it clear that monetary outcomes would not be awarded although subjects were asked to imagine that real money was involved.

The fourth investigation we wish to examine has also been referred to earlier in this section. However, its underlying conceptual structure, procedures, and results are so ingenious and interesting as to warrant more detailed consideration. One of the major purposes of the investigation by Kelley *et al.* (1970) was to determine the extent and character of cross-national differences in several aspects of bargaining behavior. Accordingly, the investigation was carried out at eight locations, including five American and three European sites (Leuven, Belgium; Paris, France; and Utrecht, the Netherlands). The bargaining task was the same at all sites, except that the instructions were translated from English into the native language of each European country. The effects of three independent variables were explored: the relative power of the bargainers, the level of difficulty of the problems over which they bargained, and incentive magnitude. For the present, we shall focus on the effects of differences in incentive magnitude.

Kelley *et al.* designed a nonzero sum, mixed-motive bargaining task in which pairs of subjects negotiated the division of resources on each of 30 trials. Each trial was identified as a "contract," and each contract consisted of an odd-numbered value (either 5, 7, 9, or 11 points in one set; or 13, 17, 19, or 23 points in a second set). On each trial the value of the contract to be negotiated was determined by the suit of a card drawn from a deck. Once the contract to be negotiated was determined ("9," for example) subjects could either attempt to reach agreement about how they would divide this amount between them (without splitting it in half) or they could decline to divide it and, instead, take an "independent" (external) value available to each of them. The independent value was also determined by the draw of a card on each trial.

Each subject knew his own independent value, but was prevented from seeing the independent value card that the other had drawn. However, subjects were allowed to say anything they wished about their independent values and were not required to be truthful in doing so. This created a condition of uncertainty, since one could never be sure of the other's independent value or whether the other was being deceptive or truthful. Also, if one player chose to take his independent value on any given trial, the other was required to take his also, and this terminated the negotiations on that trial.

If subjects succeeded in reaching five consecutive agreements (without taking their independent value) a set of increased contract values was introduced, and it was retained for as long as the players continued to reach agreement. However, the independent values associated with the second set of contract values were also increased (approximately twofold), thereby increasing the temptation to take them in order to increase one's personal gain.

The Kelley *et al.* (1970) bargaining task placed subjects in the following dilemma: by reaching five consecutive agreements, they could qualify for the higher set of contract values that, in turn, could result in increased outcomes. However, because their independent values also increased at the higher contract level, it was tempting to take this option—or to suspect that it would be taken by the other party. But, once the independent value was taken by one or both parties, they would be forced to revert to the smaller set of contract values, and would again have to reach agreement on five consecutive trials before gaining access to the larger contract values. The dilemma thus pitted long-term against short-term gain.

Superimposed upon the basic task was the incentive magnitude variable. Subjects either bargained for imaginary money (points) or for amounts of real money which were comparable across the sites at which the investigation was conducted. The results revealed that agreements occurred significantly more often, outcomes were significantly greater, and subjects were better able to maintain long runs of agreements (thereby qualifying them for, and keeping them in, the larger set of contract values) in the money than in the points condition. Moreover, this pattern of results was found to be consistent across the eight different locations at which the investigation was conducted.

Based on systematic observations of what bargainers said to one another throughout the exchange, Kelley *et al.* (1970) determined that the enhanced bargaining outcomes in the money condition resulted from the fact that these subjects more frequently established and invoked rules for reaching and remaining on the higher payoff schedule and less frequently misrepresented or threatened to take their independent values. Furthermore, subjects in the real money condition developed rules early, and these rules seemed to sustain them when dealing with more difficult contracts. When difficult contracts arose in the low incentive condition, on the other hand, subjects became significantly more competitive—with the result that their outcomes decreased further. In short, the negotiations proceeded more effectively and the bargainers capitalized more on the integrative aspects of the situation when larger incentives were at stake.

In interpreting their results, Kelley *et al.* (1970) proposed that increased incentives are most likely to induce cooperation if cooperation provides a relatively assured means of attaining greater outcomes while exploitative behavior carries with it a risk of incurring heavy costs. In the money condition of the experiment, the costs of exploitation were grounded in the risk that such action would either prevent the pair from reaching the higher payoff schedule or, once there, would throw them back onto the lower schedule. At the same time, greater outcomes were relatively assured if pair members could work out and maintain a cooperative relationship.

In terms of incentives, an important implication to be drawn from the Kelley *et al.* findings is that *competitive behavior may be constrained by a reward structure which unambiguously increases the risk of loss associated with such behavior and at the same time holds out the promise of enhanced gains for successful cooperation.*

One illustration of the beneficial effects of such a reward structure is provided by Iklé (1964), who pointed out that the early negotiations for the formation of the European Coal and Steel Community were modeled along these lines. Here, says Iklé (1964), an emphasis on community spirit enabled the member nations to "focus on their common interests, and to maximize the advantages of their joint undertaking, rather than to exchange separate gains and losses with each other [p. 119]." Some of the gains derived from the establishment of a strong sense of community spirit in these negotiations were: agreements in principle could be made more easily, leaving the details to be worked out by experts or technicians; negotiators were able to disregard rigid rules of protocol related to agenda—they were free to establish and revise partial agreements, and they were able to dispense with the pettifoggery of negotiation languages, which, according to Iklé, often leads to "wasted verbiage."

THE NUMBER OF ISSUES AT STAKE, THEIR FORMAT, PRESENTATION, AND PROMINENCE

Issue Number

Bargaining exchanges vary widely in terms of the number of issues that may be at stake. Sometimes parties convene to bargain over a single issue, such as the price to be paid for a hookah in a Persian fleamarket. On other occasions bargainers may come together to deal with a multiplicity of issues, as in the case of international negotiations between two ideologically opposed powers involved in a recurrent border dispute.

Perhaps the most general and most obvious point to be made about the effects of the number of issues at stake in any bargaining exchange is that, other things being equal, *an increase in the number of issues is likely to require an increase in the amount of time needed to reach overall agreement.* But even this elementary rule will not always hold, because other factors—such as incentive magnitude, the presence of unresolved intangible issues, or the level of difficulty of the issues—may have a still greater effect on the amount of time needed to reach agreement. One can readily imagine, for example, a situation in which a single, highly important and difficult issue requires more time than, say, a set of five relatively smaller or less difficult ones. To this point Kelley *et al.* (1970), in the investigation discussed in the previous section, found that more difficult issues (contracts) typically required an increased amount of time before agreement could be reached; moreover, the relative frequency of reaching agreement decreased as issues became more difficult. And other factors, such as the availability and use of threat (Froman & Cohen, 1969), the nature of prenegotiation contacts between the opposing parties (Bass, 1966; Druckman, 1967, 1968b), the relationship between a bargainer and his constituents (Lamm and Kogan, 1970) and personality characteristics of the bargainers (Druckman, 1967), have also been found to markedly affect both the amount of time needed to reach agreement, and the number of issues agreed upon in a given bargaining period.

Issue Format and Presentation

Among the more intriguing questions to arise when one considers the effects of the number of issues at stake are those pertaining to *how* the issues are approached or treated by the bargainers. For example, are multiple issues likely to be treated as singles? Broken into subsets? Considered in their entirety? Furthermore, if issues are differentiated, which are likely to be dealt with first, which postponed, and for what reasons? Under what conditions will bargainers tend to adopt one or the other of these approaches? Finally, how is each approach likely to affect bargaining effectiveness?

The results of two investigations provide a framework for answering some of these questions. In one, Kelley (1966) designed an expanded Bilateral Monopoly-type bargaining task (the Classroom Negotiation paradigm) consisting of five unlabeled numerical issues. The issues differed in their incentive magnitudes and relative importance (or priority rankings) for each bargainer. Opposing interests were created by providing subjects with inverted outcome distributions on each issue. Thus, settlement at a higher level for one party resulted in a smaller outcome for the other, and vice-versa. Each issue could be settled at any one of 20 predetermined points, with the result that 20^5 different contract combinations were possible. However, for a contract to be consummated, agreement had to be reached over the entire set of five items within a given time period that was unknown to the subjects. Since it is usually the case that bargainers have only incomplete information about each other's outcomes and priorities, subjects were kept uninformed of the other's outcome schedule. Subject pairs confronted the same type of bargaining problem (though it consisted of different issues) on six repeated occasions (sessions) during a 10-week period.

Kelley found that the percentage of pairs reaching agreement on one item, before settling the others, was relatively high during the first session (67%), but this percentage declined appreciably during the subsequent sessions (25%, 9%, 9%, 0%, and 9%, respectively). More than half (62%) of the pairs attempting to deal with the issues singly or on a subset basis in the first session were unable to reach an agreement covering all five issues in that session and hence failed to conclude a contract. In contrast, it was found that the percentage of pairs making five-item offers increased over the six sessions (23%, 27%, 54%, 50%, 63%, and 77%, respectively). When questioned at the end of the experiment, most pairs reported that they preferred dealing with all five issues at one time, rather than singly or in subsets.

In interpreting these findings, Kelley (1966) points out that premature agreement on any issue or subset has the effect of limiting one's latitude for making subsequent tradeoffs, thereby reducing the total number of available contract options that approximate a given overall outcome. An analysis of the overall values of five-item offerings made by individual bargainers tends to support this view. Approximately 50% of such offers yielded total outcomes falling within a range of plus or minus five points of previous five-item offers made by a bargainer. Kelley concluded that the generation of such alternatives was only possible by treating the issues as a package rather than on a one-by-one basis.

In many respects Kelley's results coincide with those obtained by Froman and Cohen (1970), who examined the relative effectiveness of "logrolling" versus "compromise" as techniques for dealing with multiple issues. Compromise involves negotiating each issue separately, without coupling it to other issues. Logrolling permits the trading of concessions on one or more issues in return for concessions on these or others by the opposing party. The investigators had subjects bargain (for real money) over four, 4-stepped, opposing interest numerical issues, until they reached agreement or until 30 min had elapsed. In one condition subjects were required to resolve the issues one at a time (compromise); in the second they were free to work on several at once (logrolling). The results revealed that logrolling led to a more equitable, significantly higher joint outcome distribution and required significantly fewer moves for completion of the bargaining sequence. Froman and Cohen (1970) conjectured that conflicting interests may be narrowed by logrolling, because the resources to be distributed (at a given time) are increased. They concluded that "strict adherence to an agenda, and the resolution of issues seriatim . . . are probably inefficient and result in raising the level of conflict in the system [p. 183]." The findings of Kelley, and of Froman and Cohen, differ in one important respect, the question of whether a set of issues can most effectively be treated as a total set (as Kelley's findings suggest) or whether the delineation of subsets might not be more effective. Kelley holds to the position that it is probably better to deal with the whole set in its entirety, in order to keep one's options open. On the other hand, Froman and Cohen's results seem to suggest that the formation of subsets may be just as effective. Perhaps the difference between the two approaches becomes pronounced as the number of issues increases from a few (say four or five) to a substantially larger slate (perhaps 25–30 or even more), as is often the case in educational, labor–management, community, and international negotiations. In such instances, one might suppose that the formation of subsets of related issues would be likely to facilitate agreements when the overall slate is unmanageably large.

Although we know of no data to support our view, we strongly suspect that *as the number of issues in a dispute grows, the pressures toward differentiating among them are likely to increase,* if for no reason other than the accompanying difficulty of dealing with an excessive number of issues simultaneously. Frequently, issues are differentiated in terms of their importance or relatedness to one another (i.e., subsets of related issues may be formed, with those that are deemed to be extraneous temporarily held in abeyance). However, the point at which differentiation pressures begin to operate—whether at 5, 10, 20, or more issues—is by no means clear, and this probably varies as a function of the type of issue involved, the personal characteristics of the bargainers, and situational factors.

Iklé (1964) points out that in international negotiation (as well, we suspect, as in other areas), pressures toward differentiation are reflected in the emergence of "package deals" and "tie-ins." Package deals involve proposals to settle several related issues simultaneously. Tie-ins involve the introduction of issues that may be extraneous to a given set, with the stipulation that settlement of the set is contingent upon a satisfactory agreement on the extraneous issue(s) as well. Iklé's views correspond to Fisher's (1964) proposal that it is often better to separate or fractionate large issues into smaller, more workable ones, in order to alleviate the negative effects of excessive commitment that are often associated with attempting to resolve large or all-encompassing issues.

A major question raised by the alternatives outlined above pertains to the order in which issues should be considered. If differentiations are to be made, which issues should be taken up first and which postponed until a later time? Here there seem to be two schools of thought. One holds that it is better to consider the more important issues first and leave the lesser ones until later. A potential difficulty arising from this approach is that if the more important issues are also the more difficult ones and if the parties are unable to reach agreement at this level, then resolution of the later issues may be tainted by the earlier failures. Here, opposition and resistance generated by early intense conflict may proliferate or spill over onto relatively minor issues. On the other hand, if early agreement can be reached on major issues, then this may facilitate less problematic bargaining on those considered later.

The second school of thought holds that it is better to work on issues of lesser importance first, because the increased likelihood of successful resolution at this level may aid the development of cooperation and may facilitate recognition of common interests. However, this approach may also have undesirable effects. As both Kelley (1966) and Iklé (1964) point out, reaching agreements too early on less important issues may close out options that could otherwise prove to be useful as tradeoffs on larger or more important issues. In addition, if bargainers experience a sense of failure in dealing with relatively simple issues, their confidence in their ability to settle the more difficult ones may be seriously undermined.

Unfortunately there is little or no empirical evidence by which to evaluate the relative usefulness of the above alternatives. Furthermore, such assessments are complicated by the fact that differing situational factors, strategic objectives, and issue characteristics may render a given approach useful in some situations but useless or harmful in others. Until more systematic evidence is generated, trial and error approaches (with their frequent reliance on such haphazard criteria as "What has worked before will work again") will probably continue to take their toll in many bargaining exchanges. As Fisher (1964) contends, if increasingly complex, multifaceted disputes are to be resolved more effectively via negotiation, bargainers must begin to exercise "issue control"—they must begin to consider more consciously the *formulation*, as well as the substance, of the issues with which they deal.

Issue Format and Presentation in the Prisoner's Dilemma Game

Experiments conducted by Evans and Crumbaugh (1966a), Crumbaugh and Evans (1967), and Orwant and Orwant (1970), concerning the effects of abstract versus nonabstract versions of the PD game, have each shown that cooperation may be both increased and sustained for a longer period when an issue is presented in concrete rather than abstract terms. In each of these experiments, subjects engaging in nonmatrix versions of the PD game (where the meaning of their choices was carefully explained, and choices were presented as analogs of realistic choice dilemmas) behaved significantly more cooperatively than those engaging in matrix (more abstract) versions of the same task. Moreover, inasmuch as Evans and Crumbaugh (1966a) found that the matrix versus nonmatrix distinction overrode the effects of the opposing party's initial behavior (hostile or neutral) and the contingency or noncontingency of his cooperativeness, there is reason to suspect that abstractly presented issues may have a rather general tendency to increase competitiveness, irrespective of the opposing party's behavior.

To gain a better understanding of the implication of these findings, it may be useful to reconsider the PD game, the problems that grow out of it, and the extent to which similar problems arise in other types of bargaining exchanges. As Deutsch (1958) points out, the dilemma of trust versus suspicion is normally heightened in the PD game because neither party can count on the other to refrain from defecting for personal gain. The temptation to defect creates a relatively high degree of uncertainty about the other party's behavior, in a context that provides little or no opportunity to exercise control over it. Moreover, because successful defection deprives the other of an equitable share of outcomes, concerns with safeguarding against exploitation are likely to become salient. As a result, each party may become "primed" to attribute exploitative motives to the other and to act defensively or preemptively. In short, there is a considerable likelihood in the PD game (where procedures designed to aid cooperation are normally absent) that competitive expectations will often be confirmed, that the ability to establish a sufficient amount of trust to sustain coordinated effort will be impeded, and that the parties will frequently become engaged in mutually destructive deadlock.

One of the difficulties with the PD paradigm thus stems from the fact that its usual presentation in abstract (matrix) rather than concrete terms may raise the already dramatic uncertainty and apprehension about the other party's behavior to an even higher (artifactual) level, and this may lead to still greater reliance on competitiveness in order to defend against an apparent increased risk of being exploited.

The pressures toward competitive behavior, as generated by abstract presentation of the PD game, are more likely to be constrained in other types of bargaining exchanges by a variety of factors, although heightened competition is certainly not uncommon in such contexts either. Such conditions as third party involvement, anticipated future interaction, accountability to dependent audiences, and a host of other circumstances not normally present in the conventional PD game may constrain bargainers from responding competitively to the uncertainty and apprehension created by abstract issues. Nevertheless, even in such circumstances, if suspicion and motives for personal gain are dominant, and if the parties have little power to exercise control over each other's behavior, abstractly presented issues would seem to be likely inducers of competition, because of their potential for increasing uncertainty and suspicion.

A second feature of the PD format that may influence competitiveness is the fact that the standard matrix version provides only two response alternatives. This creates a situation in which one is forced to choose between leaving oneself vulnerable (by behaving cooperatively) or suffering the consequences of mutual loss (by acting competitively). There are no intermediary possibilities. What would happen, then, if the number of available choices in the PD paradigm were to be increased? Would competition increase or diminish? Several experiments have been conducted in an attempt to answer just these questions.

Dolbear, Lave, Bowman, Lieberman, Prescott, Rueter, and Sherman (1969) found that the stability of cooperation was significantly greater with a 2-choice PD matrix than a 30-choice matrix. Also noted was a near significant tendency for the amount of cooperation (reflected in joint payoffs) to be greater when fewer choices were available. The investigators concluded that limiting the number of alternatives may be a better way to increase outcomes than providing opportunities for more differentiated choice, because the latter makes it more difficult to achieve maximum outcomes and remain at this level.

Standing in direct opposition to these findings, however, are the results obtained by Pilisuk, Potter, Rapoport, and Winter (1965) and Pilisuk, Skolnick, Thomas, and Chapman (1967). In two separate experiments it was found that cooperation was increased significantly by expanding the number of available choices in the standard PD matrix from 2 to 21 and exposing subjects to the expanded version prior to the standard one. The expanded version provided each participant with a range of moves on each trial, so that his choices were not limited to either full cooperation or full competition but could be made at intermediary levels as well. This version thus involved graduated decisions rather than the single or total decisions called for in the standard two-choice format.

In interpreting their results, Pilisuk and his colleagues pointed out that slowing the pace of the decision process, by leaving room for intermediary decisions, allows the parties more time for cognitive reappraisal of the conflict, with the result that they gain increased awareness of their cooperative interdependence. As their results reveal, once such awareness developed, cooperation was not only likely to increase but was also likely to persist when the subjects switched to a standard matrix format later in the sequence. In explanation, Pilisuk suggests that, when response alternatives are limited, the parties are likely to be prevented from developing mutual trust (as a result of their lessened ability to influence each other), from using their choices to communicate intentions without being fully committed to them, and from recognizing that they share a common fate requiring a measure of cooperation.

The foregoing analysis suggests an important implication for bargaining, be it in the laboratory (as in the PD game) or in more natural settings. This implication, supported by Blake and Mouton (1961b) and discussed more recently by Kelley (1966), is that *the provision of additional or intermediary options may enable bargainers to retain greater flexibility, both in terms of their cognitive appraisal of the situation and their capacity to develop alternate courses of action.*

Issue Prominence

Prominence, says Schelling (1960), is yet another factor that may influence the ease or difficulty of reaching agreement, for it affects both the noticeability and likelihood of adopting a particular solution. Prominence refers to the extent to which an alternative may be qualitatively differentiated from the other solutions that are available. Characteristics such as uniqueness, precedent, symmetry, simplicity, roundedness of numbers, and obviousness or conspicuousness may cause a solution to become a focal point of interest.

This, in turn, may help bargainers to coordinate their activities and form mutually congruent expectations. In a sense, prominence facilitates zeroing-in on solutions that possess intrinsic or distinctive attributes. The "50-50 split," "splitting the difference," rounding the purchase price of an automobile from $2507.63 to $2500.00, and the return to status quo are each illustrations cited by Schelling of solutions that may enable opposing parties to resolve one of the key problems of bargaining—coordinating their discrepant expectations in order to reach agreement.

Although Schelling's ideas about prominence have a great deal of intuitive appeal and, in fact, are quite consistent with the principles of Gestalt psychology, there has been lamentably little research on this subject. And while the few investigations that have been conducted are clearly supportive of Schelling's position, they also indicate that prominence is complexly determined, and interacts with both situational factors and the nature of the relationship between the parties.

There are, of course, the results of Schelling's own informal but ingenious experiments, requiring subjects to make independent decisions about how to divide a specified resource (coordinate), without the benefit of communication, but with structurally prominent alternatives either suggested by or incorporated in a series of different problems. In one problem, for example, Schelling (1960) presented eight subjects with a roadmap consisting of a network of roads, a centrally located bridge-crossing, several buildings placed in different areas, and a pond. Subjects were asked to select a meeting place with an imaginary other. All but one subject chose the central bridge-crossing.

In another problem, Schelling (1960) gave his subjects the following instructions:

> You are to meet somebody in New York City. You have not been instructed where to meet; you have no prior understanding with the person on where to meet; and you cannot communicate with each other. You are simply told that you will have to guess where to meet and that he is being told the same thing and that you will just have to try to make your guesses coincide [p. 56].

Schelling found that an absolute majority of his subjects chose to meet at the information booth at Grand Central Terminal, and *all* selected noon as the meeting time. He noted that this startling convergence of choices may have occurred because respondents, who were all residents of New Haven, Connecticut, may have assumed that the other party was similar to themselves in this respect, and therefore also likely to choose this location because of its familiarity to New Haven commuters.

In a third problem, 41 subjects were asked to divide $100 (imaginary) into two piles. They were informed that if they succeeded in allocating the same amount to each pile they would each receive $100; but if they failed they would receive nothing. Thirty-six of the 41 subjects chose a 50–50 split, suggesting that principles of both symmetry and equity enabled them to set this particular division apart from all others. Schelling concluded from these experiments and several others that it is possible for individuals to concert their intentions and expectations and, with the aid of clues suggested structurally or by virtue of shared background, to thereby coordinate their activities. For a more extensive analysis of the problem of coordination than is possible here, the reader is referred to Raven and Rubin (in press), as well as Roby and Rubin (1973), and Rubin, Greller, and Roby (1974).

Schelling's notion of prominence was tested more formally by Willis and Joseph (1959) and Joseph and Willis (1963). In the first experiment, Willis and Joseph had 80 pairs of subjects engage in two separate 50-trial sequences of 2-, 3-, or 4-choice, two-person matrix games. Among the factors manipulated in the experiment was the ordering of the matrices used. Two conditions were created. In one, the 2-choice matrix was employed first, followed by the 3-choice matrix (2–3 condition). In the second condition a 3–4 sequence was followed. Payoffs were determined on the basis of subjects' joint choices, and in order to receive an outcome greater than zero, subjects had to match choices on each trial. It is important to note that *only* in the 3-choice matrix was there a structurally prominent solution (yielding 20 to each player).

The relevant questions explored in the experiment concern the frequency with which the structurally prominent alternative in the 3-choice matrix was chosen, given either prior exposure to some other matrix (the 2–3 condition) or no prior exposure (the 3–4 condition). If Schelling's prominence proposition is correct, the investigators reasoned, the structurally prominent alternative should have been chosen more frequently than the others, and this tendency should have been particularly apparent when subjects were exposed first to the matrix containing the prominent solution (the 3-4 condition).

The results revealed, contrary to Schelling's proposition, that structural prominence failed to promote coordination. Instead, subjects in both the 2–3 and 3–4 conditions fell into a pattern in which one party became dominant in the first 50-trial sequence, and this was carried over to the second sequence. Approximately 75% of the subjects who gained the initial advantage in the first sequence also won the largest amount in the second sequence, regardless of the matrices used. In short, structural prominence was not operative. The results of this experiment, however, were confounded by the fact that subjects did not receive complete information about the payoff structure of the game. They were not informed of the other person's outcomes for each choice, and this appeared to produce some confusion among them. In some cases subjects even reported that they thought their partners were receiving the same outcomes as they on each trial. This, of course, suggests one possible explanation why structural prominence failed to operate. Not knowing the other's outcome, or supposing it to be the same as one's own, seems to have had the effect of eliminating structural prominence.

A second experiment was conducted in order to explore the matter further (Joseph & Willis, 1963). Their hypothesis was that by correcting the problem of insufficient information about reward structure, structural prominence would enable the parties to reach agreement more readily when a prominent solution was available than when not. In one condition, a 5-choice matrix was used during the first 3 of a series of 6 independent exchanges. This matrix provided a central and therefore prominent solution because it consisted of an odd number of choices. In a 6-choice matrix condition, no central position was suggested. Several other variables were manipulated, including induced prominence (created by informing half of the subjects that a particular alternative had been chosen most frequently in a previous run of the experiment).

The results provided strong confirmation of the structural prominence hypothesis. Subjects reached a greater number of agreements with the 5-choice than with the 6-choice matrix. More than half of these agreements were at the central (focal) position: apparently this solution was viewed as the fairest. Induced prominence failed to yield significant effects. Several complex interaction effects indicated that structural prominence was reacted to differently by men and women in different conditions. The investigators interpreted these interactions by suggesting that personality differences associated with sex may also influence the use of structurally prominent solutions and that such effects may be pronounced among males when heightened conflicts of interest exist.

In brief, although Schelling's prominence proposition seems to be borne out by the experimental evidence, it also appears that this is a highly complex phenomenon, influenced by the nature of the relationship between the parties, their personalities, and other situational factors. Clearly, further research is needed to clarify the conditions in which structural and other forms of prominence operate or fail to do so.

CONCLUDING COMMENT

One of the most creative challenges in the entire bargaining process involves the formulation of issues in terms that, minimally speaking, are likely to ease rather than block agreement, and at the same time carry a potential for increasing the satisfaction of the parties with their respective outcomes.

This idea, certainly not a novel one, has been either proposed or alluded to: by Fisher (1964), in his discussion of issue control; by Deutsch (1969), in his formulation of constructive conflict; by Sherif and Sherif (1969), in their analysis of superordinate goals; and by Walton and McKersie (1965), in their explication of integrative bargaining. An assumption common to each of these viewpoints is that it is often possible to utilize conflicts of interest—and therefore the issues at stake in them—as springboards for the creation of new, perhaps previously undefined or unanticipated, alternative solutions.

Although Deutsch's (1969) contention, namely that conflict intensification is likely to have a debilitating effect on the capacity to use intellectual resources, is borne out by both experimental and popular literature, it would seem that there are mechanisms by which a constructive process of issue control may be engendered. As we suggested in Chapter 4, third-party intervention is one such mechanism—provided, of course, that the third party is sufficiently competent, authoritative, and trustworthy and that the opposing bargainers become accountable more to him than to egoistic or external influences. Altering the definition of the situation, by providing various types of prenegotiation activities or instructional sets that induce the pursuit of common rather than unilateral interests, may be another device. Elimination of public access or visibility, in order to alleviate pressures toward excessive commitment, may also be useful for increasing receptiveness to issue control.

In general, then, how should issues be manipulated so as to increase bargaining effectiveness?

1. *Whenever possible, intangible issues should be converted into more manageable tangible ones.* As Gallo (1968) has pointed out, intangible issues of honor, face, and self-esteem can rarely, if ever, be negotiated effectively on their own terms, because of their nonspecificity, and the tendency to induce excessive ego involvement, commitment, and proliferation to other issues. Thus whenever possible, intangible issues should be recast in concrete dimensions, fractionated into their tangible components, and negotiated in operational terms. This is not to say that such intangibles may be ignored. As we have seen, without satisfactory resolution they are likely to recur throughout a bargaining exchange and thereby interfere with effective resolution of more tangible issues.

2. *Incentive and reward structure should be manipulated so as to avoid "winner take all" (zero sum) outcomes.* The empirical evidence clearly indicates that bargainers are likely to become resistant or retaliatory when it appears that they are being forced to accept what they view as an inequitable share of available outcomes. This serves to prolong a bargaining exchange and intensify conflict and may often increase the bargainers' costs as well as those of others who are dependent on them. Related to this is the demon-

strable likelihood that reward structures that are viewed as highly competitive, or as strengthening the bargainers' competitive motivational orientations, will in the long run reduce bargaining outcomes. In some cases such reward structures may even induce a willingness among bargainers to accept a loss or defeat, as long as that loss or defeat is smaller than that which can be imposed on the opposing party. This of course makes it clear that highly competitive reward stuctures may in and of themselves generate intangible issues.

3. *Variables such as the number of issues to be dealt with, their sequencing, format, abstractness, manner of presentation, and the display or arrangement of alternative solutions should be consciously formulated, whenever possible.* Of course, since the absence of such conscious formulation is likely to affect bargaining adversely, there is always the possibility that bargainers may wish to deliberately slow down, confuse, or blow up the proceedings, or make the issues more ambiguous. We suspect that such strategies are likely to interfere with bargaining effectiveness rather than enhance it. It is by creatively sizing or fractionating issues, expanding the range of alternative outcomes, coupling them to existing or new issues, forming subsets, package deals, or tie-ins, that the likelihood of reaching a mutually satisfactory agreement may be increased.

7

Bargainers as Individuals

As bargainers enter into relationships with one another, they bring with them variations in prior experience, background, and outlook that may affect the manner and effectiveness with which they interact. Individual differences in background (such as a bargainer's sex, race, age, status, etc.), as well as individual differences in personality (such as a bargainer's inherent cooperativeness, authoritarianism, cognitive complexity, risk-taking propensity, etc.), may selectively shape the course of bargaining. It is the purpose of this chapter to systematically explore these variations in individual background and personality, and to integrate the findings of approximately 200 relevant experimental studies.

Kurt Lewin (1936) has suggested that an individual's behavior may be considered as a function of two parameters: E (environment) and P (person). E is comprised of all aspects of, and elements in, the individual's physical and social environment. In terms of our analysis of bargaining, E consists of the set of external structural pressures that act both to drive and to restrain the behavior of each party to the bargaining relationship. These various pressures have been discussed at length in Chapters 4–6.

The focus of our concern in this chapter is Lewin's second major parameter, P. P consists of the individual's needs, beliefs, and values, the set of enduring predispositions he carries with him from situation to situation. In terms of our bargaining analysis, P may be thought of as the array of pressures, internal to the bargainer, that drive him to perceive his environment, and to behave, in stable, characteristic ways. These complex driving pressures, represented as variations in background and personality, shape the way each bargainer perceives and reacts to his physical and social environment. They shape the information he habitually seeks out and attends to about the other's preferences and intentions, the extent to which he trusts and believes the other. Variations in bargainers' background and personality also shape the information each elects to disclose about his own preferences and intentions, and the extent to which this information represents an honest, open, and trustworthy disposition toward the other. Finally, we may expect individual differences among bargainers to shape the particular strategy they employ with each other, as well as the kind and quality of agreement they habitually ask for and accept.

INTERPERSONAL ORIENTATION

Before beginning our examination of the experimental literature, we wish to digress for a moment, in order to introduce a conceptual distinction that may prove useful in attempting to understand the vast array of relevant research.

An overview of the bargaining studies concerned with individual difference variables leads us to posit the existence of a bargaining world comprised of two fundamentally different types of people, who reside at or near the two opposite poles of a dimension we shall refer to as *interpersonal orientation*, or IO. Depending on their location along this hypothetical continuum, we expect bargainers to view and react to their physical and social environment—and to bargain—in very different ways.

Let us first consider the bargainer who is located near the upper end of the interpersonal orientation continuum *(high IO)*. This is an individual who is, first and foremost, *responsive to the interpersonal aspects of his relationship with the other. He is both interested in, and reactive to, variations in the other's behavior.* Such variations provide the high IO individual with the important information he seeks about the other party: what the other prefers and expects, how he intends to behave, what he is really like. One consequence of this perspective is that, given changes in bargaining situational factors (discussed in Chapters 4–6), the high IO individual is likely to attribute the resulting variation in the other's behavior to the other's personality—rather than to the particular situation in which both bargaining parties are immersed. The high IO individual thus takes the other's behavior very, perhaps unduly, personally. He is sensitive and reactive to the other's cooperativeness or competitiveness, to the distribution of power and dependence in the relationship; he pays close attention to the other's adherence and deviation from norms of equity, exchange, reciprocity, and so forth. All aspects of his relationship with the other party are of interest and importance for the high IO bargainer.

In order to understand the consequences of this perspective for the manner in which bargaining develops, let us separately consider the ways in which a bargainer whose basic predisposition is either cooperative or competitive might be expected to behave. The high IO individual who is *cooperatively* disposed enters into the bargaining relationship with a posture that is both trusting and trustworthy. (By "trusting" we mean, following the work of Deutsch, 1960a, and Rapoport and Chammah, 1965a, that he expects his cooperative gestures to result in reciprocation rather than exploitation on the part of the other; by "trustworthy" we mean that the bargainer plans to respond to the other's cooperative gestures with reciprocation rather than exploitation.) Given that the other acts cooperatively, we may expect the bargaining relationship to flourish. Our cooperative high IO individual will seek out information about the other party that will further his belief that the other is a likable, attractive, and—most importantly—cooperative person ("He's a fine fellow"). But, given that the other behaves in a competitive or exploitative way (even if only occasionally, or because of miscoordination), we may expect the cooperative high IO bargainer to dramatically alter his perception of the other's true nature ("He's sneaky and not to be trusted"), and to respond to the other's defection with defensive and retaliatory behavior of particular intensity.

The high IO bargainer who is *competitively* oriented, on the other hand, enters into the bargaining relationship with an eye to taking advantage of the other. He is both suspicious of the other party (expecting him to respond to cooperative overtures with exploitation rather than reciprocation) and untrustworthy (planning to respond to the other's cooperative gestures with exploitation rather than reciprocation). Given that the other behaves cooperatively, the competitive high IO bargainer comes to view him as a sucker and a fool (the other is seen as behaving as he does not because he *has* to, but because he *wants* to), and systematically attempts to exploit him ("He really is a fool"). On the other hand, in the presence of another who is also competitive, we may expect the competitive high IO individual to develop an impression of the other as a similar, if rather malevolent, character ("He's a bastard like me"), and to behave competitively, in order to defend himself against the possibility that the other will fare better than he.

Let us now turn to the bargainer who is situated near the lower end of the interpersonal orientation continuum *(low IO)*. This individual is characterized, first and foremost, by a *nonresponsiveness to interpersonal aspects of his relationship with the other. His interest is neither in cooperating nor competing with the other, but rather in maximizing his own gain—pretty much regardless of how the other fares.* He is not interested in discovering the other party's true nature. The other, for him, is a nonperson, a "machine"—wholly rational, perhaps, or simply a person who can be expected to reason and behave just as he himself does. Variations in the other's behavior are seen as reflecting not so much the other's particular idiosyncratic way of behaving (his personality) as the particular set of environmental constraints that have impelled him to act as he does. As a consequence of this perspective, given changes in bargaining situational factors, the low IO individual is likely to attribute the resulting variation in the other's behavior to these situational factors, rather than to the other's personality. He does not take the relationship personally, and is thus unlikely to respond to the other's cooperation or competition with cooperative or competitive overtures of his own. Thus, regardless of the other's behavior or disposition, the low IO's behavior is simply designed to achieve as much tangible or intangible gain for himself as he can.

In the sections that follow in this chapter, we will look in turn at what is currently known about the effects of individual differences in a bargainer's background and personality upon bargaining behavior. The background variables we will examine are: age; race; nationality; intelligence; religious affiliation; social background and social status; and sex. The personality variables under review are: risk-taking propensity; perceived locus of control; cognitive complexity; intolerance of ambiguity; self-concept; the needs for affiliation, achievement, and power; generalized trust; cooperativeness; authoritarianism; internationalism; flexible ethicality; machiavellianism; and abnormal behavior.

The experimental literature in a number of the above areas is scant, even nonexistent. In other areas the research has been extensive, highly varied, and replete with ambiguous and apparently contradictory findings. Some of the findings may indeed be irreconcilable. Others, we believe, may be understood and integrated through their relation to the dimension of Interpersonal Orientation.

INDIVIDUAL DIFFERENCES IN BACKGROUND

Age

Although a great many researchers have studied bargaining processes in college-age student populations, while others have looked at bargaining in children, only a handful of these experiments have been truly developmental in nature, in the sense of systematically examining age as a critical independent variable.

The single most general and important finding to emerge in the studies relating bargaining to age is that, all other factors held constant, *young children tend to behave like low IOs, becoming more interpersonal in their orientation as they grow older, while college students generally behave more like high IOs.*

A simple, elegant study that supports the above generalization was conducted by Fry (1967), who placed pairs of fourth-graders, eighth-graders, and college students in a multitrial coordination game. On each trial, the subjects (incommunicado at all times) were given an identical set of three objects (for example, a door key, a pencil, and a bottle top), and were asked to pick up one of the three objects so as to match the object picked up by their unseen partner. A point was given on every trial in which a correct match occurred; on mismatch trials both subjects lost a point. The game continued until 100 trials had elapsed, or until the pair reached a solution and matched on 10 consecutive trials. Fry found that college students outperformed eighth-graders and eighth-graders outperformed fourth-graders on this task. The college students seemed best able to take the role of the other, using knowledge of the other's previous choice behavior to anticipate successfully his choice on a given problem. In contrast, the fourth-graders (acting like low IOs) had great difficulty converging on a solution to the coordination task—largely, it would seem, because they were incapable of (or uninterested in) standing in the other's shoes to "see the world as he sees it."

Several experimental studies, lending support to our generalization about the relationship of age to bargaining style, have found an interaction between age and the variable of sex. Vinacke and Gullickson (1964) ran male and female triads of 7- to 8-year olds, 14- to 16-year olds, and undergraduates in the Parcheesi Coalition game. They observed no differences as a function of age in the behavior of the female triads (all of whom behaved cooperatively). Among the males, however, the youngest triads were found to behave like the females, while the two older triads were far more competitive. Similarly, Shears and Behrens (1969), using a four-person coalition game, found that male and female third-graders behaved similarly and were generally more cooperative than fourth-graders, with the lesser cooperation among fourth-graders being largely attributable to the behavior of the male tetrads. Finally, Sampson and Kardush (1965), in a PD study in which the variables of age (7–8 years versus 9–11 years), sex, class, and race were all varied, found that the younger male and female dyads behaved similarly. Only in the older groups did they observe increasing cooperation among males and increasing competition among females.

Despite the fact that two of these studies conclude that males behave more competitively as they grow older, while the conclusion of the third is that they behave more cooperatively (a contradiction which we will attempt to reconcile in our discussion of the sex variable), they each point to the same general inference, namely, that bargaining behavior becomes increasingly distinctive and diverse as a function of age. While college students and older children are likely to bargain differently, depending on their gender, younger children tend to behave in similar fashion, regardless of whether they are boys or girls.

Several additional studies are pertinent to our discussion. In a cross-cultural study of Anglo-American and Mexican children (Kagan & Madsen, 1972b), it was found that older children (8- to 10-years old) were significantly more rivalrous than younger ones (5- to 6-years old). Similarly, McClintock (1974) reported that Anglo-American and Mexican-American children became increasingly competitive with age.

McClintock and Nuttin (1969) placed all-male pairs of second-, fourth-, and sixth-grade Belgians and Americans in a "maximizing differences" variant of the PD game. Subjects were found to behave in increasingly competitive fashion with age. Close inspection of these data indicates that the older children appeared to have adopted a particular (competitive) strategy, which they employed with consistency throughout the game. The younger children, on the other hand, displayed a far more shifting and erratic behavioral pattern, one which appeared to be largely unrelated to their opponent's behavior in any kind of meaningful way. In contrast with the older subjects, for example, the second-graders were far more likely to behave cooperatively following their own prior competitive choice (probability of .74) than a prior cooperative one (probability of .37). This suggests that they were either unable or unwilling to develop a meaningful strategy—one in which they could anticipate, for example, the likelihood of the other player's responding to their competitive (exploitative) behavior with competitive (retaliatory) behavior of his own.

The McClintock and Nuttin findings bear some resemblance to a study by Tedeschi, Hiester, and Gahagan (1969b) in which third- and fourth-grade males and females were placed in a PD game modified for use with children. It was found that children were far less responsive to variations in the other's behavior than were college students (examined in an earlier comparable study by Rapoport & Chammah, 1965a). These findings, as well as those of previously cited developmental studies, may be related to Piaget's suggestion that children between the ages of 9 and 12 experience cognitive difficulty with tasks requiring them to take the role of the other, because these tasks necessitate reasoning of a relative and formal kind.

Race

Almost without exception, bargaining research has been conducted using subjects drawn from college-age, middle-class, student populations. And almost without exception these subjects have been white. Our search of the literature over the last decade has revealed only eight experimental studies that examined the relationship of race to bargaining behavior. One of these (Wilson & Kayatani, 1968) employed Caucasian and Japanese subjects in a variant of the PD game and found no differences in bargaining as a function of race. The remaining seven studies each employed black, white, or black and white pairs, and each reported a significant relationship between race and bargaining. Two general sets of findings emerge in these experiments.

First, *subjects tend to bargain more cooperatively with an opponent of the same race than with one of another race*—perhaps because similarity induces trust and reduces the need to maintain a particular face in the eyes of others. Baxter (1970) conducted a study in which whites played a PD game against either a white or a black confederate of the experimenter. One-third of the subjects were told that the other had a cooperative personality, one-third were told that the other had a competitive personality, while the remaining subjects were given no information. Regardless of the information provided about the other, these white subjects were found to consistently behave more cooperatively in interaction with a white opponent than with a black one.

Similarly, Heller (1967), in another PD experiment, found that white (and Mexican–American) subjects made a greater number of cooperative choices in the presence of a partner "of their own race" than in the presence of a black. Finally, Harford and Cutter (1966) and Sibley, Senn, and Epanchin (1968) conducted PD studies in which black and white subjects were asked to play two games, one with a partner of the same race, the other with a partner of a different race. Again cooperation was found to be greater in same-race than in different-race pairs.

Second, *blacks tend to bargain more cooperatively than whites*. Sampson and Kardush (1965) found that pairs of black bargainers made a greater number of cooperative choices in the PD game than white pairs. Furthermore, in the postexperimental interviews, blacks more frequently cited as the motive for their behavior a desire to be considerate—"to help their partner gain higher rewards for himself." In another PD experiment, Berger and Tedeschi (1969) had black and white subjects bargain with a confederate of the experimenter (whose race was *not* specified). Several times in the course of the 50-trial game, subjects were given an opportunity to unilaterally impose a penalty upon (exploit) their partner. They found that blacks made a greater number of cooperative choices than whites. In addition, however (and in apparent contradiction with their cooperative choice behavior), black subjects chose to penalize their partner more frequently than did whites.

In explanation of the Berger and Tedeschi (1969) findings and, more generally, in explanation of the observed racial differences in bargaining, it may be useful to turn once more to the dimension of interpersonal orientation. In contrast with whites, blacks behave like high IOs. They seem particularly responsive and reactive to the other's perceived orientation, as well as to variations in the distribution of power in their relationship with him.

Support for this generalization is provided by the findings of an experiment by Hatton (1967), perhaps the most elegant and interesting of the studies relating race to bargaining. Using a sample of black high-school girls who perceived whites as highly prejudiced against blacks, Hatton had these subjects play a version of the Bilateral Monopoly game. The subjects played against a confederate of the experimenter who was either black or white and who employed either a generally cooperative (yielding) strategy or a competitive (demanding) one. Hatton found that subjects behaved cooperatively in the presence of a cooperative black partner or a competitive white, behaving more competitively in interaction with a competitive black or a cooperative white.

Notice that the black subjects in the Hatton study behaved like high IOs. When playing against a black other, we may perhaps assume that they began with a generally cooperative predisposition (like cooperative high IOs). Given that this other behaved cooperatively, these cooperative subjects sought out cooperative, equitable solutions to the bargaining problem (as did the blacks in the Sampson and Kardush, 1965, experiment). However, given that their black partner behaved competitively, these subjects responded by being demanding and competitive in return.

When playing against a white other, we may assume that the high IO blacks began with a generally competitive predisposition (like competitive high IOs). After all, they were preselected for their belief that whites are prejudiced against them. Given that their white partner behaved competitively, these subjects attempted to minimize their losses by behaving in a fairly compliant, passive manner. But playing against a white who behaved cooperatively, they bargained competitively and attempted systematically to exploit her.

The above inferences may be used to reinterpret the findings of the Berger and Tedeschi (1969) study. For, if we make the not unreasonable assumption that black subjects in the presence of a white experimenter may believe they are playing against a white other player (recall that race of the other was not specified in the Berger and Tedeschi experiment), it can be seen that they behaved like competitive high IOs—defensively when the other had equal power and exploitatively when they could unilaterally impose a penalty on him (when the other was of lower relative power).

How, then, can one account for the fact that blacks behave like high IOs? While there is no experimental evidence available to support our conjecture, we suggest that it may be out of necessity that individuals in all kinds of low power or low status positions (be they blacks, members of minority nationalities, women, etc.) learn to pay close attention to interpersonal cues. For those in high power or high status positions, interpersonal sensitivity may be a luxury, while for those deprived of such positions, this sensitivity to interpersonal cues may be a necessary prerequisite for a shift in the balance of power. Moreover, it may be that one of the ways in which individuals in high status positions attempt to maintain or at least justify their advantaged status is by selectively inattending—tuning out those interpersonal cues that might argue for the desirability of a change in the status quo.

Nationality

Perhaps because of insufficient interest, but more likely because of the numerous methodological difficulties such research poses, very little attention has been given to the relationship between bargaining and cross-cultural factors (or more loosely, "nationality").

Uejio and Wrightsman (1967) had Japanese and American subjects play a PD game with a confederate of the experimenter who was described as being alternately Japanese or American. No relationship was found between the "ethnic composition" of a dyad and the frequency of cooperative behavior.

Swingle (1970a) ran English-speaking Canadians in a variant of the PD game in which they interacted with a confederate of the experimenter who behaved in unconditionally cooperative fashion. The confederate was presented as being either English-Canadian or French-Canadian, and was given bargaining power either less than, equal to, or greater than that of the subject. Swingle found that his English-Canadian subjects exploited a similar opponent (the English-Canadian) more often when this unconditionally cooperative opponent was powerful (but did *not* use this power) than when he was weaker. On the other hand, in interaction with a French-Canadian, subjects more often exploited the other when he was weaker, rather than more powerful, than them. Thus weakness in another of shared cultural background acts to minimize exploitative behavior. The same weakness in another from a different (and presumably disliked) background, however, seems to invite exploitation, and, according to the findings of an earlier study (Swingle, 1969), the maintenance of interpersonal "psychological distance."

Pepitone *et al.* (1967) reported no differences between Italians and Americans in the frequency of cooperativeness in the PD game. Kagan and

Madsen (1972b) and McClintock (1974) found that Anglo-American children behaved more competitively than Mexican children, with this cultural difference tending to increase with age. McClintock and McNeel (1966a,d) found that Belgian undergraduates behaved more competitively than Americans in a variant of the PD game. Furthermore, Belgians were more likely to rationalize their competitive behavior with an assertion of their desire to "keep the lead," while competitive American pairs more often mentioned a desire to "get as much as possible for oneself." In contrast with these results, a later PD study using Belgian and American children (McClintock and Nuttin, 1969) found that American children behaved more competitively than Belgian children; but these differences disappeared by the time children reached the sixth grade.

Finally, Kelley et al. (1970), in an interesting and ambitious study, ran a complex bargaining game (the "International Card" game) at eight laboratories—three in Europe and five in the United States. Although differences in bargaining behavior were found in these eight sites, it is not clear whether these differences were related to a bargainer's nationality or not. There was at least as much variability of bargaining behavior among the five American sites as there was between these locations and the European laboratories.

On the basis of the above findings, it is obviously not possible to draw any general conclusion about the relationship between bargainers' nationality and their bargaining effectiveness. This is true not only because of the discrepant pattern of findings to emerge, but also because of the paucity of relevant experimentation and the noncomparability of the methods employed. Only two sets of studies (Swingle, 1969, 1970a; Uejio & Wrightsman, 1967) have actually manipulated the nationality of the subject or the other. The remaining experiments have compared the behavior of subjects belonging to separate, noninteracting populations (Italians in Italy with Americans in America, for example).

Intelligence

The limited research in this area generally suggests that *intelligence* (as measured by various tests of intellectual aptitude) *is unrelated to bargaining ability or behavior.* Fry (1965), in a coordination game study similar to the one described earlier, found no relationship between IQ and the ability to solve tacit coordination problems. Similarly, Berkowitz (1968) and Wallace and Rothaus (1969) found no relationship between IQ and bargaining behavior in the PD game.

One exception to this general pattern of nonsignificance is a study by Kubicka (1968). He ran a population of Czechoslovakian adolescents in a variant of the PD game and partitioned their premeasured intelligence scores into verbal and numerical components. He found that subjects high in numerical ability tended to behave less competitively than those who were lower in this ability. Verbal ability, on the other hand, appeared to be unrelated to bargaining behavior. In addition, Kubicka reported an interesting interaction between the variables of intelligence and sex: brighter boys were more cooperative than duller ones, while brighter girls were more competitive than duller girls. Similar findings were reported in a study by Love (1967), using a population of adults.

Religion

In the only study we have found to relate religious affiliation with bargaining behavior, Arnstein and Feigenbaum (1967) ran Jewish, Quaker, and Catholic undergraduates in a PD game. They found that Jews displayed a greater number of cooperative choices than either of the other groups. Few generalizations can be proposed on the basis of this single study.

Social Background and Social Status

Given the paucity and noncomparability of the available research, few meaningful generalizations can be made about the relationship between bargaining and various premeasured social background variables (such as social class, father's occupation, family income, place of residence, etc.).

Sampson and Kardush (1965) compared the PD game behavior of children labeled as upper or lower class, based on a classification of their fathers' occupation. Using a sample of white subjects only (none of the black children employed in the remainder of the study were classified as upper class!), they found an interaction between the variables of age and class: among younger pairs, lower class subjects were more cooperative than upper class ones; among older pairs, upper class subjects behaved more cooperatively than lower class ones.

This latter finding, concerning the behavior of older children, was lent additional support by an experimental study of bargaining among college students (Gahagan & Tedeschi, 1968b). In this study students from a college with a preponderance of professional ("upper class") families were found to behave more cooperatively in a PD game than students drawn from a second college with a preponderance of working class ("lower class") families.

Apparently unrelated to the above findings are those to emerge in three additional studies of social background. One, a comparative study of bargaining behavior among kibbutz and urban Israeli children (Shapira & Madsen, 1969), found that kibbutz subjects tended to behave more cooperatively than urban subjects in a four-person board game. The second, a study of bargaining among teenagers and adults in African tribal towns (Meeker, 1970), found that "westernized" subjects (those with a "western" occupation) behaved more competitively in a PD game than those with a more traditional background. Finally, Crowne (1966), using subjects whose parents' occupations were classified either as "entrepreneurial" (risk-taking) or "bureaucratic" (according to Miller and Swanson's, 1958, criteria), found that subjects in the former grouping tended to behave more competitively in a PD game than those in the latter.

In contrast with the five above studies, each of which employed a parallel methodology (first pitting bargainers against an opponent of premeasured like background, then comparing, post hoc, the behavior of various like-background pairs) are several studies in which bargainers of differing, experimentally manipulated social status were placed together in a single, interactive setting.

Faley and Tedeschi (1971) asked ROTC cadets of high or low rank to play a PD game against another ROTC cadet (actually a confederate of the experimenter), whose rank was presented as alternately high or low. At several points in the game, the confederate sent a threat message to the subject. Regardless of a subject's own status, it was found that subjects complied more frequently with threats issued by a high status other than a low status one. Furthermore, the greatest amount of exploitative behavior developed when a high status subject played against a low status other.

Related to the Faley and Tedeschi (1971) results are the findings of a study by Grant and Sermat (1969). Status was manipulated in this experiment by providing each subject with false feedback about his opponent's game-playing skill (inferior, equal, or superior to his own). Subjects then played a variant of the PD game against a preprogrammed experimental strategy. While no overall differences in the frequency of cooperative choices were found as a function of status, subjects playing against another of superior status behaved more submissively (choosing cooperatively on turns when they predicted the other would choose competitively) than those playing against another of equal or inferior status.

Following Harsanyi's (1966a) operational definition of social status as the degree of deference obtained by the person having status (where "deference" is defined, in turn, as a willingness to comply with another's wishes), it appears that *bargainers display considerable deference toward high (or higher) status others: by frequent compliance with their threats* (Faley and Tedeschi, 1971), *and by submissive behavior* (Grant and Sermat, 1969). *When confronted with another of lower status, however, bargainers appear to behave exploitatively.* This latter inference is supported not only by the findings of the Faley and Tedeschi (1971) study but by Swingle's (1970a) earlier research as well, in which English-Canadians were found to more frequently exploit low power French-Canadians (of perceived lower status) than they did low power, but equal status, English-Canadians.

Sex

Standing in stark contrast to the limited number of experimental studies of other background variables is an enormous array of bargaining research concerned with the variable of sex. Our search of the literature has uncovered approximately 100 studies, each of which has focused, at least in part, on the relationship between sex and various aspects of bargaining behavior.

Why, one may reasonably ask, has such overwhelming attention been given to the sex variable? Surely other variables are at least as interesting and important to an understanding of the bargaining process. The answer, we believe, has to do with the relative "economy" of the sex variable: the fact that it can be easily and efficiently varied; the fact that college populations, from which most subjects in bargaining experiments are drawn, tend to be co-ed in composition; the fact that it is therefore easier to complete a bargaining experiment, the primary focus of which may actually be upon some variable other than sex, if subjects of both sexes are employed. Thus, while many bargaining researchers appear to have made exploration of the sex variable their foremost concern, it seems that at least as many have merely tacked on an analysis of this variable and have viewed sex as being of secondary importance.

Another characteristic of the research relating sex to bargaining behavior is that it has most frequently involved the use of a single bargaining paradigm, the PD game. Sixty-eight of the studies reviewed have used this one, simple game! Another 12 experiments have placed subjects in coalition games of various kinds. The remaining studies have used a variety of other, more complex bargaining formats.

Among the studies of the sex variable are a number that conclude that there is *no* systematic relationship between sex and bargaining:

1. in terms of the relative frequency with which males and females behave cooperatively in two-person games (Arnstein & Feigenbaum, 1967; Bixenstine, Potash, & Wilson, 1963; Black & Higbee, 1973; Evans & Crumbaugh, 1966b; Gallo *et al.*, 1969; Kanouse & Wiest, 1967; Lutzker, 1961; Marwell, Schmitt, & Shotola, 1971; McNeel, McClintock, & Nuttin, 1972; Meux, 1973; Miller, 1967; Novotny, 1969; Schellenberg, 1964; Sermat, 1967a; Tedeschi, Gahagan, Aranoff, & Steele, 1968c; Voissem & Sistrunk, 1971; Wilson & Insko, 1968; Wilson & Kayatani, 1968; Wyer & Malinowski, 1972);

2. in terms of the relative frequency with which males and females behave cooperatively in coalition (three- or four-person) games (Cole & Phillips, 1967; Shapira & Madsen, 1969; Vinacke, 1964);

3. in terms of the frequency with which males and females reward a like-sexed other (Callahan & Messé, 1973);

4. in terms of the extent to which males and females tend to be suspicious of another's honesty (Benton, Gelber, Kelley, & Liebling, 1969).

Also among the total array of studies are several in which sex was varied, but findings pertinent to this variable were not reported (Crombag, 1966; Druckman, 1967, 1968b; Kershenbaum & Komorita, 1970; Komorita & Mechling, 1967; Richman, 1971; Tedeschi, Aranoff, Gahagan, & Hiester, 1968b; Tedeschi, Burrill, & Gahagan, 1969a; Willis & Long, 1967).

Having separated out those studies that found no relationship between sex and bargaining and those that failed to report data concerning this relationship, we are left with a large number of experiments whose conclusions appear to be diametrically opposed.

Evidence Suggesting that Males Behave More Cooperatively than Females

The primary finding of a number of studies is that males bargain more cooperatively than females. This finding, however, should be considered in relation to the fact that almost all of these studies employed the PD game or some simple variant of this paradigm. Furthermore, most of the PD experiments required subjects to play against a "real other" player (Bedell & Sistrunk, 1973; Crowne, 1966; Gahagan & Tedeschi, 1969; Love, 1967; McClintock, Messick, Kuhlman, & Campos, 1973; Oskamp & Kleinke, 1970; Pruitt, 1967; Rapoport & Chammah, 1965a; Sampson & Kardush, 1965; Steele, 1967; Steele & Tedeschi, 1967). Two pitted subjects against a contingent experimental strategy that attempted to simulate an opponent by mirroring the subject's own choices—behaving on trial $(n + 1)$ just as the subject had behaved on trial n (Kubicka, 1968; Swingle, 1970a). The remaining PD studies had subjects play against a noncontingent experimental strategy that made a predetermined, fixed proportion of cooperative choices (Bixenstine & Blundell, 1966; Bixenstine, Chambers, & Wilson, 1964; Bonoma & Tedeschi, 1973; Gahagan & Tedeschi, 1968b; Halpin & Pilisuk, 1967).

Of the few studies employing some format other than the PD game, Crawford and Sidowski (1964) found that male dyads did better in a coordination game than female or mixed (male–female) dyads; Phillips, Aronoff, and Messé (1971) found that male triads behaved in more conciliatory fashion in a coalition game than female triads; Shomer, Davis, and Kelley (1966) reported that male dyads had greater joint payoffs in a variant of the Acme–Bolt Trucking game than female dyads.

Evidence Suggesting that Females Behave More Cooperatively than Males

In direct opposition to the above set of findings are an even greater number of experiments which conclude that females bargain more cooperatively than males. A number of these studies have been conducted by Vinacke and his colleagues (Amidjaja & Vinacke, 1965; Bond & Vinacke, 1961; Uesugi & Vinacke, 1963; Vinacke et al., 1966; Vinacke & Gullickson, 1964; Vinacke, Mogy, Powers, Langan, & Beck, 1974), as well as others (Schiavo & Kaufman, 1974), using a version of the Parcheesi Coalition game in which subjects could communicate freely. (Note that this is in contrast to most versions of the PD game, in which subjects are incommunicado.) The conclusion of these studies (and of a similar four-person coalition game, conducted by Shears & Behrens, 1969) is that females tend to behave accomodatively, discussing each problem with one another and forming alliances that lead to an equitable division of the game's rewards. Males, on the other hand, tend to behave exploitatively, seeking and demanding an inequitable division of rewards.

Also among the studies concluding that females bargain more cooperatively than males are a large number that employed the PD game. (Aranoff & Tedeschi, 1968; Conrath, 1972; Fisher & Smith, 1969; Grant & Sermat, 1969; Harford & Cutter, 1966; Horai & Tedeschi, 1969; Joseph & Willis, 1963; Lindskold & Tedeschi, 1971; Miller & Pyke, 1973; Sibley et al., 1968; Tedeschi, Bonoma, & Lindskold, 1970a; Tedeschi, Bonoma, & Novinson, 1970b; Tedeschi, Hiester, & Gahagan, 1969b, c; Tedeschi, Hiester, Lesnick, & Gahagan, 1968d; Tedeschi, Lesnick, & Gahagan, 1968e; Tedeschi, Lindskold, Horai, & Gahagan, 1969d; Tedeschi, Powell, Lindskold, & Gahagan, 1969e) Worthy of note is the fact that nearly half of these experiments were conducted by Tedeschi and his students, and that in all but two of them subjects played against a noncontingent experimental strategy.

In addition to the studies cited above, which employed a version of either the Parcheesi Coalition game or the PD game, there are two other relevant experiments; one, a version of the Acme–Bolt Trucking game, concluded that females behaved less competitively than males (Borah, 1963); the other, a complex negotiation game modified for use with children, found that females sought more equitable solutions to bargaining problems than did males (Benton, 1971).

A Proposed Reconciliation of the Findings

How, then, can one begin to reconcile the overwhelming assortment of contradictory findings relating sex to bargaining behavior? In response, we wish to turn once again to the hypothetical dimension of Interpersonal Orientation. Our argument is simple: *females tend to bargain like high IOs, while males behave more like low IOs.*

As the findings of the following studies suggest, females appear to be more sensitive than males to a number of interpersonal cues:

1. *Sex of the other.* Grant and Sermat (1969) found that females were more influenced than males by the sex of their partner in a PD game, behaving more competitively than males in the presence of a male other, and more cooperatively in the presence of another female. Kahn, Hottes, and Davis (1971), in two, more complex PD games, reported that males did not vary their behavior as a function of the other's sex, while females tended to be more cooperative with a male than with a female. (The Kahn, Hottes, & Davis, 1971, findings were partially confirmed by an earlier study of Gregovich, 1969.) Finally, Wiley (1969) found that females discriminated more on the basis of their partner's sex than did males.

2. *Sex of the experimenter.* Sermat (1967a) found that females were more influenced by the sex of the experimenter than were males.

3. *Attractiveness of the other.* Kahn, Hottes, and Davis (1971) found that females were more likely than males to vary their bargaining behavior as a function of the physical attractiveness of their partner, cooperating more often in the presence of an attractive other, and less often in the presence of an ugly one.

4. *Availability of communication.* Shotola (1970) reported that females behaved more competitively than males in a risk-taking game with no communication. When subjects were permitted to speak freely with each other, however, females behaved more cooperatively than males. Similarly, Horai, Lindskold, Gahagan, and Tedeschi (1969) found that under conditions of no communication men were more cooperative than women, this pattern being reversed when subjects received communicated promises from the other.

5. *Equity.* Benton (1971) reported that girls were more concerned with the resolution of issues of equity and distributive justice than boys. Marwell, Ratcliff, and Schmitt (1969) found that under conditions of inequity, females were less cooperative than males, while under conditions of equity, they were more cooperative than males. Similarly, Bartos (1967a) found that women were more cooperative than men when given no information about the other's inclination to be tough or soft; however, when the other was presented as either tougher or softer, women behaved more competitively

than men. Finally, Swingle (1970a), and Black and Higbee (1973), reported that females were more likely to exploit a weak opponent than males.

6. *Cooperativeness of the other.* Bixenstine, Chambers, and Wilson (1964) found that females were initially more trusting and more trustworthy than men but were less willing to forgive violations of trust. Wilson and Bixenstine (1962b), in an unpublished study reported in Bixenstine, Chambers, and Wilson (1964), found that females were more sensitive to the other's cooperativeness than males, and more often responded in kind. Similarly, Bixenstine and Wilson (1963) reported that women were less cooperative than men in the presence of a noncontingent experimental strategy that chose cooperatively on 5% of the game trials; when the strategy made 95% cooperative choices, women were more cooperative than men. Similar findings emerged in the experiments of Kahn *et al.* (1971) and Komorita (1965).

Our argument is not that males and females differ in their inherent propensity to bargain cooperatively with another, but rather that they are sensitive to different cues. Women, like high IOs (and cooperative high IOs, in particular), are highly sensitive and reactive to the interpersonal aspects of their relationship with the other. Males, like low IOs, orient themselves not to the other, but to the impersonal task of maximizing their own earnings. When earnings can best be maximized through the use of a competitive strategy, males tend to compete; on the other hand, when a cooperative strategy seems most likely to maximize own earnings, males cooperate.

The above analysis closely parallels the position taken by Komorita (1965) and by Kahn *et al.* (1971) in their insightful interpretation of the PD literature—an interpretation that enables us to reconcile many of the contradictory PD findings.

When playing a PD game against a noncontingent experimental strategy (one that chooses randomly, always makes the same choice, or makes a predetermined percentage of cooperative choices), a bargainer can best maximize his own earnings by behaving in consistently competitive fashion, regardless of how the other behaves. This is very much what males appear to do in this situation. Females, on the other hand, tend to respond to variations in the other's behavior, altering their own cooperativeness in direct relation to their partner's level of cooperation (i.e., they respond like cooperative high IOs). Recall that nearly half of the PD studies reporting females to be more cooperative than males had subjects pitted against a noncontingent experimental strategy.

When playing the PD game against either a real other or a contingent (tit-for-tat) experimental strategy (as was the case in most of the studies reporting that males were more cooperative than females), Kahn *et al.* (1971) point out that the strategy for optimizing own earnings consists of 100% cooperation. Thus, regardless of fluctuations in the other's behavior, and regardless of all interpersonal parameters, one is best off cooperating in such a situation. This is pretty much what males appear to do. Females, on the other hand, behave rather differently. Instead of overlooking the other's competitive behavior (which almost inevitably occurs in a paradigm as predisposed to competition as the PD game), they respond defensively and vindictively, choosing competitively and persisting in this behavior longer than males. Note, however, that in more cooperatively predisposed paradigms (such as the Parcheesi Coalition game), in which communication is allowed, females tend to behave more cooperatively than males. Thus, females again appear to resemble cooperative high IOs.

Before leaving our discussion of the sex variable, we wish to point out that while our interpretation of the pertinent findings may be parsimonious in its reconciliation of the data, it should be tempered by the presence of many experiments finding no relationship between sex and bargaining behavior. Also it hardly needs to be stated that the conceptual hypothesis we have proposed here requires careful experimental test.

INDIVIDUAL DIFFERENCES IN PERSONALITY

The research concerned with variations in bargainers' background has generally examined a limited number of parameters, giving some of these (the sex variable, for example) considerable attention. In contrast, studies of individual differences in personality have tended to be both fewer in number and more diverse in focus. A great many, apparently different personality variables have been selected for study within the last decade; few, however, have been the object of repeated, intensive exploration. In order to facilitate a review of this literature, we have therefore found it necessary to group related studies into the following broad classes of variables: cognitive processes (risk-taking propensity, perceived locus of control, cognitive complexity, intolerance of ambiguity); self-concept (self-esteem, self-assurance, anxiety); motives (need for achievement, power, affiliation); attitudes (generalized trust, cooperativeness, authoritarianism, internationalism, flexible ethicality, machiavellianism); special and abnormal populations (criminals, paranoids, schizophrenics). While this classificatory scheme is clearly arbitrary and nonexclusive in nature (inasmuch as some variables may belong to more than one class), it should permit a more concise overview of the relevant research.

Cognitive Processes

Risk-taking Propensity

Of the five studies examining the relationship between a general willingness to take risks (gamble) and bargaining behavior, two have reported no systematic relationship (Dolbear & Lave, 1966; Pilisuk *et al.*, 1965). The conclusion of the remaining three studies is that high risk-takers seem more interested in maximizing their own gain than mutual gain. Based on this rather tentative evidence, it thus appears that *high risk-takers behave somewhat like low IOs.*

Sherman (1967) administered the Kogan and Wallach (1964) measure of social risk preference to an undergraduate population. (The Kogan and Wallach measure investigates the chances people say they would be willing to take in a series of hypothetical social situations.) Subjects were then told that they would be participating in a PD game in which they would be able to decide which of two types of matrices would be used: one, in which cooperation would be particularly easy to establish; the second, presenting an opportunity for greater own gain through competitive behavior. High risk-takers consistently chose the latter type of matrix, one that would maximize own, rather than mutual, gain. Low risk-takers did the reverse. These findings were replicated in a later study (Sherman, 1968).

Harnett, Cummings, and Hughes (1968), using a variant of the Bilateral Monopoly game, reached a similar conclusion. High risk-takers (as measured by the Kogan and Wallach scales) were found to yield less often (make fewer concessions) than low risk-takers, under conditions of low information about the other's earning. When such information was available, differences as a function of risk-taking propensity were reduced.

Perceived Locus of Control

Rotter (1966) has posited the existence of a personality variable (locus of control), which is defined as the subjective probability that rewards are determined by self-effort (internal control) or by outside agency (external control). "Internals," he says, believe rewards are contingent upon their own behavior; "externals" attribute their success to luck, fate, chance, or other people.

Condry (1967) found no relationship between locus of control and behavior in a two-person negotiation game. In the other published bargaining study of this variable, Bobbitt (1967) administered Rotter's scale to a group of subjects, who then played a PD game against an experimental strategy. When this strategy was consistently competitive, internals behaved less competitively than externals; on the other hand, when a predominantly cooperative strategy was employed by the experimenter, internals were less cooperative than externals. Internals thus appear to be less sensitive and reactive to variations in the other's behavior than externals. *Internals behave somewhat like high risk-takers (and low IOs):* maximizing own gain by choosing competitively (exploitatively) when the other consistently cooperates; attempting to maximize own gain by initiating cooperative behavior (risk-taking) in the presence of another who is competitive, but presumably may be induced to choose cooperatively. Externals, on the other hand, like high IOs (and, more particularly, like cooperative high IOs) seem less concerned with the maximization of own gain and more concerned with interpersonal cues, making cooperative choices in direct proportion to the frequency of the other's cooperativeness.

Cognitive Complexity

This personality variable refers, most generally, to the approach taken to the processing of information: "abstract" processors are said to be high in cognitive complexity; "concrete" information processors are said to be low in cognitive complexity.

Based on the findings of the two bargaining studies which have premeasured subject's cognitive complexity, it tentatively appears that *bargainers high in cognitive complexity behave like high IOs, while those low in cognitive complexity behave more like low IOs.* Phelan and Richardson (1969) found that subjects high in cognitive complexity ("abstracts") made more cooperative choices in a PD game than those who were lower along this dimension ("concretes"). They found, moreover, that abstracts favored an equitable distribution of payoffs when the other behaved cooperatively, and a distribution that minimized own losses when the other was competitive. Concretes, on the other hand, utilized the opportunity for gain, even if it meant a decrease in outcomes for the other. Leff (1969) reported that abstracts were more cooperative than concretes in a PD game when no information was provided about the other's behavior on each trial. But when the other's behavior was known, abstracts behaved more competitively than concretes.

We interpret the above findings by assuming that concrete bargainers, like low IOs, are primarily concerned with maximizing their own earnings. Given, then, that they are in the presence of another about whom no information is provided, they should compete; while in the presence of another whose behavior is visible (and occasionally cooperative), cooperation should be the dominant strategy. (Note that this is the same argument we developed in our discussion of the sex variable findings.) Abstracts, on the other hand, like high IOs (and cooperative high IOs, in particular), are reactive to interpersonal cues, and are hence more likely to behave defensively in the presence of another about whom they have information (whose competitive as well as cooperative behavior they can witness) than in the presence of another about whose choice behavior they know nothing. Consistent with the above interpretation is Leff's (1969) observation that abstracts "indicated that they saw the experiment as less of an impersonal, rule governed exercise and as more of an interpersonal task requiring communication and cooperation [p. 4103]."

In one other pertinent study, cognitive complexity was manipulated rather than premeasured (Hammond, Todd, Wilkins, & Mitchell, 1966). Subjects were first trained to think differently (were given different "cue dependencies") about a common set of problems and were then brought together to make joint decisions. Subjects who had been trained to use a complex cognitive system (a nonlinear model) were found to be less willing to modify their position in the face of conflict with another than those who had been taught a simpler (linear) system. Note that cognitive complexity was not really considered in this study as a personality variable. It was manipulated rather than premeasured and bears no relation to the abstractness or concreteness of the subjects' thinking.

Intolerance of Ambiguity

Individuals who are intolerant of ambiguity, in contrast with those who reside near the opposite pole of this dimension, tend to prefer regularity to change, clarity to ambiguity, balance to imbalance, concreteness to abstraction, and so forth. As such, *individuals who are intolerant of ambiguity may be expected (at least in theory) to behave like those who are low in cognitive complexity—like low IOs.* The available evidence, unfortunately, does not permit us to confirm this hypothesis.

Of the six experimental studies of intolerance of ambiguity (and closed mindedness), two (Nardin, 1967—an unpublished study cited in Terhune, 1970—and Sherman, 1968) found no systematic relationship with bargaining behavior. A third study (Druckman, 1968b) premeasured subjects in terms of their closed- versus open-mindedness, but did not discuss findings pertinent to this variable.

Three experiments, however, reported a significant relationship between intolerance of ambiguity and bargaining. Pilisuk *et al.* (1965), using an expanded version of the PD game, found that subject pairs both of whom were high in tolerance for ambiguity (low in intolerance) were more likely to evolve a mutually cooperative relationship than other pairs. Druckman (1967) administered Rokeach's (1960) Dogmatism Scale to subjects (designed to measure degree of closed-mindedness), then placed them in a collective bargaining simulation game. He reported that subjects high in dogmatism tended to make fewer concessions (were less yielding), resolved fewer issues, and viewed compromise as defeat more often than those who were low in dogmatism. Similarly, Teger (1970), using a variant of Deutsch's Allocation game (Deutsch, Epstein, Canavan & Gumpert, 1967), found that subjects high in intolerance of ambiguity persevered in (tolerated) conflict longer than other.

On the basis of the above studies, it thus generally appears that *bargainers who are high in tolerance for ambiguity are more likely to behave cooperatively than those who are low.*

Self-Concept

Self-concept refers most generally to the set of feelings and beliefs a person has about how he looks in his own eyes and the eyes of others. An individual with a positive self-concept tends to have greater self-esteem and self-acceptance and tends to have less anxiety about how he looks to others than a person with a more negative view of himself.

Two of the seven relevant studies (Pilisuk *et al.*, 1965; Phillips *et al.*, 1971) have found no relation between self-concept and bargaining behavior. The general conclusion of the other experiments, however, is that *individuals with a negative self-concept tend to bargain more competitively than those with a positive view of themselves.*

Tedeschi *et al.* (1969a) found that subjects who were high in anxiety (as measured on the Manifest Anxiety Scale) behaved more competitively in a PD game than those who were less anxious. Williams, Steele, and Tedeschi (1969) reported that subjects who were concerned with the issue of self-concept made a greater number of competitive choices. Lindskold (1971) experimentally induced feelings of competence or incompetence by providing subjects with success or failure experience during the early trials of a PD game. Subjects then played the remaining trials against a simulated other (a 50% or 100% noncontingent cooperative strategy), toward whom promises or threats or both could be directed. Lindskold found that low competence subjects generally behaved more exploitatively and aggressively than high competence ones, the former making nearly exclusive use of threats in the 100% cooperation condition.

In an attempt to examine the effects of experimentally induced feelings of high or low self-esteem on bargaining behavior, Pepitone *et al.* (1967) gave subjects false feedback about their performance on a "test of creativity" (at the 97th versus 60th percentile), then ran them in a PD game. They found that bargainers who were high in manipulated self-esteem behaved more competitively than those who were low.

The findings of the Pepitone *et al.* (1967) study appear to contradict the view that bargainers with a negative self-concept (low self-esteem) tend to behave more competitively than those with positive self-regard. This apparent contradiction, however, is largely reconciled in an experiment performed by Faucheux and Moscovici (1968) in which self-esteem was not only manipulated but premeasured as well. When self-esteem was manipulated, the Pepitone *et al.* findings were replicated: highs behaved more competitively in a PD game than lows. However, when self-esteem was premeasured, and chronic highs and lows were then run in the same game, a trend in the reverse direction emerged: lows tended to behave more competitively than highs.

In explanation, Faucheux and Moscovici argued that competitive bargaining behavior was most likely to emerge among individuals who were high in anxiety. Among the premeasured subjects, it was the chronically low self-esteem individuals who were most anxious (about how they looked in the eyes of others) and who compensated for their feelings of inadequacy by taking high rewards for themselves—at the expense of the other. Among the manipulated self-esteem subjects, however, the situation was reversed. It was those subjects who were told how very competent they were (97th percentile) who felt they now had to validate the experimenter's "expert" judgment, who experienced high anxiety (about how they looked in the eyes of the experimenter), and who therefore, like chronically low self-esteem individuals, responded with competitive behavior!

Motives

Almost without exception, the research concerned with the relationship between a bargainer's motivational predisposition and his subsequent behavior has focused on the effects of one or more of three, basic motives: the need for achievement (Nach), the need for affiliation (Naff), and the need for power (Nepo). Following Terhune (1968), the need for achievement may be defined as the need or desire to attain a standard of excellence; the need for affiliation (or nurturance) as the need or desire to have friendly relations with others; and the need for power (or dominance) as the need or desire to exert control over others. Based on the findings of the several studies concerned with these three motive types, it appears that *high Nach bargainers tend to behave like low IOs, while both high Naff and high Nepo bargainers tend to act like high IOs.*

Support for the above proposition stems from a variety of sources, perhaps the most important of which is an ambitious experiment conducted by Terhune (1968) and Terhune and Firestone (1967)—the latter being an unpublished manuscript cited by Terhune (1970). A large population of male undergraduates was administered the Thermatic Apperception Test. These tests were scored for the presence of Nach, Naff, and Nepo, and only subjects who were strong in one of the three motives (while being weak in the other two) were employed. Subjects then participated in three types of experimental tasks: three one-trial PD games, in which the inherent cooperativeness of the payoff matrix was varied; a 30-trial PD game played against a real other player of the same motive type; and an "international relations" game, in which subjects of the same motive type were formed into three-man groups.

The findings of the Terhune study were as follows: First, in the three one-trial PD games, the high Nach subjects made a greater number of cooperative choices than either the high Naffs or the high Nepos, regardless of the cooperativeness of the matrix used. The high Naffs were cooperative only when the game matrix was cooperative; given a more competitive environment, they tended to behave suspiciously (expecting defection by the other) and defensively (defecting themselves). The high Nepos were consistently noncooperative, exploiting the other whenever possible. Second, few overall differences by motive type emerged in the 30-trial PD game. However, when the behavior of dyads in which both players had chosen cooperatively on the first trial was compared, high Nachs were again found to be most cooperative, and high Nepos least cooperative. Finally, no overall differences in cooperative behavior were found in the international relations game, although the greatest number of cooperative offers was initiated by high Nach triads, the fewest by high Naffs, and the greatest amount of lying was done by high Nepos.

The findings of several PD game experiments lend partial support to Terhune's observations. In one of several studies of the need for power, Marlowe (1963) reported that subjects high in the needs for aggression and autonomy (variants of the need for power, according to Terhune, 1970) behaved more competitively than those who were lower in these needs. Similarly, Higgs and McGrath (1965)—in an unpublished study cited by Terhune (1970)—found that subjects high in the need for "prominence" tended to compete. Sermat reported contradictory findings relating the need for dominance (as measured by the Minnesota Multiphasic Personality Inventory, or MMPI) to bargaining behavior. In one study (Sermat, 1967b) he found no relationship; in a later study (Sermat, 1968) he found that subjects high in the need for dominance behaved more competitively than those who were lower in this motive. Two studies of the need for achievement (Crowne, 1966; Higgs & McGrath, 1965) found no relationship with PD game behavior. Finally, a study by Noland and Catron (1969) of the need for affiliation (nurturance) reported that high Naffs (as measured by the Adjective Check List) behaved more cooperatively than others. Worthy of note is the fact that subjects in this experiment played a PD game against a noncontingent experimental strategy which was predominantly (76%) cooperative.

As we have suggested earlier, the best way to maximize one's own earnings in the PD game when playing against a real other is to consistently make the cooperative choice, pretty much regardless of what the other player does. This is exactly what high Nachs in the PD game (like low IOs) appear to be doing. In contrast, the high Naffs and high Nepos seem highly reactive to the other's expected or actual behavior. The high Naffs, like cooperative high IOs, cooperate to the extent that they expect the other to cooperate as well (as in the Noland and Catron, 1969, study). But given the expectation that the other will behave competitively (as he almost certainly will in a free play PD game), the high Naffs respond defensively and vindictively. The high Nepos, like the Naffs, are sensitive to variations in the other's behavior, but (like competitive high IOs) they use this information to exploit the other.

If our analysis is correct, one would expect to find a different patterning of cooperative behavior among the three motive types in an experimental paradigm that more readily permits cooperation than does the PD game. Such is the case in two coalition studies of the needs for achievement and nurturance (affiliation).

Chaney and Vinacke (1960) administered the Edwards Personal Preference Schedule to subjects, then formed them into triads composed of one high Nach (low in Naff), one high Naff (low in Nach), and one person intermediate in both needs. Subjects then played the Parcheesi Coalition game, with communication permitted. High Nachs consistently behaved less cooperatively than the high Naffs, formed fewer two-person alliances based on a 50–50 split of the available rewards, discussed the problem less often, and so forth. While they were most active in initiating offers to form coalitions and earned the greatest number of points, the high Nachs were generally seen as aggressive, and they formed fewer coalitions than either of the other two subject-types. These findings were replicated in a later study by Amidjaja and Vinacke (1965).

Notice that in the context of a paradigm like the Parcheesi Coalition game—in which cooperation is more readily attainable than in the PD game, and in which there is greater access to interpersonal cues—the high Naffs behave more cooperatively than the high Nachs. Note also that this general pattern of findings is very close to that which emerged in our discussion of the sex variable. As Amidjaja and Vinacke (1965) point out in their discussion of coalition game findings, men appear to bargain like high Nachs, while women act more like high Naffs. While there are no data presently available to support our conjecture, we expect that under some circumstances women may behave like high Nepos as well.

In addition to the experimental studies we have cited above, there are several others that have focused on the relationship between motives and the bargaining process. Fry (1965, 1967), in two closely related studies, used the Allport and Allport A-S Reaction study to classify subjects as either high or low in ascendance (the tendency to initiate interaction). Subject pairs with similar or different ascendance scores were then run in a tacit coordination game. While no differences in coordination ability emerged as a function of absolute ascendance level, Fry found that subject pairs with discrepant scores outperformed those with similar scores. Based on Fry's results, as well as the similar findings of an earlier study by Smelser (1961), it thus appears that under some circumstances, bargainers may be better able to coordinate their mutual expectations and intentions in the presence of another whose personal predispositions are different than, rather than similar to, their own.

Finally, brief mention should be made of a "shotgun" study by Williams *et al.* (1969), in which subjects were first given Cattell's Motivation Analysis Test, then had their various subtest scores correlated with several measures of performance in the PD game (150 correlations were computed; 14 were significant). Subjects high in Cattell's "narcissism-comfort" motive ("the level of drive to sensuous, self-indulgent satisfaction") were found to generally behave more cooperatively than those who were lower.

Attitudes

Within this most general of rubrics, we wish to consider the effects of the following attitudinal variables on the course of bargaining: generalized trust; cooperativeness; authoritarianism; internationalism; flexible ethicality; and machiavellianism. Even though we recognize that several of these attitudes overlap and interrelate in a variety of ways, we have employed this particular classification of variables in order to facilitate a review of the pertinent literature.

Generalized Trust

A number of researchers have found a systematic relationship between bargaining behavior and an individual's predisposition to trust others. It appears, most generally, that *trusting bargainers behave more cooperatively than those who are less trusting (suspicious)*.

Tedeschi *et al.* (1969c) and Schlenker, Helm, and Tedeschi (1973) found that individuals who were high in premeasured trust of others behaved more cooperatively in the PD game than those who were low. Similarly, Wrightsman (1966) found that bargainers who believed human nature to be altruistic, trustworthy, and independent chose cooperatively in the PD game more frequently than those who did not hold these beliefs. Tedeschi *et al.* (1968) reported that bargainers who (optimistically) predicted that the other would behave cooperatively in the PD game behaved more cooperatively themselves than those who (more realistically) predicted less cooperation on the part of the other player.

Focusing on the other side of the same general issue, Shure and Meeker (1965)—in an unpublished study cited by Terhune (1970)—found that suspicious bargainers behaved less "generously" than trusting ones. In a study of reactions to deceit, Benton *et al.* (1969) placed subjects in a mixed-motive game, in which one (the subject) was dependent upon the other (a confederate of the experimenter) for information that would affect both their outcomes. They found that the frequency with which subjects doubted the veracity of the information provided by the other was higher among people who were initially suspicious than among those who were initially trusting.

Four additional experimental studies found no relationship between trust (Richman, 1971), exploitativeness–accommodativeness (Murdoch, 1968), or altruism (Bixenstine & Blundell, 1966; Bixenstine *et al.*, 1966) and bargaining behavior.

Cooperativeness

Just as trusting bargainers behave more cooperatively than suspicious ones, so too (as one might reasonably expect) do *bargainers with a cooperative predisposition ("cooperators") tend to behave more cooperatively than those with the opposite attitude ("competitors")*.

Over the last decade, Morton Deutsch and others, in a number of important studies of the bargaining process, have examined the effects of an experimentally induced motivational orientation upon subsequent behavior.

The conclusion of this research has consistently been that cooperatively oriented bargainers (those who are instructed to maximize joint gain, to be concerned with the other's welfare as well as one's own, etc.) behave more cooperatively than those who are competitively oriented (instructed to beat the other, to maximize the difference in gain, etc.). Because this research has focused more on the effects of a manipulated, experimentally induced tendency to cooperate, however, rather than on inherent predispositions, it will be discussed in conjunction with an analysis of variables relating to bargainers' interdependence (Chapter 8).

Of greater pertinence to our discussion of cooperative and competitive predispositions are two articles by Kelley and Stahelski: an experimental study of cooperators' and competitors' beliefs about others (1970a) and a theoretical review of this study and other related research (1970c). Kelley and Stahelski point out that the overall tendency of cooperators to behave more cooperatively than competitors is a reflection of the fact that these two predispositional types have radically different views of the world. Based on the findings of their research, we will attempt to argue in this section that *cooperators behave like cooperative high IOs, while competitors behave more like low IOs.*

In an intriguing study of bargainers' perceptions of intentions, Kelley and Stahelski (1970a) first taught subjects the details of the PD game, then asked them to state their goals and intentions. Based on responses to this premeasure, subjects were classified as cooperators or competitors and were formed into incommunicado pairs with similar (cooperator–cooperator; competitor–competitor) or different (cooperator–competitor) predispositions. These pairs played out a multi-trial PD game, during which they were asked at several points to estimate the other's intentions (cooperative or competitive). The frequency of cooperative choice behavior and the frequency with which cooperators and competitors made various errors of perception of the other's intention at the outset of the experiment constituted the primary dependent measures.

Kelley and Stahelski found that competitors cooperated less frequently than cooperators and did not vary their behavior in relation to the type of partner with whom they were matched. Cooperators, on the other hand, tended to behave like their partner—choosing cooperatively in the presence of another they believed was a cooperator, and competitively in the presence of one they viewed as a competitor. Concerning errors of perception, Kelley and Stahelski reported that cooperators more accurately perceived the other's true intention than competitors. Competitors tended to view the world as comprised of other competitors; hence, in cooperator–competitor pairs, they mistakenly judged their cooperatively inclined partner to be a competitor like themselves. Cooperators, on the other hand, when paired with a competitive other, correctly perceived their partner's intentions as competitive and stated a feeling of little responsibility for the course of the relationship.

In their review of the implications of this PD study, Kelley and Stahelski (1970c) draw four important conclusions which they support with the findings of other research.

1. Competitors behave competitively, regardless of the other's behavior. Cooperators behave like the others with whom they interact—cooperatively in the presence of a cooperator and competitively with a competitor. Support for this conclusion is drawn from studies by Apfelbaum (1967), Stahelski and Kelley (1969)—both cited in Kelley and Stahelski (1970c)—Sermat and Gregovich (1966), and Pilisuk *et al.* (1965). Furthermore, there is some evidence suggesting that cooperators may overreact in the presence of a competitor—behaving even more competitively than their competitive partner (Swinth, 1967b; an unpublished study by Shure, Meeker, Moore & Kelley, 1966).

2. Because of cooperators' tendencies toward behavioral assimilation, their intentions are misperceived by competitors, who mistakenly judge them to be competitive (Stahelski & Kelley, 1969).

3. Cooperators are more aware of the causal role played by a competitive other than are competitors (Stahelski & Kelley, 1969; Kelley & Stahelski, 1970b).

4. Cooperators and competitors come to have different views of what others are like—cooperators see the world as being made up of both cooperative and competitive people; competitors believe that others are uniformly competitive (Kelley & Stahelski, 1970b; Stahelski & Kelley, 1969; Dorris, 1969—an unpublished study; Kelley *et al.*, 1970).

Based on Kelley and Stahelski's analysis, a clear correspondence can be drawn between cooperativeness and our dimension of Interpersonal Orientation. Competitors act like low IOs: they are insensitive to (or uninterested in) interpersonal cues; they do not vary their behavior in response to the other; they misperceive the other's intentions; they underestimate the importance of their own behavior in determining what the other does; they view the world as consisting of others just like themselves; in the PD game, at least, they tend to compete. Cooperators, on the other hand, behave like cooperative high IOs: they are interested in and sensitive to variations in the cooperativeness of the other's behavior; given that he is cooperative, they are cooperative; but given another who competes, they respond in defensive, vindictive fashion (behaving even more competitively than their competitive adversary); furthermore, they are acutely (even overly) aware of the role of the other's behavior in shaping both their outcomes.

Authoritarianism

The authoritarian personality, first described by Adorno, Frenkel-Brunswik, Levinson, and Sanford (1950), is a complex predispositional type, involving not only attitudes but cognitive processes and motives as well. An individual high in authoritarianism (scoring high on the authoritarianism, or F, scale—a *high F*) is characterized by a power orientation, obeisance to others in power, proneness to concrete thinking, and an attitude toward others which is generally suspicious and cynical.

Of the 16 experiments that have examined authoritarianism and various bargaining processes, 7 report no relationship between F-scale score and: *(1)* risk-taking behavior (Baron & Arenson, 1967); *(2)* performance in a coordination game (Fry, 1965); *(3)* behavior in the PD game (Gahagan, Horai, Berger, & Tedeschi, 1967—an unpublished study cited in Terhune, 1970; Lynch, 1968; McKeown, Gahagan, & Tedeschi, 1967; Robinson & Wilson, 1965—an unpublished study cited in Druckman, 1967; Wood, Pilisuk, & Uren, 1973). The general conclusion of the remaining studies, each of which found a significant relationship between authoritarianism and bargaining is that *low Fs bargain more cooperatively than high Fs.* Given the large proportion of studies with nonsignificant results, however, this conclusion is tentative at best.

Deutsch (1960b) ran high and low Fs in a two-trial PD game played against a simulated opponent. On the first trial, subjects were required to choose before the other player; on the second trial, they made their choice after the other (who always chose cooperatively). Deutsch found that low Fs behaved more cooperatively than high Fs. They trusted the other more frequently (making a cooperative choice on the first trial) and more often reciprocated the other's trusting behavior on the second trial with a trustworthy (cooperative) choice of their own. Similar findings have emerged in other, more recent PD experiments (Ashmore, 1969—an unpublished study cited in Kelley & Stahelski, 1970c; Berkowitz, 1968; Bixenstine & O'Reilly, 1966; Driver, 1965—an unpublished study cited in Terhune, 1970; Slack & Cook, 1973; Wrightsman, 1966).

Friedell (1968) placed high and low Fs in a two-person, two-choice "war" game in which subjects could retaliate against attacks launched by the other (but only at mutual expense). He reported that authoritarianism increased the propensity to retaliate, high Fs engaging in mutually costly retaliation more frequently than low Fs.

Smith (1967a) ran high and low Fs in a triadic conflict situation in which they were led to believe they had control over the rewards received by a second player (P2), who controlled the rewards of a third player (P3) who, in turn, had the power to reward the subject. All subjects occupied the same position in the triad (P1), while the behavior of the other two players was simulated by the experimenter. Both the power of the subject over P2 and that of P2 over P3 were varied. Smith found that as the power of P2 increased, low Fs increasingly attempted to influence P2 through the use of reward, while high Fs increasingly resorted to punishment (the witholding of reward).

In their discussion of cooperators and competitors, Kelley and Stahelski (1970c) have pointed to the presence of a rough isomorphism between cooperativeness and authoritarianism. They suggest that *high Fs behave like competitors (and, we infer, like low IOs), while low Fs act more like cooperators (whom we have likened to cooperative high IOs).* In support of their hypothesis, Kelley and Stahelski draw on the findings of several social perception (nonbargaining) studies which are beyond the scope of this book. The sense of these findings, however, is that high Fs tend to view the world as being uniformly composed of other high Fs; low Fs, on the other hand, expect others to be more heterogeneous in authoritarianism. Furthermore, while high Fs are consistently aggressive, egoistic, and exploitative in their behavior, low Fs behave more variably, in response to what the other does. In the presence of a high F other, a low F individual will thus come to behave aggressively, exploitatively, and so forth, which will heighten the high F's misperception of his low F partner and result in a self-fulfilling prophecy.

Internationalism

Closely related to authoritarianism is the internationalism scale, designed by Lutzker (1960) to measure an individual's willingness to trust other nations. It draws a number of items from the ethnocentrism scale (a precursor of the F scale) and, according to Lutzker, is correlated with authoritarianism.

Of the eight experimental studies of internationalism and bargaining, four have reported no relationship with behavior in the PD game (Bixenstine *et al.*, 1966; Pilisuk *et al.*, 1965; Sermat, 1968; Sherman, 1968). The tentative conclusion implied by the remaining studies, however, is that *bargainers who are high in internationalism (high Ints) behave more cooperatively than those who are lower (low Ints).*

Lutzker (1960) administered his internationalism scale to a group of subjects. High and low Ints were then formed into homogeneous (like attitude) pairs and were run in the PD game. Lutzker found that high Ints (both as individuals and as pairs) made a greater number of cooperative choices than low Ints. Similar findings have been reported in subsequent PD studies by McClintock, Harrison, Strand, and Gallo (1963) and Swirsky (1968).

In what is perhaps the most interesting of the bargaining studies of internationalism, McClintock, Gallo, and Harrison (1965) had high and low Ints play a two-part, assymetric version of the PD game against an experimental strategy. In the first part of the game, subjects had little control over their own and the other's payoffs, and played against a strategy that was either predominantly cooperative or competitive. In the second part of the game, subjects were given virtually total control over their own and the other's payoffs, and played against a uniformly cooperative strategy. The major finding of this study was an interaction among the three experimental variables: Given a chance to exert control over the other (in part two), low Ints tended not to vary their behavior as a function of their prior experience at the hands of the other (part one); high Ints, on the other hand, responded to a prior cooperative strategy by the other with reciprocation (cooperation), and to a prior competitive strategy with retaliation (competition). *High Ints (like high IOs, and cooperative high IOs in particular) thus appear to be more sensitive to variations in the other's behavior than low Ints (and low IOs).*

Flexible Ethicality

Also closely related to authoritarianism is a measure of "flexible ethicality," developed by Bixenstine. This measure consists of a series of story dramas in which the protagonist makes a choice involving an ethical value, to which the subject is asked to provide his reaction. Individuals who are said to be high in flexible ethicality display moderate and conventional endorsement of commonly accepted ethical principles on this measure; those who are low in flexible ethicality show more extreme and moralistic (more authoritarian) endorsement of these principles.

Of the five studies examining flexible ethicality and bargaining, only one reported no relationship (Bixenstine *et al.*, 1964). The conclusion of the remaining studies is that *bargainers who are high in flexible ethicality behave more cooperatively than those who are low.* This conclusion is supported by the findings of three PD experiments using Bixenstine's measure

(Bixenstine *et al.*, 1966; Bixenstine, *et al.*, 1963; Bixenstine & Wilson, 1963). In addition, Brumback (1963) reported that bargainers who scored low in ethicality (on a scale describing exploitative practices engaged in by a generalized business firm) behaved more competitively in a simulated "business" game than those who scored higher on this scale.

Machiavellianism

Machiavellianism, first described and measured by Richard Christie, has been defined by Geis (1965) as "the willingness and ability to use guile, deceit and other opportunistic strategies in interpersonal relations in order to manipulate other people [p. 7407]." Two *Mach scales* have been devised by Christie to assess this attitudinal predisposition. Of the 16 experimental studies we have reviewed, four have found no relationship between machiavellianism and bargaining behavior (Condry, 1967; Daniels, 1967; Lewicki, 1970; Wrightsman, 1966). Based on the findings of the remaining studies, however, it appears that *bargainers high in machiavellianism (high Machs) behave more competitively than those who are low in machiavellianism (low Machs); furthermore, high Machs tend to behave like (competitive) high IOs, while low Machs behave more like low IOs.*

Lowe (1966)—in an unpublished study cited in Christie and Geis (1970a) —Uejio and Wrightsman (1967), and Wahlin (1967) found that high Machs behaved more competitively than low Machs in variants of the PD game. Edelstein (1966)—in an unpublished study cited in Christie and Geis (1970a)—found that high Machs bluffed more frequently and took greater risks than lows in a two-person game. In another two-person bargaining game (type not specified), Wiley (1969) reported that high Machs played more strategically ("exhibited more shaping behavior") than low Machs.

Three experimental studies of machiavellianism have employed variations of the "Allocation" game, devised by Deutsch and his colleagues (Deutsch *et al.*, 1967) to examine the effects of various strategies of eliciting cooperation. Using a version of this game, Lake (1967) found that high Machs responded more rapidly than lows to changes in the other's behavior and were more likely than lows to respond to the other's aggression in like fashion (with counteraggression). Similar findings were reported by Teger (1970), who found that high Machs responded to a hostile act by the other with greater immediate retaliation than low Machs. Finally, O'Brien (1970), although finding no overall relationship between machiavellianism and behavior in the Allocation game, reported that high Machs were more sensitive to variations in their own and the other's power than low Machs.

In addition to the experiments already cited, four unpublished studies by Richard Christie, Florence Geis, and their colleagues appear in an exhaustive and entertaining review of the machiavellianism literature (Christie & Geis, 1970a). In the first of these, Geis (1965) had high, middle, and low scorers on the Mach scale negotiate the division of a number of points with one another in a three-person coalition game. In one condition, subjects had to bargain with one another in the absence of any information about their relative power positions in the group; in another condition, this information was available throughout the game. Geis found that high Machs consistently outbargained others, winning a greater number of points than low or "middle" Machs—this effect being particularly pronounced under conditions of informational ambiguity. In a recent interpretation of these findings, Geis (1970) has pointed out that high Machs (in contrast to lows) display a greater ability to test social limits without exceeding them, to opportunistically time their offers to form coalitions, and to initiate and control the group's social structure through the active making and breaking of coalitions.

Christie and Geis (1970b) described a replication of Geis' (1965) study, in which subjects played for greater stakes—the division of $10 instead of a number of points. Once again high Machs won more than lows, bargaining even more successfully when the stakes were tangible and sizable than when they were hypothetical.

Geis, Weinheimer, and Berger (1970) ran subjects in a seven-person "political" bargaining game in which either neutral or emotionally charged issues were the focus of negotiations. No differences in bargaining efficiency emerged between high and low Machs in the neutral issue game; in the emotional issues game, however, high Machs consistently won more than lows. In explanation of these findings, Geis *et al.* suggested that high Machs are better able than lows to exert personal control and restraint over potentially ego-involving aspects of the bargaining process.

Finally, Christie, Gergen, and Marlowe (1970) had high and low Machs play a variant of the PD game against a preprogrammed experimental strategy. For the first 10 trials of the game, subjects played for points; for the remaining trials ("to make things more interesting") they played either for a penny or a dollar a point. High and low Machs did not differ in their frequency of cooperativeness when the game was played for points; however, high Machs were found to behave more cooperatively than lows when the stakes were changed from points to pennies (and even more so when they were changed to dollars). High Machs thus seem willing to cooperate if it is to their advantage (and in this case to the detriment of the experimenter!).

Taken together these findings suggest that high Machs behave like competitive high IOs. Their interest in manipulating and exploiting others is facilitated by a sensitivity and responsiveness to interpersonal cues. They respond rapidly (and often effectively) to changes in the other's behavior and strategy, as well as to variations in situational demands and constraints. Compared to low Machs, highs are far more interested in, and apparently capable of, using interpersonal information (or the lack of this information) to form working hypotheses about the other's true nature, hypotheses which may then be used in the service of systematic exploitation.

Special and Abnormal Populations

Over the course of the last decade, several researchers have attempted to verify the hypothesis that gross differences in personality produce systematic variations in bargaining. Experiments have compared the bargaining behavior of students and criminals; criminals, psychotics, and students; schizophrenics and nonschizophrenics; paranoid and nonparanoid schizophrenics; and so forth. The general, if somewhat vague, conclusion we draw from this diverse collection of experiments is that *bargainers who are "mentally healthy" (relative to some comparison population which is somehow less "healthy") tend to behave like high IOs; their less healthy counterparts behave more like low IOs.* As a number of the following studies suggest, however, this conclusion must be tempered by the presence of several contradictory findings.

Bixenstine and Douglas (1967) placed pathology-free and pathology-indicative subjects (as measured by the MMPI) in a six-person PD game, in which the availability of communication was varied. When communication was prohibited, no differences emerged between the two groups; given that it was allowed, however, pathology-free (normal) subjects, in contrast to pathology-indicative ones, became increasingly cooperative, more frequently using the communication channel to talk about the game and to agree upon a coordinated, collective strategy. Similar findings emerged in a study by Solomon (1962), in which he reported that normals performed better in a tacit coordination game than regressed schizophrenics. Solomon's (1962) study is described a little later in this chapter in greater detail.

Contradicting Bixenstine and Douglas' (1967) finding that normal subjects behave more cooperatively (under certain circumstances) than pathology-indicative ones are the results of two studies. Harford (1965) found that schizophrenics behaved more cooperatively (trustingly) than college students. Knapp and Podell (1968) reported no differences in cooperation between students and psychotics. In this latter experiment, Knapp and Podell had three grossly different subject populations (college students, psychotic mental hospital patients, and criminal inmates of a state prison) play a PD game against a noncontingent cooperative or competitive strategy. When the strategy was competitive, no behavioral differences emerged among the three groups; given a cooperative strategy, however, students and psychotics became increasingly cooperative (although not differentially so), while criminals did not. Supporting Knapp and Podell's report that students are more cooperative than criminals is Berger and Tedeschi's (1969) finding that juvenile delinquents behaved more aggressively than other boys. On the other hand, Scodel and Minas (1960) found that criminals and students did not differ in behavior in the PD game.

Two experimental studies of bargaining behavior in schizophrenic and nonschizophrenic subject populations present contradictory findings. Travis (1965)—in an unpublished study cited in Terhune (1970)—reported that schizophrenic mental patients behaved less cooperatively than nonschizophrenic patients in the PD game. On the other hand, Nichols (1967) found no differences in behavior in a tacit bargaining game.

Presenting a pleasant contrast to the rather murky set of findings that have emerged in the preceding experiments is the work of Leonard Solomon and his colleagues. Solomon has conducted a number of interesting studies relating schizophrenia to bargaining behavior which yield a highly consistent and interpretable pattern of results.

In the earliest of these experiments, Solomon (1962)—in an unpublished manuscript—set out to explore the ability of hospitalized schizophrenics to shift interpersonal perspective. Subjects were pairs of normals, "regressed" schizophrenics (predicted not to leave the hospital in the foreseeable future), and "remitted" schizophrenics (predicted to leave within 6 months). The task consisted of a multitrial tacit coordination game, on each trial of which the incommunicado subjects attempted to match their choices among three colored lights. The criterion of successful coordination was seven successive matches. Solomon found that regressed schizophrenics required a greater number of trials to reach criterion than either remitted patients or normals. The regressed subjects, Solomon pointed out, tended to treat the game as if it were impersonal or a game of chance, and appeared to be less capable of "taking the role of the other."

In order to explore further the nature of the regressed schizophrenics' inability to shift interpersonal perspective, Solomon (1966)—in an unpublished study cited in Fry (1967)—had schizophrenics play the Solomon (1962) coordination game against a confederate of the experimenter. The confederate was programmed to employ either a "tracking" strategy (mimicking the pattern of choices emitted by the subject) or a "cueing" one (in which the confederate attempted to initiate a choice pattern). Successful coordination with a cueing strategy clearly requires a greater ability to take the role of the other than coordination with a tracking one. Subjects in this study were preselected on the basis of their level of adjustment prior to the manifest appearance of schizophrenia (good versus poor premorbid case histories). Solomon found that patients had greater difficulty coordinating (required a greater number of trials to reach criterion) when playing against a cueing than a tracking other; this was especially true of schizophrenics with a poor premorbid history.

Klein and Solomon (1966) ran paranoid and nonparanoid schizophrenics in a variant of the PD game played against an experimental confederate. The confederate first assumed a noncontingently exploitative strategy, then shifted to a conditionally cooperative pattern. Klein and Solomon found that both paranoids and nonparanoids behaved competitively (defensively) in the presence of an exploitative other, but, given a cooperative shift in the other's strategy, paranoids persistently competed, while nonparanoids attempted to cooperatively modify their pattern of play. Paranoids thus appear to be less sensitive and reactive to changes in the other's behavior than nonparanoids.

Harford and Solomon (1969), in an article based on Harford's thesis (1965), set out to see whether the persistent noncooperative behavior of paranoids in the Klein and Solomon (1966) study was due to the nature of the other's prior competitive behavior or to a general cognitive inability on the part of paranoids to adapt to change. Paranoid and nonparanoid schizophrenics played a PD game against a confederate who employed one of two experimental strategies: the "lapsed saint" (a shift from unconditional to conditional cooperation) or the "reformed sinner" (a shift from unconditional competition to conditional cooperation). They found that nonparanoids behaved more exploitatively, overall, than paranoids. Of greater interest was the fact that nonparanoids responded differentially to the two strategies, cooperating more frequently with the "reformed sinner" than with the "lapsed saint"; paranoids cooperated with both strategies.

Finally, one of Solomon's students (Freilich, 1972) had paranoid and nonparanoid schizophrenics play a PD game against a consistently benevolent or malevolent experimental strategy. Paranoids were further classified as being either passive (submissive, constricted, rigidly suspicious, prone to use the defense mechanism of reaction formation) or aggressive (arrogant, aggressively suspicious, prone to use the defense mechanism of projection). She found, overall, that paranoids were more suspicious than nonparanoids. Furthermore, while nonparanoids became less competitive in the presence of a benevolent other, paranoids displayed comparatively far less change in behavior. With respect to the passive–aggressive distinction, Freilich reported that a benevolent experimental strategy led to increased trust in passive paranoids, and to increasing suspicion in aggressives. This latter finding is supported by the results of an earlier PD study of subjects who habitually employ the defense mechanism of projection or reaction formation (Lynch, 1968).

Taken together, Solomon's studies of schizophrenia and bargaining indicate that relatively healthy patients (those who are remitted, those with good premorbid histories, nonparanoids) are more sensitive and responsive to interpersonal cues (like high IOs) than less healthy patients (those who are regressed, those with poor premorbid histories, paranoids), who act more like low IOs.

CONCLUDING COMMENT

The fact that approximately 200 experimental studies have been devoted, at least in part, to an exploration of the relationship between individual difference variables and bargaining is testimony to the importance social psychologists have ascribed to the effects of background and personality. Embedded within this impressively large array of experiments are numerous contradictory findings—many of which we have attempted to reconcile

Table 7–1

Summary of the Individual Differences in Background and Personality that Appear to Lie at Opposite Ends of the Interpersonal Orientation (IO) Continuum

High IOs	*Low IOs*
Older children and college students	Young children
Blacks	Whites
Females	Males
Low risk-takers	High risk-takers
Externals	Internals
Abstract thinkers	Concrete thinkers
Persons high in needs for affiliation and power	Persons high in need for achievement
Cooperators (premeasured)	Competitors (premeasured)
Persons low in authoritarianism	Persons high in authoritarianism
Persons high in internationalism	Persons low in internationalism
Persons high in machiavellianism	Persons low in machiavellianism
"Normals" (remitted schizophrenics, nonparanoids, patients with good premorbid histories)	Abnormals (regressed schizophrenics, paranoids, patients with poor premorbid histories)

through the introduction of a theoretical construct: Interpersonal Orientation.

Although a number of the individual difference variables and findings do not lend themselves readily to an IO interpretation, at least as many do—or so we have argued. The distinction between persons who are high or low in IO has permitted us to organize a collection of what, at first glance, may appear to be a rather peculiar assortment of "odd bedfellows" (see Table 7-1).

Assuming that our interpretation of the evidence has been appropriate, several interesting questions arise. *(1)* What is it about young children, whites, men, high risk-takers, and others that inclines them to behave like low IOs, while their counterparts tend to behave more like high IOs? *(2)* As shown in Table 7-2, why do some high IOs typically behave cooperatively (showing the characteristics of externals, high Naffs, low Fs, etc.), while others behave more competitively (showing the characteristics of high Nepos, high Machs, etc.)? *(3)* Most importantly, by means of what underlying principles may the particular association of odd bedfellows at opposite ends of the IO continuum be best explained? What characteristics, in other words, do the members of these distinct clusters have in common? While answers to these questions are beyond the scope of the present analysis, we believe they clearly warrant further consideration.

Even after partitioning out those findings that can be partially integrated through the IO distinction, one is left with a surprisingly large number of experiments that find no systematic relationship between individual difference parameters and bargaining behavior. This fact may be explained, at least in part, by Terhune's (1970) observation that structural variables seem

Table 7–2

Summary of the Further Distinction of High IOs into Cooperative and Competitive

Cooperative High IOs	Competitive High IOs
Blacks (bargaining with blacks)	Blacks (bargaining with whites)
Persons high in need for affiliation	Persons high in need for power
Externals	Persons high in machiavellianism
Abstract thinkers	
Cooperators (premeasured)	
Persons low in authoritarianism	
Persons high in internationalism	
Females??	

to exert a more prepotent (or at least more visible) effect on what bargainers do to and with one another than do individual difference variables. In our brief discussion of the directions toward which we believe bargaining research should move (Chapter 10), we will consider several alternative conceptual methodological approaches that may better elucidate the role of individual difference variables in the bargaining process.

8

Interdependence

One of the more important distinguishing features of bargaining is the fact that it is a voluntary relationship. Bargainers come together in an attempt to resolve their conflict(s) of interest not because they have to but because they choose to. Each can make a variety of offers and demands, and each is free to leave the relationship—or threaten to do so—at any time. And it is precisely because bargaining is a voluntary relationship that it is also one of mutual dependence, that is, interdependence. In pushing for an agreement that is as personally advantageous as possible, bargainers must be careful not to tear the delicate fabric that binds them together, thereby driving the other away from the relationship and terminating the very process in which both chose to participate in the first place. Bargainers, in short, need each other. Neither can hope to satisfy his own needs and interests in the relationship without the consent of the other.

Although interdependence "bonds" may be said to characterize any true bargaining relationship, both the nature and the strength of these bonds may vary as a function of the explicit or implicit contract formed by the participants and the degree of mutuality of their preferences for reaching agreement. For example, when opposing bargainers have equally strong preferences for reaching agreement, their interdependence bonds are likely to be quite different than when this preference is asymmetrical, as when one party enters into bargaining largely to gain a public platform for his position, rather than to reach agreement on the substantive issues as stake. However, even in this case the parties are rightfully viewed as interdependent, because so long as one finds it desirable to use the exchange as his platform he depends on the other to allow this to occur.

Over the course of the last decade, students of the bargaining process have devoted considerable research attention to variables affecting the nature of bargainers' interdependence and the consequences of particular patterns of interdependence for bargaining effectiveness. Indeed the experimental studies concerned with factors affecting interdependence number in the hundreds. Despite this fact, we know of no attempt to review this massive literature or to consider it in the context of an organizing conceptual framework. It is the purpose of this chapter to present such a framework and to use it as a guide in the review, analysis, and interpretation of the experimental literature.

THE PARAMETERS OF INTERDEPENDENCE IN BARGAINING

Our review of the research concerned with the multitude of variables that affect interdependence leads to the proposal of a rather simple conceptual framework, comprised of three parameters: (1) bargainers' *motivational orientation* (cooperative versus individualistic versus competitive; (2) the distribution of *power* in their relationship (equal versus unequal); and (3) bargainers' *interpersonal orientation* with respect to one another (high versus low). We believe that these parameters, considered singly and in concert or interaction with one another, are likely to exert a profound impact on interdependence and on the effectiveness with which bargainers function.

Motivational orientation (MO) refers most generally to one bargainer's attitudinal disposition toward another and may be usefully described in terms of three extreme cases (following Deutsch, 1960a). A bargainer has a *cooperative* MO to the extent that he has a positive interest in the other's welfare as well as in his own. A *competitive* MO denotes an interest in doing better than the other, while at the same time doing as well for oneself as possible. A bargainer with an *individualistic* MO is simply interested in maximizing his own outcomes, regardless of how the other fares. As Deutsch (1973) has pointed out [p. 182], a number of other motivational orientations can be posited to exist as well. These three MOs are, however, of special interest, both because they represent extreme cases and because they have been the focus of considerable bargaining research.

MO has been systematically varied in a number of ways, including the manipulation of experimental instructions, the introduction of variations in the reward structure of the experiment, the premeasurement of subjects' attitudes, and the introduction of payoff matrix variations. As our subsequent analysis of the literature will suggest, however, regardless of the particular manner in which MO has been varied, *a cooperative MO tends to lead to*

*more effective bargaining than an individualistic, and especially a com-
petitive, MO (Proposition 1).*

Following Thibaut and Kelley's (1959) analysis, "power" refers most generally to the ability of one individual (bargainer) to move another through a
range of outcomes. Thus, the broader the range of outcomes—positive or
negative—through which B can be moved by A, the greater A's power is said
to be. Two or more bargainers have equal power to the extent that each can
move the other(s) through an equivalent range of outcomes. Two or more
bargainers have unequal power to the extent that one can move the other(s)
through a broader range of outcomes than he (they) can move him.

As in the case of MO, the distribution of power in the bargaining relationship has been varied in a number of ways, including the manipulation of the
actual or perceived status of the participants, and the introduction of
variations in experimental reward structure and payoff matrices. In our subsequent analysis of this segment of the literature, we will attempt to demonstrate support for the proposition that *equal power among bargainers tends
to result in more effective bargaining than unequal power (Proposition 2).* In
addition, to anticipate further our discussion of the power parameter, it
appears that support for several related propositions can also be demonstrated. *Under conditions of unequal relative power among bargainers, the
party with high power tends to behave exploitatively, while the less powerful
party tends to behave submissively, unless certain special conditions prevail
(Proposition 3).* In addition, it appears that *the smaller the discrepancy in
bargainers' power, the more effectively they are likely to function (Proposition 4).* Finally, with respect to the total amount of power available to
bargainers, it appears that *the smaller the total amount of power in the
system, the more effectively bargainers are likely to function (Proposition 5).*

The third parameter of interdependence, *Interpersonal Orientation* (IO),
denotes the extent to which bargainers are sensitive to interpersonal aspects
of their relationship with one another. A High IO bargainer is one who has
been so sensitized, and is therefore likely to be especially reactive to variations in the other's behavior. A low IO bargainer, on the other hand, is
relatively insensitive to the interpersonal aspects of his relationship with the
other, and is therefore likely to be less responsive to variations in the other's
behavior.

While we know of no attempts to systematically measure or vary IO per
se, a number of experimental studies have measured or manipulated variables which, in turn, are likely to exert a profound impact on bargainers'
IO. As described in the previous chapter, for example, it appears that the
findings with respect to a great many individual difference variables can be

fruitfully analyzed in relation to their implications for IO. Variations in the availability or use of communication channels, moreover (discussed in Chapter 5), while in no way representing direct manipulations of IO, are nevertheless likely to have an important effect on bargainers' sensitivity to interpersonal cues—since the very act of communication provides each bargainer with information about the other.

Rather than reintroduce individual difference and communication variables for the purposes of the present analysis, however, we will restrict this chapter's discussion of factors affecting IO (and therefore interdependence) to variables that have not been considered elsewhere in the book. These variables include the availability to bargainers of information about the possibility of meeting the other in the future, the other's prior behavior, and the nature of the bargainers' interdependence. Based on our analysis of experiments manipulating variables such as these, we will attempt to demonstrate support for the general proposition that *bargainers who are induced to be high in IO tend to function more effectively than those who are induced to be low in IO (Proposition 6)*.

The preliminary model we have developed with respect to the three parameters of MO, power, and IO may be likened to a complex factorial model. Thus, just as we expect each of the parameters, considered alone, to display a "main effect" in relation to bargaining effectiveness, so too do we expect the three parameters—considered in relation to one another—to display "interaction effects." The interaction propositions we wish to test (but for which empirical evidence is often scant or nonexistent) are as follows:

Bargainers will tend to function most effectively when they share a cooperative MO and are of equal power, functioning least effectively when they share a competitive MO and are again of equal power—MO × Power (Proposition 7).

Bargainers will tend to function most effectively when they share a cooperative MO and are high in IO, functioning least effectively when they share a competitive MO and are again high in IO—MO × IO (Proposition 8).

Bargainers will tend to function most effectively when they are of equal power and high in IO, functioning least effectively when they are of unequal power and are again high in IO—Power × IO (Proposition 9).

Bargainers will tend to function most effectively when they share a cooperative MO, are of equal power, and are high in IO, functioning least effectively when they share a competitive MO, are again of equal power, and are again high in IO—MO × Power × IO (Proposition 10).

Given these three parameters of interdependence, let us now turn to a review and analysis of the experimental literature and consider the extent to which the general propositions we have advanced are indeed supported.

MOTIVATIONAL ORIENTATION (MO)

As suggested earlier, the effects of MO on bargaining have been studied in several ways: by varying the MO subjects are given through experimental instructions, by manipulation of the experimental reward structure, by pre-measurement of subjects' attitudes, and by manipulation of payoff matrices. Studies employing each of these methodologies will be considered in turn.

Variation in MO through Motivational Induction

Almost without exception, experiments in which MO (cooperative, competitive, individualistic) has been varied through experimental instructions have yielded results which indicate that a cooperative MO leads to more cooperation (greater bargaining effectiveness) than either an individualistic or competitive MO.

The earliest and perhaps archetypal study of MO and bargaining was conducted by Deutsch (1958, 1960a). Both members of a pair of subjects were given a cooperative, an individualistic, or a competitive MO, and played a PD game for either 1 or 10 trials in one of several communication and choice simultaneity conditions (i.e., they made their choices simultaneously, sequentially, or with freedom to "reverse"). Deutsch manipulated MO in his instructions to subjects, and because these manipulations have been employed in one form or other in so many subsequent bargaining studies, they are reproduced verbatim below:

Cooperative MO

Before you start playing the game, let me emphasize that in playing the game you should consider yourself to be partners. You're interested in your partner's welfare as well as in your own. You do have an interest in whether your partner wins or loses. You do care how he does and he does care how you do. His feelings make a difference to you and your feelings make a difference to him. You want to win as much money as you can for yourself and you do want him to win. He feels exactly the same way, he wants you to win too. In other words, you each want to win money and you also want your partner to win too [Deutsch, 1960a, p. 130].

Individualistic MO

Before you start playing the game, let me emphasize that in playing the game your *only* motivation should be to win as much money as you can for yourself. You are to have no interest whatsoever in whether the other person wins or loses or in how much he wins or loses. This is *not* a competitive game. You both can win, you both can lose, or one can win and the other can lose. You don't care how he does and he doesn't care how you do. Assume that you don't know each other and that you'll never see each other again. His feelings don't make any difference to you and your feelings don't make any difference to him. You're not out to help him and you're not out to beat him. You simply want to win as much money as you can for yourself and you don't care what happens to him. He feels exactly the same way [Deutsch, 1960a, p. 131].

Competitive MO

Before you start playing the game, let me emphasize that in playing the game your motivation should be to win as much money as you can for yourself and also to do better than the other person. You want to make rather than lose money but you also want to come out ahead of the other person. Assume that you don't know each other and that you'll never see each other again. His feelings don't make any difference to you and your feelings don't make any difference to him. Except that you're out to beat him and he's out to beat you [Deutsch, 1960a, p. 131].

Deutsch found that the MO variable produced sharp differences in subjects' behavior, regardless of the other variables manipulated. Thus, a cooperative MO led to greater cooperation and mutual gain than an individualistic MO, which in turn led to greater cooperation and mutual gain than a competitive MO. Subjects given a cooperative MO, moreover, expected the other to behave more cooperatively than those given an individualistic, and especially a competitive, MO.

Other studies employing the PD game have reported similar findings. For example, Griesinger and Livingston (1973), Kanouse and Wiest (1967), as well as Radlow, Wiedner, and Hurst (1968) used Deutsch's induction to establish a cooperative or competitive MO and found greater cooperation in the former condition than the latter. Alexander and Weil (1969) manipulated MO somewhat differently. Subjects were first shown a list of plays in a 20-trial PD game between "Al" and "Bob." Al's choices were consistently cooperative, while Bob's were consistently competitive. Subjects were then asked to rate Al and Bob on an adjective check list. In one set of experimental conditions, this check list emphasized personal, nongame related traits (PAL), while in the other set of conditions the list emphasized traits that were particularly appropriate in a competitive game situation (PLA). Having completed one of these two check lists, subjects then played a PD game together.

The investigators found that subjects given the PAL list subsequently behaved more cooperatively in the PD game than those given the PLA list. Why? Presumably because the PAL list heightened the salience and virtues of cooperation, while the PLA list enhanced the salience of competition. That this was indeed the effect of the check list manipulation is reflected by the finding that subjects given the PAL list rated Al more positively than Bob, while those given the PLA list did the reverse.

Experiments employing paradigms other than the PD game have yielded similar findings. Crawford and Sidowski (1964), using the "Minimal Social Situation" paradigm, found that subject pairs given a cooperative MO— following Deutsch's (1960a) general procedure—functioned more effectively (made a greater number of correct choices) than those given a competitive MO. Willis and Hale (1963) had subjects engage in a 50-trial coordination game in which, in order to win points, both had to make the same one of three possible choices. Subjects were given one of several versions of a cooperative, individualistic, or competitive MO, manipulated via the experimental instructions. It was found that pairs given a competitive MO had greater difficulty coordinating their choice behavior than those given either a cooperative or an individualistic MO.

Using the Acme–Bolt Trucking game, Deutsch and Lewicki (1970) conducted several experiments in order to assess the conditions under which a strategy of brinksmanship (similar to the one commonly used in the game of "chicken") is likely to prove effective. The availability to subjects of a brinksmanship strategy was manipulated by providing them with a "lock"—a device by means of which a subject's truck could be locked irreversibly in forward gear. In one of the Deutsch and Lewicki "chicken" experiments (the others will be discussed subsequently, in relation to the power parameter), both members of a pair of subjects were given a lock. In addition, subject pairs in some conditions were given a cooperative MO ("social problem-solving" instructions), while others were given a competitive MO ("chicken" instructions). Deutsch and Lewicki found that subjects given the former (cooperative) MO functioned far more effectively than those given the latter. A cooperative MO resulted in significantly fewer collisions, higher joint outcomes, and a smaller difference in outcomes between Acme and Bolt than a competitive MO.

Summers (1968), using a "cognitive conflict" paradigm, selected subjects on the basis of their beliefs about "the determinants of the status of minority citizens," and formed them into pairs with opposite viewpoints. On each of 10 trials, dyads were presented with a history of a hypothetical nation whose educational, economic, and political opportunities for minorities varied. They were asked to discuss each history and record their opinions, both before and after discussion. Subjects were given either a cooperative or "persuasive" MO. In the former, they were to "seek mutually acceptable joint predictions," while in the latter (really a variant of a competitive MO) they were to "convince the other of the merits of one's point of view." Summers found that subjects given a cooperative induction compromised more and showed greater belief change than those receiving a "persuasive" induction.

Finally, Schiavo and Kaufman (1974) had subject triads play a version of the Parcheesi Coalition game. Following Deutsch's (1960a) general procedure, subjects were given either a cooperative or an individualistic MO, or no motivational induction at all. Schiavo and Kaufman found that triads given a cooperative MO behaved more accommodatively than triads in either of the other conditions, forming a greater number of three-way coalitions, and rating both themselves and the others as more cooperative.

Overall, the research cited above lends support to Proposition 1. The three studies that provide exceptions to this general pattern, moreover (finding either no differences as a function of MO or a reversal), each have special characteristics that may help explain their lack of support and that may shed further light on factors that alter the effects of MO.

The first of these studies, conducted by Messick and McClintock (1968), was a test of six types of "decomposed" PD matrices, under two conditions of "interpersonal set" and three conditions of information about own and other's outcomes. Subjects participated in pairs, and interpersonal set was manipulated by characterizing the other player as either "partner" (cooperative MO) or "opponent" (competitive MO) in the experimental instructions. Messick and McClintock found no differences in choice behavior as a function of interpersonal set. Notice, however, the relative weakness of their MO manipulation, in contrast to that used by Deutsch and others. It is perhaps no surprise (as the authors themselves observed) that MO produced no systematic effects.

A related problem is apparent in Gallo's (1966) experiment. Gallo manipulated four variables in a paper-and-pencil version of the Acme–Bolt Trucking game. One of the variables (instructions) was manipulated by informing half of the subjects that they were taking part in a "decision-making" study, in which they were to make as much for themselves as possible, without regard for the other player—individualistic MO; the remaining subjects were told they were participating in a "test of social intelligence," in which "the more 'socially intelligent' an individual is, the more likely it would be that he would win more money than his opponent [p. 17]"—competitive MO. Gallo found no differences in overall joint pay as a function of this instructional variable.

Again, in interpreting these findings of no differences, the strength of Gallo's manipulation may be questioned. Subjects were not told how they *ought* to behave, but rather how people in their role typically *do* behave. Gallo's data, moreover, were based on an unusually small sample—two dyads in each of the 16 experimental conditions in his study—and were collected using a rather artificial version of the original Trucking game. Finally, close inspection of Gallo's data indicates that while there were no overall differences in joint pay, MO did differentially affect pay in the second half of the game, with competitive MO dyads achieving a poorer joint outcome than individualistic pairs.

The only experiment to find a reversal in the effects of MO was conducted by Schenitzki (1963). In this important study, subjects participated in a version of the Bilateral Monopoly game under either "individual goal" or "group goal" conditions. Subjects in the former condition (individualistic MO) were told to maximize their own profits, without regard for the other's outcome; those in the latter condition (cooperative MO) were told to cooperate with their partner to maximize joint profit. Schenitzki found that maximum joint profits were obtained significantly more often by pairs in the individualistic than in the cooperative MO condition. However, this finding emerged only under conditions of no communication. When subjects were permitted to communicate freely, differences as a function of MO disappeared.

In interpreting Schenitzki's findings, we believe it is important to consider the particular experimental paradigm employed. The Bilateral Monopoly game (unlike many other paradigms, such as the PD and Acme–Bolt Trucking games) is ideally suited for the study of opening offers and concession making. Each bargainer, working from his own profit table, typically begins by making an extreme opening offer, which is subsequently followed by concessions, until agreement near the midpoint is reached. When no communication can occur, other than that of an offer or counteroffer, Kelley and Schenitzki (1972) point out that the value of an agreement is directly related to the magnitude of a bargainer's initial offer: the greater the bargainers' initial demands, the more likely they are to attain a maximum joint profit agreement. As it turns out, the individualistic MO bargainers in Schenitzki's study tended to make greater initial demands than did those with a cooperative MO. When free communication was permitted, however, initial differences in the size of opening offers were offset by the availability of communication. Thus, we would argue that the absence of communication, coupled with the particular characteristics of the Bilateral Monopoly game, may have contributed to the reversal reported by Schenitzki. The implications of this important study will be considered in greater detail in Chapter 9.

Variation in MO through Reward Structure

A number of experiments have manipulated MO either by varying the reward structure of the experiment or by coupling this manipulation with a motivational induction. Without exception, these experiments lend support to Proposition 1.

Wallace and Rothaus (1969) had pairs of volunteers from two neuropsychiatric wards play a 10-trial PD game under two MO conditions: half of the subjects were told that the single player who won the most points would win a $2 bonus (competitive MO), while the remaining subjects were told that the group winning the most points (in comparison with other groups) would win a $2 bonus for each player (cooperative MO). In addition, half of the subjects were members of intragroup dyads (both from the same ward) while half were members of intergroup dyads (from different wards). Wallace and Rothaus found that intragroup dyads behaved more cooperatively than intergroup dyads. Moreover, within intragroup dyads those subjects given a cooperative MO behaved more cooperatively than those given a competitive MO.

Gallo and Dale (1968), in a study briefly discussed in Chapter 5, varied reward structure (and MO) by means of a rather interesting and unusual manipulation. Pairs of subjects played a 50-trial PD game and were given choice feedback by the experimenter at the end of each trial. While the experimenter was providing this feedback, he attempted to bias subjects' behavior by varying his facial expression and tone of voice. In half the conditions this bias was in the form of approval for cooperation and disapproval for competition (cooperative MO); in the remaining conditions this bias was reversed (competitive MO).

By biasing subjects' behavior toward cooperation or competition, Gallo and Dale implicitly varied reward structure (and MO), since what was prob-

MOTIVATIONAL ORIENTATION (MO)   207

ably varied at the same time was reward in the eyes of the experimenter. As one might expect, significantly more cooperation emerged in the cooperative bias than in the competitive bias condition.

This same general pattern of findings with respect to reward structure has also emerged in paradigms more complex than the PD game. In a study employing the Acme–Bolt paradigm, Krauss (1966) manipulated reward structure (MO) by introducing bonuses which were either positively or negatively correlated with the other's profits. In cooperative (MO) conditions each subject received a bonus in which 20% of the other player's profits was added to the subject's own profit. In competitive conditions each player had 20% of the other player's losses added to his own profits. Krauss found that subjects given a cooperative MO achieved higher joint outcomes and used their gates less frequently than those given a competitive MO.

In two parallel nonbargaining experiments, Raven and Eachus (1963) and Crombag (1966) had three-person groups participate in a "nonverbal intelligence test," requiring them to level a triangular board as quickly as possible. The triangular board was set on three set screws, so that each subject (sitting at a different table corner) could raise or lower the board levels of the other two by turning his screw. Half of the triads (cooperative MO) were told that their objective should be to level the board as a group, a prize being awarded to the group that succeeded in solving the problem first. In the remaining triads (competitive MO) each subject was told that his objective should be to level his corner of the board before the other two, a prize being awarded to the one group member who could level his corner first. Subjects in both conditions were permitted to communicate freely.

Both Raven and Eachus, and Crombag, found that, in contrast with triads given a competitive MO, those given a cooperative MO required less time to level the board, communicated more frequently, enjoyed the task more, saw the others as facilitating rather than hindering performance, and generally evaluated the others more positively. Groups given a cooperative MO thus functioned more effectively than those given a competitive MO.

Shapira and Madsen (1969), in a four-person board game not unlike the Raven and Eachus paradigm, studied the behavior of Israeli kibbutz and urban children. Subjects were seated around a board on top of which four circles had been drawn, one in front of each subject. A pen mounted to a metal cylinder was located at the center of the board, and had four strings attached to it—each controlled by a different subject. In the "group reward" (cooperative MO) condition, the subjects' task was, by pulling their strings, to draw a line over all four circles within 1 min. If they succeeded in doing this, each would receive a prize. In the "individual reward" (individualistic

MO) condition, on the other hand, the subjects were each assigned a circle and told that a prize would be awarded to each subject whenever a line was drawn through his circle within the 1 min of playing time.

The investigators found no differences in behavior, as a function of MO, for kibbutz children: They performed effectively in either situation. Urban children, however, performed far more effectively in cooperative than in individualistic MO conditions. Those given an individualistic MO appear to have converted a four-way (nonconstant sum) coordination problem into a four-way (constant sum) "tug of war." As a result, few of the urban, individualistic MO children received a prize.

Rubin (1971b) manipulated MO and relative power in a study of the nature and success of influence attempts in a complex four-party bargaining relationship with the following characteristics: The bargaining process in which the four parties (A, B, X, and Y) were engaged was mixed-motive in nature; A and B had equal power, as did X and Y; A and B had greater power than X and Y; A and X were "allied" with each other, as were B and Y, these dyads being each engaged in potentially cooperative relationships; and A and B could interact with each other indirectly, via their respective allies, X and Y; whenever they did, A and B were dependent for the quality of their outcomes on the behavior of X and Y.

An analogy may be drawn, Rubin argued, between a bargaining system with the above characteristics and certain instances of international and familial conflict. For example, it was suggested that the relationships among the USA (A), the USSR (B), Israel (X), and the Arab nations (Y) in the ongoing Middle East crisis—or among Mother (A), Father (B), Son (X), and Daughter (Y) in certain familial conflicts—contain interactional characteristics roughly analogous to this type of four-party system.

Subjects participated in a 20-trial, four-party card game. At the beginning of each trial, A and B had to decide which of two types of games they wished to play on that turn. In one (the "separate pairs" game), A and B could choose to interact directly with each other, while X and Y simultaneously did the same. The number of points each player won or lost was then determined by the color and point value of the cards used in the two dyads. In the second game (the "foursome") A and B could choose to interact via their respective teammates, X and Y. A and B passed cards to X and Y, accompanied by a stated promise or threat if they wished, and the number of points won or lost by the four parties was determined by the color and point value of the cards used by X and Y. X and Y could either use the cards they were passed or use one of their own cards.

Rubin was particularly interested in the effects, upon the use of influence and overall bargaining effectiveness, of A's and B's MO and the relative power of X and Y vis-à-vis their respective allies, A and B. The findings with respect to the latter variable will be discussed subsequently, in the context of the power parameter. MO, however, was varied by manipulating the experimental instructions A and B received, as well as the reward structure of the experiment. Following Deutsch's (1960a) procedure, subjects in the A and B roles were asked to adopt either a cooperative or competitive MO toward each other. In addition, subjects given a cooperative MO were told that their pay would be determined by the number of points they made, with any difference in point totals being subtracted from both A's and B's scores; those given a competitive MO were told that any difference in point totals would be added to the score of the player with the greater number of points and subtracted from the score of the player with the smaller number of points. X and Y, in all conditions, were given an individualistic MO.

Rubin found, as hypothesized, that when A and B were given a cooperative, rather than a competitive, MO: they more frequently invested resources in X and Y that were earmarked for cooperative use; they were more willing to take risks in their investments in X and Y—by passing them high point value cards; they transmitted a greater number of both promises and threats; X and Y behaved more cooperatively; and the total four-party system functioned more effectively, in terms of final outcomes received.

One other relevant study, although not a bargaining experiment per se, was conducted by Jones and Vroom (1964). Pairs of subjects were given the task of solving three 20-piece jigsaw puzzles in succession, in a short period of time. Both members of a pair of subjects had a duplicate set of pieces with which to work. Subjects in cooperative MO condiditions were told that if, between them, all three puzzles were solved, both would receive a monetary reward. Subjects in competitive MO conditions, on the other hand, were told that only one of them (the first person to solve the three puzzles successfully) would receive a reward. Jones and Vroom found that dyads given a cooperative MO displayed greater division of labor, more effective performance, greater liking for their partner, and greater satisfaction with their performance than dyads given a competitive MO.

Variation in MO through Premeasurement of Attitudes

Our review has yielded only four experiments in which MO has been varied by classifying subjects as cooperative, competitive, or individualistic on the basis of a pretest. The findings of each of these studies lend either direct or indirect support to Proposition 1.

McNeel (1973) characterized subjects as having either an "own gain" (individualistic) or "relative gain" (competitive) goal orientation on the basis of their performance in an initial series of PD and "maximizing difference" games. When subjects subsequently played a PD game against a conditionally cooperative other, McNeel found that those with a premeasured individualistic orientation behaved more cooperatively than subjects with a competitive orientation.

Benton *et al.* (1969) conducted a two-person, two-choice card game, in which subjects (in the role of the "recipient") played against an experimental confederate (the "declarer"). At the beginning of each of 64 trials, the recipient and declarer each drew a card from the top of a shuffled deck. After observing the color of his card (black or red), the recipient passed his card to the declarer, who noted the color of the cards and then announced to the recipient that the cards were the same or different in color. The recipient (subject) then stated his acceptance or doubt of the accuracy of the declarer's announcement.

Outcomes in this game were derived as follows: (1) declarer states that the cards are the same in color and the recipient accepts this statement = +2 for the recipient and 0 for declarer; (2) declarer states that cards are the same in color and recipient doubts this statement = +1 for recipient and −1 for declarer; (3) declarer states that the cards are different in color and the recipient accepts this statement = 0 for recipient and +2 for declarer; (4) declarer states that the cards are different in color and the recipient doubts this statement = −1 for recipient and +1 for declarer (if the cards really are different) or = +1 for recipient and −1 for declarer (if the cards really are the same color). Thus, the payoffs were constructed so that cards of the same color favored the recipient, while cards of different color favored the declarer. Doubting by the subject, moreover, resulted in both players being penalized one point in relation to the score of the true state. The expression of doubt or mistrust, in other words, guaranteed a joint loss.

Prior to beginning the game, subjects were asked the following question: "How trustworthy do you believe the other participants will be during the task you are about to begin? [p. 173]." On the basis of subjects' responses, they were classified as either "initially trusting" (cooperative MO) or "initially suspicious" (competitive MO). Benton *et al.* (1969) found that the rate of doubting for cooperative MO subjects was significantly lower than the rate for those with a competitive MO. Of greater importance, in terms of our discussion of bargaining effectiveness, was the finding that joint outcomes were significantly higher when subjects began with a cooperative as compared with a competitive MO.

In two important and ingenious studies of the perception of cooperative and competitive intentions, Kelley and Stahelski (1970a,b) classified subjects as "cooperators" or "competitors" on the basis of their choice of goals prior to participation in a PD game. One of these studies (1970a) has already been described in some detail in Chapter 7. Recall that Kelley and Stahelski found that subjects with an initially cooperative rather than competitive MO more accurately perceived the other's true intentions and chose cooperatively with greater frequency (especially when the other chose cooperatively as well).

In a subsequent, related experiment, designed more specifically to assess the attribution of intentions, Kelley and Stahelski (1970b) asked subjects with an initial premeasured cooperative or competitive MO to make several judgments on the basis of a hypothetical sequence of moves in the PD game. More specifically, after being instructed in the rules of the PD game, subjects were shown a two-trial sequence of moves (the moves by players A and B on trial n and the move by A on trial $n + 1$) and, on the basis of this pattern, were asked to judge why A made the particular choice he did on trial $n + 1$. Subjects were shown a total of eight 2-trial move patterns and were asked to provide judgments with respect to each. These patterns were as follows (where C = a "cooperative" choice, and K = a "competitive" one): C–C, C (i.e., A chooses C on trial n as does B; on trial $n + 1$, A chooses C again); C–C, K; C–K, C; C–K, K; K–C, C; K–C, K; K–K, C; K–K, K.

Kelley and Stahelski (1970b) found that subjects beginning with a cooperative MO, regardless of pattern, displayed greater variance in their expectations of how a typical person would behave than did competitive MO subjects, who more consistently expected a typical person to behave competitively, like themselves. Cooperators thus appeared to have a more realistic view of the world of others—as comprised of both cooperators and competitors—than did competitors. Perhaps of greater interest in terms of the present analysis was the finding that attributions about A's behavior in particular patterns varied as a function of subjects' MO. Thus cooperative MO subjects presented with the C–K, K pattern were more likely than those with a competitive MO to view A's choice on trial $n + 1$ as reflecting a cooperative (but defensive) intention, rather than an unequivocally exploitative one. Similarly, cooperative MO subjects presented with pattern K–K, C were more confident that A's choice on trial $n + 1$ reflected a cooperative intention than were subjects with a competitive MO. In general, subjects with a cooperative rather than competitive MO appear to have been more sensitive to the potential variability of the other's behavior, more aware of the dominating influence of a competitor, and better able to modify their perceptions (and presumably their behavior) accordingly. The effect of a cooperative MO is thus to increase adaptability to changing circumstances and thereby increase the likelihood of effective bargaining.

Variation in MO through Matrix Manipulation

Perhaps the most direct way of varying MO, as we have seen, is by altering the experimental instructions or incentive structure (or both) with which subjects are provided. Another method involves premeasuring subjects' cooperative or competitive goals and relating these to subsequent behavior and perceptions. Still another method of varying MO, we would argue, involves the introduction of systematic manipulations of matrix values. While researchers have typically varied matrix values in order to manipulate the size of perceived or actual conflict in a bargaining relationship, we believe that the effect of such variations has been to manipulate MO indirectly as well. Thus, it seems not unreasonable to argue that matrix variations, by altering conflict size, systematically affect each person's orientation toward the other, as well as his expectation about the other's orientation toward him. More specifically, matrix variations that engender high conflict are likely to induce a competitive MO, while low conflict matrices are more likely to induce a cooperative MO. Therefore, if Proposition 1 is correct, the greater the conflict produced by matrix variations, the more likely a competitive (rather than cooperative) MO should be, and the less likely bargainers should be to function effectively.

Without exception, experimental manipulations of conflict size through matrix variations have employed the PD paradigm or some variant of this game. Recall the general matrix representation of the PD game in Chapter 3, Figure 3-1. If both players choose cooperatively, each receives outcome a; if both choose competitively, each receives outcome d; and if one player chooses cooperatively while the other makes a competitive choice, the former receives outcome b while the latter receives outcome c. By increasing or decreasing the value of one or more of these four outcomes, researchers have attempted to vary the size of conflict. Thus, in order to decrease conflict size, PD researchers have done one or more of the following: increase the reward for mutually cooperative behavior (increase a); increase the reward (decrease the cost) associated with exploitation by the other (increase b); decrease the temptation to defect and behave exploitatively oneself (decrease c); decrease the reward (increase the cost) associated with a mutually competitive choice (decrease d). Conversely, conflict size has been increased by doing one or more of the following: decreasing the value of outcome a, decreasing the value of outcome b, increasing the value of outcome c, increasing the value of outcome d.

Of the 25 studies we have reviewed which have used one or more of the above variations to manipulate conflict size in the PD game, only four report no differences in bargaining effectiveness (Dolbear & Lave, 1966; Kershenbaum & Komorita, 1970; Lave, 1965; Tedeschi *et al.*, 1969b). The remaining 21 experiments, however, have consistently demonstrated that the greater the conflict size, the less effectively bargainers are likely to function in terms of joint outcomes obtained, the frequency of cooperative behavior, liking for the other, and satisfaction with own performance (Aranoff & Tedeschi, 1968; Bixenstine & Blundell, 1966; Ells & Sermat, 1966, 1968; Fisher & Smith, 1969; Guyer, 1968a,b; Guyer & Rapoport, 1969, 1972; Horai *et al.*, 1969; Jones, Steele, Gahagan, & Tedeschi, 1968; Kelley & Grzelak, 1972; Komorita & Mechling, 1967; Lindskold, Bonoma, & Tedeschi, 1969; Miller, 1967; Miller & Pyke, 1973; Oskamp & Perlman, 1965; Scodel, 1962; Steele & Tedeschi, 1967; Terhune, 1968; Worchel, 1969). Given the plausibility of our assumption that the effects of conflict size upon bargaining effectiveness are mediated by the MO which conflict size indirectly shapes, it seems reasonable to conclude that matrix variations that produce low conflict lead to the development of a cooperative MO between bargainers, which in turn may lead to greater bargaining effectiveness than occurs under conditions of high conflict.

Motivational Orientation: Summary

Considered together, the research reviewed in the preceding sections provides substantial support for Proposition 1. Regardless of the particular method by which MO has been varied, it appears that a cooperative MO leads to more effective bargaining than an individualistic, and especially than a competitive, MO. Indeed, 44 of the 51 studies reviewed lend partial or complete support to this conclusion.

POWER

The effects of the distribution of power upon bargaining effectiveness have been assessed in two primary ways: by varying the actual or perceived status of the parties, or by varying experimental reward structure or payoff matrices. It should be obvious that both methodologies conform to Thibaut and Kelley's (1959) definition of power in terms of the range of outcomes (positive and/or negative) through which one person can be moved by another. Status variations represent indirect manipulations of relative power, inasmuch as they vary the power each party believes he (and the other) can, or is entitled to, exercise. Similarly, reward structure and matrix variations have been used to manipulate the distribution of power, by directly varying either the initial allocation of resources among the parties or the ability to help or hinder the other or both. Studies employing each of these methodologies will be considered in the following sections, in the context of the particular power proposition to which they pertain.

The Effect of Equality versus Inequality of Power

Of the 27 experimental studies we have reviewed, 19 provide unequivocal support for Proposition 2, five report no differences as a function of power equality, and three report findings in the opposite direction—with equal power bargainers functioning less effectively than those with unequal power.

Status Variations

Rekosh and Feigenbaum (1966) and Faley and Tedeschi (1971) manipulated status in the PD game and had subjects play against an experimental confederate. In the first study, status was varied by informing subjects that the other was either a peer (another undergraduate) or a graduate student. Subjects in the Faley and Tedeschi experiment were ROTC cadets; status was varied by selecting subjects who were high or low in ROTC cadet rank and leading them to believe they had been paired with another of equal or different rank.

Rekosh and Feigenbaum found that subjects made cooperative choices with greater frequency when playing against a peer (with equal power) rather than a graduate student (with higher relative power). Similarly, Faley and Tedeschi found that high status subjects behaved more cooperatively when the other was also of high rather than lower status; and low rank cadets behaved more cooperatively—although not significantly so—when the other was also of low rather than higher status.

In a similar, more recent experiment, Baranowski and Summers (1972) had subjects play a PD game against a fictitious other who was described as being of equal status (another undergraduate) or higher status (a member of the faculty). Subjects in the former group chose cooperatively more often, and showed a greater tendency to reciprocate the other's cooperation, than those in the latter condition.

Using a paper-and-pencil version of the Acme–Bolt Trucking game, Borah (1963) varied status by informing both members of some dyads that they were playing against another like themselves; the remaining subjects were led to believe that the other considered himself to be superior and of higher status. As one might expect, given the apparent illegitimacy of the other's "assertion" of superiority in the latter condition, Borah found that dyads functioned more effectively when status was equal rather than unequal. Thus, subjects in the equal status condition achieved higher median and joint outcomes and lost less time in deadlock than those in the unequal status (low relative power) condition.

The one experiment finding no differences in bargaining effectiveness as a function of status was conducted by Lindskold, Gahagan, and Tedeschi (1969). Subjects played a PD game against an experimental strategy, either alone or in groups of three. As in the previously cited study by Tedeschi and his colleagues, status was varied by preselecting subjects on the basis of their ROTC rank. In one condition, triads were formed that consisted of an ROTC officer and two subordinates of equal rank. Subjects in this condition were told to indicate privately their preferred choices before each trial, and to discuss their choices before making a collective decision—the officer being empowered to make the decision in case of conflict. In a second condition, triads consisted of three equal rank cadets, and each triad was told to find its own method for making a collective choice decision before each trial. In the third condition, subjects (in this case non-ROTC students) played alone against the experimental strategy.

Lindskold, Gahagan, and Tedeschi found no differences in the frequency of cooperative choice as a function of group size and relative status. In particular, equal status triads were no more likely to choose cooperatively than those whose members had unequal status. Note, however, that status was varied not between bargainers (as in the four other studies), but within a bargaining team. Moreover, the lack of differences observed between the two triad conditions may have been attributable not to the insignificance of the status variable, but to some other source—the fact, for example, that the decision-making process was structured differently in the two conditions.

Reward Structure and Matrix Variations

Most of the studies to vary power equality (22) have done so by manipulating either payoff matrices or experimental reward structure. Of these studies, 15 lend support to Proposition 2, four report no differences as a function of power equality, and three indicate a reversal.

Several of the studies whose findings lend support to Proposition 2 have employed the PD paradigm. Deignan (1970), McClintock *et al.* (1973), Sheposh and Gallo (1973), Solomon (1960), Swingle (1970a), and Tedeschi, Lindskold, *et al.* (1969) each had subjects play variants of the PD game in which power was varied by manipulating matrix values. Thus, matrices in which the outcomes to both players were symmetrical were contrasted with those in which outcomes favored one player over the other. In general, the findings of these studies indicate that bargainers with equal power behave more cooperatively (make a cooperative choice with greater frequency) than those with unequal power.

Similar findings have emerged in PD studies in which power has been varied not by manipulating matrix values but by differentially allocating initial resources or control over the experimental situation. Pepitone, Maderna *et al.* (1970) initially awarded $2 to only one player (unequal power) or $2 to neither (equal power) and found greater cooperation in the latter condition than the former. Similarly, Aranoff and Tedeschi (1968) awarded one member of a pair of subjects an initial advantage of 0, 25, 50, 100, or 500 points. They found that the greater the magnitude of a subject's advantage, the lower the frequency of mutual cooperation. Finally, Swingle and Mac-Lean (1971) permitted one player, neither, or both players in a PD game to suspend play for a period of time. The presence of unilateral (unequal) power resulted in less cooperation than did either of the equal power conditions.

Support for Proposition 2 has also been obtained using paradigms more complex and interesting than the PD. Deutsch and Krauss (1960), for example, in their original Acme–Bolt Trucking studies, varied relative power by providing one member, neither, or both members of a bargaining pair with a "gate." Since a gate may be used to move the other through a negative range of outcomes, to be in possession of a gate is to be "in power."

Notice that the gate manipulation is more conceptually complex than might appear at first glance. Thus, Deutsch and Krauss' single independent variable, number of gates (0, 1, or 2), may be perhaps more appropriately considered as two variables: equality of power (0 and 2 gates versus 1 gate) and amount of power (0 gates versus 1 gate versus 2 gates). The findings with respect to the latter variable will be considered subsequently, in the context of Proposition 5. The variable of power equality, however, is clearly relevant to the present discussion.

While Deutsch and Krauss were not explicitly interested in the effects of power equality upon bargaining effectiveness, their data nevertheless permit us to draw tentative inferences with respect to this variable. Thus, the finding that the mean joint payoff was 203.31 (¢) in the 0-gate condition, −405.88 in the 1-gate condition, and −875.12 in the 2-gate condition, leads us to conclude that mean joint outcomes and bargaining effectiveness were greater when bargainers had equal power (0 or 2 gates) rather than unequal power (1 gate)—means of −335.90 and −405.88, respectively. Whether these means are significantly different, of course, cannot be determined from their data, although their direction certainly lends support to Proposition 2.

Deutsch and Lewicki's (1970) Acme–Bolt study of the game of "chicken" can be analyzed similarly. Recall that subjects in this experiment were provided with a "lock"—a device that can irreversibly lock one's own truck in forward gear. Deutsch and Lewicki had pairs of subjects play either a 1-trial or a 20-trial game in one of three conditions: 0 locks, 1 lock, or 2 locks. The mean joint payoffs for the 1-trial game were as follows: 0 locks = − 3.5 cents, 1 lock = − 12.6¢, 2 locks − 16.3¢. Thus, outcomes were greater (less negative) under equal (0 locks and 2 locks combined) than under unequal power conditions—although Deutsch and Lewicki did not test for the significance of this difference. Consideration of the 20-trial game data leads to an identical conclusion: Pairs with equal power attained higher joint payoffs than those with unequal power.

In a rather ingenious version of the Acme–Bolt Trucking game, Swingle (1968a) provided each of a pair of subjects with a model train and asked each to try to beat the other through a single "train tunnel." Relative power was manipulated by varying the speed of subjects' trains. In one of three experimental conditions ("absolute power"), one subject had complete control over the attainment of his goal; in the second ("illusory power"), one subject had more power than the other but the weaker player "retained power to inflict mutual loss"; in the third condition, subjects had equal power. Swingle found that equal power pairs established a pattern of cooperative alternation significantly sooner than those in which one player had absolute or illusory power. Equal power pairs thus bargained more effectively than those with unequal power.

Komorita and Barnes (1969) tested the effects of relative power in the Bilateral Monopoly game. The cost of making an offer was varied so that the cost was $2 for the buyer and 0 for the seller, 0 for buyer and $2 for seller, $2 for both, or 0 for both. Thus power was equal in two of the conditions (2–2 and 0–0) and unequal in the others (2–0 and 0–2). As in the Deutsch and Krauss, and Deutsch and Lewicki experiments, Komorita and Barnes were primarily interested in the effects of amount of power. Their data, however, permit us to reach several tentative conclusions about the effects of equality of power. Thus, Komorita and Barnes found that pairs with equal power (2–2 and 0–0) reached agreement more often, required fewer trials to do so, and made larger concessions than those with unequal power (2–0 and 0–2). Note that it was pairs in the low equal power condition (2–2) that functioned most effectively overall—not unlike the 0-gate and 0-lock pairs in the Trucking experiments.

A final study in support of Proposition 2 was conducted by Kelley, Beckman, and Fischer (1967), using Kelley's rich and interesting "Game of 9's." This game consists of three participants: two players (subjects) and a dealer (experimenter). The players' task, on each turn, is to reach agreement about the division of 9 points (9–0, 8–1, 7–2, 6–3, 5–4, etc., with point splitting not permitted). In order to make a profit on any turn, however, each player's share of an agreement must be greater than a certain "break-even" value, or *Minimum Necessary Share* (MNS). A player's MNS on each turn is determined by a card, ranging in value from 1 to 9, which he is passed by the dealer. Thus, depending on the MNS card he receives, a player can be placed in a relatively difficult or advantageous position with respect to reaching agreement. A player may say anything he wishes about his MNS cards but may not show them to the other at any time. Finally, each player can unilaterally terminate negotiations at any point, in which case both he and the other receive a score of 0 on that turn.

Of the several independent variables studied by Kelley *et al.*, one is of particular importance for the present discussion—the relative value of the MNS cards given to subjects by the experimenter. On some problems (trials), subjects were given equal MNS cards, while on others one subject had a lower (more advantageous) MNS card than the second. The investigators found that on equal-MNS problems, subjects required less time to reach agreement and quit the relationship less frequently than they did on unequal-MNS problems. Thus, once again it appears that equal power results in more effective bargaining than does unequal power. (The findings of Kelley *et al.* have been replicated in a more recent study by Holmes, Throop, & Strickland, 1971.)

Standing in direct contrast to the findings of the preceding studies are several experiments that have reported either no differences as a function of power equality, or a reversal. Perhaps most damaging to the plausibility of Proposition 2 are the latter studies, and we will therefore consider them first.

Komorita, Sheposh, and Braver (1968) and Tedeschi, Bonoma, and Novinson (1970b) conducted PD experiments in which it was found that subjects in unequal power conditions made cooperative choices with greater frequency than those with equal power. Komorita, Sheposh, and Braver manipulated relative power by introducing a third choice into a modified PD matrix which resulted in greater loss to the other than to oneself. Depending on the particular condition, this choice was made available to either one or both players. Tedeschi, Bonoma, and Novinson varied relative power by permitting subjects in some conditions to unilaterally threaten and punish the other (a confederate); in other conditions, subjects were informed that both players had this capability.

Given the findings of the original Deutsch and Krauss (1960) research—namely, that the 2-gate (bilateral threat) condition resulted in lower joint outcomes than the 1-gate (unilateral threat) condition—the results of these two PD studies should come as no surprise. Note, however, that two variables—equality and amount of power—were implicitly manipulated. It is therefore unclear whether the obtained results were due to one, the other, or both variables. And while it is at least possible to estimate the effect due to power equality in the Deutsch and Krauss experiments—by comparing the 0-gate and 2-gate conditions with the 1-gate condition—such a comparison cannot be made in these two studies, since only two conditions were studied.

The other experiment to report greater cooperation in unequal than equal power conditions was conducted by Cheney (1969), using the Acme–Bolt Trucking game. According to Cheney, two types of power relationships were established between Acme and Bolt: equal, "wherein both players had the same amounts of control over their own and the other player's earnings [p. 2146]" and unequal, "wherein one player had the ability to partially determine the other's wins or losses [p. 2146]." Unfortunately the summary of Cheney's procedure does not explain in any detail the particular way in which "control over earnings" was manipulated. It is therefore impossible to consider the implications of his findings for Proposition 2.

Let us now briefly consider the four studies that reported no differences as a function of power equality. Schellenberg (1964) had pairs of subjects play a PD game using a symmetrical (equal power) or asymmetrical (unequal power) matrix. While he found no significant differences in frequency of cooperative choice as a function of power, it is perhaps noteworthy that the means fell in the direction predicted by Proposition 2: Pairs in the symmetrical condition behaved cooperatively more often than those in the asymmetrical condition.

Hornstein (1965) tested the effects of threat potential in a version of the Bilateral Monopoly game. Pairs of subjects participated in a "real estate" game in which agreement had to be reached with the other about "the number of acres and the cost per acre to be used in the sale of a piece of land [p. 283]." Relative power was manipulated by varying each subject's "threat potential"—the percentage by which each could reduce the other's profits on a turn. Six conditions were run, in which the threat potential (power) available to bargainers was as follows: 90–90, 50–50, 10–10, 90–10, 50–10, or 20–10. Note that subjects had equal power in the first three conditions and unequal power in the others.

Hornstein's experiment permits consideration of a number of issues with respect to the distribution of power: the effects of equality versus inequality, the effects of total amount of power in the system, and the effects of discrepancy in power. His findings with respect to the two latter issues will be discussed subsequently. With respect to the effects of power equality, Hornstein found no significant overall differences in bargaining effectiveness. However, inspection of his mean data indicates a pattern lending tentative support to Proposition 2. Thus, pairs with equal power (90–90, 50–50, and 10–10) tended to obtain higher profits and reach agreement more often than those with unequal power (90–10, 50–10, and 20–10).

Graeven (1970) investigated the effects of relative power on the resolution of intergroup conflict. Subjects observed a discussion between two groups concerning the legalization of marijuana and were then asked to represent one of the groups in negotiation with a spokesman for the other position. Graeven reported no differences, as a function of relative power, in subjects' "role expectations" or "behavioral intentions." Unfortunately, as in the Cheney (1969) experiment, the reader is given no idea of the manner in which power equality was varied, hence it is unclear how to interpret the reported findings.

Finally, Kelley, Shure *et al.* (1970) examined the effects on bargaining effectiveness of several variables, in the "International Card" game (briefly described in Chapter 6). Relative power was manipulated by varying the "independent value" cards subjects were given, where the independent value referred to the outcome a subject could receive by terminating the bargaining relationship on any turn. Half the subject pairs received cards which were equal in value, while the remaining pairs received cards distributed so that one player had higher values (higher power) than the other. Kelley and his colleagues hypothesized that unequal power would "interfere with the establishment and maintenance of agreements and would act to the detriment of the pair's outcomes [p. 416]." This hypothesis was not supported, however; the conditions did not differ in their disruptive effects.

One possible explanation for this finding of no differences has been suggested by the authors themselves, and relates to the structure of the experimental task. Subjects were led to believe that their independent value cards had been determined randomly, although in fact they were not. Moreover, while the subjects could say anything they wished about their cards, they were never permitted to show them to each other. Thus, the subjects had every reason to believe that the other's independent value cards were comparable to their own and had no way to ascertain that in some conditions the other was either more or less powerful than themselves. Therefore the lack of differences as a function of power may have been attributable to subjects' insensitivity to the distribution of power in their relationship.

Equality of Power: Summary

While the evidence in support of Proposition 2 is less conclusive than that obtained with respect to the first proposition, it nevertheless appears that equal power among bargainers is generally likely to result in more effective bargaining than is unequal power. As has already been pointed out, however, the power parameter is complex, and its component effects are difficult to tease out from the array of studies in which variables other than equality alone have been manipulated. It is to a consideration of these other power variables that we now turn.

The Effect of Power Inequality on the Behavior of the Participants

We have already seen, in support of Proposition 2, that an unequal distribution of power generally results in less effective bargaining, overall, than does an equal distribution. Unequal power, moreover, appears to affect differentially the behavior of the more powerful and less powerful parties. Bargainers with high power relative to that of their adversary tend to behave manipulatively and exploitatively, while those with low relative power tend to behave more submissively (Proposition 3).

Our review of the literature has uncovered 28 studies, each of which is addressed, directly or indirectly, to Proposition 3. These studies vary considerably in the paradigms they have employed, the manner in which relative power has been varied, and the particular way in which the consequences of power inequality have been assessed. The studies have varied, moreover, in the extent to which they have considered the consequences of power inequality from the vantage point of one party only (the one with either greater power or lesser power) or from the vantage points of both. Rather than review each of these diverse studies in detail, we shall instead briefly summarize their findings with respect to Proposition 3.

Four experiments have reported either that high power bargainers behave more cooperatively (less exploitatively) than those with lower power (Garfield, 1970; Marwell et al., 1969; Schellenberg, 1964) or that no differences exist as a function of role (Motivans, 1968). The remaining 24 studies, however, provide direct or indirect support for Proposition 3.

Thirteen of these experiments have employed the PD game or some variant of this paradigm and have reported support for the proposition in terms of: frequency of cooperative choice (Burrill, 1968; Gahagan & Tedeschi, 1969; Grant & Sermat, 1969; Johnson & Ewens, 1971; Pepitone, Maderna *et al.*, 1970; Scodel, 1961; Stevens, 1970; Swingle, 1970a; Tedeschi *et al.*, 1969d; Thibaut & Gruder, 1969; Wiley, 1969); compliance with threat by the low power party (Faley & Tedeschi, 1971); or scores on a scale of "exploitation–accommodation" (Murdoch, 1968). Four Acme–Bolt experiments have provided support for Proposition 3, in terms of choice and outcomes (Cheney, 1969; Deutsch & Krauss, 1960; Deutsch & Lewicki, 1970; Swingle, 1968a), as have four studies employing some variant of the Bilateral Monopoly paradigm. Two of these latter experiments measured choice and concessions (Komorita & Barnes, 1969; Silver, 1969), one measured threat use (Hornstein, 1965), and the fourth assessed compliance with threat by the less powerful party (Michener & Cohen, 1973).

Support for Proposition 3 is also evident in more complex paradigms. Kelley *et al.* (1967), using Kelley's Game of 9's, found that bargainers with high power obtained higher profits than those with lower power, with the latter tending to quit the relationship more frequently. Similarly, Kelley, Shure *et al.* (1970) found, in the International Card game, that the high power party obtained greater profit and employed threat more often than his less powerful adversary. Finally, Hermann and Kogan (1968) report that bargainers with low power were more willing to compromise (in a group discussion task) than those with higher power.

It appears in general that power inequality tends to induce, or be related to, dominant or exploitative behavior on the part of the more powerful bargainer and submissive behavior (or attempts at withdrawal) by the weaker. There are certain conditions, however, under which power inequality is likely to have rather different consequences. In particular, consider the situation in which three or more bargainers are involved, at least two of the parties view themselves as relatively disadvantaged with respect to obtaining some outcome, and these less powerful parties do not consider it fruitless to join together in the collective pursuit of the outcomes they seek. Under these conditions we might expect the less powerful parties to form a coalition and resist the demands of their more powerful adversary, rather than submit to them. Indeed, as the coalition literature makes abundantly clear (see the review of this material in Chapter 4), unless the less powerful parties believe that their resources are simply insufficient to offset those of the more powerful, unless the latter is able to block the formation of alliances, or unless the conflict among potential coalition partners is sufficiently intense, coalitions are likely to form, thereby offsetting an initial power disadvantage and transforming submission into resistance. The generalization suggested by Proposition 3 is therefore likely to hold only, or especially, when conditions favorable to the formation of coalitions among the less powerful do not exist.

The Effect of Variations in the Extent of Power Discrepancy

Bargainers, we have seen, tend to function more effectively when they jointly possess equal rather than unequal power (Proposition 2). Unequal power, moreover, tends to result in an asymmetric distribution of outcomes, in which the party with higher power behaves exploitatively, while the less powerful party behaves submissively—unless the possibility of coalition formation exists (Proposition 3). Given the support for both propositions, it stands to reason that the greater the discrepancy between bargainers' power, the less effectively they are likely to be able to function as a unit. Expressed in other words, the more closely the bargaining relationship approximates one of power equality, the more bargaining effectiveness should increase (Proposition 4).

In order to test the validity of Proposition 4 it is obviously necessary to examine those experimental studies in which the degree of power discrepancy in the bargaining relationship has been systematically varied. Of the nine studies we have reviewed, seven indicate support for our proposition, while two indicate that the smaller the discrepancy in power, the less effective bargaining is likely to be. The findings with respect to each of these experiments will be considered in turn.

Aranoff and Tedeschi (1968) had pairs of subjects play a 200-trial PD game in which one player, chosen at random, was awarded either no initial advantage or an initial advantage of 25, 50, 100, or 500 points. As the size of this initial advantage (power discrepancy) decreased, the authors found, the frequency of mutual cooperation increased. Solomon (1960), in an earlier PD experiment (first reported in Deutsch, 1958), had subjects play a six-trial game against a simulated other. On each of the first five trials, the subject chose first and announced his choice before the other made his move. Power inequality was manipulated by providing subjects with one of four game matrices, which differed in the extent to which the subject's payoffs were dependent upon the other's choice. Solomon found that as power inequality decreased, subjects were more likely both to expect trustworthy behavior on the part of the other and to make a trusting (cooperative) choice themselves.

A rather different source of support for Proposition 4 flows out of the work of John Thibaut and his colleagues. Thibaut has argued (1968) that when one bargainer (P) has greater control over the division of outcomes than another (X), P will be tempted to become exploitative, thereby threatening X (an "internal threat" to the relationship). On the other hand, when X has available a highly attractive alternative to his relationship with P, X will be tempted to become disloyal by quitting the relationship, thereby threatening P (an "external threat" to the relationship). Thus, P and X each have access to a form of power which they can exercise if they choose: P has control over the outcomes in the relationship, while X has control over the continuation of the relationship. When one bargainer possesses power while the other does not, Thibaut suggests, the result is likely to be ineffective bargaining, manifested either by exploitation or withdrawal. However, it is when *both* forms of power are present in the relationship, when power is both high *and* relatively equal that, paradoxically, bargainers are likely to function most effectively. Why? Because each party may be threatened by the choice that the other is tempted to make, which in turn increases the likelihood that a contract (or set of rules) will be developed which explicitly forbids such threatening behavior. Each side agrees to forego the use of power, and bargaining effectiveness is likely to result.

In one of the earliest tests of this intriguing and important hypothesis, Thibaut and Faucheux (1965) randomly assigned pairs of subjects to each of two positions (P and X) and had them play a nine-trial, face-to-face matrix game. Subjects were told to compete not with each other but with other subjects in the same power position as themselves. On each trial, subjects were to bargain over the division of points represented in the two-choice possibilities of a 2 x 2 game matrix. After reaching tentative agreement in open discussion, each subject recorded his actual decision about what he would play, scores were announced, and the next trial began. Each trial presented subjects with the choice of either bargaining over the division of points (in which case player P was permitted to determine, within limits, the allocation of points) or taking an "external alternative" (which guaranteed the subjects a fixed number of points).

On each of the last three trials, subjects were permitted, although not required, to form contractual agreements governing their own and the other's behavior. If they wished, subjects could invoke one or more of three predetermined rules on these trials. The two which concern us here are the EA-rule: "It is prohibited to play the external alternative on this trial if a tentative agreement has been reached to play within the matrix [p. 94]" and the D-rule: "If on this trial a tentative agreement has been reached concerning the division and distribution of points between the partners, it is prohibited in the actual play to change the distribution agreed upon [p. 94]."

Power was manipulated in this experiment by varying (1) the number of points P could take for himself whenever P and X bargained over the division of outcomes in the matrix ("internal threat") and (2) the number of points X (and/or P) could receive by taking the external alternative ("external threat"). Thibaut and Faucheux found that exploitation by P was most likely to occur when P had high power with respect to the division of outcomes while X had low power (a relatively unattractive external alternative), that is, when the discrepancy in power was large. Of greater interest and importance was their finding that contracts were most likely to be formed, especially contracts containing both the EA and D rules, when both subjects had high and relatively equal power. That the formation of contracts was in turn related to bargaining effectiveness is reflected by the finding that, over trials, contractual dyads displayed a significantly greater reduction in the discrepancy between the outcomes to P and X than dyads that did not form contracts. Thus, it was when both players had the capability of threatening the other that rules were invoked which served to regulate the conflict and increase bargaining effectiveness.

Subsequent "contractual norm" research has lent additional support to the findings of Thibaut and Faucheux. Thibaut, Gruder, and Wells (in an experiment described in Thibaut, 1968), had two dyads play the Thibaut and Faucheux game against each other, with one member of each dyad serving as spokesman. They found, as before, that conflict regulating contracts were formed most frequently when both dyads had high and relatively equal power. Thibaut and Gruder (1969), similarly, in another double dyad experiment, found that contracts were likely to form when the discrepancy in the parties' power was relatively small. As Thibaut and Gruder conclude: "When mutual threat is high and credible, the contractual agreements are reached through mutual recognition by the parties that contracts provide and will enforce an exchange of threat reduction [p. 64]."

In yet another replication and extension of the Thibaut and Faucheux research, Murdoch (1967) manipulated power (or threat) discrepancy by varying the *perceived* exploitativeness and disloyalty of P and X in a two-person game. Prior to beginning the game, X was given "evidence" that P was either fair or exploitative, and P was provided with evidence that X was either loyal or disloyal. Murdoch found as hypothesized that pairs were most likely to form contracts to their mutual advantage when P was portrayed as exploitative, and X as disloyal. Thus, regardless of whether threat is manipulated by varying the structure of the game or the concomitant perception of the other, the presence of high power coupled with a relatively small discrepancy in power appears to lead to more effective bargaining than does a relationship characterized by a larger power discrepancy.

One final experiment lending at least partial support to Proposition 4 was conducted by Vitz and Kite (1970). Subjects were asked to imagine that they were the representatives of two different hypothetical nations that had to band together in an alliance in order to deter an external threat. In order to deter this threat, subjects had to make contributions to a "defense fund." If the size of the threat proved to be greater than the defense fund, the players would lose everything and the game would end. If, on the other hand, the alliance of players succeeded in maintaining a defense fund greater than the "threat," each player would get to keep whatever resources he had left at the end of the game. This two-person, mixed-motive game ("Crisis") consisted of a total of five trials.

In order to study some of the conditions affecting conflict within an alliance that has already formed, Vitz and Kite manipulated the discrepancy in resource strength (power) among the two subjects. Four experimental discrepancy conditions were created, defined in terms of the difference between the proportion of total resources controlled by the two players: .04, .31, .57, .84. Thus, in all conditions one subject had greater power than the other, but the magnitude of this inequality was systematically varied. Vitz and Kite found that the amount of conflict in the subjects' relationship (as measured by postexperimental questionnaire ratings and content analysis of communication between subjects about the allocation of resources) was greater in the .31 than in the .04 discrepancy condition, lending apparent support to Proposition 4. It was also found, however, (as the experimenters hypothesized) that as power discrepancy increased beyond .31 (.57 and .84 conditions), conflict *decreased*. Thus conflict within the alliance was greater when power discrepancy was intermediate in size than when it was either very small or very large.

Vitz and Kite interpreted these findings by suggesting that conflict size in a power discrepant relationship varies as a function of two parameters: the importance of the discrepancy (the greater the discrepancy, the greater its importance); and the pressure to reduce the discrepancy (where, following Festinger's, 1954, social comparison theory, the greater the discrepancy the less the pressure to reduce it). Multiplicative combination of the predictions for these two parameters then leads to a model which predicts that conflict should be greatest under conditions of moderate discrepancy in power.

While the above prediction is both provocative and persuasive, in light of the experimental support it received its applicability to Proposition 4 should be tempered by at least two considerations. First, the Vitz and Kite study was structured in such a way that social comparison processes were likely to be of special importance. Subjects were not explicitly competing with each other, as is often the case in bargaining relationships. Rather they were members of an alliance, asked to work together for a common goal of mutual importance. The comparability of the other's resources with one's own was thus likely to be a more salient issue in subjects' eyes than is perhaps typical of most bargaining relationships. Second, and perhaps of greater importance, the Vitz and Kite study provides no direct measure of bargaining effectiveness. While it seems not unreasonable to expect the amount of conflict in a relationship to be inversely related to bargaining effectiveness, it is impossible to assess the plausibility of this expectation by inspection of the Vitz and Kite data. Bargaining effectiveness, per se, was simply not assessed.

In addition to the Vitz and Kite study, which provides only partial support for Proposition 4, there are two experiments that report a reversal. In three of the six conditions in Hornstein's (1965) previously described study, power was unequal and the degree of discrepancy was varied (90–10, 50–10, 20–10). Hornstein found that the greater the discrepancy in subjects' threat potential, the higher the joint profits attained and the greater the number of agreements concluded. In explanation of this unexpected finding, he suggested that "bargainers' threat potentials acted as cues that facilitated or hindered them in their efforts to come to an agreement [p. 291]." Thus, when the discrepancy in threat potential was large, subjects were able to use this information to agree on the share of the profits that each player would receive. When the power discrepancy was small, on the other hand, the information provided about the allocation of resources was less useful. As Hornstein points out: "The ambiguity regarding who should acquiesce and who should receive what share of the profits interfered with the negotiations and resulted in fewer agreements as well as less profits [pp. 291–292]."

Our interpretation of Hornstein's findings is somewhat different. As the experimenter himself observed, profits and losses in this game were fictional, and subjects may therefore have been relatively uninvested in the quality of their outcomes. Ordinarily one might expect an increasing discrepancy in power to lead to a heightening of concerns with intangible issues and to be accompanied by exploitation on the part of the stronger party and submission on the part of the weaker (unless resistance is possible). In the absence of real monetary incentives, however, one might expect these same concerns to be minimized, with an increasing power discrepancy acting not as the source of greater conflict in the relationship but as a source of information about the manner in which resources should be allocated. We suspect, in other words, that were Hornstein's study to be replicated using real rather than fictional outcomes, the results would turn out rather differently and might even lend further support to Proposition 4.

The other experiment to report a reversal of findings as a function of power discrepancy was conducted by Rubin (1971b), and has already been described in some detail. The relative power of X and Y vis-a-vis their respective allies, A and B, was manipulated by varying the cards (resources) X and Y were given. A and B, in all conditions, were given pairs of red and black cards from Ace through 10. X and Y, however, were given pairs of red and black cards either from Ace through 3 (high discrepancy, or low counterpower, conditions) or from 5 through 7 (low discrepancy, or high counterpower, conditions). Note that in both conditions, A and B had greater power than X and Y, although the magnitude of this power discrepancy was varied.

Rubin found as hypothesized that when the power discrepancy in favor of A and B was small, X and Y were less likely to use the cards invested in them by A and B; A and B, in turn, were more likely to accompany the cards sent to X and Y with a promise or threat message. In general, the four-party system functioned more effectively when the power discrepancy was large rather than when it was small.

In order to understand the meaning of Rubin's findings with respect to Proposition 4, it is important to bear in mind that his experiment examined bargaining in an unusually complex relationship. The fact that four parties rather than two were interconnected permitted a variety of alliances and loyalties to develop. X and Y could, if they wished, band together to resist A and B's influence attempts. Indeed they were far more likely to do this when the discrepancy in power was relatively small, leading A and B to transmit a greater number of promises and threats in this condition, perhaps in the belief that X and Y needed to be persuaded via reward and punishment. We suspect that X and Y would have been far less resistant, under conditions of low power discrepancy, had they *not* been permitted to band together. Rubin's findings, in other words, may have been due to the particular properties of his experimental paradigm—a paradigm rather different and more complex than the ones that have been employed traditionally.

Amount of Power

The preceding discussion of the power parameter has demonstrated in a variety of ways that bargainers tend to function far more effectively when they have equal rather than unequal power. As the discrepancy in power increases, effectiveness tends to decrease and is accompanied by an asymmetric allocation of resources in which the more powerful party generally behaves exploitatively and the less powerful behaves submissively. Still at issue, however, is the extent to which bargaining effectiveness may vary as a function not of power equality per se but of the total amount of power in the relationship.

Our review of the literature indicates general, although not conclusive, support for the assertion that bargainers are likely to function more effectively the smaller the total amount of power, particularly coercive power, in the system (Proposition 5). Of the 17 studies reviewed, 11 lend support to this proposition while 6 report a reversal of findings.

Some of the most persuasive evidence in support of Proposition 5 comes from research using the Acme–Bolt Trucking paradigm. Beginning with the work of Deutsch and Krauss (1960), a number of investigators have examined the effects of threat capability on bargaining behavior by providing neither, one, or both players with a gate (0 versus 1 versus 2 gates). Deutsch and Krauss' findings with respect to the effects of number of gates (amount of power) were clear-cut and compelling: Mean joint and individual outcomes were significantly higher in the 0-gate than in the 1-gate or 2-gate conditions.

These findings have been replicated in subsequent research by Borah (1963) and Shomer et al. (1966), who compared 0- and 2-gate conditions only, in terms of mean and median joint outcomes, and by Deutsch and Lewicki (1970), who compared 0-lock, 1-lock, and 2-lock conditions in terms of mean joint outcomes. In general, the Acme–Bolt research has indicated that the greater the amount of coercive power in a relationship, the less effectively bargainers are likely to function. Why? Perhaps because the effect of increasing total power is to heighten each party's expectation that the other will use this power for coercive purposes, and this in turn may lead to the pre-emptive use of power for purposes of defense.

In an attempt to check the validity of the Deutsch and Krauss findings, Tedeschi et al. (1970) created unilateral and bilateral threat conditions in a modified PD game. On each of 30 trials of a 150-trial game played against a simulated other, subjects either had unilateral power to punish the other's noncompliance (as in the Acme–Bolt 1-gate condition), or both the subject and the other had coercive power (the 2-gate condition). The experimenters found that subjects in the equivalent of the 2-gate condition rated the other as more potent and exercised their coercive power with significantly greater frequency than those in the 1-gate condition. In interpreting these results, Tedeschi, Bonoma, and Novinson suggest that the simulated other in the 2-gate condition may have been seen as possessing greater counterpower, and that it therefore seemed "fair" to punish him. "There is some inhibition," they write, "against 'attacking' and imposing costs upon a relatively helpless adversary; but when the adversary is armed . . . then the inhibition is removed [p. 74]."

Schellenberg's (1965) PD research provides a somewhat different line of support for Proposition 5. In order to test the hypothesis that "increases in dependence by either or both parties will be associated with increased collaboration and decreased exploitation and disengagement [p. 158]," pairs of subjects played a PD variant in which a third choice was added. Payoffs resulting from this third choice remained constant, regardless of the other's choice, thereby serving as a measure of "disengagement" from the relationship. By manipulating the values in the 9 cells of the game matrix, Schellenberg attempted to vary both the attractiveness of the bargaining relationship (high versus low) and the attractiveness of the alternative to the relationship (high versus low). He found that when subjects were highly dependent on the relationship (high relationship attractiveness, low alternative attractiveness), they were most likely to choose cooperatively and were least likely to make the disengagement response. On the other hand, when the alternative was high in attractiveness and the relationship low in attractiveness, disengagement occurred most often and cooperation least often. Thus, the greater bargainers' dependence on their relationship (the less their overall power), the more effectively they were likely to function.

Support for Proposition 5 is also evident in research using a variety of other more complex paradigms. Berkowitz, Hylander, and Bakaitis (1973) varied the availability of destructive, retaliatory potential in a two-person production game. The less the magnitude of this coercive power, the more cooperatively subjects behaved over trials. Komorita and Barnes (1969), in the Bilateral Monopoly study described earlier, varied the cost to buyer and seller of making an offer to be either $2 or $0, creating four conditions: 2–2, 2–0, 0–2, 0–0. Their findings conform to the pattern observed earlier by Deutsch and Krauss (1960): Agreement was reached more rapidly, and the concession rate was greater in the 2–2 than in the 2–0 or 0–2, than in the 0–0 conditions. The greater the potential cost to bargainers (the less the overall power in the relationship), the more effectively they were likely to function.

Harford, Solomon, and Cheney (1969) provided none, 1, 2, or all 3 members of a triad with coercive power and found that, as the number of people armed with punitive power increased, the amount of competitive behavior increased as well. Smith (1967a) studied the effects of direct and indirect power in the triad by providing each subject with direct control over the outcomes of a second player, who controlled the outcomes of a third, who in turn controlled the subject's own outcomes. Subjects thus had direct power with respect to one player and indirect power with respect to the other; the amount of both direct and indirect power was manipulated to be high or low. Smith found that subjects who had high direct control were more likely to punish the intermediary (the person over whom this control could be exercised) than were those low in this form of power. Similarly, subjects who had high indirect control over the behavior of the third party were more likely to punish the intermediary than were those low in indirect power. The greater the amount of power in this three-party system, the less effectively it tended to function.

In a subsequent investigation of triadic relations, Smith (1968a) manipulated not amount of power per se but its precision. The precision of power, he and others have argued, has important consequences for the degree to which power is usable. Thus, if two people (A and B) have access to an identical range of power—extending, for example, from 0 through 100 units of control—but A's power is imprecise (he can impose outcomes of 0 or 100 only and nothing in between) while B's is precise (he can impose any outcome from 0 through 100), B has far more usable power than A. In a sense, then, B may be said to have greater power than A.

Smith asked subjects to take the role of a "manager" in a three-person group containing a "worker" and "supervisor" as well, both of whom were fictitious. The subject's task was to elicit the best possible work performance from the worker, over whom the subject had no direct control. Instead, the subject-manager was given direct control over the pay received by the supervisor, who controlled pay to the worker, who in turn determined the subject's own pay. Precision of power was manipulated by informing subjects that the supervisor could pay the worker 0¢ or 12¢ on each trial or, alternately, anything from 0¢ through 12¢, and that the worker's performance on each trial would be scored either all-or-nothing (0¢ or 12¢) or on a 13-point scale (0¢ through 12¢). Smith found that a subject (manager) punished the other over whom he had direct control (the supervisor) with greater frequency when the worker had precise rather than imprecise control over the subject's pay. No differences were observed as a function of the supervisor's precision of control over the worker. These results thus lend at least partial support to Proposition 5: When the worker's control was precise and his power usable (and therefore greater), coercion was most likely to occur.

Support for Proposition 5 is of course not unequivocal. Morrison *et al.* (1971), for example, reported that bargainers were more likely to choose cooperatively in a PD game when both, rather than neither, possessed a "shock" switch. It is noteworthy, however, that no significant differences as a function of amount of power emerged with respect to three of their four dependent measures: number of shocks administered, total joint outcome, and difference in outcomes.

Hornstein (1965), whose research has already been discussed in conjunction with several other power propositions, found that threat was used more often in the 50–50 than in either the 10–10 or 90–90 "threat potential" conditions. Threat and aggression were more likely to occur between bargainers who had intermediate power to harm one another than between those who each possessed either a lot or only a little coercive power. In explanation, he suggested that the threat potential in the 90–90 condition was too dangerous to be used, while in the 10–10 condition it was too insignificant. These results, of course, fly in the face of the research by Deutsch and Krauss (1960) and a host of others, whose findings indicate that when coercive power is available it will tend to be used—often to the mutual detriment of the parties involved. However, as we noted earlier, Hornstein's subjects played for fictitious stakes, and the generalizability of his findings must therefore be questioned.

Of greater seriousness with respect to the validity of Proposition 5 are the findings to emerge in the research of Thibaut and his colleagues (Murdoch, 1967; Thibaut, 1968; Thibaut & Faucheux, 1965; Thibaut & Gruder, 1969). This important work, discussed in the context of Proposition 4, has indicated that it is when bargainers possess power that is both high and relatively equal that they are most likely to function effectively. It is when both parties to a relationship possess coercive power that rules and norms are likely to emerge which act to regulate the conflict.

In order to reconcile these findings with those that suggest the reverse—namely, that increasing the amount of power in a bargaining relationship leads to conflict escalation—we would argue for the importance of a distinction having to do with the comparability of bases of power. In each, if not all of the studies lending support to Proposition 5, bargainers have had a comparable basis of power: One or both has been placed in possession of a gate, a lock, or some other shared currency of power. In the research by Thibaut and his colleagues, on the other hand, the bases of power have been noncomparable: One party has been given control over the allocation of resources (an internal threat to the relationship), while the second has been in control of the relationship's continuity (an external threat). We suspect that when power among bargainers is comparable, an increase in the overall amount of power acts to heighten the concern with intangible issues (such as self-esteem and loss of face), thereby escalating the conflict. Where power is noncomparable, the same increase in amount of power sensitizes bargainers to the differences in their respective strengths and weaknesses, thereby paving the way for a process of accommodation based on mutual respect and restraint. Jack Spratt and his wife can lick the platter clean as long as one prefers fatty meat and the other lean—and each acknowledges the acceptability of the other's preference. But if both Mr. and Mrs. Spratt prefer either fat meat or lean, the possibilities for a mutually acceptable settlement—and a clean platter—are greatly reduced.

The Power Parameter: Summary

In this section, the 60 or so different power studies under consideration have been referred to in a total of approximately 80 different instances. That our four propositions relating to power have some degree of validity is suggested by the fact that support for them has been obtained in about 60 of these 80 instances. The propositions are obviously interrelated, and a number of experiments have therefore been discussed in relation to two or more propositions. What is perhaps less obvious is the fact that some of these experiments have lent support to one proposition while failing to do so in the case of others—hence the justification for having considered each study in relation to all the propositions to which it was applicable.

All too often, we believe, bargaining researchers have neglected the possibility that a single experimental manipulation of power may simultaneously vary or confound such issues as the equality of power, the total amount of power in the relationship, the degree of power discrepancy, and its consequences for the parties with greater or lesser power. The power parameter is both complex and nonmonolithic. And it has been in order to distinguish its various effects on bargaining effectiveness that we have advanced not one, but four, separate propositions.

INTERPERSONAL ORIENTATION (IO)

IO may be manipulated, at least indirectly, in a variety of ways. Manipulations of communication availability, for example, by varying the type and amount of interpersonal information to which the parties have access, are likely to affect IO—which in turn may affect the quality of bargaining. Similarly, individual difference variables may be analyzed in terms of their consequences for IO and bargaining effectiveness. Still other variables that are likely to affect IO include: the perceived similarity or attractiveness of the other; the possibility of meeting the other sometime in the future (anticipated future interaction); information about the other's past behavior; and information about the nature of the parties' interdependence.

Although each of the above variables, as well as others, is likely to affect bargaining effectiveness indirectly through its effects on IO, we shall (for the sake of parsimony) restrict the present analysis to those variables which have not already been considered elsewhere. Thus, since communication availability and individual difference factors have already been discussed (Chapters 5 and 7, respectively), they will not be considered further. Similarly, perceived similarity or attractiveness, we shall argue, may be considered most appropriately in terms of the interaction of MO and IO and hence will be considered later in the chapter. It is to the remaining three classes of independent variables (anticipated future interaction, the other's past behavior, and information about the parties' interdependence) that the present analysis will be directed.

Anticipated Future Interaction

It seems not unreasonable to expect bargainers who have been led to believe they will meet one another in the future to be higher in IO than those who have no such expectation. Anticipated future interaction should, after all, heighten bargainers' concerns with how they look in the eyes of the other and should thereby heighten their sensitivity to a variety of interpersonal cues. Given the assertion of Proposition 6—that high IO bargainers will function more effectively than those who are lower in IO—we might expect greater bargaining effectiveness to occur when the parties anticipate future interaction than when they do not.

Two experiments lend clear support to this proposition. Slusher, Roering, and Rose (1974) had subjects play a one-trial PD game and led them to believe this was the first of three such games in which they would participate. Half of the subjects were told that the remaining games would be played with the same partner, with whom the results of prior sessions could be discussed. The remaining subjects were told they would have a different partner, whom they would not meet, in each of the remaining games. Slusher, Roering, and Rose found that subjects who anticipated future interaction with their partner behaved more cooperatively than those who expected to remain anonymous.

Marlowe, Gergen, and Doob (1966) had subjects play a 30-trial PD game against a confederate who chose cooperatively on 24 of the trials. The subjects were either led to expect they would meet with their partner after the game (to "discuss their behavior") or were given no such expectation. It was found that subjects who were led to anticipate further interaction with the other were significantly less exploitative in their choice behavior than those who did not expect to meet the other.

Standing in direct contrast to the findings of the above studies, however, are the results of another PD experiment conducted by Swingle (1969). English- and French-Canadian subjects played a 100-trial game against a confederate who employed a tit-for-tat strategy with probability (.90). The subjects were led to expect either that they would meet him after the session or that they would remain anonymous. Regardless of subjects' background, Swingle found, those in anonymous conditions behaved more cooperatively than subjects who anticipated future interaction.

How may the contradictory findings of the above studies be reconciled? An experiment by Gruder (1969) suggests an answer to this question. Subjects in this "intergroup negotiation" game were told they had been arbitrarily chosen to bargain as the "spokesman" of their dyad (team) against the spokesman for another dyad. (Actually, both the subject's teammate and the spokesman for the other team were simulated.) On the basis of preprogrammed written information, the subjects were led to believe that the other spokesman was either "fair and reasonable" or "exploitative and unreasonable." The subjects, in addition, were either led to anticipate a future meeting with the other spokesman or not. Gruder found, in support of Slusher et al. and Marlowe et al., that subjects playing against a "fair" other whom they expected to meet were more compromising and yielding than those playing without this expectation. In support of Swingle, however, it was also found that subjects playing against an "exploitative" other whom they expected to meet were more competitive and demanding than those who did not anticipate such a meeting.

Gruder's findings have been replicated (Gruder, 1971) and have been further supported by the results of a study conducted by Michelini (1971). The latter investigator conducted a PD experiment in which the positivity or negativity of prior interaction was varied, as well as the anticipation of future interaction. Michelini found that subjects who anticipated future interaction following a positive prior experience expressed greater liking for their partner than those who expected to remain anonymous. Conversely, subjects who had been exposed to a negative prior interaction experience expressed greater dislike for their partner when they expected to meet her than when they did not.

It thus appears that the effects of anticipated future interaction on bargaining are a function of its interaction with perception of the other. Anticipated future interaction leads to greater cooperation when the other is seen as cooperative, and to greater competition when the other is seen as competitive, than occurs when no future meeting is expected. A possible explanation, then, for the discrepant findings of Marlowe et al. (1966) and Swingle (1969), in particular, is that the other was seen as more cooperative in the former study than in the latter. That this may indeed have been the case is suggested by the fact that subjects in the Marlowe et al. experiment played against a strategy that cooperated on 80% of the trials, whereas subjects in the Swingle study played against a potentially less cooperative, tit-for-tat strategy.

Information about the Other's Past Behavior

Just as one might expect IO to be heightened by the anticipation of future interaction, so too might it be heightened as a function of information provided about the other party's past behavior. Bargaining researchers have typically varied the availability and nature of information about the other's past behavior in one of two rather different ways: either by introducing information prior to the bargaining session (in the form of prenegotiation experience) or by introducing information during the session itself (typically in the form of posttrial feedback about the other's previous choices, moves, etc.). The findings to emerge using these two methods have rather different implications for the validity of Proposition 6, and so will be considered separately.

Availability of Information Prior to the Bargaining Session

Bass (1966) and Druckman (1967, 1968b), in research described in Chapter 5, provided subjects with one of two rather different types of experience prior to their participation in an intergroup negotiation task. Either subjects were asked to meet beforehand with the other members of their team in order to formulate their objectives (unilateral conditions) or they were permitted to meet for the same purpose with the other team (bilateral conditions). In each of the three studies it was found that subjects in the bilateral conditions bargained far more effectively (in terms of the time taken to resolve issues, the number of unresolved issues, the frequency of concessions, etc.) than those in unilateral conditions.

In another study designed to assess the effects of prior experience on bargaining, Hall and Williams (1966) compared the decision-making behavior of established and ad hoc groups. Groups of subjects, ranging in size from six to nine members, were shown a portion of the film *12 Angry Men* and were asked to predict (first as individuals and then as a group) the order in which the 11 jurors, initially voting "guilty" in the film, shifted their votes to "not guilty." Half of the subject groups were composed of members with previous ingroup activity (established), while the members of the remaining groups had no previous ingroup activity and little if any knowledge of one another (ad hoc). The investigators found that the established groups reached more accurate group decisions, utilized their resources more effectively, and were more creative than ad hoc groups.

Prior to taking part in a PD game, Harrison and McClintock (1965) had subjects participate in a "reaction-time" task in which both subjects either won or lost on 85 of the 100 trials. Subjects then played a 60-trial PD game either immediately afterwards or after a delay of one week. Finally, a control condition was run in which subjects were given no prior experience. Harrison and McClintock found that subjects who were jointly successful in the reaction-time task, as well as those who were not successful and played the PD game after a one week delay, made cooperative choices in the PD game with greater frequency than control subjects. Thus, it was a prior rewarding encounter with the other—but also a nonrewarding encounter coupled with a delay before obtaining the dependent measure—that led to more effective bargaining than did no prior encounter at all.

Michelini (1971), in another PD study, asked female subjects to discuss and reach consensus on a topic with an experimental confederate, prior to taking part in the PD game. The topic for discussion was " Does a married college-educated woman owe it to her family to stay at home or to herself to pursue her career aspirations?" In one condition (positive prior interaction), the confederate was instructed to behave cooperatively and display similar opinions; in the other (negative prior interaction) condition, the confederate continually expressed opinions at odds with those of the subject. Michelini found that subjects in the former condition subsequently behaved more cooperatively than those in the latter.

Finally, Pruitt (1968) had subjects participate in a "decomposed" PD game for three blocks of three trials each. On each trial, the subjects were told, one of the players would be given a number of money chips which he could distribute between himself and the other in any way he wished. These money chips were worth more to the other (1.5 × the value sent) than to the distributor of these resources. The other player, actually the experimenter, was given control over the allocation of money chips during blocks 1 and 3 of the game, while the subject had control for block 2.

Pruitt varied the subjects' prior experience with the other by manipulating the amount of money (in chips) that the latter sent to the subjects during block 1. He found, as hypothesized, that subjects provided the other with greater reward during block 2 the more the other had given in the past and the more the other had given in relation to his initial resources. Thus, as in the Harrison and McClintock (1965) study, it appears that prior experience with the other is especially likely to enhance bargaining effectiveness when the other is seen in a favorable light (as generous, competent, cooperative, etc.).

Availability of Information during the Bargaining Session

Standing in direct contrast to the findings of the above studies, each of which lends support to Proposition 6, are the results of a considerably larger body of research in which the availability of posttrial feedback has been varied. Almost without exception, posttrial feedback has been manipulated in these experiments by providing some subjects with veridical information about the choices made both by themselves and by the other on the immediately preceding trial (joint choice or outcome feedback), while providing other subjects with no information about the other's previous choice (own choice or outcome feedback only).

The findings of the posttrial feedback research are rather consistent. Of the 20 studies we have reviewed, 10 report greater bargaining effectiveness when subjects are provided with own rather than joint feedback. Nine of these experiments employed the PD game or some variant (Gallo, Irwin, & Avery, 1966; McClintock & McNeel, 1966a, c; McClintock & Nuttin, 1969; Messick & Thorngate, 1967; Rapoport, 1969; Swensson, 1967; Tedeschi, Lesnick, & Gahagan, 1968e; Willis & Hale, 1963), the tenth (Smith & Emmons, 1969) being based on the Acme–Bolt Trucking game. Only 3 studies have reported support for Proposition 6 (Bixenstine et al., 1966; Cole & Schneider, 1964; Siegel & Harnett, 1964), with the remaining 7 experiments reporting no consistent effects as a function of feedback (Leff, 1969; Harnett et al., 1968; McNeel, 1973; Messick & McClintock, 1968; Pilisuk, Winter, Chapman, & Haas, 1967; Smith, 1968b; Suppes & Carlsmith, 1962). Proposition 6 thus receives very little additional support from the feedback research. If anything, there appears to be stronger evidence for the conclusion that an experimentally induced high IO leads to less bargaining effectiveness than does a low IO.

In interpreting the above pattern of findings it is important to bear in mind that 9 of the 10 studies finding greater bargaining effectiveness with own rather than joint feedback employed variants of a single experimental paradigm—the PD game. As we have argued throughout this volume, a competitive choice tends to dominate in the PD game. Thus, other things being equal, the other player is more likely to make a competitive choice than a cooperative one. When no feedback is available with respect to the other's previous choice (own feedback only), the subject is relatively unaware of the other's general tendency to behave competitively and is likely to attempt simply to maximize his own gain. When feedback about the other's prior competitive behavior is available, on the other hand (joint feedback), this information is likely to heighten a view of the other as a competitor and is likely to lead in turn to the arousal of competitive feelings and behavior on the part of the subject.

We wish to argue, in other words, that the pattern of findings observed with respect to posttrial feedback is attributable not to the effect of IO per se, but rather to the interaction of IO with a second variable: the particular experimental paradigm employed. When this paradigm is "competitively loaded," the effect of experimentally inducing a high IO may be to increase the likelihood of competitive behavior. When the paradigm provides greater latitude for cooperative behavior, on the other hand, we might expect a high IO to lead to greater cooperation and bargaining effectiveness than a low IO. The Bilateral Monopoly game is a good example of such a paradigm, inasmuch as cooperative, conciliatory behavior is probably more likely to occur here than in the PD game. In this regard it is noteworthy that one of the few feedback experiments to provide unequivocal support for Proposition 6 was the Bilateral Monopoly study conducted by Siegel and Harnett (1964).

More generally, we wish to suggest that IO—unlike the other two parameters of interdependence, each of which displays a simple main effect with respect to bargaining effectiveness—tends to exert its most important effects in interaction with other variables. As we shall see when we turn to the interaction of MO and IO in particular, this interaction is often robust and compelling. Before concluding our discussion of the feedback variable, however, we wish to further document our point by briefly describing a study in which the effects of IO are best understood in terms of its interaction with a second variable.

Bixenstine *et al.* (1966) had subjects play a modified PD game in groups of six. At the end of the first 20 trials the experimenter announced a recess during which subjects were either permitted to talk with one another or were asked to remain silent. The game was then played for 20 additional trials. Half of the subject groups were given joint choice feedback at the end of each trial, while the remaining groups were given own choice feedback only. The investigators found that during the second block of 20 trials (after the communication manipulation) cooperative choices were made with greatest frequency when subjects had been given joint feedback and had been allowed to communicate during the recess. When joint feedback was available and communication was not allowed, however, competition occurred most often. In other words, feedback about the other's behavior (an experimentally induced high IO) was most likely to lead to cooperation when communication was present and was most likely to elicit competition when communication was absent.

The Bixenstine *et al.* experiment is important for two reasons. First, it documents yet another variable, in addition to the particular paradigm employed, with which IO interacts. Second, it helps explain why studies in which information has been made available prior to the bargaining session lend support to Proposition 6 while most of the studies in which information has been made available during the session do not. Prior to bargaining—that is, prior to the development of a bargaining stance from which it may be awkward or costly to retreat—the availability of interpersonal experience (such as communication before the second block of trials in the Bixenstine *et al.* study) provides each party with the opportunity to discover, at relatively minimal cost, something more about what the other is like. Prenegotiation experience may help the parties to develop a more realistic, less stereotypic view of each other before positional lines are drawn and commitment processes have begun to operate at full strength. Once bargaining begins, however, there is all too often a tendency to downplay the importance of interpersonal information, except as this information serves to further bolster a stereotypic view of the other. The availability of interpersonal information during the bargaining session itself (such as joint feedback) is therefore likely to encourage a "self-fulfilling prophecy" view of the other and, as in a relationship in which communication is not permitted, may lead to increased rigidity in the parties' perceptions of one another.

Information about the Nature of the Parties' Interdependence

It seems not unreasonable to expect that a high IO might be experimentally induced by informing subjects that they are playing against a real other person rather than an imaginary other or a machine. Similarly, it seems not unreasonable to expect that bargainers who are sensitized to the fact that they are interdependent should be higher in IO than those who are not so sensitized. In general, then, bargainers who have been provided with information about the nature of their interdependence should be higher in IO, and therefore likely to bargain more effectively, than those who are not provided with such information.

Only three of the seven experiments in which the "reality" of the other player has been varied lend support to Proposition 6. In one, Sidowski and Smith (1961) had subjects take part in a version of the "Minimal Social Situation"—a paradigm originally developed by Sidowski, Wyckoff, and Tabory (1956). The Minimal Social Situation (MSS) paradigm typically consists of two subjects, seated in separate rooms, neither of whom is aware that another is involved. Each subject has two buttons, about which he is told nothing except that he can push them in any manner or order he wishes. On each turn the subject can either make points, indicated on a counter in front of him, or receive electric shock. His task is to try to make as many points as possible and, of course, avoid being shocked. Unknown to the subject, one of his buttons is wired so as to deliver a point to the other person, while the other button is wired to deliver electric shock. The other person's buttons are similarly wired so as to deliver shock or points to the first. Neither subject can reward or shock himself; his buttons only control the shocks and points that the *other* receives.

Sidowski and Smith had pairs of subjects engage in the MSS for 400 trials. Subjects were given one of four types of instructions: being led to believe that there was no opponent or that their opponent was a machine, the experimenter, or another subject (the last was in fact the case). The investigators found that subjects in the "machine opponent" condition took significantly longer to evolve a pattern of mutual reward, in which each subject consistently pressed the button delivering points to the other, than subjects in the three remaining conditions.

In the only other experiments of this general type to report support for Proposition 6, Brayer (1964) had subjects play a two-person, zero sum game against a program. Subjects were led to expect either that their opponent was rational or that his choices were purely random. It was found that subjects who expected their opponent to be rational made "minimax" choices with greater frequency than those who expected to play against a random opponent. Brayer's findings have been recently replicated by Fox (1972).

Other experiments, however, have reported a rather different pattern of results. Halpin and Pilisuk (1967) had subjects play a 200-trial PD game against an opponent who was described as either a preset program controlled by a computer, a like-sexed other, or a computer program that was designed to be responsive to the subject's own choices. They found that even though subjects in all three conditions actually played against an identical 70% randomized cooperative strategy, those in the like-sexed other condition were far less accurate in their predictions of the other's choice on each trial than subjects in either of the two computer program conditions.

Rapoport and Cole (1968), also using the PD paradigm, had subjects play against a programmed strategy. Subjects were told either that their opponent was, indeed, a programmed strategy or that their opponent was a live other. The findings indicated that subjects in the former condition behaved more cooperatively and obtained a significantly larger number of points than those in the latter (real other) condition. Lacey and Pate (1960), similarly, have reported that subjects playing a simple matrix game against a machine tend to learn the correct solution more rapidly than those playing against a human opponent, with subjects in the latter condition tending to choose in relation to their own previous plays and the anticipated plays of the other. Kanouse and Wiest (1967), finally, had subjects play a PD game against an opponent whom they were either told was real or were asked to imagine was real. They found no differences in the frequency of cooperation as a function of this manipulation.

Clearly the findings of the studies in which the reality or rationality of the other has been varied lend very little support to Proposition 6. While these findings cannot readily be explained away, it is perhaps noteworthy that none of the experiments in support of our proposition employed the PD game, whereas two of the three studies reporting a reversal did. Again, as we have already argued, given the dominance of a competitive choice in the PD paradigm, it should come as no surprise that subjects playing this game against a real other should expect greater competition, and therefore be likely to behave more competitively themselves, than subjects playing against an imagined other or a machine.

Experiments in which the subjects' *awareness* of their interdependence has been varied lend clearer support to Proposition 6. Fry, Hopkins, and Hoge (1970), Kelley, Thibaut, Radloff, and Mundy (1962), and Smith and Murdoch (1970), for example, in three separate MSS experiments, either kept subjects completely ignorant of the social nature of their task or informed them that there was a real other person who controlled the subject's outcomes and whose outcomes were in turn controlled by the subject. All three experiments reported that subjects required a significantly smaller number of trials to reach solution (a pattern of consistent mutual reward) when they were aware rather than unaware of their mutual dependence.

In another related study, Guyer and Rapoport (1969) had pairs of subjects play one of several variants of the PD game under one of two information conditions: Either subjects were provided with a complete matrix which displayed the potential outcomes both to them and to the other or they were provided with an incomplete matrix which displayed only their own outcomes. It was found that subjects given the complete matrix achieved maximum joint outcomes significantly more often than those given the incomplete one. Thus, by making the subjects more aware of their interdependence, bargaining effectiveness was increased.

Related to Guyer and Rapoport's research are Pruitt's (1967, 1970) investigations using the "decomposed" PD game. A decomposed PD matrix is one in which both the subject's and the other's outcomes are presented as being a direct result of the subject's own behavior, regardless of the other's choice. Thus, by comparing a standard PD matrix (in which the outcomes to both the subject and the other are displayed) with one or more of its many possible decompositions (in which the same outcomes are presented as a function of the subject's choice alone), it is possible to assess the effects on behavior of the particular manner in which interdependence is portrayed to the subject.

Pruitt (1967) exposed pairs of subjects either to a standard PD game or to one of several decomposed variants. Subjects played against a real other and each knew that the other had the same (complete or decomposed) payoff matrix as he. It was found, in support of Proposition 6, that some decompositions resulted in less overall cooperation than the complete matrix parent PD. Other decompositions, however, elicited greater cooperation than the PD. In explanation, Pruitt hypothesized that decompositions of the same parent outcome matrix may have different psychological consequences for subjects, motivating them to behave more cooperatively than the parent PD in some circumstances, and more competitively in others. Pruitt obtained further support for this explanation in subsequent research (1970).

Thus, while there is evidence, in support of Proposition 6, that the very act of increasing awareness of interdependence tends to result in a higher IO and greater bargaining effectiveness, this evidence must be qualified by the findings of Pruitt's research. It may not be the awareness of interdependence per se, so much as the particular manner in which this interdependence is portrayed to the parties involved, that is responsible for its effects on bargaining behavior. It therefore appears once again that the consequences of an experimentally induced IO can be best understood not in terms of its simple main effects but rather in its interaction with other variables.

The IO Parameter: Summary

In addition to considering the impact of variations in MO and power upon bargaining effectiveness, we have suggested that it may be useful to consider the role of yet another parameter: IO. While we know of no attempt to vary IO directly, and while in none of the studies discussed in the preceding sections was IO directly assessed, we would argue that it is nevertheless possible to consider the impact of IO by analyzing those variables whose effects on bargaining are likely to be mediated by the often unwitting manipulation of Interpersonal Orientation.

We have found only partial support for the proposition that an experimentally induced high IO tends to result in more effective bargaining than a low IO. Of the 45 different studies reviewed, 23 have reported support for Proposition 6, fourteen have reported findings exactly the reverse of those predicted, and 8 have found no differences as a function of (what we have described as) IO. The reason for this lack of clear support of Proposition 6, we believe, is because the effects of IO may be observed most clearly when it is considered in interaction with other variables. It is to a consideration of these expected and observed interaction effects that several of the remaining sections of this chapter will be addressed.

THE INTERACTION OF MO AND POWER

Just as the three parameters of interdependence, considered alone, have been shown to have important consequences for bargaining effectiveness, so too might we expect their effects to occur in interaction with one another. We have seen that a cooperative MO is likely to result in greater bargaining effectiveness than an individualistic, and especially a competitive, MO (Proposition 1). Similarly, it has been demonstrated that equal power among bargainers tends to result in more effective bargaining than unequal power (Proposition 2). What, then, of the interaction of these two parameters? What are the consequences for bargaining effectiveness likely to be when MO and power are considered not alone but in concert? In response, we wish to argue that bargainers will tend to function most effectively when they share a cooperative MO and are of equal power, functioning least effectively when they share a competitive MO and are again of equal power (Proposition 7).

When bargainers share a cooperative MO and are of equal power, conditions are most favorable for the effective resolution of a conflict of interest. Each party has an interest in the other's welfare as well as in his own. Each wishes to maximize not only his own outcomes but the other's also. The parties thus share an attitude of trust which is likely to facilitate the development of a close and mutually beneficial understanding, as well as a relationship which is relatively free of concerns with intangible issues—such as the loss of face in the other's eyes. The bargainers' shared trust, moreover, is likely to lead them toward the exploration of a fair and equitable allocation of resources, a search that is strongly buttressed by the fact that they are of comparable power. The important decision about what constitutes a "fair share" should be quite simple to make. If the parties are truly cooperative in their orientation and do indeed have comparable control over resources and outcomes, they can simply "split the pot down the middle!" The problem of coordination, so often a thorn in the side of bargainers (even those with the most charitable intentions), is easy to resolve. The bargainers trust each other, and the maintenance of this attitude is greatly facilitated by the comparability of their power.

When the bargainers share a cooperative MO but are unequal in power, they are confronted with a potentially difficult, although not insoluble, coordination problem. Given their shared attitude of trust, how should resources be allocated in relation to those differences in power which do in fact exist in the relationship? Perhaps they should be divided equitably, with each party receiving an outcome that is proportional to his power. The potential difficulty with such a solution stems from the fact that one party must then settle for less than the other, possibly endangering the mutual trust that characterizes the relationship. So, perhaps resources should be divided not equitably, but equally, with both parties receiving identical outcomes. The potential difficulty with this solution is that it ignores the fact that the bargainers do indeed differ in their ability to control the other's outcomes. Thus, while cooperative MO bargainers of unequal power, given their trusting attitude toward each other, are indeed capable of functioning very effectively, their ability to do so may be hampered by the issue of resource allocation, and they may be expected to function less effectively than bargainers who share the same orientation but have equal power as well.

A shared individualistic MO, regardless of power equality, is likely to result in bargaining that is less effective than a cooperative MO but more effective than a competitive MO. We therefore expect an individualistic MO to be intermediate with respect to its consequences for bargaining effectiveness; rather than consider it further, let us instead turn briefly to the two extreme situations in which bargaining is likely to prove extremely ineffective.

When bargainers share a competitive MO, each is out to beat the other. Each party not only wishes to maximize his own outcomes but to minimize the other's as well. The resulting attitude of mutual suspicion and distrust is likely to foster a climate in which each party hopes to exploit the other, and the bargainers are thus likely to function very ineffectively. When power is unequal, however, the outcomes of this ineffective bargaining are in a sense overdetermined. The more powerful party is likely to be relatively successful in his attempts to manipulate and exploit the weaker, who in turn will tend to behave passively and submissively, unless he has the option to withdraw from the relationship or successfully form an alliance with others like himself. Under conditions of power inequality, therefore, bargainers sharing a competitive MO will tend to view one another as noncomparable (one is stronger than the other after all) and will tend to lock into a pattern of ineffective bargaining characterized by exploitation on the one hand and submission on the other.

It is when competitively oriented bargainers are of equal power, however, that all hell is likely to break loose. It is in this situation that conditions are least favorable for effective bargaining. The same equality of power which facilitated the resolution of conflict when the parties shared a cooperative MO will now lead to a ferociously intense struggle over intangible issues. If both are equally powerful (or equally weak), why should one give in to the competitive, exploitative behavior that the other is likely to display? Expressed in other words, the comparability of the other's power with one's own (following the social comparison theory of Festinger, 1954) is likely to increase the salience of a win or a loss, both in one's own eyes and in the eyes of the other. The very equality of power, and resulting basis of comparability among the bargainers, which was the key to an equitable allocation of resources when the parties shared a cooperative MO, is now the basis for increasing tension and the emergence of a host of costly intangible issues.

Unfortunately, remarkably few experiments have been conducted that provide a test of Proposition 7. Rubin (1971b), in a study described earlier, varied both MO and relative power in a relationship consisting of four parties: A, B, X, and Y. A and B were asked to adopt either a cooperative or a competitive MO toward each other, and X and Y were given either high or low counterpower with respect to their allies, A and B. Rubin found that the four-party system functioned most effectively when A and B were cooperatively oriented and X and Y had low counterpower, functioning least effectively when A and B were competitive while X and Y had high (relatively equal) power.

That bargaining should have been least effective when the parties had a competitive MO and were of relatively equal power seems quite plausible and clearly supports Proposition 7. It was in this condition, replete with negative affect, that bargainers could trust neither their opponents nor their teammates and hence obtained the poorest joint outcomes. More troubling with respect to the validity of Proposition 7 are Rubin's findings with respect to the conditions of greatest bargaining effectiveness. One might have expected the greatest overall effectiveness to have occurred when MO was cooperative and X and Y's counterpower was high, rather than low. In explanation, it should be pointed out that the relationship under consideration in Rubin's study consisted not of two but of four parties—thereby increasing the likelihood that A and B would experience problems of coordination in their attempts to influence their allies' behavior. Expressed in other words, increasing the equality of X and Y's power in relation to A and B's, because of the complexity inherent in a relationship consisting of four interdependent parties, may have served to hamper rather than facilitate A and B's attempts to manage the conflict effectively. Had these coordination difficulties not been present, the system might indeed have functioned most effectively under conditions of cooperative MO and (relatively) equal power.

The only other study whose findings bear on Proposition 7 was conducted by Deutsch and Lewicki (1970). In one of several experiments reported in this paper, subjects were given equal power (each had a "lock") and either a cooperative or a competitive MO. It was found that subjects given a competitive MO had a significantly greater number of collisions and achieved significantly poorer outcomes than those given a cooperative MO. Thus, equal power in the presence of a shared cooperative MO resulted in greater bargaining effectiveness than the same equality of power accompanied by a competitive orientation—in support of Proposition 7. Unfortunately, because power equality was held constant in the Deutsch and Lewicki study, it is not possible to test fully its implications for the accuracy of our proposition.

On the basis of only two studies—neither of which provides a particularly direct test of the interactive effects of MO and relative power—it is obviously impossible to draw conclusions about the validity of Proposition 7. Clearly, although this has not yet been done, it would be easy enough to design research in which MO and power equality are jointly varied. We would argue the need for such research if the potentially important interactive effects of these two parameters of interdependence are to be better understood.

THE INTERACTION OF MO AND IO

In our discussion of Proposition 6 it was suggested that the effects of IO may be best understood in terms of its interaction with other variables, such as the particular bargaining paradigm employed or the availability of communication. As we shall argue in the present section, one of the most important variables with which IO interacts is MO. When bargainers share a cooperative orientation and are high in IO, they will tend to function most effectively, functioning least effectively when they share a competitive MO and are again high in IO (Proposition 8).

By experimentally creating a high IO, the salience of interpersonal information is increased and bargainers are induced to react to features of their interactive environment in extreme, highly variant fashion. And when this "environmental feature" is the parties' MO, in particular, the result is an intensification of those tendencies that MO generates in its own right. We have suggested that a cooperative MO tends to engender a shared attitude of trust and a search for a fair and equitable division of resources. In the presence of a high IO, this trusting attitude, equitable resource allocation, and thus bargaining effectiveness should all be enhanced. The bargainers' cooperative intentions are buttressed by the availability of corroborative information about one another. Each party's trusting attitude is reinforced and justified by information which indicates that the other is trustworthy. A desire for equitable resource allocation is bolstered by information which indicates that the other shares the same desire. Thus, although a cooperative MO may lead to effective bargaining even when IO is low, conditions are maximally favorable for the emergence of effective bargaining when, in addition, IO is high.

When bargainers share an individualistic MO, regardless of IO level, it seems not unreasonable to expect them to function with an intermediate degree of effectiveness. However, it is when they share a competitive orientation and are once again high in IO that *in*effective bargaining should be most likely to occur. The distrust and suspicion already engendered by a competitive MO are likely to be further intensified by the heightened salience of interpersonal information. To not only suspect the other of having competitive, exploitative intentions but have these worst suspicions confirmed by information about the other's behavior is to escalate the conflict and greatly reduce the chances of its effective management. Therefore, the ineffective bargaining to which a competitive MO leads in the presence of little or no interpersonal information (low IO) is likely to be exacerbated even further when IO is high.

Unlike Proposition 7 (and Propositions 9 and 10), for which little experimental evidence has been available to date, a number of bargaining studies permit at least a partial test of the validity of Proposition 8. Willis and Hale (1963) and Kanouse and Wiest (1967), for example, independently manipulated MO (and indirectly IO) in variants of the PD game. IO was varied in the former study by manipulating the availability of feedback, while in the latter study subjects were led to believe that they were playing either against a real other or against an imaginary other. Both experiments yielded a significant effect due to MO (in support of Proposition 1), and Willis and Hale found an effect due to IO (in support of Proposition 6), but in neither study was a significant interaction between the two variables reported.

A larger body of research, however, reveals a rather different picture. A number of experiments have been conducted in which the interaction of MO and IO has been perhaps unwittingly varied by manipulating the perceived friendliness of the other. In these studies, pairs of friends, enemies (non-friends), or complete strangers have typically been preselected and then asked to work together on some bargaining task. When a subject is led to believe that the other bargainer is either his friend *or* his enemy, we wish to argue, he is provided with interpersonal information that is likely to induce a high IO. Each knows something more about his partner than is possible when the other is a total stranger (the latter being an example of an experimentally induced low IO). Moreover, to think of another as one's friend is to like and trust him, to expect him to behave cooperatively, and probably to behave cooperatively oneself. Conversely, if the other is known to be an enemy, he can be expected to behave competitively, and one is likely to be suspicious of his intentions and to behave competitively oneself. Thus, to be told that another is your friend is to be provided simultaneously with information that is likely to foster a high IO and a cooperative MO. Conversely, information that another is your enemy is likely to induce a high IO and a competitive MO. Finally, information that the other is a total stranger is likely to result in a low IO and, probably, an individualistic MO.

As Byrne (1969) and others have amply demonstrated, similarity and liking are closely related. In particular, perceived similarity tends to lead to trust and liking for the other, whereas perceived dissimilarity tends to engender dislike and suspicion. Hence the preceding argument may be extended to include those bargaining studies in which perceived similarity, rather than friendliness per se, has been manipulated. The perception of another as highly similar to oneself in attitudes, beliefs, or values should result in a high IO and a cooperative MO. The presence of a dissimilar other, conversely, should induce a high IO and a competitive MO. And the presence of another about whom no information is available concerning similarity–dissimilarity should result in a low IO and an individualistic MO.

Of the 17 bargaining studies in which the perceived attractiveness or similarity of the other has been varied, only 4 have reported no consistent differences (Bartos, 1967a; Fisher & Smith, 1969; Oskamp & Perlman, 1966; Wyer, 1969). However, the remaining experiments, involving manipulations of either perceived friendliness or perceived similarity, lend clear support to Proposition 8 and will be considered in turn.

Manipulations Of Perceived Friendliness

Morgan and Sawyer (1967) had pairs of fifth and sixth graders engage in a simple bargaining task. The subjects faced each other across a "Bargaining Board" with seven pairs of "pockets." The seven pockets on one subject's side contained from 0 to 6 nickels, while those on the other's side contained from 0 to 6 quarters, arranged in exactly the reverse order. The subjects' task was, through the open exchange of offers and counteroffers, to reach agreement on a single pair of pockets—each subject then winning the money in the pocket on his side of the board. If agreement was not reached, the subjects were told, neither would win anything.

On the basis of a previously administered sociometric inventory, half the dyads were composed of friends and half of nonfriends (the person a boy would "least like to sit next to"). Finally, before beginning the game, a questionnaire was administered in which subjects estimated the most and least they expected to win. In half the dyads, this information was exchanged (read aloud to subjects), while in the remaining dyads it was not made available.

Morgan and Sawyer found that nonfriends who were given no information about the other's expectations required significantly more time to reach agreement than did friends with or without knowledge of the other's expectations. Furthermore, although a number of solutions to the bargaining problem were possible, the Bargaining Board was deliberately constructed in such a way that two types of solution were particularly likely to occur: equal (5 nickels versus 1 quarter) and equitable (3 nickels versus 3 quarters). Morgan and Sawyer found in this regard that it was when friends had no information about each other's expectations, that outcomes tended to be equal. For nonfriends, on the other hand, outcomes tended to be equal regardless of the presence or absence of information about the other's expectations.

In explanation of their results, the investigators suggest that fifth- and sixth-grade boys, regardless of whether they are friends or not, strongly prefer equal to equitable outcomes. Friends, however, although they prefer an equal allocation of resources, are willing to settle for an unequal but equitable division when one believes that the other might prefer it. Nonfriends, on the other hand, regardless of the information with which they are provided, will not settle for anything but strict equality. As Morgan and Sawyer express this point: "For nonfriends, equality appears to be more than merely the preference it is for friends, but closer to a requirement [p. 148]." Friends thus appear far more flexible and trusting in their approach to resolving a conflict of interest than nonfriends, who tend to adhere rigidly to a single solution, and the former are therefore likely to bargain far more effectively.

We might note in passing, however, that the very "flexibility" which characterizes bargaining among friends may also be the source of miscoordination and ineffectiveness. To the extent that each party is overly concerned with "being nice" to the other and focuses more on what he thinks the other would like than on a clear statement of his own preferences, the relationship runs the danger of foundering on a sea of good intentions. As Schenitzki (1963) has found in his Bilateral Monopoly study, one of the "pathologies" of cooperation is that bargainers expend too much time and energy trying to "get inside the other's head" and, paradoxically, such bargainers achieve fewer maximally beneficial joint agreements than those who are more individualistic in their orientation. Similarly, Morgan and Sawyer (1967) observe that "in the absence of information friends develop and act upon false expectations about the other's preference [p. 147]." Thus, although liking for another is likely to increase the flexibility of one's bargaining posture and outlook, and although this is generally likely to enhance bargaining effectiveness, it may also lead to problems of miscoordination that have serious adverse effects.

In a more recent study employing a paradigm not unlike the Morgan and Sawyer Bargaining Board, Benton (1971) divided male and female preadolescents into same-sex dyads, and had each dyad member rank 15 toys in their order of desirability. The subjects were then seated at opposite ends of a bargaining table and were asked to reach agreement over the choice of one of four pairs of toys. The toys were paired in such a way that one child's first choice corresponded to the other's last. On the basis of a prior sociometric inventory, in which the subjects were to indicate the children they would most and least like to sit next to in class, dyads were constituted consisting of friends, nonfriends, and "neutrals" (children not mentioned in response to the sociometric questionnaire).

Benton found that males, regardless of their degree of friendship, tended to seek out and achieve equitable agreements. For females, however, friendship had more important consequences: Friends evaluated each other more favorably than nonfriends, exchanged more information about their toy preferences, emitted a greater number of emotional responses (such as giggling, sighing, and laughing), and rated themselves as less dissatisfied with bargaining outcomes. The results for neutrals were intermediate with respect to each of these dependent measures. Thus for the female children at least, perceived friendship led to apparently greater bargaining effectiveness than neutrality and, especially, than perceived enmity. As Benton (1971) points out with respect to the latter group: "The bargaining behavior of the pairs of female nonfriends was awkwardly competitive and strained. It was characterized by numerous periods of silence interspersed with infrequent comments . . . practically no exchange of information . . . and a relatively quick resolution which showed little relationship to the child's previous productivity [p. 77]."

Prior to beginning a PD game played against an experimental confederate, Baxter (1970) presented subjects with a personality description which led them to believe that the other had either a cooperative or a competitive personality; in addition, some subjects received no such description (no information). He found that subjects behaved more cooperatively in the cooperative information than in the no information condition, behaving least cooperatively when they were told the other had a competitive disposition. Similarly, McClintock and McNeel (1967) gave subjects either no prior experience with the other before participating in a variant of the PD paradigm or had them play a prior 10-trial game in which the other (a programmed strategy) behaved in systematically friendly or hostile fashion. They found that subjects indicated greater liking for the other and chose more cooperatively in the presence of a friendly other than in the presence of a hostile or unfamiliar one. Riker and Niemi (1964), moreover, in a three-person game, constituted triads of friends, casual acquaintances, or strangers and found that friends were least likely to form two-way coalitions to the exclusion of the third member.

Finally, two "friendliness" experiments have been conducted by Swingle, both of which suggest an important qualification to Proposition 8. Swingle (1966) had subjects play a simple two-person game against a liked, neutral, disliked, or strange (no previous acquaintance) experimental confederate. One player (the transmitter) was seated in front of a table on which one of four colored lights came on. His task was to tell the other player (the respondent) which one had lit up and the respondent, in turn, was to press one of four buttons. If the respondent pressed the correct button and the whole process was completed in 1½ sec, the respondent earned one point. The transmitter, however, could affect the respondent's earnings by varying the amount of time he allowed to elapse (the latency) before calling out the light color. Finally, the players were told they were in competition, with the winner to be awarded "one extra point toward his psychology course grade."

The game was divided into four 25-trial phases. During Phase 1, the confederate was put in the role of transmitter, while the subject served as respondent. During Phase 2 these roles were reversed. During Phase 3 the subject once again served as respondent (as in Phase 1), but the confederate behaved in such a way that the subject made only 40% of his Phase 1 score; the other was thus made to appear uncooperative. Finally, during Phase 4 the subject once again called out the lights (as in Phase 2).

In support of Proposition 8, Swingle found (Phase 2) that subjects tended to transmit information more rapidly when playing against a liked other than when playing against a strange, neutral, or a disliked other. In Phase 4, however, after having been subjected to the confederate's noncooperative behavior during Phase 3, a rather different pattern emerged: Subjects playing against a liked other, who had previously exploited them, displayed a greater latency before transmitting than those playing in the three other conditions. Cooperation with a friend followed by the friend's betrayal thus led to revenge.

Related findings have emerged in a more recent study by Swingle and Gillis (1968). Subjects played a 100-trial PD game against a programmed opponent who either chose cooperatively at first and then switched to competition for the remainder of the game or began competitively and became more cooperative. One day prior to the experiment, subjects were asked to make sociometric ratings of their classmates and, on the basis of these ratings, were led to believe that their partner was someone they liked, disliked, or had no previous association with. The investigators found in support of Proposition 8 that subjects paired with a "liked other" behaved more cooperatively than those paired with a "stranger," with subjects in the "disliked other" condition behaving most competitively. In addition they observed an intriguing interaction between other's strategy and his attractiveness rating. Subjects playing against a liked confederate who switched from competition to cooperation became increasingly cooperative, while those playing against a liked other who switched from cooperation to competition became more competitive (vengeful). This pattern did not emerge when a subject's partner was either disliked or a stranger.

Taken together, the findings of Swingle's research indicate that bargainers are indeed likely to function more effectively in the presence of a friend than a stranger—and especially a nonfriend or enemy. Given an act of betrayal by a friend, however, the tables may "turn with a vengeance." An exploitative act by a person one trusts is likely to lead to greater suspicion and competitive, retaliatory behavior than the same act performed by someone who is a total stranger or, for that matter, someone who is roundly disliked. As we saw in Chapter 7, in our discussion of the individual differences literature, a cooperative high IO individual tends to make attributions of trustworthiness to his partner and tends to behave cooperatively himself. Given the betrayal of this trust, however, the cooperative high IO bargainer is likely to behave even more vindictively than one who is either a competitive high IO or a low IO.

Manipulations of Perceived Similarity

The findings of six "perceived similarity" studies lend unequivocal support to Proposition 8. Four of these experiments employed the PD game, and in each it was found that the perception of high similarity led to greater cooperation than the perception of low similarity (Deignan, 1970; Kaufman, 1967; Tornatzky, 1970; Tornatzky & Geiwitz, 1968). Kaufman, moreover, found that high similarity more often resulted in expectations of cooperation by the other than did low similarity. And Tornatzky and Geiwitz reported that subjects high in perceived similarity behaved more cooperatively over trials, while those low in perceived similarity behaved more competitively.

Lewicki (1970), in a study of the effects of cooperative or exploitative behavior on subsequent behavior in a different relationship, first had subjects play against a confederate in a two-person game in which they were induced to cooperate with or exploit the other. The subjects were then asked to complete a series of self-descriptive paragraphs, on the basis of which they were paired with a "new" other who was said to be similar or dissimilar or about whom no information was available. The subject and the new other (a programmed strategy) played a 50-trial version of Deutsch's Allocation game. Lewicki found, as predicted, that subjects made significantly more exploitative and defensive choices in their subsequent relationship when they had earlier been induced to behave exploitatively. More pertinent with respect to our proposition was his finding that cooperative choices were made with the greatest frequency in the condition in which the subject had previously been cooperative and was paired with someone who was perceived as highly similar.

Finally, Krauss (1966) ran pairs of subjects in the Acme–Bolt Trucking game with bilateral gates. Among the variables manipulated in this study were: the subject's attitude toward his partner, varied by presenting each subject with a set of the other's self-ratings which were either highly similar or dissimilar to the subject's own; and "attitudinal anchoring," manipulated by describing the subject's self-rating as a source of either highly reliable or insufficient information (strong versus weak anchoring). Krauss found that bargaining effectiveness, as measured by gate use and average time taken to complete a trip, was greatest when subjects were strongly anchored in the belief that they were highly similar. Conversely, bargaining was least effective when the subjects thought they were highly dissimilar and this attitude was again strongly anchored.

MO–IO Interaction: Summary

The evidence accumulated in the preceding sections points to the validity of Proposition 8: Thirteen of the 19 studies reviewed have reported findings which indicate that an experimentally induced high IO coupled with a cooperative MO on the one hand or a competitive MO on the other is likely to result in bargaining that is, respectively, most effective and least effective. We would point out, however, that none of these experiments was designed for the express purpose of testing this particular interaction. Rather, we have attempted to test the validity of our proposition by reading between the lines. As in the case of the potentially important but largely untested interaction of MO and power, further research, specifically designed to test Proposition 8, is necessary.

THE INTERACTION OF POWER AND IO

Just as IO appears to interact with MO, so too do we expect it to interact with power—by further intensifying those tendencies that the power parameter generates in its own right. In particular, we wish to argue that bargainers will tend to function most effectively when when they are of equal power and high in IO, functioning least effectively when they are of unequal power and are again high in IO (Proposition 9).

When bargainers possess comparable power (other things being equal), their relationship is in a sense a "democratic" one. Each is just as powerful and just as weak as the other. Given the absence of pressures likely to heighten the importance of intangible issues (such as a competitive MO), we might therefore expect the parties to resolve their conflict of interest with relative ease—by attempting to allocate available resources equally. When the bargainers, in addition, share an experimentally induced high IO, the ease with which they are able to settle their dispute should be further enhanced: Both are sensitive to interpersonal information which is likely to increase their awareness both of the comparability of their control and of the salience of an equal division of outcomes. The effect of coupling equal power with a high IO is thus to facilitate the resolution of problems of coordination. So, although equal power may lead to effective bargaining even when IO is low, conditions are maximally favorable for effective functioning when IO is high.

When bargainers have noncomparable power, on the other hand, their relationship is "undemocratic." One party is stronger than the other and, given the opportunity, is likely to take advantage of this reality through attempts at exploitation. The weaker party, unless he can withdraw from the relationship or seek an alliance with others like himself, is in turn likely to be forced to behave in passive, submissive fashion. Bargaining, considered in terms of the mutual gains or losses in the relationship, is therefore likely to prove rather ineffective. When the bargainers, in addition to having unequal power, are provided with an experimentally induced low IO, the outcomes of this ineffective exchange are likely to be overdetermined: The more powerful party will probably be quite successful in his attempts to manipulate and exploit the weaker who, in turn, will probably display little resistance. So, although bargaining is quite ineffective in this situation, it is at least unlikely to be exacerbated by the arousal of a host of other intangible issues.

A rather different pattern may be expected to occur when the bargainers share a high IO. With both parties sensitized to interpersonal information, the salience of their power inequality is likely to be heightened. While this heightened salience may induce the more powerful party to behave even more exploitatively than he would have in the absence of this interpersonal information, it may also promote greater resistance on the part of the weaker. Given constant reminders of the other's superior strength, as well as disturbing indications that his powerful opponent hopes to lose no opportunity to use that power to the full, why should the weaker party passively submit? Thus, when power inequality is coupled with a high IO, a host of costly intangible issues may arise that make ineffective bargaining even more likely to occur than when unequal power is coupled with a low IO.

As we saw in the case of Proposition 2, for which considerable evidence was obtained, equal power among bargainers is generally likely to result in more effective bargaining than unequal power. The simple argument behind Proposition 9, therefore, is that in the presence of a high IO these tendencies toward effective or ineffective bargaining as a function of power are likely to be further magnified. Unfortunately we are aware of no research to date that permits a direct or indirect test of this proposition, and its validity must therefore remain unsubstantiated.

THE INTERACTION OF MO, POWER, AND IO

Just as we have argued that the three parameters of interdependence, considered alone or two at a time, display "main" and "simple interaction" effects with respect to bargaining effectiveness, so too do we expect all three parameters to act in concert. In particular, we expect that bargainers will tend to function most effectively when they share a cooperative MO, are of equal power, and are high in IO, functioning least effectively when they are competitively oriented, again of equal power, and again high in IO (Proposition 10).

A cooperative MO predisposes bargainers to develop a shared attitude of trust as well as a desire to allocate resources fairly and equitably. The effective bargaining that is likely to result should be further enhanced when the parties possess comparable power, since problems associated with the coordination of resource allocation will probably be reduced. Finally, when the bargainers in addition share an experimentally induced high IO, their trusting attitude and their search for a fair division of outcomes are likely to be further bolstered by the availability of buttressing, mutually supportive interpersonal information. The other, it is clear, is worthy of one's trust and can be counted on to approach the conflict of interest with an eye to maximizing mutual rather than individual gain. Thus it is when a cooperative MO is coupled with equal power and a high IO that conditions for effective bargaining are most favorable.

On the other hand, bargainers who approach a dispute with a shared competitive MO are out to manipulate and exploit the other if they possibly can. Given this shared orientation, the parties are likely to develop a relationship characterized by a climate of mutual distrust and suspicion. When the bargainers, in addition, share a high IO, the worst suspicions of each are likely to be confirmed, and an already costly and ineffective relationship is likely to deteriorate even further. Finally, the possession of comparable power, rather than facilitating the coordination of resource allocation, is instead—in the face of a competitive MO buttressed by a high IO—likely to bring to the fore a plethora of intangible issues whose resolution may be close to impossible. Why should a bargainer display any willingness to make concessions when he suspects the other of being wholly untrustworthy, when this perception is reinforced by corroborative interpersonal information, and when the other is no stronger or weaker than he? Thus it is when a competitive MO is coupled with equal power and a high IO that conditions for effective bargaining are most unfavorable.

CONCLUDING COMMENT

The three parameters of interdependence that we have discussed— motivational orientation (MO), power, and interpersonal orientation (IO)— clearly exert a robust influence on the quality of the bargaining exchange. A number of the propositions, advanced at the beginning of this chapter in the context of a "factorial model" of interdependence, have been lent support by a review of the experimental literature. Others, however, have received less support or have gone untested because of the paucity of pertinent research.

In general it appears that the most important determinant of bargaining effectiveness is MO. Cooperative and competitive orientations, despite variations in power and IO, are likely to result in extremely effective and ineffective bargaining, respectively. Power, or more accurately the distribution of power, is clearly an important determinant of effectiveness also, but its effects tend to be muddied by the fact that power is a complex, multidimensional parameter. As we have seen, simple experimental manipulations of one dimension of power have all too often simultaneously varied other dimensions as well, making it exceptionally difficult to sort out the precise impact of this parameter. IO, finally, appears to exert its most powerful effects upon bargaining not alone but in concert with other variables, intensifying and increasing the variance of tendencies that may already exist.

The propositions and model of interdependence we have advanced are meant to represent nothing more than a preliminary step in the direction of better understanding the nature of the fabric that binds bargainers together. Despite the appearance of an extraordinary number of bargaining studies within the last decade or so, considerable additional, and rather different, research is necessary if we are to judge the acceptability of this (or some other) model of interdependence.

9

Social Influence and Influence Strategies

As we have attempted to indicate throughout the book, bargaining is fundamentally an interpersonal process. Bargainers do things to and with one another. Through the offers and counteroffers they make and the social postures they continually display, bargainers shape the outcomes of their interaction in strategic fashion.

A central characteristic of the bargaining relationship is the fact that each party is dependent upon the other for the quality of the outcomes that he himself receives. A division of resources, after all, can be reached only by mutual consent. But dependence with respect to outcomes goes beyond the mere exchange or division of resources. Important intangible as well as tangible issues are at stake, having to do with how one looks in the eyes of one's opponent, one's constituents, and the various other audiences who are spectators to the bargaining process. Bargainers want and need to believe that they are capable of moving others through a range of outcomes—of exerting influence. They need to believe that they look good, or at least not foolish, in the eyes of others. These needs are fundamentally social. They can be satisfied only by obtaining the respect, positive regard, esteem, and so forth of others—especially of the adversary with whom the bargainer continually interacts.

In attempting to decide on the kind of bargaining stance to adopt, each party must acquire information about the other's true preferences, intentions, and social perceptions: "what he wants," "what he will settle for," and "what he thinks of me." Even as he is in the process of acquiring this important information, however, the bargainer must tentatively adopt a particular posture and disclose information about his own preferences, intentions, and perceptions—information that may be used by the other to fashion his own strategy. Bargainers, thus, are influenced by the information they obtain or are exposed to about the other and, in turn, exert influence themselves through the information they disclose. *It is this exchange of information, the attributions to which it leads, and the ways in which it is shaped for the purposes of mutual social influence, that represents the fundamental strategic issue in bargaining.*

Information about a bargainer's preferences, intentions, and perceptions of the other is conveyed in often complex, interconnected fashion—a "coded language" that must be systematically broken apart, then pieced together, if it is to be understood. Any given "move," if interpreted closely and carefully enough, may be found to provide information about what a bargainer wants, what he will settle for, and what he thinks of his adversary.

How then, through what kinds of explicit and implicit channels, is this information conveyed in bargaining relationships? Based both on our review of the relevant literature, as well as on a conceptual analysis of the bargaining process, it appears that there are three interrelated ways in which preferences, intentions, and perceptions are transmitted.

First, as our review of the experimental literature will demonstrate, the course of bargaining is largely determined by the initial offers and counteroffers made by each side. Early moves and gestures are critical in the creation of the psychological setting within which the "game" is to be played. It is here that rules and norms are first implanted, issues such as trust and bargaining toughness are considered for the first time, and the division of resources to which each party aspires is presented for the other's consideration. It is during these early encounters that bargainers begin to exchange information about their disposition toward the other, as well as the subjective utility scale that each uses to judge the attractiveness of potential outcomes.

Second, apart from their opening gestures, it is through the arrangement of offers and counteroffers that bargainers attempt to forge an acceptable agreement. Moves convey information in two important ways: (1) When considered independent of the particular sequence in which they are patterned, moves present a picture of a bargainer's overall cooperativeness: the extent to which a mutually satisfactory agreement is of greater importance to him than one that maximizes own gain at the expense of (or without regard for) the other. (2) When analyzed in terms of the ways in which they are strung together, moves describe the magnitude, rate, and timing with which concessions are made, and the extent to which these concessions are contingent upon the behavior of the other. The detailed patterning of offers and counteroffers, in the form of concessions, provides each bargainer with important information about the other's preferences and intentions (his utilities, flexibility, toughness, etc.). In addition, to the extent that the other's moves appear to be made in response to the bargainer's own behavior, information is conveyed about the bargainer's ability to exert influence systematically.

Finally, in order to increase the likelihood of an offer being acceptable to the other side, bargainers often accompany their offers with a variety of other more explicitly articulated influence attempts. While the availability and effectiveness of accompanying appeals and demands is shaped largely by numerous structural constraints (discussed in Chapters 4–6), it nevertheless appears—following French and Raven's (1959) useful analysis of social power—that bargainers can attempt to influence one another in six ways:

By emphasizing his similarity with the other and attempting to engender feelings of solidarity ("referent" power), a bargainer can increase the acceptability of his offer. Where bargainers have, or appear to have, a common opponent—a threatening or intervening third party, for example—referent influence may be used to increase the likelihood of a particular agreement being concluded.

For "expert" power to be effective, one bargainer must be able to convince the other that he possesses superior knowledge or ability. Since, as Raven and Kruglanski (1970) point out, such a state can occur only if a high degree of trust exists in the relationship, expert influence is unlikely to be used effectively by most bargainers, especially at points early in the exchange. Note, however, that in the hands of a mutually acceptable third party, this form of influence may be instrumental in the resolution of conflict.

To the extent that one bargainer can convince the other that he has a right to make a particular offer or demand ("legitimate" power) the likelihood of this offer being accepted is increased. By appealing to "oughts" of various kinds (rules, precedents, norms of reciprocity, fair play, etc.), each party can attempt to goad or prod the other into agreement. Or for that matter, he can "shame" the other into acceptance of an offer by pointing to signs of his own weakness, inability, or dependency (Dorris, 1972). As Raven and Kruglanski (1970) indicate, however, legitimate influence can work only if there is mutual acceptance of the basis of legitimacy. For this reason, as in the case of expert power, appeals to legitimacy are more likely to be effective in the hands of an accepted third party than in the hands of one's adversary.

By pointing out contingencies about which the other has little or no awareness, by providing him with information ("informational" power), a bargainer can attempt to make his offer stick. Such informational appeals, however, can be effective only if there is some minimal degree of trust in the relationship. To the extent that bargainers feel that they have very different basic values, information may be seen as "misinformation" and may intensify mutual suspicion.

Finally, to the extent that one bargainer can successfully impose reward or punishment on the other ("reward" or "coercive" power), in relation to the other's performance or nonperformance of some behavior, he can increase the likelihood that his offer will prove acceptable. Through the language of promises and threats, respectively, reward and coercive influence provide the other with important information about preferences, intentions, and social perceptions. An important difference between these two bases of influence and the four we briefly described above resides in the fact that the first four depend for their effectiveness on the agent's ability to engender a variety of private beliefs in the other: the belief that the agent is fundamentally like oneself (referent), knows more (expert), has a right to make certain appeals or demands (legitimate), and is providing accurate information (informational). The effectiveness of promises and threats, on the other hand, depends not on the other's private beliefs, but on the influence agent's ability to mediate reward and punishment by maintaining surveillance over the other's behavior.

More than 100 experimental studies have examined the effects of social influence and influence strategies in bargaining. In order to facilitate a review and integration of this extensive literature, we will consider it in relation to the conceptual framework outlined above. First we will examine the findings that concern the effects of opening moves upon the course of bargaining. Next we will consider issues related to the overall patterning of moves and countermoves. Finally, we will review the research concerned with the appeals and demands which accompany moves, confining our analysis to the only two bases of influence that have received experimental attention in the bargaining literature: promises and threats.

THE LANGUAGE OF OPENING MOVES

One of the ways in which bargainers influence the outcomes of their interaction is through the array of moves and gestures that they exchange and display during the early moments of their relationship. These early moves and gestures convey information about each party's initial preferences, intentions, and perceptions, and are instrumental in shaping the psychological climate that will prevail throughout the bargaining relationship.

Opening Moves and Cooperation

Almost without exception, experimental studies of opening moves in bargaining have focused on a single important strategic issue, having to do with the effects of early cooperative or competitive overtures upon the course of bargaining. The general conclusion of this research is that *the early initiation of cooperative behavior tends to promote the development of trust and a mutually beneficial, cooperative relationship; early competitive behavior, on the other hand, tends to induce mutual suspicion and competition.*

A number of experiments, employing the PD game or some variant of this paradigm, have examined the effects of opening moves by having subjects play against an initially cooperative or competitive experimental strategy. Three of these studies have found no differences as a function of the other's initial behavior (Bixenstine *et al.*, 1963; Bixenstine & Wilson, 1963; Sermat, 1964). The others, however, have reported findings in the expected direction.

Crumbaugh and Evans (1967), Michelini (1971), Oskamp (1970), Sermat and Gregovich (1966), and Tedeschi, Hiester, Lesnick, and Gahagan (1968d) found that initial cooperative behavior by an experimental strategy induced greater subsequent cooperation by subjects than did initially competitive behavior. Using a somewhat different manipulation of the other's behavior, Kaufman (1967) had subjects play a 100-trial version of the PD game in which no feedback was provided about the other's choices. At the end of the fiftieth trial, half the subjects were informed that the other player had behaved cooperatively so far, while the remainder were told that the other had behaved in predominantly competitive fashion. Subjects given "cooperative" feedback were found to behave more cooperatively in the second half of the game than those given competitive feedback.

In a complex experimental study of betrayal and reconciliation, Komorita and Mechling (1967) had subjects play a PD game against another who behaved cooperatively for either 4 or 10 trials before "betraying" subjects by: choosing competitively for 2 consecutive trials, then choosing cooperatively (repenting) for 3 consecutive trials, and finally mirroring the subject's previous response (playing tit-for-tat) for the remainder of the game. Komorita and Mechling found that subjects required fewer trials to reach a criterion of 5 consecutive cooperative choices when betrayal was preceded by 10 rather than by 4 initial cooperative trials.

In an interesting and important study of the development of trust, Swinth (1967b) had subjects play a version of the PD game against an experimental strategy in which several low risk (low payoff) "commitment" trials were followed by a high risk (high payoff) "test" trial. One of two experimental strategies was employed by the experimenter during the commitment trials, in an attempt to induce cooperation: an initiating strategy (in which the other chose cooperatively, regardless of the subject's own behavior) or a responding strategy (in which the other responded in kind to the subject's previous choice). Swinth found that subjects who successfully established trust at any point in the commitment trials were far more likely to be cooperative on subsequent test trials than those who did not establish trust. In addition he found that trust was established with far greater difficulty by subjects who were exposed to a responding strategy rather than an initiating one by the other. Bargainers, it would appear, do not want to take the risks involved in making a unilaterally trusting, cooperative overture to the other. These risks, after all, consist not only of tangible costs but of important intangibles as well. Rather than offer one's hand in friendship, only to incur the risk of having it slapped away, it may be safer—and is certainly easier—to offer no hand at all.

In yet another PD-type study to examine the effects on later cooperation of opening moves by a simulated other, Sermat (1967a) had subjects play against a strategy that was initially either cooperative or competitive for 30 trials, then conditionally cooperative (tit-for-tat) for 200 trials. He found that a cooperative other induced greater subsequent cooperation than a competitive one. In addition, and of particular interest in light of Swinth's (1967b) results, was the finding that subjects in the cooperative pretreatment showed a powerful and enduring tendency to retaliate when the other had defected first and a strong tendency to cooperate when they themselves had defected first. Thus, the early establishment of a trusting relationship has important consequences for the way in which subsequent defection is viewed. One's own defection may be seen as a temporary "aberration," a momentary submission to temptation—forgivable, understandable, and likely to be followed by guilt-induced repentance and cooperation. Defection by the other, however, is likely to be seen as a betrayal of one's trust—betrayal which, because of the social costs it implies, is likely to be followed by prolonged and vindictive retaliatory behavior.

Lock-in Effects

In addition to the above studies, each of which has examined the development of cooperation by varying the initial behavior of a simulated other, a number of PD-type experiments have considered the consequences of early behavior by live, freely interacting bargaining pairs. The findings of these studies consistently point to the importance of what Pilisuk and Rapoport (1964b) have called the "lock-in" effect: the tendency of bargaining pairs to initiate a pattern either of mutual cooperation or of mutual competition early in their relationship and then to persist in one or the other of these patterns for the remainder of their interaction.

Komorita (1973), Oskamp (1970), Rapoport and Chammah (1965a), and Terhune (1968) each found that later cooperation in the PD game was highest among bargaining pairs who both chose cooperatively on the first trial; the fewest cooperative choices tended to appear among subjects who began by defecting and who were the victims of defection in return. Pilisuk, et al. (1965) and Pilisuk and Skolnick (1968), using an interesting expanded version of the PD game, reported a similar tendency for bargainers to lock in to a cooperative or competitive pattern early in their relationship.

In the paradigm developed by Pilisuk and his colleagues, subjects were presented with an arms race–disarmament dilemma in which anywhere from 0 to 20 "missiles" (represented by poker chips) could be converted into "factories," and vice versa. Players' outcomes were determined by the number of missiles or factories produced by each side. These outcomes, represented in a 20 × 20 matrix, conformed to the general principles of the PD game. The joint production of factories (a mutually cooperative choice) led to a positive outcome for both players, although not as high an outcome as could be obtained by producing missiles in the presence of the other's factories. On the other hand, the joint production of missiles (mutual competition) resulted in mutually costly, negative outcomes.

Using this paradigm, Pilisuk and his colleagues classified subject pairs, on the basis of their behavior on the last five game trials, as resembling one of three characteristic types: Doves (cooperators), Hawks (competitors) and Mugwumps (intermediates). In a post hoc analysis it was found that Doves were more cooperative on the very first trial of the game than either Mugwumps or Hawks. Stated in other words, if a pair had an early experience of mutual cooperation, it was likely to evolve into a Dove pair, especially if both players simultaneously made cooperative, trusting gestures.

The robustness of the lock-in effect can be seen not only in the PD game and its variants, but in more complex paradigms as well. Deutsch et al. (1967) reported a cooperative lock-in pattern in their Allocation game (described in greater detail on pp. 273–274). Subjects in this study played against a simulated other who attempted to elicit cooperation by employing one of several different strategies. In three of these conditions the other began by making a noncontingent cooperative choice on trial one, then responded in differing, contingently cooperative fashion on each of the subsequent trials. Deutsch *et al.* reported that of the 45 subjects run in these three conditions, more than one-third (18) had to be eliminated because they did not experience the different strategies. Instead these subjects tended to choose cooperatively on trial one (as did the other) and followed this choice with consistently cooperative behavior for the remainder of the game.

Based on our own experimental knowledge of the Acme–Bolt Trucking game (Brown, 1968; Deutsch, Canavan, & Rubin, 1971) it appears that the lock-in effect operates in this paradigm as well. Bargaining pairs that are unable to solve the coordination problem implicit in this game tend to initiate, and then persist in, a variety of competitive behaviors (deadlocking, the use of threat for purposes of coercion, withdrawal from the relationship, etc.). Other pairs, however, manage to work out a cooperative alternation solution early in their relationship and then adopt a mutually cooperative stance for the remainder of the game.

The findings of the various studies we have reviewed strongly underscore the importance of opening moves in the establishment of trust and the subsequent maintenance of cooperation. One of the reasons, we suspect, for the importance of this early period in the life of the bargaining relationship is the fact that, despite the frequency of ritualized posturing, positions are relatively fluid. Jaws are not yet set as firmly in place as they are later in the exchange. Bargainers often seem to consider it acceptable and appropriate for opening moves to be used to test limits and to explore a variety of behaviors with one's adversary before committing oneself to a particular posture. (Teger, 1970, for example, has found that a hostile act performed early in a relationship is far less likely to induce a retaliatory response than one performed after a period of interaction.) Hence the potential psychological costs involved in trusting the other, considerable as they are, may not be as great in the early moments of the relationship as they are once positional lines have been drawn. And, once established, mutual trust may help commit bargainers to a cooperative pattern that prevails throughout their interaction.

The Extremity of Initial Offers

Opening moves in bargaining may be used to convey information not only about each party's disposition toward the other (his cooperativeness) but also about his subjective utilities. Initial offers and counteroffers inform bargainers about the division of resources to which each aspires and, in so doing, specify the range of outcomes that are possible in the relationship. Beginning with extreme initial offers, bargainers can and do make systematic concessions, as they attempt to approach a mutually acceptable division of resources. In order for bargainers to reach an optimal division of these resources, however, they must begin by informing the other about the upper limit of their utility scale—their level of aspiration.

Several experimental studies employing the Bilateral Monopoly paradigm have examined the effects of extreme versus moderate opening offers upon bargaining outcomes. The general conclusion reached in this research is that *bargainers attain higher and more satisfactory outcomes when they begin their interaction with extreme rather than more moderate demands.* (It is perhaps worth noting that paradigms like the PD game cannot be effectively used to study the extremity of opening offers. Players generally have only two choices available to them, rather than a wide range from which to select. In addition, these two choices have clear cooperative or competitive implications for the relationship: An offer represents either a cooperative or a competitive gesture, rather than a neutral or exploratory one. Hence, the effects of opening exchanges of information about subjective utilities can not be conveniently analyzed.)

In studies of opening offers and concessions, Chertkoff and Conley (1967), and more recently Hinton, Hamner, and Pohlen (1974), have found that bargainers achieved higher outcomes when they made extreme rather than moderate initial demands. Komorita and Brenner (1968) reported that a strategy of making an initial offer at the level one expected to settle at eventually was an ineffective means of reaching agreement. Bargainers achieved higher outcomes when they made extreme initial demands, coupled with gradual concessions, than when they made a large initial concession and remained firmly at that level. Similarly, Chertkoff and Baird (1971), in a variant of Kelley *et al.*'s (1967) Game of 9's found that the more extreme a confederate's initial demands (the greater the extremity of his stated "break-even point," or CL_{alt}), the more often subjects complied and the greater their concessions.

Liebert, Smith, Hill, and Keiffer (1968), in a study of the effects of information and magnitude of initial offer, had subjects play a version of the Bilateral Monopoly game against a programmed experimental strategy that made either an extreme or moderate initial demand. In addition, half of the subjects were given information about the range of profits attainable by both themselves and their opponent, while the remaining subjects knew only their own possible profits. The investigators found that given no information about the other's utilities, as is often the case in bargaining relationships, extreme initial demands by the other led to higher outcomes for him than more moderate demands. On the other hand, when subjects had information about both their own and the other's possible profits, extreme initial demands by the other led to more extreme counterdemands (and poorer outcomes for him) than more moderate demands—largely, it would appear, because the demanding other was now seen as selfish and unreasonable. Overall, it was found that bargaining behavior was affected more by the other's initial offer than by his subsequent concession rate. Based on this result, and a similar finding reported by Pruitt and Drews (1969), it thus appears that opening moves are critical in shaping the course of subsequent interaction. Indeed, initial demands accounted for 67% of the variance in subsequent demands in the Pruitt and Drews study.

In one final study, Benton *et al.* (1972) had subjects play a two-person game, involving the division of monetary outcomes, against a programmed other. The other followed one of three concession schedules, making an initial demand that was either extreme or minimal and was maintained throughout or making an extreme initial demand followed by gradual concessions. The investigators found that bargaining effectiveness (as measured by average pair earnings) was greatest when subjects confronted a strategy that coupled an extreme initial demand with subsequent concessions. Subjects in this condition reported feeling most satisfied with and responsible for their outcomes.

The preceding research generally suggests that bargainers fare better when they begin with extreme rather than moderate opening demands. But why should this be so? First of all, by making extreme initial demands, a bargainer avoids the pitfall of adopting a stance that may prove to be too "generous"; he is thus less likely to accept a smaller division of the resources than the other is willing to offer. Second, by making extreme initial demands, the bargainer often gives himself more time to assemble information about the other's preferences and intentions. Third, he communicates his expectations of how he should be treated by the other—namely that he should not be exploited. Finally, his extreme initial offers provide the other with valuable information about his subjective utilities.

It should be pointed out that a bargainer's initial offers, in addition to representing an assertion of his own subjective utilities, are likely to influence the magnitude of the other's subjective utilities as well. Rubin and DiMatteo (1972) have demonstrated this in a recent Bilateral Monopoly study. Subjects in this experiment were placed in the role of the seller and played against a noncontingent programmed strategy which acted as the buyer. The investigators were interested in assessing the conditions affecting the magnitude of three subjective utility parameters: aspiration level (AL), defined as the profit a bargainer would like to attain; CL, defined as a bargainer's point of subjective neutrality; and CL_{alt}, the lowest profit at which a bargainer would be willing to settle. Among the independent variables manipulated in this design was the magnitude of the buyer's offers, varied by exposing subjects to a strategy that yielded them a potential profit ranging either from $840 to $900 (high offers) or from $370 to $430 (low offers). For purposes of the present analysis, it is important to bear in mind that the magnitude of the strategy's initial offer was greater in the high offer than in the low offer condition.

Rubin and DiMatteo found that subjects exposed to a high (attractive) initial offer from the buyer bargained more toughly, attained greater profit for themselves, and were more satisfied with their outcomes than subjects exposed to a lower initial offer. With respect to subjective utilities, it was found that subjects receiving a high initial offer set their AL, CL, and CL_{alt} far higher than those receiving a lower offer. (Yukl, 1974, has reported similar results with respect to AL.) Thus initial offers, in addition to providing a bargainer with information about the other's subjective utilities, are likely to provide information about, and thereby shape, his own as well. And as we shall see in our discussion of concession making in bargaining, the exchange of (extreme) initial offers, through the information about subjective utilities it provides, is critical to the development of an optimal agreement.

THE OVERALL PATTERN OF MOVES AND COUNTERMOVES

Opening moves, we have argued, have important consequences for the subsequent development of the bargaining relationship. As we shall attempt to demonstrate in this section, however, the course of bargaining is shaped not only by these early gestures but by the moves and countermoves that follow in their wake. Considered without regard for the particular ways in which they are pieced together, the overall configuration of these moves conveys important information about each party's general disposition toward the other. Thus, a bargainer who is invariably cooperative is reacted to very differently than one who never sways from a competitive stance. On the other hand, when considered in terms of the particular order in which they are sequenced, moves convey information both about each party's perceptions of the other and about the preferences and intentions of each with respect to possible divisions of resources. A bargainer who never sways from a cooperative stance is seen and reacted to differently than one who appears to undergo a shift in the course of bargaining from a competitive to a more cooperative position.

Overall Cooperativeness

The PD game and its variants seem to be particularly well suited for an examination of the influence of overall cooperativeness. By simulating the behavior of a second player in this paradigm, researchers can systematically vary the other's overall cooperativeness—the frequency with which he makes cooperative choices—and then examine its effects on subjects' behavior. Our review of the bargaining literature has uncovered a great many experimental studies of this type.

Eight experiments have found no systematic relationship between the overall cooperativeness of a simulated other and behavior in PD-type games (Gahagan & Tedeschi, 1968a; Lindskold & Tedeschi, 1971; McClintock et al., 1965; McClintock et al., 1963; McKeown et al., 1967; Phelan & Richardson, 1969; Tedeschi, Burrill, & Gahagan, 1969; Wilson & Wong, 1968). Two experiments have reported that a noncooperative other induced greater cooperation in subjects than a cooperative one (Lindskold, 1971; Sermat, 1964).

The remaining experimental studies (numbering 22), however, have found that the greater the cooperativeness of a simulated other in a PD game, the greater a subject's own cooperativeness (Bonoma, Horai, Lindskold, Gahagan, & Tedeschi, 1969; Deutsch, 1958; Gahagan, Long, & Horai, 1969; Gruder & Duslak, 1973; Heller, 1967; Kleinke & Pohlen, 1971; Knapp & Podell, 1968; Komorita, 1965; Komorita et al., 1968; Lave, 1965; Lynch, 1968; Pruitt, 1968, 1970; Shure & Meeker, 1968; Solomon, 1960; Swingle & Coady, 1967; Tedeschi, Aranoff, & Gahagan, 1968a; Tedeschi, Aranoff, Gahagan, & Hiester, 1968b; Tedeschi, Hiester, & Gahagan, 1969c; Whitworth & Lucker, 1969; Wilson, 1969; Wyer, 1971).

The general conclusion implied by the above research is that *cooperation begets cooperation; and, conversely, noncooperation begets noncooperation.* But why should this be so? Bargainers, we have argued, are often concerned with intangible issues having to do with how they look in the eyes of others. In the presence of an adversary who behaves in consistently competitive fashion, the need to maintain or not lose face emerges as a central theme in the relationship and drives the bargainer to defend himself through competitive behavior. On the other hand, to the extent that one's adversary chooses to cooperate, a bargainer's need to maintain face (to look tough) is dramatically reduced, and he can and does risk the reciprocation of cooperation.

Given the development and maintenance of mutual cooperation, it would appear that bargainers should be better able to work for and attain an optimally satisfactory division of resources. Yet an intriguing study by Schenitzki (1963) suggests that this may not always be the case. Schenitzki had pairs of bargainers play a version of the Bilateral Monopoly game in which they were given information about their own range of profits only and could communicate only by means of written offers and counteroffers. In addition, subjects were explicitly instructed either to maximize their joint profits (cooperative induction) or to maximize their own profits without regard for the other (individualistic induction). While one might reasonably expect cooperative induction pairs to have obtained the maximum joint payoff (MJP) more frequently than individualistic pairs, Schenitzki found exactly the reverse: Bargainers given the individualistic induction obtained MJP more often than those who had been explicitly told to maximize joint gain.

In explanation of these paradoxical findings, Kelley and Schenitzki (1972) suggested that cooperatively oriented bargainers, in their attempts to obtain MJP, may have tried too hard to take account of the other's profits as well as their own, and in so doing may have made important judgmental errors. In the absence of information about the other's subjective utilities, these bargainers were so concerned with giving their partner what he appeared to want that they failed to communicate adequately their own utilities. Individualistically oriented bargainers, on the other hand, concentrated on presenting the series of offers and counteroffers that were most beneficial to them, without regard for the other, and thereby managed to obtain implicitly the optimal division of resources that the cooperative bargainers were explicitly striving for. Schenitzki's research, as well as the related findings of a study by Morgan and Sawyer (1967), suggests that in the absence of information about the other's subjective utilities, bargainers are most likely to reach an optimal agreement if they each focus on the clear and honest presentation of their own needs and preferences and avoid trying to "get inside the head" of the other. The bargainer, for example, who sets his opening offers at a level below that of the outcome to which he really aspires (perhaps because he likes the other or because he doesn't want to appear greedy) may end up settling for a less satisfactory agreement than he might otherwise have obtained by being more "selfish." And if both bargainers act in this fashion, they may jointly obtain a less than maximal division of resources. Hence, *one of the potential pathologies of an otherwise beneficial, mutually cooperative relationship is the possibility that cooperators, in their concern with taking the role of the other, may develop and act upon incorrect expectations about the other's preferences and intentions, and the result may be mutually detrimental miscoordination.*

The Patterning of Concessions

We have seen that bargainers influence each other by varying the cooperativeness implicit in their overall array of moves. Another important way in which bargainers exert influence is by varying the particular sequence in which these moves are arranged. By starting tough and then systematically softening his position, by making (positive) concessions, a bargainer can communicate his willingness to settle for a particular division of resources. Even in the relatively simple PD paradigm, a bargainer can in effect make positive concessions by following a spate of competitive choices with cooperative ones. On the other hand, by increasingly toughening his position (or in the PD game, by shifting from cooperative to competitive, or contingently cooperative, behavior) a bargainer can make negative concessions and can convey his unwillingness to settle for a particular offer made by the other. Finally, by adopting either a consistently tough or a consistently soft stance throughout his relationship with the other, a bargainer can elect to make no concessions at all.

A number of experimental studies employing one or more variants of the PD game have examined the effects of shifts in the cooperativeness of a simulated other upon subjects' cooperation. Three of these studies have found no systematic relationship between shifts in the other's cooperativeness and subject behavior (Bobbitt, 1967; Rapoport & Cole, 1968; Schellenberg, 1964). The conclusion reached by the others is that a sequential change in the other's behavior from low to high cooperativeness induces greater cooperation than either a shift from high to low or a pattern of high unchanging cooperativeness (Bixenstine & Wilson, 1963; Harford, 1965; Harford & Hill, 1967; Harford & Solomon, 1967; Oskamp, 1970; Rapoport & Mowshowitz, 1966; Scodel, 1962; Sermat, 1964, 1967a; Swingle, 1968b; Swingle & Coady, 1967; Swingle & Gillis, 1968; Wilson, 1971; Wilson & Insko, 1968). Based on this research it thus appears that *a bargainer who makes (positive) concessions is more likely to elicit cooperation from the other than one who makes either negative concessions or no concessions at all.*

The above generalization receives additional support from the findings of several experiments that examined the effects of contingent experimental strategies upon subject behavior. Pilisuk and Skolnick (1968) had subjects play the previously described arms race–disarmament game against a simulated other who employed one of two experimental strategies: "matching" (the number of missiles produced by the other was equal to the number produced by the subject on the previous trial); or "conciliatory" (the number of missiles produced by the other was equal to one less than the subject's number on the previous trial). Pilisuk and Skolnick found that the conciliatory strategy was more likely to induce cooperation than the matching one.

In a study of strategies of inducing cooperation, Deutsch *et al.* (1967) had subjects play a board game known as the Allocation game against a simulated other. On each of 60 trials, both the subject and the other could choose (allocate) one of seven different colored pegs: *black* (an individualistic choice that earned money for the subject, regardless of what the other did); *blue* (a cooperative choice that earned money for the subject only if the other player also chose blue on that trial); *white* (an altruistic choice that awarded the other money from one's own earnings); *red* (an aggressive choice that when used in an "attack," initiated by the use of an *orange* peg, earned money for the subject by taking money away from the other); *green* (a defensive choice that could neutralize the effects of a red on a one-to-one basis); and *beige* (a "disarmament" choice which voluntarily destroyed one's accumulated supply of red pegs). In an attempt to influence the subject's behavior, the other employed one of five strategies: *turn-the-other-cheek* (the subject's choice of red or orange on the previous trial was matched by white, while all other peg choices were responded to with blue); *nonpunitive* (a previous choice of black was matched by black; white by white; red or orange by green; and blue, green, or beige by blue); *deterrent* (orange matched by orange; black, green, or red matched by red; and blue, white, or beige matched by blue); *reformed sinner–turn the other cheek* (red and orange chosen on the first 15 trials, followed by beige on trial 16, then the turn-the-other-cheek strategy for the remaining trials; or *reformed sinner–nonpunitive* (red and orange pegs chosen on the first 15 trials, then beige, then the nonpunitive strategy for the duration of the game.

The findings of this complex and interesting study lend support to our generalization about concessions. Subjects in the two reformed sinner conditions, in which the other shifted from an initially competitive to a contingently cooperative stance, were induced to behave more cooperatively than subjects in the three other conditions, in which no competitive-to-cooperative shift took place. Of additional interest are Deutsch *et al.*'s findings that the nonpunitive strategy elicited far more cooperation than the deterrent one. (Gruder & Duslak, 1973, and Komorita *et al.*, 1968, have reported a similar result.) Thus it appears that one is more likely to induce an adversary to cooperate by meeting his aggression with defensive behavior than with counteraggression.

Deutsch *et al.* also found that the turn-the-other-cheek strategy was least effective in inducing cooperation: It resulted in systematic exploitation by subjects. Although Marwell, Schmitt, and Bøyesen (1973) have obtained evidence to the contrary, indicating that a pacifist strategy may elicit cooperation (at least among Norwegian subjects), other studies lend additional support to the Allocation game findings (Meeker & Shure, 1969; Shure *et al.*, 1965). Assuming that a pacifist strategy tends to be ineffective more often than not, the question arises of why this should be so. A recent experiment by Bixenstine and Gaebelein (1971) suggests one possible answer.

Subjects in this PD study played against a contingent strategy that was programmed to match their prior cooperative or competitive behavior in tit-for-tat fashion, either immediately or gradually. The investigators expected the greatest cooperation to be elicited when subjects played against a strategy that was quick to reciprocate cooperation and slow to reciprocate competitive behavior (retaliate). Instead they found that subjects exploited the other in this condition, taking advantage of his "eagerness to cooperate" by choosing competitively on these occasions. The condition that elicited the greatest cooperation was one in which the strategy was again slow to compete but was now also slow to respond to cooperation by subjects with like behavior. Because the other was slow to reciprocate cooperation, his cooperative behavior may have appeared all the more valuable, and subjects' temptation to defect was therefore reduced. As Bixenstine and Gaebelein (1971) conclude: "Turning the other cheek (or being slow-to-compete) is fine, but for maximum influence in producing mutually beneficial behavior, it is best wed to a cautious exposure of one's cheek to begin with [p. 164]!"

The role of concession making can also be seen in the Acme–Bolt Trucking game. Bargainers typically begin by deadlocking in the middle of the one-lane section of road, taking a relatively tough stance. After some jockeying back and forth and some loss of time and money for both parties, we might expect to see one player (perhaps Acme) reverse his truck, allowing the other (Bolt) to go through the one-lane section first, before completing the trip himself. On a subsequent turn we might expect the bargainers to once again meet in the middle, with Bolt backing up this time in order to permit Acme through first. This pattern of alternation, one which represents the optimal solution to the mutual coordination problem posed by the game, is a clear example of reciprocated concession making. Beginning with a relatively intransigent stance, one bargainer eventually decides to run the risk of trusting the other and makes a unilateral concession. This concession, if reciprocated, can lead to a mutually beneficial solution to the bargaining problem. However, if not reciprocated—if the concession maker is "betrayed" by his adversary—the result may well be a mutually destructive conflict that is difficult to resolve.

A number of experiments have examined the concession-making process in variants of the Bilateral Monopoly game. The general conclusions reached by these studies are first, that the rate and magnitude of concessions by a simulated other tend to be reciprocated in kind (Chertkoff & Conley, 1967; Druckman, Zechmeister, & Solomon, 1972; Komorita & Barnes, 1969; Pruitt & Johnson, 1970). Second, a strategy of starting tough and then gradually making concessions is a more effective means of reaching an optimal division of resources than one in which a softer stance is maintained throughout (Benton *et al.*, 1972; Druckman *et al.*, 1972; Komorita & Brenner, 1968; Schenitzki, 1963; Yukl, 1974). In addition, two studies have found no overall relationship between concession making and bargaining behavior (Hatton, 1967; Pruitt & Drews, 1969).

Kelley (1966) studied the concession-making process in a complex and more realistic version of the Bilateral Monopoly game—the "Classroom Negotiation" paradigm. A pair of bargainers was given a set of five issues to negotiate simultaneously. The outcome a bargainer received was determined by the overall contract reached on these five issues, where each issue contained 20 possible agreements represented as entries in a table of profits. Furthermore, while each party was provided with a table of his own potential profits, he was given no information about the other's, the latter information being obtained only by the series of offers and written communications that the bargainers exchanged. Finally, although the bargainers had a conflict of interest with respect to all five of the issues, some of them were of greater importance (yielded more favorable outcomes) to one party than to the other.

Kelley found that bargaining pairs were most likely to settle on a mutually favorable contract when they behaved in keeping with what Kelley and Schenitzki (1972) have described as the "systematic concessions model." According to this formulation, each party begins by proposing contracts for which his own profits are high. As these offers and counteroffers are rejected by the other, he then proposes contracts that are somewhat less profitable (i.e., he makes concessions). Each time a bargainer makes a concession, he thereby increases the set of contracts he considers acceptable. Concessions continue in a stepwise, systematic fashion until bargainers reach the point where their two sets of acceptable contracts first overlap. This is the point of maximum joint profit and represents the optimal settlement.

One implication of the systematic concessions model is the fact that a favorable agreement is more likely to be reached if all issues are juggled simultaneously, thereby presenting to the other an integrated rather than segmented picture of one's shifting preferences. Froman and Cohen (1970) have lent support to this notion in their study of "logrolling" and "compromise." They found that bargainers attained higher outcomes when they traded concessions on multiple issues (logrolling) than when they negotiated each issue separately, in relative isolation of agreements reached on other issues (compromise).

Concession Making: Summary

Considered as a whole, the research suggests that the concession-making process has two important consequences for the bargaining relationship. First, *concessions convey vital information about a bargainer's subjective utilities. They allow each party to gauge the other's preferences and intentions and, in turn, permit each party to present or misrepresent information about his own.* For example, a bargainer who makes frequent concessions will probably be viewed as willing to settle for less than one who makes concessions only occasionally. Similarly, a bargainer who makes concessions up to a certain point and then refuses to move beyond this point will probably be seen as being close to some "cutoff point" on his utility scale (his CL_{alt}), below which he will leave the relationship rather than settle. On the other hand, a bargainer who makes negative concessions may be seen as threatening to toughen his position unless a particular offer is accepted. Thus, concessions may be shaped in a variety of ways, each of which has important consequences for the way in which one's preferences and intentions are viewed by the other. And, as we have seen in our examination of Kelley's (1966) research and several Bilateral Monopoly studies, when concessions are made systematically—especially when they are coupled with extreme opening demands—they are instrumental in the attainment of an optimal division of resources.

Second, *concessions convey important information about a bargainer's perceptions of his adversary. They allow each party to find out how he looks in the other's eyes. And to the extent that a bargainer believes he is seen as capable and effective, we may expect him to behave in increasingly cooperative fashion.* Consider the findings of the numerous studies which have shown that a bargainer who makes positive concessions is more likely to elicit reciprocated concessions from the other than one who makes either negative concessions or none at all. The reason these findings hold, we would argue, has to do with the implications of concession making for a bargainer's self-concept. An adversary who follows a stance of initial toughness with a softening of demands may be seen as communicating a perception of the bargainer as a worthy opponent—an opponent who is effective, persuasive, and to whom one must gradually yield. Thus a bargainer may come to see the other's positive concessions as a reflection of his own bargaining effectiveness. To the extent that he views himself in this fashion, we may expect the bargainer's concern with how he looks in the other's eyes to be sharply reduced and to be followed by an increasing willingness to reciprocate. Conversely, the other's making of negative concessions or none at all may be seen by the bargainer as a reflection of his own incompetence—since he seems to be incapable of influencing the other to make offers that are increasingly attractive. Given this belief, we may expect the bargainer to become increasingly concerned with the apparent loss of face he has incurred in the other's eyes and to become increasingly competitive and vindictive as a result.

The general point we have been emphasizing here, namely, that bargainers are more likely to behave cooperatively when they feel they are capable of exerting systematic influence with respect to their adversary, is indirectly borne out by the findings of a number of PD experiments. These studies have compared the relative effectiveness of contingent (generally tit-for-tat) and noncontingent (100% cooperative, 100% competitive, or random) experimental strategies in inducing cooperation. Two studies have reported no differences as a function of a strategy's contingency (Minas, Scodel, Marlowe, & Rawson, 1960; Oskamp & Perlman, 1965). The conclusion reached by many others, however, is that a contingent experimental strategy is far more likely to induce cooperation than a noncontingent one—even if the other cooperates 100% of the time (Baranowski & Summers, 1972; Crumbaugh & Evans, 1967; Deutsch, 1958; Gallo, 1969; Gallo et al., 1966; Gruder & Duslak, 1973; Kahn et al., 1971; Komorita, 1965; Kubicka, 1968; Lave, 1965; McNeel, 1973; Oskamp, 1974; Scodel, 1962; Sermat, 1970; Solomon, 1960; Tedeschi, Aranoff, & Gahagan, 1968a; Tedeschi, Aranoff, Gahagan, & Hiester, 1968b; Whitworth & Lucker, 1969; Wilson, 1969, 1971).

The fact that subjects tend to behave more cooperatively in the presence of another whose behavior is contingent upon, rather than independent of, their own behavior constitutes powerful evidence in support of our general argument. *A bargainer wants to believe he is capable of shaping the other's behavior, of causing the other to choose as he (the other) does.* In the presence of an adversary whose behavior appears to vary favorably in response to the bargainer's own moves and countermoves, the bargainer may come to view himself as competent and may be expected to behave in increasingly cooperative fashion. On the other hand, in the presence of an opponent whose offers appear to be unrelated to the bargainer's behavior—even if these offers are consistently cooperative—the bargainer may see himself as fundamentally incompetent at the task of persuading the other and may come to behave in increasingly defensive or exploitative fashion. Thus *by making positive concessions, bargainers may communicate their perception of the other as a strong, worthy, and tough opponent and in so doing may increase the likelihood of inducing positive concessions in return.*

Related to the above observations are the findings of several studies that reported that subjects were more likely to cooperate in the presence of a contingently cooperative experimental strategy than in the presence of a live, freely interacting opponent (Gallo, 1969; Oskamp, 1970, 1974; Pilisuk, Kiritz, & Clampitt, 1971; Pilisuk & Skolnick, 1968; Pilisuk, Skolnick, & Overstreet, 1968). Oskamp (1971) has suggested that these results may have been due to a tendency for live opponents to behave more variably than a programmed strategy. Hence, under some circumstances, subjects may actually come to view themselves as more capable of influencing the behavior of a simulated adversary than a live one!

ACCOMPANYING APPEALS AND DEMANDS: PROMISES AND THREATS

Bargainers can and do attempt to increase the likelihood of a particular offer being acceptable to the other side by accompanying their offer with a variety of appeals and demands. Two of these influence attempts, promises and threats, appear to be used with considerable frequency and have been the object of extensive bargaining research; consequently they will be the focus of our attention in this section. In keeping with Deutsch (1973), Kelley (1965b), Sawyer and Guetzkow (1965), Schelling (1960), and others, we shall define a "threat" as an expressed intention to behave in a way that appears detrimental to the interests of another. A "promise," conversely, is an expressed intention to behave in a way that appears beneficial to the interests of another.

We have suggested in Chapter 2 that the bargaining relationship is essentially a voluntary one, in which each party has two important kinds of choices available to him. First, he can choose which of several possible agreements to ask for and which, if any, to accept. Second, he can decide whether, and for how long, to remain in interaction with the other. Because bargainers can make these two kinds of choices, and because each knows that the other can make them as well, both parties have the capacity to exert leverage on the other through the use of threats and promises. A bargainer can threaten to leave the relationship unless a particular offer is accepted. Or he can threaten not to make further concessions, or even to make negative concessions, unless a particular demand is met. Similarly, a bargainer can promise to remain in the relationship if a particular concession is made by his adversary. Or he can promise to come to an immediate agreement (minimizing mutual costs of time, energy, money, etc.) if a proposed offer is accepted. He can even promise to "sweeten the kitty" by making compromises on another issue of issues, or by making side payments of various kinds. Regardless of the particular promise or threat used, however, and regardless of the manner in which it is deployed, these influence attempts are possible because of the fact that the parties, by definition, have the power to impose both beneficial and harmful outcomes on each other.

Promises and threats convey information about a bargainer's preferences and intentions. A bargainer's very willingness to back up a threat or promise with the punishment and reward respectively implied by these influence attempts communicates information about his subjective utilities—namely, that he wishes to reject a particular offer or have another accepted by his adversary. A bargainer who promises an elaborate side payment, rather than a token one, if agreement is reached is likely to be seen by his adversary as in need of having a particular offer accepted—so much so that he is willing to attempt a "bribe" in order to get what he wants. Similarly, a bargainer who threatens to break off the relationship immediately, unless a particular demand is met, may well be viewed as displaying a stronger need than another who only intimates that he will not "look kindly" on the rejection of some offer. Thus, *by carefully observing the frequency, intensity, and timing with which threats and promises are made, the recipient can attempt to gauge the other's true preferences and intentions.* Conversely, of course, the transmitter of a threat or promise may use these influence attempts not only to convey his true preferences or intentions but to misrepresent them deliberately, in order to prod the other into a personally advantageous settlement.

Promises and threats also convey important information about the transmitter's perceptions of the other. Implicit in both forms of influence is the notion that the sender views his own interests and the other's as opposed. Otherwise why would the use of a threat or promise be deemed necessary? In addition, both forms of influence tend to personalize the bargaining relationship, firmly entrenching the implied consequences of the other's behavior in the hands of a promiser or threatener who wishes to have his interests given priority. In terms of their relative consequences, promises seem to convey a more positive view of the other than threats. After all, the bargainer who elects to make a promise, thereby rewarding the other for the performance of a particular behavior, presumably communicates more positive regard for his adversary than he might have had he chosen to threaten him with punishment. On the other hand, as Raven and Kruglanski (1970) point out, the affective consequences of promises and threats may vary as a function of their magnitude. Under some circumstances, to make too small a threat may be to convey the insulting notion that the other can be easily goaded into submission. Conversely, a large threat may be seen, perhaps, as a sign of respect for one's opponent. Similarly, while a small promise may communicate some degree of liking for the other, too large a promise may be seen as a bribe.

Based on our review of the relevant literature, it appears that a number of generalizations may be suggested about the conditions under which promises and threats are used and the consequences their use has for the course of bargaining. These generalizations, as well as the pertinent experimental findings, will be considered in turn.

Limiting Conditions

While we know of no findings that lend direct support to this generalization, it nevertheless appears that *promises and threats are likely to be used to the extent that a bargainer believes he cannot successfully exert influence in other ways.*

One of the characteristics of the Acme–Bolt Trucking game is the availability to bargainers of alternate routes that permit each party to avoid interaction with the other. By taking his alternate route on a particular trial, a bargainer can in effect opt out of the relationship and can thereby convey his dissatisfaction with the other's behavior. In the absence of these alternate routes, however, the ways in which bargainers can influence each other's behavior are reduced, and they are constrained to remain in the relationship and develop alternative means of exerting influence.

Shomer *et al.* (1966) had pairs of subjects play a version of the Trucking game in which either both players or neither player had alternate routes available. In addition, subjects in some experimental conditions were each provided with threat capability in the form of a "gate" which, when closed by the bargainer who controlled it, prevented the other from reaching his destination via the main route. Subjects in the remaining conditions had no such threat capability. Shomer *et al.* found that subjects in the no threat condition obtained higher joint profits than those with bilateral threat capability. In addition, they reported that among the pairs given threat capability, subjects with no alternate route showed greater improvement in joint performance over the course of the game than those who had available this form of withdrawal—and means of expressing dissatisfaction. Thus, when constrained to remain in interaction, some subjects learned to cooperate, despite the presence of threat capability. Indeed, as the findings of a second study by Shomer *et al.* demonstrated, while some of the pairs with no alternate route used threat for purposes of coercion, others learned to use it to facilitate cooperation.

Smith and Anderson (1972) had subjects play the Shomer *et al.* (1966) version of the Acme–Bolt Trucking game. Some pairs were permitted to communicate while others were not, and neither player had an alternate route. They found that when subjects could communicate, they obtained higher joint profits when they did not have threat capability than when they did. On the other hand, when communication was not permitted, joint profits were higher in threat than in no threat conditions. The latter finding suggests that when the bargainers could not exert influence through communication or by withdrawal, they tended to convey their preferences and intentions in other ways—in this case through the use of threat.

Kelley *et al.* (1967) conducted a series of experiments in which subjects were to divide a reward between them. In order to obtain an agreement which was profitable, a subject had to exceed his "minimum necessary share" (MNS), a value which the experimenter privately provided him with at the beginning of each problem. The bargainers were free to make a variety of offers and concessions, to threaten and lie, and to terminate the interaction on any trial. The investigators found that as subjects were pushed close to their MNS values, they made use of threats and lies with increasing frequency. In other words, when bargainers found themselves unable to reach a satisfactory agreement through the pattern of offers and counteroffers they employed, and as they neared the point of being prodded into an unprofitable division of resources, they resorted increasingly to the use of threats.

Finally, Rubin (1971b) had subjects play a complex, four-party bargaining game (described in Chapter 8) in which two of the parties (A and B) were encouraged to interact indirectly with each other, using their respective "allies" (X and Y) as intermediaries. On any trial in which A and B elected to interact in this fashion, they could attempt to influence X and Y's behavior in a number of ways: by earmarking a resource for cooperative or competitive use, by varying the value of this resource, and by accompanying the resource with a message that either promised reward for compliance or threatened punishment for noncompliance. X and Y did not have to use the resources they received in the manner in which A and B intended; betrayal of one's ally was thus possible.

Rubin found that promises and threats were used rather infrequently—on only 23% of the turns on which they could be transmitted. When they were used, moreover, he found that A and B sent both promises and threats with the greatest frequency on trials in which they displayed maximal trust of their allies—by investing high value, cooperative resources in X and Y. In explanation it was suggested that when A and B were trusting they may have experienced greater vulnerability at the hands of their intermediaries than others who were either more conservative or competitive in their choice behavior. As a consequence, A and B may have felt the greatest need to gain control over the quality of their outcomes through the use of promises and threats.

Relative Frequency of Use

More direct evidence is available in support of the following generalization: *Bargainers tend to transmit promises with greater frequency than threats.*

Radlow and Weidner (1966) ran subjects in a modified PD game in which messages of contingent promise or threat could be exchanged or in which communication was prohibited. They found that promises were exchanged more often than threats. Moreover, subjects behaved more cooperatively when promises and threats could be sent than when no communication was available. Similarly, Cheney, Harford, and Solomon (1972) examined the effects of communicating threats and promises that were contingent or non-contingent upon behavior in the Acme–Bolt Trucking game. Depending on experimental condition, bargaining pairs were provided with promise messages only, threats only, both promises and threats, or neither. They found that subjects made greater use of promises than of threats and greater use of contingent than of noncontingent messages. In addition, as in the Radlow and Weidner study, it was found that subjects behaved more cooperatively when promises and threats could be sent than when no communication was available.

Rubin and Lewicki (1973), in a nonbargaining study, had subjects take part in a hypothetical influence situation in which they were asked to imagine that they were students who had each been assigned a partner for collaborative work on a group project. The partner attempted to persuade the subject to work on his project topic by making one of eight contingent statements, four of which were promises and four of which were threats. Subjects then rated both the other and the statements themselves on a number of attributes and were asked to order any four of the eight statements into a four-step influence strategy designed to elicit optimal compliance. The investigators found that, given the opportunity to develop a strategy, subjects selected more than twice as many promises for use as threats. Similar findings have emerged in a more recent unpublished study in which two live bargainers were required to exchange influence messages in a PD game (Lewicki & Rubin, 1974).

In contrast with the pattern of results reported in each of the above studies, Lindskold (1971) found that threats were used more frequently than promises in an attempt to influence the behavior of a 50% cooperative experimental strategy. An experiment by Gruder (1969), however, helps reconcile this apparent contradiction. Gruder had subjects bargain against a preprogrammed other who was presented as being either competitive and exploitative (like Lindskold's 50% cooperative other) or fair and compromising—perhaps more the way a real other bargainer might be initially expected to behave. Given an opportunity to accompany their offers with a number of prepared appeals and demands, he found that subjects who viewed the other as competitive tended to use more threatening messages than those who had been led to believe that the other was cooperative. The latter subjects tended to employ offers of willingness to cooperate and personal appeals.

Effects on Compliance

In general it appears that *threats, and to a lesser extent promises, tend to increase the likelihood of immediate compliance and concession making by the other.*

Almost all of the research concerned with this issue has been conducted by Tedeschi and his colleagues, using the following general paradigm (see Tedeschi, Bonoma, & Brown, 1971). Subjects play a PD game against a simulated other who on certain "influence" trials transmits a standardized promise or threat message. The magnitude of the promise or threat is manipulated by varying the size of the implied reward or punishment. "Credibility" is manipulated by varying the frequency with which a promise or threat is enforced. Subjects are generally given three response options from which to choose on an influence trial, denoting the intentions to comply or not comply or the decision not to disclose one's intentions. On "noninfluence" trials, the simulated other generally behaves in 100% competitive fashion. The major dependent measures in the Tedeschi paradigm are the frequency of compliance on influence trials (the focus of our attention at present), the frequency of compliance on noninfluence trials, the frequency with which the three response options are chosen, and subjects' ratings of the other on a number of adjectival dimensions.

A number of studies have found that the greater the credibility of a promise, the more likely its transmitter is to obtain immediate compliance (Gahagan, 1970; Gahagan & Tedeschi, 1968a, b; Horai, Lindskold, Gahagan, & Tedeschi, 1969; Schlenker *et al.*, 1973). This finding, however, is offset by the presence of a number of other experiments by these same authors that have reported no differences as a function of a promiser's credibility (Brown, Smith, & Tedeschi, 1971; Lindskold & Bennett, 1973; Lindskold & Tedeschi, 1971; Lindskold, Tedeschi, Bonoma, & Schlenker, 1971; Tedeschi, Lindskold, Horai, & Gahagan, 1969d; Tedeschi, Powell, Lindskold, & Gahagan, 1969e).

The findings with respect to the immediate impact of threats are more conclusive. Of the studies reviewed, only one reported no relationship between the credibility of a threat and immediate compliance (Lindskold, Bonoma, & Tedeschi, 1969). Each of the remaining experiments found that the frequency of immediate compliance varied as a direct function of the availability of threat (Black & Higbee, 1973), threat magnitude (Bonoma *et al.*, 1970; Bonoma & Tedeschi, 1973; Gahagan, Tedeschi, Faley, & Lindskold, 1970; Lindskold, Bonoma, & Tedeschi, 1969), threat credibility (Mogy & Pruitt, 1974), or as a direct function of both magnitude and credibility (Faley & Tedeschi, 1971; Horai & Tedeschi, 1969; Horai, Tedeschi, Gahagan, & Lesnick, 1969).

We wish to note in passing that while the above studies lend support to our generalization about the immediate impact of promises and threats, acceptance of this generalization should be tempered by the fact that the findings were based on a single experimental paradigm in which the procedures used and independent variables studied were often virtually identical. Experimental study and replication of these findings clearly needs to be conducted employing a paradigm that is more complex and interesting than the PD game.

Given these reservations, however, and accepting the validity of our generalization, one may reasonably ask why a threat should be better able to elicit immediate compliance than a promise. Consider the case of the transmitter who wishes to influence another to perform behavior X, where X is one of a number of behaviors (four, for example) from which the recipient can choose. A typical promise in this situation might take the form: "If you do X, I will reward you." This statement conveys the information that the recipient will be rewarded for the performance of X. *The consequences of engaging in any of the three other possible behaviors, however, are not specified*—one or more of them may be rewarded, punished, or not reinforced. By way of contrast, consider the typical threat: "If you do not do X, I will punish you." Here the recipient is unambiguously told that if he does anything other than X (that is, if he engages in any of the three other behaviors) he will be punished; *only the consequences of performing X are ambiguous*—his action may be rewarded, punished, or not reinforced. Notice that in these two examples the threat conveys unequivocal information about the consequences of performing three of the four behaviors, while the promise conveys this information about the consequences of performing only one of the four. Thus it may be that in the eyes of the recipient a threatener is seen as more powerful, as exerting greater control over his (the recipient's) outcomes, than a promiser. Given such a perception, we might reasonably expect an individual to display greater immediate compliance to a threat than to a promise.

Affective Consequences

Over the course of the bargaining relationship, the use of promises tends to elicit general liking for the transmitter, while the use of threats tends to elicit greater hostility.

Of the three studies reviewed which have examined the perceptions of a promiser, Brown *et al.* (1971) and Lindskold *et al.* (1971) found that the transmitters of highly credible promises were rated more favorably than the transmitters of less credible ones. Similarly, Evans (1964) reported that another who made promises was seen as more trustworthy than one who made none.

In one of several studies that compared the perceptions of promisers and threateners, Dustin and Arthur (1968) had subjects play a PD game against a simulated other who sent a promise or a threat after each trial. They found that subjects displayed significantly greater resistance (made a greater number of competitive choices) in the presence of a threatening other than a promising one. Dunn (1972), Lewicki and Rubin (1973, 1974), Rubin and Lewicki (1973), and Rubin, Lewicki, and Dunn (1973) found that the transmitter of a promise was liked more and was seen as friendlier, more cooperative, more persuasive, and more likely to elicit compliance than the transmitter of a threat. Similar findings have been reported more recently by Heilman (1974). Promisers, as compared with threateners, were rated as more reasonable, more easy-going, more considerate, more likable, less nasty, more trustworthy, friendlier, gentler, and wiser.

A number of experiments have found that a threatener tends to evoke hostility in the other. Five studies by Tedeschi and his colleagues reported that bargainers were more likely to defect on noninfluence trials, the greater the magnitude of the threat they received (Bonoma *et al.*, 1970; Lindskold, Bonoma, & Tedeschi, 1969), and the greater the credibility of this threat (Horai & Tedeschi, 1969; Horai, Tedeschi, Gahagan, & Lesnick, 1969). In addition, it was found that the greater the magnitude of a threat, the greater a subject's tendency to lie—by indicating an intention to cooperate on influence trials, and then competing (Gahagan *et al.*, 1970).

In their Trucking game studies, Deutsch and Krauss (1960, 1962) reported that bargainers with bilateral threat capability used the availability of communication to convey their mutual distaste and displeasure with far greater frequency than those not provided with this threat potential. Similarly, Gumpert (1967) and Smith and Anderson (1972) found that subjects with bilateral threat capability in the Trucking game viewed their partners as less cooperative and felt less friendly toward them than those with no threat.

Effects on Bargaining Outcomes

Finally, our review of the literature indicates support for the following generalization: *Over the course of the bargaining relationship, the use of promises tends to increase the likelihood of bargainers reaching a mutually favorable agreement, while the use of threats tends to reduce this likelihood.*

Several studies have compared the effects of promises and threats on bargaining outcomes. Cheney *et al.* (1972) and Radlow and Weidner (1966) found that subjects who transmitted promises behaved more cooperatively and bargained more effectively than those who transmitted threats. Similarly, Lewicki and Rubin (1974) reported that bargaining pairs exchanging promises tended to achieve higher joint profits than those that employed threats.

In yet another experimental attempt to compare the relative effects on outcomes of promises and threats, Rubin *et al.* (1973) informed subjects that they would be taking part in a study of "supervisor–worker relations." Subjects were assigned the role of worker, while the experimenter acted as the supervisor. The supervisor's task was to oversee the performance of the worker, who in turn had the job of decoding a series of anagrams which were either easy or difficult to solve. The supervisor's pay was completely determined by the worker's performance, the former receiving twice as much for each difficult anagram correctly decoded by the worker as for each easy one. The worker was paid a standard fee at the beginning of each of three sets of trials, regardless of the number or difficulty of the anagrams correctly solved. In addition, the supervisor could augment or reduce the worker's fee by 40%, by sending (and enforcing) a promise or threat message at the beginning of each trial. These messages were devised, of course, to persuade the worker to choose to work on the difficult rather than easy problems. Depending on condition, subjects, at the beginning of each trial, were sent a contingent promise, a contingent threat, or a control message that simply asked the worker to decode the difficult anagrams (but did not specify the consequences of compliance or noncompliance).

Rubin, Lewicki, and Dunn found that subjects complied more often, by choosing to work on the difficult anagrams, when the supervisor sent them a promise rather than a threat or a control message. Of greater interest was the finding that subjects correctly decoded many more anagrams when they were sent a promise than a threat, decoding an intermediary number when they received the control message. Thus even though subjects had only to agree to work on the difficult words in order to receive the promised reward or avoid the threatened punishment, they went out of their way to help the other when he sent a promise (by solving as many words as they could), and actively hindered the other when a threat was sent (by solving far fewer words in an identical list). Consequently the experimenter's "earnings" were greater in the promise than in the control message condition, and his outcomes were poorest when a threat was sent. The data thus suggest that a threat is not only less effective than a promise but is also less effective than a communication in which no contingency is specified. As Rubin et al. (1973) conclude: "The carrot is better than the stick, but even better than the stick is no stick at all [p. 142]."

Of the 11 studies of the effects of threats alone which we have reviewed, only one reported no differences in choice behavior as a function of the availability of threat (Tornatzky & Geiwitz, 1968). The general conclusion reached by the others, however, is that the use of threats tends to reduce sharply the magnitude of joint bargaining outcomes in the Trucking game (Borah, 1963; Deutsch & Krauss, 1960, 1962; Deutsch & Lewicki, 1970; Froman & Cohen, 1969; Gallo, 1966; Gumpert, 1967; Shomer et al., 1966), as well as in variations of the Bilateral Monopoly game (Hornstein, 1965; Kelley, 1966).

Promises and Threats: Summary

Our review has suggested that promises and threats have a number of important consequences for the course of bargaining. In addition, however, it should be remembered that the course of bargaining itself has important consequences for the use and interpretation of both these forms of influence. When the conflict of interest in a relationship is relatively small, promises and threats (as Deutsch & Lewicki, 1970, Harris, 1969, and others have experimentally demonstrated) may be used effectively as an aid in the co-ordination of mutual expectations and intentions. This is especially likely to be true when other means of influence are unavailable. On the other hand, when a conflict of interest is large, these same promises and threats may end up serving destructive purposes. Promises may be seen as bribes, threats may become the "gateways to the use of punitive power [Gumpert, 1967]," and both forms of influence may serve only to exacerbate further an already treacherous situation. Thus, in the last analysis, it may be that promises and threats either need not be used, as when bargainers are cooperatively disposed toward one another, or should not be used (when a conflict of interest is viewed by bargainers as relatively large).

CONCLUDING COMMENT

We have suggested that bargainers' attempts to influence each other's behavior may be analyzed in relation to three dimensions: the language of opening moves and gestures, the overall patterning of moves and counter-moves, and the use of accompanying appeals and demands. Opening moves are important because they are largely responsible for establishing the climate of the setting in which bargaining occurs. Concessions, similarly, as a result of their frequency, timing, and strategic patterning, have important consequences for bargaining effectiveness. Finally, accompanying appeals and demands, through the information they convey about each party's preferences, intentions, and attitudes toward the other, are likely to affect the quality of the exchange.

Social influence in bargaining is often exerted systematically and self-consciously, as when a bargainer deliberately selects the one strategy he believes will be most likely to accomplish his goal or goals. But the tangible and intangible outcomes of bargaining are also shaped in less clearcut, rational, and volitional ways. Unwitting glances, mannerisms, and gestures, private fears and fetishes, may be as instrumental in influencing the other as a bargainer's best-laid, most shrewdly considered strategic plan. The experimental literature has given overwhelming attention to the antecedents and consequences of strategic behavior in bargaining. While such consideration is clearly important, it may be that if we are truly to understand the inner workings of the bargaining process, we must also learn how to study and analyze the more ambiguous and unwitting processes by which influence is exerted as well.

10

Afterthoughts

That social psychologists consider bargaining to be a domain worthy of serious study is perhaps attested to no better than by the fact that more than 1000 experimental and nonexperimental articles and books devoted to bargaining have appeared since 1960. By undertaking the task of reviewing, consolidating, and integrating a substantial portion of this massive literature, we have attempted to inch our collective understanding of the bargaining process, its implications, and applications one step closer to realization. Yet, despite the overwhelming attention given to the study of bargaining, and despite our own attempts to summarize the state of present knowledge, it is apparent that understanding of this complex and fascinating process is far from complete. Answers to old and important questions are soon followed by new queries. Analysis of some issues paves the way for the formulation of other, perhaps more central and important issues that are yet to be fully understood. Indeed, as we have come to know more about the bargaining process, we have come to understand how little is really known!

That knowledge tends to beget informed ignorance, of course, is reason not for despondency but for renewed scientific enthusiasm. Out of our ignorance of the bargaining process and the host of questions and issues for future research to which this ignorance has given rise may come further knowledge and greater insight than before. It is for this reason that we view the prospects for continued research in the area of bargaining with considerable excitement and zest.

The purpose of this final chapter, therefore, is to formulate briefly several of the questions and issues to which our review of the literature has given rise, in the hope that bargaining research may be stimulated to move in new and different directions. Using Chapters 4–9 as a guide, we wish to pose a number of specific questions to which only future research can provide answers. Finally, we wish to close by briefly considering several more general experimental and theoretical issues.

SOME QUESTIONS SUGGESTIVE OF FUTURE RESEARCH IN BARGAINING

In Chapter 4 it was suggested that there are three social structural components that are likely to be of particular importance in bargaining: the presence of audiences; the availability of third parties; and the number of participants involved in the exchange (with the accompanying tendency, as number increases, to form coalitions). The reason these components shape behavior as they do, we have argued, is because bargainers share an underlying need for positive evaluation that renders them accountable to a variety of others.

With respect to audience effects, the following questions may be posed: How are various audience characteristics, such as size, composition, identity, relationship with bargainers, dependency, and the extent and nature of its demands, likely to influence bargaining behavior? What are the consequences for bargaining effectiveness of various characteristics of audience feedback, including its clarity or ambiguity, unanimity or dividedness, verbal or nonverbal expression? Under what circumstances is negative audience feedback likely to evoke increased competitiveness, and to what extent may this competitiveness be offset by variations in situational and individual difference parameters? In what ways should an audience's evaluative feedback be conveyed (by explicit announcement, tacit suggestion, etc.) so as to maximize bargaining effectiveness? Under what conditions are "abstract referents" such as national honor, reputation, and history likely to become salient "audiences" in the minds of bargainers? How do such abstract referent "audience" effects differ from those induced by the physical presence of real others? What are the differential effects of tangible versus intangible dependency on an audience? Under what circumstances is the presence of accountability to an audience likely to facilitate or hinder effective bargaining? What are the "minimal" conditions under which audience accountability pressures tend to exert themselves? To what extent are loyalty, commitment, and advocacy typical reactions to the presence of accountability pressures, and what causes such reactions to vary? What kinds of bargainers, in what circumstances, are most likely to be responsive to audience accountability pressures? Finally, how are variations in prenegotiation experience with an audience, and the extent to which one identifies with an audience, likely to affect a bargainer's responsiveness to the accountability pressures generated?

Unanswered questions with respect to the role and effectiveness of third parties include the following: How should a third party intervene so as to alter the degree of accountability and loyalty to audiences, as well as the commitment to and advocacy of their positions? Under what circumstances should third party interventions be made privately rather than in public? To what extent do the timing, content, modality, and formality of third party interventions affect the likelihood of effective bargaining? What are some of the individual difference and situational factors that may increase bargainers' susceptibility to the influence of third parties? Under what conditions are third party interventions, designed to structure, filter, or tutor communication, likely to prove useful? When are such attempts to structure communication likely to be rejected, and why? What kinds of third party attributes (authoritativeness, expertise, integrity, etc.) are necessary, and which sufficient, for the enhancement of bargaining effectiveness? With what sorts of issues, both tangible and intangible, are third party interventions likely to prove most and least effective? What type of third party behavior is likely to contribute to his being viewed as neutral? What are the situational factors that are likely to detract from this view? Do the effects of third party neutrality differ when bargaining is formal or informal, long-term or short-term? Under what circumstances, and with what kinds of bargainers, may the mere presence of a third party increase bargaining effectiveness? Do bargainers need to view themselves as having freedom of choice in order for third party interventions to be effective? Finally, how may a third party go about increasing bargainers' accountability, loyalty, and commitment to him, as well as advocacy of his positions?

With respect to the formation of coalitions in multiparty bargaining, the following questions may be posed. Under what circumstances are coalitions likely to form, even though it is clear that they are insufficient to offset the strength of the more powerful party? What kinds of individual difference and situational factors are likely to induce the formation of such "futile" coalitions, and what types of secondary gains may be derived from them? Under what conditions is a more powerful bargainer apt to disrupt the formation of alliances among the weaker parties? What are the consequences for bargaining effectiveness of such active attempts at disruption? How may potential or existing coalition partners reduce the effectiveness of attempts at disruption by a more powerful party? Under what circumstances is the introduction of a "common enemy" likely to lead to coalition formation? What attributes and behavior of this common enemy will heighten or reduce this tendency? What factors contribute to contention among potential or existing coalition partners? Finally, under what conditions does an increase in the number of bargaining parties not result in the formation of coalitions?

There are four physical components of bargaining structure, we suggested in Chapter 5, that are of particular importance in bargaining: the location and accessibility of the bargaining site; physical arrangements at the site proper; the availability and use of communication channels; and the presence of time limits. Some unanswered questions concerning these four components are as follows:

Under what circumstances are the issues of site selection and public visibility likely to become vehicles for the emergence of conflict over intangibles? How are a bargainer's attempts to control site characteristics likely to affect compliance or resistance on the part of his adversary? When such attempts at site control are met with resistance, what form is this resistance likely to take? To what extent does bargaining behavior vary, in terms of toughness, concession making, responsiveness to the other, use of threat, etc., when an individual bargains either on his own or the other party's "home turf"? What sorts of interpersonal perceptions and expectations are fostered by the presence of a home turf, and how may these be altered? To what extent do factors such as prior bargaining history, anticipated future interaction, and conflict intensity regulate the importance of site neutrality? What are the consequences for bargaining effectiveness of conducting negotiations under conditions of either high or low public visibility? What steps may be taken by bargainers to counteract the effects of public visibility? What factors are likely to affect bargainers' responsiveness to a third party's attempts at the modification of site location and accessibility? Finally, how may the issues of site neutrality and openness be best used to gain a strategic advantage in bargaining?

To what extent are variations in physical arrangements, such as seating, interpersonal distance, bodily orientation, visual contact, etc., likely to affect bargaining and reflect the climate of the exchange? What kinds of physical arrangements are likely to announce, crystallize, or reduce existing status differences between bargainers? What kinds of seating and other physical arrangements are likely to be chosen when bargainers have either equal or unequal power or bargain under conditions of high or low conflict intensity? What sorts of suggested site arrangements may be introduced or accepted through third party intervention? Finally, when are such interventions likely to increase bargaining effectiveness, and when not?

How may "communicational isolation" be altered through physical arrangements? Under what conditions is it appropriate or inappropriate to do so? How, exactly, does communicational isolation influence bargainers' perceptions of one another? When should communication between conflicting parties be reduced or avoided in order to increase the likelihood of agreement? What consequences does subtle nonverbal behavior (gestures, facial expressions, etc.) have for the manner in which a bargaining relationship evolves? To what extent may bargaining effectiveness be enhanced through the use of third parties who encourage the use of communication for cooperative ends? Must such encouragement be given bilaterally for bargaining effectiveness to result? What are the effects of permitting a third party to filter communication, by screening out certain forms of communication and permitting others to enter into the exchange? How may an experimenter's instructions concerning the availability and mode of communication be used to affect the content of what subjects in bargaining experiments communicate to one another? Finally, in what subtle ways do an experimenter's instructions influence bargaining behavior?

Under what conditions do time limits tend to serve constructive ends, thereby increasing bargaining effectiveness? When will the opposite tend to be true? What sorts of bargainers are likely to prove especially susceptible to time pressure? Can bargaining effectiveness be increased through the introduction of deadlines by a third party? Under what circumstances are such interventions likely to be acceptable to the bargainers? Finally, how may a bargainer use the presence of time limits in order to gain a strategic advantage?

Chapter 6 was concerned with the consequences for bargaining effectiveness of the following issue components: intangibility; incentive magnitude, reward structure, and number; format, presentation, and prominence. Further consideration of each of these factors leads us to pose the following questions for future research:

Are there intangible issues or concerns (such as "morality," "equity," etc.) that, rather than interfering with bargaining effectiveness, may actually enhance it? How may such intangibles be introduced or formulated so as to counteract the divisive effects of other issues? What is the nature of the underlying process by which intangible issues become fused to tangible ones? Under what conditions, exactly, do intangible issues become equally or more important than the tangible issues at stake? What are the conditions that regulate the intensity of status struggles? What sort of behavior by bargainers can offset the tendency of intangible issues to "swamp" more tangible ones? Finally, what kinds of third party interventions (structural, interpersonal, etc.) may be employed in order to separate tangibles from intangibles?

Under what conditions are issues having low incentive value likely to be assigned higher importance rankings than those having high incentive value?

To what extent does the willingness to take risks vary as a function of incentive magnitude? What consequences does this risk-taking propensity have for bargaining effectiveness? What sorts of individual difference factors tend to interact with incentive magnitude and reward structure? What is the maximum number of issues over which effective bargaining can take place? Finally, how does this number vary as a function of such factors as incentive magnitude, issue importance ranking, time constraints, and the number of possible alternative solutions to each issue?

When should the most important issue(s) be negotiated first, when last, and when throughout the exchange? Under what circumstances should issues be considered sequentially rather than simultaneously? What issue properties are conducive to the formation of subsets? How may bargainers be taught or induced to consider alternative approaches to the negotiation of multiple issues, such as fractionation, coupling, packaging, and the treatment of issues as "singles"? Under what circumstances are tradeoffs likely to prove effective, and how will they vary as a function of such factors as timing and the symmetry of importance rankings? When is it useful to present an issue concretely or clearly rather than in more abstract or vaguer terms? Finally, under what conditions is the presence of a central, prominent solution likely to intensify rather than reduce a conflict of interest?

Chapters 4–6 were written on the basis of a relative paucity of experimental evidence. Hence numerous questions have been raised about the effects of structural components, which only future research can answer. The material reviewed in Chapters 7–9, on the other hand, seems to have tapped issues of more central concern to bargaining researchers, as reflected by the hundreds of experimental studies concerned with individual differences, interdependence, and bargaining strategy. As a result, many of the propositions advanced in Chapters 7–9 appear to be more solidly grounded in laboratory research, have been set forth with greater confidence, and therefore lead to fewer specific unanswered questions than those in Chapters 4–6. Several important unresolved issues remain, nevertheless.

Perhaps the single most important question to be raised with respect to Chapter 7 concerns the validity of our interpersonal orientation (IO) formulation. To what extent may the host of background and personality differences among bargainers really be better understood and integrated through recourse to a dimension (IO) that distinguishes bargainers on the basis of their sensitivity and reactivity to variations in the other's behavior? Assuming the validity of our IO construction, several additional questions arise: How may the strange concatenation of individual difference characteristics, which seem to align themselves at opposite ends of the IO continuum, be best explained? Assuming that high IO bargainers may be further distinguished on the basis of their presumed cooperative or competitive orientation, would it be conceptually useful to make a similar distinction in the case of low IO individuals? Can a scale be developed that assesses a bargainer's IO a priori, rather than merely using IO as a post hoc analytic tool? Assuming the existence of a psychometric tool for the measurement of IO, would the characteristic tendencies of bargainers to behave like high or low IOs continue to be observed? And finally, most generally, under what conditions is the IO formulation likely to break down? For example, under what conditions is a cooperatively oriented high IO bargainer likely to become so oversensitive to variations in the behavior of a truly cooperative other that he mistakenly behaves competitively, perhaps even more so than a bargainer who is actually competitive to begin with or lower in IO?

With respect to our discussion of interdependence among bargainers (Chapter 8), the single most important issue for future research concerns the validity of our proposed three-factor model. Can the complexity of bargaining interdependence really be best understood in terms of the main and interaction effects attributable to three factors: motivational orientation, power, and interpersonal orientation? If not, what kind of model might do a better, more parsimonious job of accounting for the existing experimental data? Might not an alternative formulation be possible, for example, in which motivational orientation is considered under the broader rubric of IO—where cooperative and competitive orientations denote a high IO, while an individualistic motivational orientation denotes a low IO?

Our three-factor model and the propositions that have been generated suggest several more specific questions. Under what circumstances, exactly, is the presence of equal power in a bargaining relationship likely to either heighten or minimize the importance of intangible issues? Is it indeed true that bargainers will tend to function most and least effectively when they are of equal power and share either a cooperative or a competitive motivational orientation, respectively? And is it true, as proposed in Chapter 8, that bargainers will function most effectively when they are of equal power and high in IO, functioning least effectively when they are of unequal power and are again high in IO? Finally, can experimental support be demonstrated for the proposition that bargainers will tend to function most and least effectively when they are of equal power, high in IO, and share either a cooperative or a competitive motivational orientation, respectively?

Chapter 9 reviewed the extensive literature concerned with the effects of social influence and influence strategies in bargaining. Preferences, intentions, and perceptions, it was argued, are typically communicated in three interrelated ways: through the language of opening moves, through the overall pattern of moves and countermoves, and through accompanying appeals and demands. While substantial evidence has been obtained in support of a number of generalizations, several important unanswered questions remain: Under what circumstances are opening moves and gestures likely to be *unimportant* with respect to bargaining outcomes? What, exactly, are the conditions in which the early initiation or overall maintenance of cooperative behavior is likely to lead to the reduction of bargaining effectiveness? When, if ever, does it make sense for bargainers to begin their interaction by making moderate rather than extreme opening offers? How can bargainers be induced to view themselves as competent and strong, without at the same time encouraging them to adopt an intransigent stance toward their adversary? For what reasons, and under what conditions, are threats more likely to be employed by bargainers than promises? How may this tendency be altered? What functions, other than influence, do threats and promises provide? How may influence attempts such as promises and threats be framed so as to increase their effectiveness while not at the same time inducing the other to overreact or increasing the salience of intangible issues? Finally, in what ways and with what consequences is the quality of bargaining shaped by subtle, often unwitting influence attempts as well as by more obvious, consciously formulated strategic plans?

SOME GENERAL RECOMMENDATIONS

Apart from the many questions to which our review of the bargaining literature has given rise, it has provided us with the enthusiastic hindsight and wisdom of "Monday morning quarterbacks." We therefore cannot resist the temptation to close by suggesting a few general proscriptions and prescriptions for future research in bargaining. These recommendations are concerned with the general issues of experimental design and theory building in bargaining and will be considered in turn.

Issues for Research Design

First of all, social psychologists interested in the study of bargaining need to find a way of developing richer and more interesting laboratory paradigms than are presently available. As we have labored to indicate throughout the book, the PD game has given rise to hundreds of experimental studies, despite its obvious simplicity and many limitations. Similarly, other paradigms (such as the Acme–Bolt Trucking game, the Parcheesi Coalition game, and the Bilateral Monopoly game) have been latched onto with considerable, if lesser, zeal even though they represent only partial and largely incomplete abstractions of the bargaining process. If researchers are to understand the complex dynamics of bargaining, we believe it essential that they (we) create paradigms that incorporate this complexity, thereby permitting the examination of a spate of important and as yet largely unstudied issues. Indeed several such complex paradigms already exist (for example, Kelley *et al.* (1967) Game of 9's, and Kelley, Shure, *et al.*'s (1970) International Card game), although researchers have not yet found them fashionable or intriguing enough to warrant serious attention.

Second, and related to the first point, social psychologists need to become far more imaginative in their development of dependent variables. "Mean joint outcome" and "frequency of cooperative choice" are valid measures of bargaining effectiveness. But surely there are other, perhaps more complex indices that may be employed to assess bargaining effectiveness as well. How useful it would be, for example, if researchers would begin consistently treating behavior in multitrial games as the data of a single, complex, sequential bargaining episode—rather than as a series of independent, unrelated events. All too often, moreover, potentially valuable measures of bargainers' preferences, expectations, intentions, and attitudes toward one another have been tacked onto a design simply because it is expedient or convenient to do so. The time has come to move such measures and others out of the dark recess known as "supplementary analysis" back into the forefront of researchers' attention, where they belong.

Third, it has all too often been the case that researchers have premeasured or manipulated independent variables because of "economic" considerations rather than the theoretical merits of the issues which these variables attempt to spread apart. To cite just one example of what is meant, consider the variable of sex, which has often been manipulated not because an experimenter is interested in bargaining differences as a function of this factor but because an insufficient number of subjects of one sex are available to complete his experimental design! Clearly bargaining researchers need to pay more attention to the development of independent variables that are, at least to them, intrinsically interesting and important in their own right.

Fourth, with respect to the issue of subject selection, we desperately need to conduct more research in which subjects are drawn from something other than a college-age, middle-class, student population. Bargaining research can and should be geared to something more profound than the "social psychology of the college sophomore." The world is filled with people of all ages and backgrounds, almost all of whom have been engaged in one bargaining encounter or another, have found these encounters interesting, and would therefore be willing to participate in laboratory bargaining research. Why not take experimental advantage of the fact that bargaining is such an important, intriguing, and pervasive process in the lives of so many?

Fifth, while it is clear that individual difference variables are likely to exert a profound effect on the manner in which bargainers behave, it is also clear that many of these effects are obscured in the laboratory by the presence of more visible situational variables. If social psychologists are to understand the potentially important role of individual differences in background and personality, we need to develop alternative methods for assessing their effects. Terhune (1970), for example, has argued for the importance of six research needs that, if met, are likely to highlight individual differences more clearly. These needs include the development of more complex (including longitudinal) designs, greater attention to incentives and "personal utilities," improved psychometric tools for the measurement of individual difference variables, a multidimensional view of personality, the development and use of more specific behavioral indices, and a conscious attempt to consider the interaction of individual difference and situational variables [pp. 221–225].

Finally, social psychologists need to adhere more closely to the "multi-trait–multimethod" approach to research proposed some years ago by Campbell and Fiske (1959). In order to understand the bargaining process, and in order to increase our confidence in this understanding, we need to consider the effects of multiple variables, using a variety of methods. That bargaining researchers have explored the effects of a great many independent variables is abundantly clear; that they have systematically exploited all available methods of study is less so. Bargaining, after all, goes on all around us, all the time, in innumerable contexts. Yet how often have we taken advantage of this fact and left the experimental laboratory in search of real bargaining incidents? Clearly there is a need for more, much more, observation of as well as intervention in the bargaining process as it occurs in reality. Why not take advantage of its omnipresence to formulate more deliberately and self-consciously field experiments and field studies that run parallel to the themes of our laboratory work? Why not conduct more research based on the anecdotal, historical, and archival accounts of the countless recorded divorce proceedings, instances of plea bargaining, as well as international, labor–management, and other disputes? Only in this way, by reaching beyond the laboratory to the outer world, can we hope to converge upon a true understanding of the bargaining process.

Issues for Theory Development

While various theorists, over the years, have articulated many of the ideas they believe should be incorporated in a theory of bargaining, it is clear that no such theory yet exists. This is also true of the present volume of course. A review of the literature, no matter how extensive, is simply not equivalent to a theory. And while we are not yet prepared to propose a single organizing conceptual framework, we nevertheless wish to exploit our knowledge of the literature for the purpose of outlining what we believe are some of the more important elements to be incorporated in such a theory.

First, a theory of bargaining will almost certainly have to include a clear conceptualization of the process of information seeking and disclosure. This process, after all, is what we believe bargaining is largely about. It is through the selective, strategic exchange of information that bargainers attempt to discover the other's true preferences, expectations, and intentions, while at the same time revealing as little as possible about their own. And it is the quality and content of this information exchange, as well as the influence attempts to which it leads, that is ultimately responsible for the effectiveness with which bargaining proceeds.

Second, a true theory of bargaining should somehow incorporate an understanding of the process of coordination, since it is through the dynamics of this process that information seeking and disclosure takes place. Coordination is the mechanism by means of which bargainers attempt to transform their divergent interests into a mutually agreed upon, convergent solution. That coordination is a ubiquitous and important process in bargaining can be seen by the fact that attempts to converge on a solution are all too often fraught with difficulty, even when bargainers share the most coopera- tive and benevolent of intentions.

Third, a theory of bargaining will probably need to systematically in- corporate the notion of image management. As we have suggested through- out this volume, bargainers wish to look competent and strong in their own eyes and in the eyes of salient others, even as they wish to avoid appearing inept and weak. Bargainers are thus continually involved in "managing" the image they hope to convey to a variety of audiences: their adversary, his constituency, their own constituency, and indeed themselves. The manner in which the needs for approval and accountability with respect to each of these audiences is translated into behavior is likely to have a profound effect.

Fourth, given the abundance of evidence accounted for by our Inter- personal Orientation formulation, it would appear that a theory of bargaining should include some clear understanding of the circumstances under which bargainers are likely to be either highly sensitive or "immune" to variations in the other's behavior. As we have seen, an individual who is, or can be induced to become, highly reactive to the interpersonal aspects of the bargaining relationship is likely to behave very differently than one who is exclusively concerned with maximizing own gain regardless of how the other fares. As a result, Interpersonal Orientation is likely to have important consequences for bargaining and its effectiveness.

Fifth, a theory of bargaining should include a clear understanding of why and how it is that certain issues, be they tangible or intangible, become highly salient in the minds of bargainers, while others, apparently equal in importance, fall by the wayside. Why is it, we need to know, that certain issues exercise greater "pull" than others, and how does the pull of these issues become translated into the language of perceived gains and losses that ultimately shapes bargaining?

Finally, a true theory of bargaining must be able to incorporate with equal facility and validity the knowledge we have gained both in the laboratory and in the world of real and eventful bargaining incidents. Laboratory research has influenced the behavior of practitioners, just as the knowledge gleaned from countless, live, everyday bargaining encounters has shaped the development of laboratory experimentation. Only if this process continues and grows, and only if theorists build upon this process, is a theory likely to develop that truly comprehends bargaining for what it is: a gateway to the analysis of social interaction.

Bibliography

Adams, J.S. Inequity in social exchange. In L. Berkowitz (Ed.), *Advances in experimental social psychology*, Vol. 2. New York: Academic Press, 1965.

Adorno, T.W., Frenkel-Brunswik, E., Levinson, D.J., & Sanford, R.N. *The authoritarian personality*. New York: Harper, 1950.

Alexander, C.N., Jr., & Weil, H.G. Players, persons, and purposes: Situational meaning and the prisoner's dilemma game. *Sociometry*, 1969. 32, 121–144.

Amidjaja, I.R., & Vinacke, W.E. Achievement, nurturance, and competition in male and female triads. *Journal of Personality & Social Psychology*, 1965, 2, 447–451.

Anderson, R.E. Status structures in coalition bargaining games. *Sociometry*, 1967, 30, 393–403.

Anonymous. 2 sides sit silently 4½ hours at Korean truce meeting. *The Evening Bulletin*, Philadelphia, Friday, April 11, 1969. P. 10.

Apfelbaum, E. Representations du partenaire et interactions a propos d'un dilemme de prisonnier. *Psychologie Française*, 1967, 12, 287–295.

Apfelbaum, E. On conflicts and bargaining. In L. Berkowitz (Ed.), *Advances in experimental social psychology*, Vol. 7. New York: Academic Press, 1974.

Appelgren, L. An attrition game. *Operations Research*, 1967, 15, 11–31.

Aranoff, D., & Tedeschi, J.T. Original stakes and behavior in the prisoner's dilemma game. *Psychonomic Science*, 1968, 12, 79–80.

Argyle, M., & Dean, J. Eye-contact, distance and affiliation. *Sociometry*, 1965, 28, 289–304.

Arnstein, F., & Feigenbaum, K.D. Relationship of three motives to choice in the prisoner's dilemma. *Psychological Reports*, 1967, 20, 751–755.

Ashmore, R.D. Personality-attitude variables and characteristics of the protagonist as determinants of trust in the prisoner's dilemma. Unpublished manuscript, 1969.

Atkinson, R.C., & Suppes, P. Applications of a Markov model to two-person noncooperative games. In R.R. Bush & W.K. Estes (Eds.), *Studies in mathematical learning theory*. Stanford, California: Stanford Univ. Press, 1959.

Atthowe, J.M., Jr. Interpersonal decision making: The resolution of a dyadic conflict. *Journal of Abnormal & Social Psychology*, 1961, 62, 114–119.

Aubert, V. Competition and dissensus: Two types of conflict and of conflict resolution. *Journal of Conflict Resolution,* 1963, **7,** 26–42.

Axelrod, R. Conflicts of interest: An axiomatic approach. *Journal of Conflict Resolution,* 1967, **11,** 87–99.

Axelrod, S., & May J.G. Effect of increased reward on the two-person non-zero-sum game. *Psychological Reports,* 1968, **23,** 675–678.

Baker, K.A. An experimental analysis of third party justice behavior. *Dissertation Abstracts,* 1970, **30,** 5521–A.

Baker, R.A., Ware, J.R., Spires, G.H., & Osborn, W.C. The effects of supervisory threat on decision making and risk taking in a simulated combat game. *Behavioral Science,* 1966, **11,** 167–176.

Ball, G.W. Nixon's appointment in Peking—Is this trip necessary? *The New York Times Magazine,* February 13, 1972. Pp. 11, 50–55.

Banks, M.H., Groom, A.J.R., & Oppenheim, A.N. Gaming and simulation in international relations. *Political Studies,* 1968, **16,** 1–17.

Baranowski, T.A., & Summers, D.A. Perception of response alternatives in a prisoner's dilemma game. *Journal of Personality & Social Psychology,* 1972, **21,** 35–40.

Baron, R.A., & Arenson, S.J. Authoritarianism and exposure to another's behavior in a risk-taking situation. *Psychonomic Science,* 1967, **9,** 461–462.

Bartos, O.J. A model of negotiation and the recency effect. *Sociometry,* 1964, **27,** 311–326.

Bartos, O.J. Concession-making in experimental negotiations. *General Systems,* 1965, **10,** 145–156.

Bartos, O.J. How predictable are negotiations? *Journal of Conflict Resolution,* 1967, **11,** 481–496. (a)

Bartos, O.J. *Simple models of group behavior.* New York: Columbia Univ. Press, 1967. (b)

Bartos. O.J. Determinants and consequences of toughness. In P. Swingle (Ed.), *The structure of conflict.* New York: Academic Press, 1970.

Bass, B.M. Effects on the subsequent performance of negotiators of studying issues or planning strategies alone or in groups. *Psychological Monographs,* 1966, **80** (Whole No. 614).

Bass. B.M., & Dunteman, G. Biases in the evaluation of one's own group, its allies, and opponents. *Journal of Conflict Resolution,* 1963, **7,** 16–20.

Baxter, G.W., Jr. The effects of information about other player and race of other player upon cooperation in a two-person game. *Dissertation Abstracts,* 1970, **30,** 4544–4545–A.

Baxter, G.W., Jr. Prejudiced liberals? Race and information effects in a two-person game. *Journal of Conflict Resolution,* 1973, **17,** 131–161.

Becker, G.M., & McClintock, C.G. Value: Behavioral decision theory. *Annual Review of Psychology,* 1967, **28,** 650–651.

Bedell, J., & Sistrunk, F. Power, opportunity costs, and sex in a mixed–motive game. *Journal of Personality & Social Psychology,* 1973, **25,** 219–226.

Benton, A.A. Productivity, distributive justice, and bargaining among children. *Journal of Personality & Social Psychology,* 1971, **18,** 68–78.

Benton, A.A., Gelber, E.R., Kelley, H.H., & Liebling, B.A. Reactions to various degrees of deceit in a mixed–motive relationship. *Journal of Personality & Social Psychology,* 1969, **12,** 170–180.

Benton, A.A., Kelley, H.H., & Liebling, B. Effects of extremity of offers and concession rate on the outcomes of bargaining. *Journal of Personality & Social Psychology,* 1972, **24,** 73–83.

Berger, S.E., & Tedeschi, J.T. Aggressive behavior of delinquent, dependent, and "normal" white and black boys in social conflicts. *Journal of Experimental Social Psychology,* 1969, **5,** 352–370.

Berkowitz, N.H. Alternative measures of authoritarianism, response sets, and prediction in a two–person game. *Journal of Social Psychology*, 1968, **74**, 233–242.

Berkowitz, N.H., Hylander, L., & Bakaitis, R. Defense, vulnerability, and cooperation in a mixed–motive game. *Journal of Personality & Social Psychology*, 1973, **25**, 401–407.

Bernard, J. Some current conceptualizations in the field of conflict. *American Journal of Sociology*, 1965, **70**, 442–454.

Birdwhistell, R.L. *Introduction to kinesics*. Louisville, Kentucky: Univ. of Louisville Press, 1952.

Birmingham, R.L. The prisoner's dilemma and mutual trust: Comment. *Ethics*, 1969, **79**, 156–158.

Bishop, R.L. Game–theoretic analyses of bargaining. *Quarterly Journal of Economics*, 1963, **77**, 559–602.

Bixenstine, V.E., & Blundell, H. Control of choice exerted by structural factors in two–person, non–zero–sum games. *Journal of Conflict Resolution*, 1966, **10**, 478–487.

Bixenstine, V.E., Chambers, N., & Wilson, K.V. Effect of asymmetry in payoff on behavior in a two-person non–zero–sum game. *Journal of Conflict Resolution*. 1964, **8**, 151–159.

Bixenstine, V.E., & Douglas, J. Effect of psychopathology on group consensus and cooperative choice in a six–person game. *Journal of Personality & Social Psychology*, 1967, **5**, 32–37.

Bixenstine, V.E., & Gaebelein, J.W. Strategies of "real" opponents in eliciting cooperative choice in a prisoner's dilemma game. *Journal of Conflict Resolution*, 1971, **15**, 157–166.

Bixenstine, V.E., Levitt, C.A., & Wilson, K.V. Collaboration among six persons in a prisoner's dilemma game. *Journal of Conflict Resolution*, 1966, **10**, 488–496.

Bixenstine, V.E., & O'Reilly, E.F., Jr. Money versus electric shock as payoff in a prisoner's dilemma game. *Psychological Record*, 1966, **16**, 251–264.

Bixenstine, V.E., Potash, H.M., & Wilson, K.V. Effects of level of cooperative choice by the other player on choices in a prisoner's dilemma game: Part I. *Journal of Abnormal & Social Psychology*, 1963, **66**, 308–313.

Bixenstine, V.E., & Wilson, K.V. Effects of level of cooperative choice by the other player on choices in a prisoner's dilemma game: Part II. *Journal of Abnormal & Social Psychology*, 1963, **67**, 139–147.

Black, T.E., & Higbee, K.L. Effects of power, threat, and sex on exploitation. *Journal of Personality & Social Psychology*, 1973, **27**, 382–388.

Blake, R.R., & Mouton, J.S. Comprehension of own and of outgroup positions under intergroup competition. *Journal of Conflict Resolution*, 1961, **5**, 304–310. (a)

Blake, R.R., & Mouton, J.S. Loyalty of representatives to ingroup positions during intergroup competition. *Sociometry*, 1961, **24**, 177–183. (b).

Blake, R.R., & Mouton, J.S. Overevaluation of own group's product in intergroup competition. *Journal of Abnormal & Social Psychology*, 1962, **64**, 237–238. (a)

Blake, R.R., & Mouton, J.S. Comprehension of points of communality in competing solutions. *Sociometry*, 1962, **25**, 56–63. (b)

Blau, P.M. *Exchange and power in social life*. New York: Wiley, 1964.

Blumstein, P.W. An experiment in identity bargaining. *Dissertation Abstracts*, 1970, **31**, 3034–3035–A.

Bobbitt, R.A. Internal–external control and bargaining behavior in a prisoner's dilemma game. *Dissertation Abstracts*, 1967, **27**, 3266–3267–B.

Bonacich, P. Putting the dilemma back into prisoner's dilemma. *Journal of Conflict Resolution*, 1970, **14**, 379–387.

Bond, J.R., & Vinacke, W.E. Coalitions in mixed–sex triads. *Sociometry*, 1961, **24**, 61–75.

Bonoma, T., Horai, J., Lindskold, S., Gahagan, J.P., & Tedeschi, J.T. Compliance to contingent threats. *Proceedings of the 77th Annual Convention of the American Psychological Association,* 1969, **4**, 395–396.

Bonoma, T.V., Schlenker, B.R., Smith, R., & Tedeschi, J. Source prestige and target reactions to threats. *Psychonomic Science,* 1970, **19**, 111–113.

Bonoma, T.V., Tedeschi, J.T., & Lindskold, S. A note regarding an expected value model of social power. *Behavioral Science,* 1972, **17**, 221–228.

Bonoma, T.V., & Tedeschi, J.T. Some effects of source behavior on target's compliance to threats. *Behavioral Science,* 1973, **18**, 34–41.

Borah, L.A., Jr. An investigation of the effect of threat upon interpersonal bargaining. *Dissertation Abstracts,* 1961, **22**, 2089.

Borah, L.A., Jr. The effects of threat in bargaining: Critical and experimental analysis. *Journal of Abnormal & Social Psychology,* 1963, **66**, 37–44.

Borch, K. A utility function derived from a survival game. *Management Science,* 1966, **12**, 287–295.

Borgatta, M.L. Power structure and coalitions in three person groups. *Journal of Social Psychology,* 1961, **55**, 287–300.

Borgatta, M.L., & Borgatta, E.F. Coalitions in three–person groups. *Journal of Social Psychology,* 1963, **60**, 319–326.

Boulding, K.E. Review of T.C. Schelling, "The strategy of conflict." *Contemporary Psychology,* 1961, **6**, 426–427.

Boulding, K.E. *Conflict and defense: A general theory.* New York: Harper, 1962.

Boulding, K.E. Towards a pure theory of threat systems. *American Economic Review,* 1963, **53**, 424–434.

Bower, J.L. Group decision making: A report of an experimental study. *Behavioral Science,* 1965, **10**, 277–289.

Boyle, R., & Bonacich, P. The development of trust and mistrust in mixed-motive games. *Sociometry,* 1970, **33**, 123–139.

Brayer, A.R. An experimental analysis of some variables of minimax theory. *Behavioral Science,* 1964, **9**, 33–44.

Brew, J.S. An altruism parameter for prisoner's dilemma. *Journal of Conflict Resolution,* 1973, **17**, 351–367.

Brody, R.A. Deterrence strategies: An annotated bibliography. *Journal of Conflict Resolution,* 1960, **4**, 443–457.

Broskowski, A.T. The effects of reciprocity relationships on the bargaining behavior of the dyad. *Dissertation Abstracts,* 1968, **29**, 363–B.

Brown, B.R. The effects of need to maintain face on interpersonal bargaining. *Journal of Experimental Social Psychology,* 1968, **4**, 107–122.

Brown, B.R. Face–saving following experimentally induced embarrassment. *Journal of Experimental Social Psychology,* 1970, **6**, 255–271.

Brown, B.R., & Garland, H. The effects of incompetency, audience acquaintanceship, and anticipated evaluative feedback on face–saving behavior. *Journal of Experimental Social Psychology,* 1971, **7**, 490–502.

Brown, B.R., Garland, H., & Freedman, S. The effects of constituency feedback, representational role, and strategy of the other on concession–making in a bilateral monopoly bargaining task. Paper presented at the meeting of the Eastern Psychological Association, Washington, D.C., May 1973.

Brown, R., Smith, R.B., & Tedeschi, J.T. Impressions of a promisor after social deprivation or satiation. *Psychonomic Science,* 1971, **23**, 135–136.

Brumback, G.B. Exploitative game behavior as a function of the individual's exploitative value judgments and of his opponent's strategy and success. *Dissertation Abstracts*, 1963, **24**, 1268–1269.

Bruning, J.L., Sommer, D.K., & Jones, B.R. The motivational effects of cooperation and competition in the means–independent situation. *Journal of Social Psychology*, 1966, **68**, 269–274.

Buchanan, J.M. Simple majority voting, game theory, and resource use. *Canadian Journal of Economics & Political Science*, 1961, **27**, 337–348.

Buchler, I.R., & Nutini, H.G. (Eds.). *Game theory in the behavioral sciences*. Pittsburgh: Univ. of Pittsburgh Press, 1969.

Buckley, J.J., & Westen, T.E. The symmetric solution to a five–person constant-sum game as a description of experimental game outcomes. *Journal of Conflict Resolution*, 1973, **17**, 703–718.

Burrill, D.A. The measurement of power in asymmetrical two–person non–zero sum games. *Dissertation Abstracts*, 1968, **28**, 3893–B.

Byrne, D. Attitudes and attraction. In L. Berkowitz (Ed.), *Advances in experimental social psychology*, Vol. 4. New York: Academic Press, 1969.

Caldwell, M. Coalitions in the triad: Introducing the element of chance into the game structure. *Journal of Personality & Social Psychology*, 1971, **20**, 271–280.

Callahan, C.M., & Messé, L.A. Conditions affecting attempts to convert fate control to behavior control. *Journal of Experimental Social Psychology*, 1973, **9**, 481–490.

Campbell, D.T., & Fiske, D.W. Convergent and discriminant validation by the multitrait–multimethod matrix. *Psychological Bulletin*, 1959, **56**, 81–105.

Campbell, R.J. Team composition and group decision–making in a collective bargaining situation. *Dissertation Abstracts*, 1961, **21**, 3539–3540.

Caplow, T.A. A theory of coalitions in the triad. *American Sociological Review*, 1956, **21**, 489–493.

Caplow, T.A. Further development of a theory of coalitions in the triad. *American Journal of Sociology*, 1959, **64**, 488–493.

Caplow, T.A. *Two against one: Coalitions in triads*. Englewood Cliffs, New Jersey: Prentice–Hall, 1968.

Chacko, G.K. Bargaining strategy in a production and distribution problem. *Operations Research*, 1961, **9**, 811–827.

Chamberlain, N. *Collective bargaining*. New York: McGraw–Hill, 1951.

Chamberlain, N.W. *The labor sector*. New York: McGraw–Hill, 1965.

Chaney, M.V., & Vinacke, W.E. Achievement and nurturance in triads varying in power distribution. *Journal of Abnormal & Social Psychology*, 1960, **60**, 175–181.

Cheney, J.H. The effects upon the bargaining process of positive and negative communication options in equal and unequal power relationships. *Dissertation Abstracts*, 1969, **30**, 2146–2147–A.

Cheney, J., Harford, T., & Solomon, L. The effects of communicating threats and promises upon the bargaining process. *Journal of Conflict Resolution*, 1972, **16**, 99–107.

Chertkoff, J.M. The effects of probability of future success on coalition formation. *Journal of Experimental Social Psychology*, 1966, **2**, 265–277.

Chertkoff, J.M. A revision of Caplow's coalition theory. *Journal of Experimental Social Psychology*, 1967, **3**, 172–177.

Chertkoff, J.M. Coalition formation as a function of differences in resources. *Journal of Conflict Resolution*, 1971, **15**, 371–383.

Chertkoff, J.M., & Baird, S.L. Applicability of the big lie technique and the last clear chance doctrine to bargaining. *Journal of Personality & Social Psychology*, 1971, **20**, 298–303.

Chertkoff, J.M., & Conley, M. Opening offer and frequency of concession as bargaining strategies. *Journal of Personality & Social Psychology*, 1967, **7**, 181–185.

Chidambaram, T.S. Coordination problems in competitive situations. *Dissertation Abstracts*, 1967, **28**, 2513–B.

Christie, R., & Geis, F.L. (Eds.). *Studies in machiavellianism*. New York: Academic Press, 1970. (a)

Christie, R., & Geis, F. The ten dollar game. In R. Christie & F.L. Geis (Eds.), *Studies in machiavellianism*. New York: Academic Press, 1970. (b)

Christie, R., Gergen, K.J., & Marlowe, D. The penny–dollar caper. In R. Christie & F.L. Geis (Eds.), *Studies in machiavellianism*. New York: Academic Press, 1970.

Clarkson, G.P.E. Decision making in small groups: A simulation study. *Behavioral Science*, 1968, **13**, 288–305.

Coddington, A. Game theory, bargaining theory, and strategic reasoning. *Journal of Peace Research*, 1967, **4**, 39–44.

Cohen, A. Situational structure, self–esteem, and threat-oriented reactions to power. In D. Cartwright (Ed.), *Studies in social power*. Ann Arbor, Michigan: Institute for Social Research, Univ. of Michigan, 1959.

Cole, M., & Schneider, A. Amount of reward and information in a two–person game. *Canadian Journal of Psychology*, 1964, **18**, 197–208.

Cole, S.G. An examination of the power–inversion effect in three–person mixed–motive games. *Journal of Personality & Social Psychology*, 1969, **11**, 50-58.

Cole, S.G. Conflict and cooperation in potentially intense conflict situations. *Journal of Personality & Social Psychology*, 1972, **22**, 31–50.

Cole, S.G., & Phillips. J.L. The propensity to attack others as a function of the distribution of resources in a three person game. *Psychonomic Science*, 1967, **9**, 239–240.

Coleman, J.S. Introduction: In defense of games. *American Behavioral Scientist*, 1966, **10**, 3–4.

Coleman, J.S. Games as vehicles for social theory. Paper presented at the sixty–third meeting of the American Sociological Association, Session 7. Boston, 1968.

Condry, J.C., Jr. The effects of situational power and personality upon the decision to negotiate or not in a two person bargaining situation. *Dissertation Abstracts*, 1967, **27**, 2612–A.

Conrath, D.W. Experience as a factor in experimental gaming behavior. *Journal of Conflict Resolution*, 1970, **14**, 195–202.

Conrath, D.W. Sex role and "cooperation" in the game of chicken. *Journal of Conflict Resolution*, 1972, **16**, 433–443.

Contini, B. The value of time in bargaining negotiations: Some experimental evidence. *American Economic Review*, 1968, **58**, 374–393.

Cook, J.O. Laboratory study of endogenous social change. *Psychological Reports*, 1968, **22**, 1108.

Cook, M. Experiments on orientation and proxemics. *Human Relations*, 1970, **23**, 61–76.

Coombs, C.H. A reparameterization of the prisoner's dilemma game. *Behavioral Science*, 1973, **18**, 424–428.

Coombs, C.H., & Pruitt, D.G. Components of risk in decision making: Probability and variance preferences. *Journal of Experimental Psychology*, 1960, **60**, 265–277.

Coombs, C.H., & Pruitt, D.G. Some characteristics of choice behavior in risky situations. *Annals of the New York Academy of Science,* 1961, **89**, 784–794.

Cope, V.M. The effects of sequences of winning and losing on level of aspiration in two-person competitive situations. *Dissertation Abstracts,* 1968, **28**, 4266–A.

Cottrell, N.B. Means-interdependence, prior acquaintance, and emotional tension during cooperation and subsequent competition. *Human Relations,* 1963, **16**, 249–262.

Crawford, T., & Sidowski, J.B. Monetary incentive and cooperation/competition instructions in a minimal social situation. *Psychological Reports,* 1964, **15**, 233–234.

Crombag, H.F. Cooperation and competition in means-interdependent triads: A replication. *Journal of Personality & Social Psychology,* 1966, **4**, 692–695.

Cross, J.G. A theory of the bargaining process. *American Economic Review,* 1965, **55**, 67-94.

Crowne, D.P. Family orientation, level of aspiration, and interpersonal bargaining. *Journal of Personality & Social Psychology,* 1966, **3**, 641–645.

Crumbaugh, C.M., & Evans, G.W. Presentation format, other–person strategies, and cooperative behavior in the prisoner's dilemma. *Psychological Reports,* 1967, **20**, 895–902.

Cullen, D.E. *Negotiating labor–management contracts.* Ithaca, New York: New York State School of Industrial and Labor Relations, Cornell Univ., 1965.

Daniels, V. Communication, incentive, and structural variables in interpersonal exchange and negotiation. *Journal of Experimental Social Psychology,* 1967, **3**, 47–74.

Davis, J.H., Cohen, J.L., Hornik, J., & Rissman, A.K. Dyadic decision as a function of the frequency distributions describing the preferences of members' consitituencies. *Journal of Personality & Social Psychology,* 1973, **26**, 178–195.

Deep, S.D., Bass, B.M., & Vaughan, J.A. Some effects on business gaming of previous quasi–T group affiliations. *Journal of Applied Psychology,* 1967, **51**, 426–431.

Deignan, G.M. Perceptual, interpersonal and situational factors in cooperation and competition. *Dissertation Abstracts,* 1970, **31**, 1371–A.

Deutsch, M. An experimental study of the effects of cooperation and competition upon group process. *Human Relations,* 1949, **2**, 199–232.

Deutsch, M. Trust and suspicion. *Journal of Conflict Resolution,* 1958, **2**, 265–279.

Deutsch, M. The effect of motivational orientation upon trust and suspicion. *Human Relations,* 1960, **13**, 123–139. (a)

Deutsch, M. Trust, trustworthiness, and the F scale. *Journal of Abnormal & Social Psychology,* 1960, **61**, 138–140. (b).

Deutsch, M. Some considerations relevant to national policy. *Journal of Social Issues.* 1961, **17**, 57–68. (a)

Deutsch, M. The face of bargaining. *Operations Research,* 1961, **9**, 886–897. (b)

Deutsch, M. Cooperation and trust: Some theoretical notes. In M.R. Jones (Ed)., *Nebraska symposium on motivation,* 1962. Lincoln, Nebraska: Univ. of Nebraska Press.

Deutsch, M. Bargaining, threat, and communication: Some experimental studies. In K. Archibald (Ed.), *Strategic interaction and conflict: Original papers and discussion.* Berkeley: Institute of International Studies, 1966.

Deutsch, M. Conflicts: Productive and destructive. *Journal of Social Issues,* 1969, **25**, 7–41.

Deutsch, M. *The resolution of conflict.* New Haven: Yale Univ. Press, 1973.

Deutsch, M., Canavan, D., & Rubin, J. The effects of size of conflict and sex of experimenter upon interpersonal bargaining. *Journal of Experimental Social Psychology,* 1971, **7**, 258–267.

Deutsch, M., Epstein, Y., Canavan, D., & Gumpert, P. Strategies of inducing cooperation:

An experimental study. *Journal of Conflict Resolution*, 1967, **11**, 345–360.

Deutsch, M., & Krauss, R.M. The effect of threat upon interpersonal bargaining. *Journal of Abnormal & Social Psychology*, 1960, **61**, 181–189.

Deutsch, M., & Krauss, R.M. Studies of interpersonal bargaining. *Journal of Conflict Resolution*, 1962, **6**, 52–76.

Deutsch, M., & Lewicki, R.J. "Locking–in" effects during a game of chicken. *Journal of Conflict Resolution*, 1970, **14**, 367–378.

Diesing, P. Bargaining strategy and union–management relationship. *Journal of Conflict Resolution*, 1961, **5**, 369–378.

Dolbear, F.T., Jr., & Lave, L.B. Risk orientation as a predictor in the prisoner's dilemma. *Journal of Conflict Resolution*, 1966, **10**, 506–515.

Dolbear, F.T., Jr., & Lave, L.B. Inconsistent behavior in lottery choice experiments. *Behavioral Science*, 1967, **12**, 14–23.

Dolbear, F.T., Lave, L.B., Bowman, G., Lieberman, A., Prescott, E., Rueter, F., & Sherman, R. Collusion in the prisoner's dilemma: Number of strategies. *Journal of Conflict Resolution*, 1969, **13**, 252–261.

Dorris, J.W. The effects of nonverbal cues on interpersonal judgments in a bargaining situation. Unpublished manuscript, Univ. of California, Los Angeles, 1969.

Dorris, J.W. Reactions to unconditional cooperation: A field study emphasizing variables neglected in laboratory research. *Journal of Personality & Social Psychology*, 1972, **22**, 387–397.

Douglas, A. *Industrial peacemaking*. New York: Columbia Univ. Press, 1962.

Driver, M.J. A structural analysis of aggression, stress, and personality in an inter-nation simulation. Paper No. 97, January 1965, Institute for Research in the Behavioral, Economic, and Management Sciences, Purdue University, Lafayette, Indiana.

Druckman, D. Dogmatism, prenegotiation experience, and simulated group representation as determinants of dyadic behavior in a bargaining situation. *Journal of Personality and Social Psychology*, 1967, **6**, 279–290.

Druckman, D. Ethnocentrism in the inter-nation simulation. *Journal of Conflict Resolution*, 1968, **12**, 45–68. (a)

Druckman, D. Prenegotiation experience and dyadic conflict resolution in a bargaining situation. *Journal of Experimental Social Psychology*, 1968, **4**, 367–383. (b)

Druckman, D. The influence of the situation in interparty conflict. *Journal of Conflict Resolution*, 1971, **15**, 523–554. (a)

Druckman, D. On the effects of group representation. *Journal of Personality & Social Psychology*, 1971, **18**, 273–274. (b)

Druckman, D., Zechmeister, K., & Solomon, D. Determinants of bargaining behavior in a bilateral monopoly situation: Opponent's concession rate and relative defensibility. *Behavioral Science*, 1972, **17**, 514–531.

Dunlop, J.T., & Chamberlain, N.W. (Eds.). *Frontiers of collective bargaining*. New York: Harper and Row, 1967.

Dunlop, J.T., & Healy, J.J. *Collective bargaining: Principles and cases*. Homewood, Illinois: Irwin Press, 1955.

Dunn, L. The effects of sex of transmitter and sex of recipient upon the effectiveness of promises and threats. Unpublished manuscript, Tufts Univ., Medford, Massachusetts, 1972.

Dunn, R.E., & Goldman, M. Competition and noncompetition in relationship to satisfaction and feelings toward own–group and nongroup members. *Journal of Social Psychology*, 1966, **68**, 299–311.

Dustin, D.S., & Arthur, T.B. Resistance to threat. *Psychonomic Science*, 1968, **10**, 403–404.

Edelstein, R. Risk–taking, age, sex, and machiavellianism. Unpublished manuscript, New York Univ., New York, 1966.

Edwards, W. Behavioral decision theory. *Annual Review of Psychology*, 1961, **12**, 473–498. (a)

Edwards, W. Costs and payoffs are instructions. *Psychological Review*, 1961, **68**, 275–284. (b)

Eisenman, R.L. A profit–sharing interpretation of Shapley value for n-person games. *Behavioral Science*, 1967, **12**, 396–398.

Eiser, J.R., & Tajfel, H. Acquisition of information in dyadic interaction. *Journal of Personality & Social Psychology*, 1972, **23**, 340–345.

Ells, J.G., & Sermat, V. Cooperation and the variation of payoff in non-zero-sum games. *Psychonomic Science*, 1966, **5**, 149–150.

Ells, J.G., & Sermat, V. Motivational determinants of choice in chicken and prisoner's dilemma. *Journal of Conflict Resolution*, 1968, **12**, 374–380.

Ellsworth, P.C., & Carlsmith, J.M. Effects of eye contact and verbal content on affective response to a dyadic interaction. *Journal of Personality & Social Psychology*, 1968, **10**, 15–20.

Emerson, R.M. Power–dependence relations: Two experiments. *Sociometry*, 1964, **27**, 282–298.

Emshoff, J.R. A computer simulation model of the prisoner's dilemma. *Behavioral Science*, 1970, **15**, 304–317.

Emshoff, J.R., & Ackoff, R.L. Explanatory models of interactive choice behavior. *Journal of Conflict Resolution*, 1970, **14**, 77–89.

Estes, W.K. Review of R.D. Luce, "Individual choice behavior: A theoretical analysis." *Contemporary Psychology*, 1960, **5**, 113–116.

Evan, W.M., & MacDougall, J.A. Interorganizational conflict: A labor-management bargaining experiment. *Journal of Conflict Resolution*, 1967, **11**, 398–413.

Evans, G. Effect of unilateral promise and value of rewards upon cooperation and trust. *Journal of Abnormal & Social Psychology*, 1964, **69**, 587–590.

Evans, G.W., & Crumbaugh, C.M. Effects of prisoner's dilemma format on cooperative behavior. *Journal of Personality & Social Psychology*, 1966, **3**, 486–488. (a)

Evans, G.W., & Crumbaugh, C.M. Payment schedule, sequence of choice, and cooperation in the prisoner's dilemma game. *Psychonomic Science*, 1966, **5**, 87–88. (b)

Exline, R.V. Explorations in the process of person perception: Visual interaction in relation to competition, sex, and the need for affiliation. *Journal of Personality*, 1963, **31**, 1–20.

Exline, R.V., Thibaut, J., Brannon, C., & Gumpert, P. Visual interaction in relation to machiavellianism and an unethical act. *American Psychologist*, 1961, **16**, 396.

Faley, T., & Tedeschi, J.T. Status and reactions to threats. *Journal of Personality & Social Psychology*, 1971, **17**, 192–199.

Faucheux, C., & Moscovici, S. Self–esteem and exploitative behavior in a game against chance and nature. *Journal of Personality & Social Psychology*, 1968, **8**, 83–88.

Ferguson, C.E., & Pfouts, R.W. Learning and expectations in dynamic duopoly behavior. *Behavioral Science*, 1962, **7**, 223–237.

Festinger, L. A theory of social comparison processes. *Human Relations*, 1954, **7**, 117–140.

Fishburn, P. Utility theory. *Management Science,* 1968, **14,** 335–378.

Fisher, R., & Smith, W.P. Conflict of interest and attraction in the development of coopera-tion. *Psychonomic Science,* 1969, **14,** 154–155.

Fisher, R. Fractionating conflict. In R. Fisher (Ed.), *International conflict and behavioral science: The Craigville papers.* New York: Basic Books, 1964.

Flament, C. Representation in a conflictual situation. An intercultural study. *Psychologie Française,* 1967, **12,** 297–304.

Flynn, J.C. Cooperative and non-cooperative game strategies as a function of perceived differential ability in the triad. *Dissertation Abstracts,* 1962, **22,** 2463–2464.

Fouraker, L.E. Level of aspiration and group decision making. In S. Messick & A.H. Brayfield (Eds.), *Decision and choice: Contributions of Sidney Siegel.* New York: McGraw–Hill, 1964.

Fouraker, L.E., & Siegel, S. *Bargaining behavior,* New York: McGraw–Hill, 1963.

Fouraker, L.E., Siegel, S., & Harnett, D.L. An experimental disposition of alternative bilateral monopoly models under conditions of price leadership. *Operations Research,* 1962, **10,** 41–50.

Fox, J. The learning of strategies in a simple, two-person zero-sum game without saddlepoint. *Behavioral Science.* 1972, **17,** 300–308.

Fox, J., & Guyer, M. Equivalence and stooge strategies in zero-sum games. *Journal of Conflict Resolution,* 1973, **17,** 513–533.

Frank, J.D. *Sanity and survival: Psychological aspects of war and peace.* New York: Random House, 1967.

Freilich, N. The effect of interpersonal unpredictability and malevolence upon interpersonal suspicion in paranoid schizophrenics. Unpublished doctoral dissertation, Boston Univ., Boston, Massachusetts, 1972.

French, J.R.P., Jr., & Raven, B.H. The bases of social power. In D. Cartwright (Ed.), *Studies in social power.* Ann Arbor, Michigan: Univ. of Michigan Press, 1959.

Frey, R.L., Jr., & Adams, J.S. The negotiator's dilemma: Simultaneous in-group and out-group conflict. *Journal of Experimental Social Psychology,* 1972, **8,** 331–346.

Friberg, M., & Jonsson, D. A simple war and armament game. *Journal of Peace Research,* 1968, **5,** 233–247.

Friedell, M.F. A laboratory experiment in retaliation. *Journal of Conflict Resolution,* 1968, **12,** 357–373.

Friedland, N., Arnold, S.E., & Thibaut, J. Motivational bases in mixed-motive interactions: The effects of comparison levels. *Journal of Experimental Social Psychology,* 1974, **10,** 188–199.

Froman, L.A., Jr., & Cohen, M.D. Threats and bargaining efficiency. *Behavioral Science,* 1969, **14,** 147–153.

Froman, L.A., Jr., & Cohen, M.D. Compromise and logroll: Comparing the efficiency of two bargaining processes. *Behavioral Science,* 1970, **15,** 180–183.

Fry, C.L. Personality and acquisition factors in the development of coordination strategy. *Journal of Personality & Social Psychology,* 1965, **2,** 403–407.

Fry, C.L. A developmental examination of performance in a tacit coordination game situa-tion. *Journal of Personality & Social Psychology,* 1967, **5,** 277–281.

Fry, C.L., Hopkins, J.R., & Hoge, P. Triads in minimal social situations. *Journal of Social Psychology,* 1970, **80,** 37–42.

Gahagan, J.P. Effects of promise credibility, outside options and social contact on inter-personal conflict. *Dissertation Abstracts,* 1970, **30,** 3546–A.

Gahagan, J., Horai, J., Berger, S., & Tedeschi, J. Status and authoritarianism in the prisoner's dilemma game. Paper presented at the meeting of the Southeastern Psychological Association, Atlanta, April 1967.

Gahagan, J.P., Long, H., & Horai, J. Race of experimenter and reactions to threat by black preadolescents. *Proceedings of the 77th Annual Convention of the American Psychological Association*, 1969, **4**, 397–398.

Gahagan, J.P., & Tedeschi, J.T. Strategy and the credibility of promises in the prisoner's dilemma game. *Journal of Conflict Resolution*, 1968, **12**, 224–234. (a)

Gahagan, J.P., & Tedeschi, J.T. Demographic factors in the communication of promises. *Journal of Social Psychology*, 1968, **76**, 277–280. (b)

Gahagan, J.P., & Tedeschi, J.T. Shifts of power in a mixed–motive game. *Journal of Social Psychology*, 1969, **77**, 241–252.

Gahagan, J., Tedeschi, J.T., Faley, T., & Lindskold, S. Patterns of punishment and reactions to threats. *Journal of Social Psychology*, 1970, **80**, 115–116.

Gallo, P.S., Jr. The effects of different motivational orientations in a mixed motive game. *Dissertation Abstracts*, 1964, **24**, 4303–4304.

Gallo, P.S., Jr. Effects of increased incentives upon the use of threat in bargaining. *Journal of Personality & Social Psychology*, 1966, **4**, 14–20.

Gallo, P.S., Jr. Prisoners of our own dilemma? Paper presented at the meeting of the Western Psychological Association, San Diego, April 1968.

Gallo, P.S. Personality impression formation in a maximizing difference game. *Journal of Conflict Resolution*, 1969, **13**, 118–122.

Gallo, P.S., Jr., & Dale, I.A. Experimenter bias in the prisoner's dilemma game. *Psychonomic Science*, 1968, **13**, 340.

Gallo, P.S., Jr., Funk, S.G., & Levine, J.R. Reward size, method of presentation, and number of alternatives in a prisoner's dilemma game. *Journal of Personality & Social Psychology*, 1969, **13**, 239–244.

Gallo, P.S., Jr., Irwin, R., & Avery, G. The effects of score feedback and strategy of the other on cooperative behavior in a maximizing differences game. *Psychonomic Science*, 1966, **5**, 401–402.

Gallo, P.S., Jr., & McClintock, C.G. Cooperative and competitive behavior in mixed-motive games. *Journal of Conflict Resolution*, 1965, **9**, 68–78.

Gallo, P., & Sheposh, J. Effects of incentive magnitude on cooperation in the prisoner's dilemma game: A reply to Gumpert, Deutsch and Epstein. *Journal of Personality & Social Psychology*, 1971, **19**, 42–46.

Gallo, P.S., Jr., & Winchell, J.D. Matrix indices, large rewards, and cooperative behavior in a prisoner's dilemma game. *Journal of Social Psychology*, 1970, **81**, 235–241.

Gamson, W.A. A theory of coalition formation. *American Sociological Review*, 1961, **26**, 373–382. (a)

Gamson, W.A. An experimental test of a theory of coalition formation. *American Sociological Review*, 1961, **26**, 565–573. (b)

Gamson, W.A. Coalition formation at presidential nominating conventions. *American Journal of Sociology*, 1962, **68**, 157–171.

Gamson, W.A. Experimental studies of coalition formation. In L. Berkowitz (Ed.), *Advances in experimental social psychology*, Vol. 1. New York: Academic Press, 1964.

Gamson, W.A. Game theory and administrative decision-making. In C. Press & A. Arian (Eds), *Empathy and ideology: Aspects of administrative innovation*. Chicago: Rand-McNally, 1966.

Gardin, H., Kaplan, K.J., Firestone, I.J., & Cowan, G.A. Proxemic effects on cooperation, attitude, and approach–avoidance in a prisoner's dilemma game. *Journal of Personality & Social Psychology*, 1973, **27**, 13–18.

Garfield, F.B. The effects of the opponent's payoffs on choice behavior in a two person nonzero sum game. *Dissertation Abstracts*, 1970, **30**, 3546–3547–A.

Garrett, J., & Libby, W.L., Jr. Role of intentionality in mediating responses to inequity in the dyad. *Journal of Personality & Social Psychology*, 1973, **28**, 21–27.

Geis, F.L. Machiavellianism in a three-person game. *Dissertation Abstracts*, 1965, **25**, 7407–7408.

Geis, F. Bargaining tactics in the con game. In R. Christie & F.L. Geis (Eds.), *Studies in machiavellianism*. New York: Academic Press, 1970.

Geis, F., Weinheimer, S., & Berger, D. Playing legislature: Cool heads and hot issues. In R. Christie & F.L. Geis (Eds.), *Studies in machiavellianism*. New York: Academic Press, 1970.

Geiwitz, P.J. The effects of threats on prisoner's dilemma. *Behavioral Science*, 1967, **12**, 232–233.

Gillis, J.S., & Woods, G.T. The 16PF as an indicator of performance in the prisoner's dilemma game. *Journal of Conflict Resolution*, 1971, **15**, 393–402.

Goffman, E. *The presentation of self in everyday life*. New York: Doubleday (Anchor), 1959.

Goffman, E. *Behavior in public places*. New York: Free Press, 1963.

Gouldner, A. The norm of reciprocity: A preliminary statement. *American Sociological Review*, 1960, **25**, 161–179.

Graeven, D.B. Intergroup conflict and the group representative: The effects of power and the legitimacy of the power relation on negotiations in an experimental setting. *Dissertation Abstracts*, 1970, **31**, 3037–A.

Grant, M.J., & Sermat, V. Status and sex of other as determinants of behavior in a mixed-motive game. *Journal of Personality & Social Psychology*, 1969, **12**, 151–157.

Gregovich, R.P., Jr. Sex differences in the prisoner's dilemma game. *Dissertation Abstracts*, 1969, **29**, 2357–A.

Gregovich, R.P., & Sidowski, J.B. Verbal reports of strategies in a two-person interaction: A note. *Psychological Reports*, 1966, **19**, 641–642.

Griesinger, D.W., & Livingston, J.W., Jr. Toward a model of interpersonal motivation in experimental games. *Behavioral Science*, 1973, **18**, 173–188.

Gross, D.E., Kelley, H.H., Kruglanski, A.W., & Patch, M.E. Contingency of consequences and type of incentive in interdependent escape. *Journal of Experimental Social Psychology*, 1972, **8**, 360–377.

Gruder, C.L. Effects of perception of opponent's bargaining style and accountability to opponent and partner on interpersonal mixed-motive bargaining. *Dissertation Abstracts*, 1969, **29**, 4555–4556–A.

Gruder, C.L. Social power in interpersonal negotiation. In P. Swingle (Ed.), *The structure of conflict*. New York: Academic Press, 1970.

Gruder, C.L. Relationships with opponent and partner in mixed-motive bargaining. *Journal of Conflict Resolution*, 1971, **15**, 403–416.

Gruder, C.L., & Duslak, R.J. Elicitation of cooperation by retaliatory and nonretaliatory strategies in a mixed-motive game. *Journal of Conflict Resolution*, 1973, **17**, 162–174.

Gumpert, P. Some antecedents and consequences of the use of punitive power by bargainers. Unpublished doctoral dissertation, Teachers College, Columbia Univ., New York, 1967.

Gumpert, P., Deutsch, M., & Epstein, Y. Effect of incentive magnitude on cooperation in the prisoner's dilemma game. *Journal of Personality & Social Psychology*, 1969, **11**, 66–69.

Guyer, M.J. An analysis of duopoly bargaining. *General Systems*, 1966, **11**, 215–224.

Guyer, M. Response–dependent parameter changes in the prisoner's dilemma game. *Behavioral Science*, 1968, **13**, 205–219. (a)

Guyer, M.J. The effects of response-dependent parameter changes in the prisoner's dilemma game. *Dissertation Abstracts*, 1968, **28**, 3074–B (b)

Guyer, M., Fox, J., & Hamburger, H. Format effects in the prisoner's dilemma game. *Journal of Conflict Resolution*, 1973, **17**, 719–744.

Guyer, M.J., & Hamburger, H. A note on the enumeration of all 2 × 2 games. *General Systems*, 1968, **13**, 205–208.

Guyer, M., & Rapoport, A. Information effects in two mixed-motive games. *Behavioral Science*, 1969, **14**, 467–482.

Guyer, M., & Rapoport, A. Threat in a two-person game. *Journal of Experimental Social Psychology*, 1970, **6**, 11–25.

Guyer, M.J., & Rapoport, A. 2 × 2 games played once. *Journal of Conflict Resolution*, 1972, **16**, 409–431.

Guyer, M., & Zabner, M. *Experimental games: A bibliography (1965–1969)*. Ann Arbor, Michigan: Mental Health Research Institute, Univ. of Michigan, 1969. Communication #258.

Guyer, M., & Zabner, M. *Experimental games: A bibliography (1945-1964)*. Ann Arbor, Michigan: Mental Health Research Institute, Univ. of Michigan, 1970. Communication #265.

Halberstam, D. *The best and the brightest.* New York: Random House, 1972.

Hall, E.T. *The hidden dimension.* New York: Doubleday, 1966.

Hall, J., & Williams, M.S. A comparison of decision-making performances in established and ad hoc groups. *Journal of Personality & Social Psychology*, 1966, **3**, 214–222.

Halpin, S.M., & Pilisuk, M. Probability matching in the prisoner's dilemma. *Psychonomic Science*, 1967, **7**, 269–270.

Hamburger, H. Separable games. *Behavioral Science*, 1969, **14**, 121–132.

Hamburger, H. Take some—A format and family of games. *Behavioral Science*, 1974, **19**, 28–34.

Hammond, K.R., Todd, F.J., Wilkins, M., & Mitchell, T.O. Cognitive conflict between persons: Application of the "lens model" paradigm. *Journal of Experimental Social Psychology*, 1966, **2**, 343–360.

Hammond, L.K., & Goldman, M. Competition and non-competition and its relationship to individual and group productivity. *Sociometry*, 1961, **24**, 46–60.

Hamner, W.C. The influence of structural, individual, and strategic differences on bargaining outcomes: A review. In D.L. Harnett & L.L. Cummings (Eds.). *Bargaining behavior and personality: An international study.* In preparation, 1974.

Harford, T.C., Jr. Game strategies and interpersonal trust in schizophrenics and normals. *Dissertation Abstracts*, 1965, **26**, 2903.

Harford, T., & Cutter, H.S.G. Cooperation among Negro and white boys and girls. *Psychological Reports*, 1966, **18**, 818.

Harford, T., & Hill, M. Variations in behavioral strategies and interpersonal trust in a two-person game with male alcoholics. *Journal of Clinical Psychology*, 1967, **23**, 33–35.

Harford, T., & Solomon, L. "Reformed sinner" and "lapsed saint" strategies in the prisoner's dilemma game. *Journal of Conflict Resolution*, 1967, **11**, 104–109.

Harford, T., & Solomon, L. Effects of a "reformed sinner" and a "lapsed saint" strategy upon trust formation in paranoid and nonparanoid schizophrenic patients. *Journal of Abnormal Psychology*, 1969, **74**, 498–504.

Harford, T., Solomon, L., & Cheney, J. Effects of proliferating punitive power upon cooperation and competition in the triad. *Psychological Reports*, 1969, **24**, 355–360.

Harnett, D. L. Bargaining and negotiation in a mixed-motive game: Price leadership bilateral monopoly. *Social Economic Journal*, 1967, **33**, 479–487.

Harnett, D.L., Cummings, L.L., & Hamner, W.C. Personality, bargaining style, and payoff in bilateral monopoly bargaining among European managers. *Sociometry*, 1973, **36**, 325–345.

Harnett, D.L., Cummings, L.L., & Hughes, G.D. The influence of risk–taking propensity on bargaining behavior. *Behavioral Science*, 1968, **13**, 91–101.

Harris, M.G.P. The effects of threat on cooperative behavior under high and low conflict of interest. *Dissertation Abstracts*, 1969, **29**, 3218–A.

Harris, R.J. A geometric classification system for 2×2 interval-symmetric games. *Behavioral Science*, 1969, **14**, 138–146. (a)

Harris, R.J. Note on "optimal policies for the prisoner's dilemma." *Psychological Review*, 1969, **76**, 363–375. (b)

Harris, R.J. An interval-scale classification system for all 2×2 games. *Behavioral Science*, 1972, **17**, 371–383.

Harrison, A.A., & McClintock, C.G. Previous experience within the dyad and cooperative game behavior. *Journal of Personality & Social Psychology*, 1965, **1**, 671–675.

Harsanyi, J.C. Bargaining model for the cooperative n-person game. In A.W. Tucker & R.D. Luce (Eds.), *Contributions to the theory of games*. Vol. IV. Princeton, New Jersey: Princeton Univ. Press, 1959.

Harsanyi, J.C. On the rationality postulates underlying the theory of cooperative games. *Journal of Conflict Resolution*, 1961, **5**, 179–196.

Harsanyi, J.C. Measurement of social power, opportunity costs, and the theory of two-person bargaining games. *Behavioral Science*, 1962, **7**, 67–80. (a)

Harsanyi, J.C. Measurement of social power in n-person reciprocal power situations. *Behavioral Science*, 1962, **7**, 81–91. (b)

Harsanyi, J.C. Bargaining in ignorance of the opponent's utility function. *Journal of Conflict Resolution*, 1962, **6**, 29–38. (c)

Harsanyi, J.C. Models for the analysis of balance of power in society. In E. Nagel, P. Suppes, & A. Tarski (Eds.), *Logic, methodology, and philosophy of science: Proceedings*. Stanford, California: Stanford Univ. Press, 1962. (d)

Harsanyi, J.C. Rationality postulates for bargaining solutions in cooperative and in non-cooperative games. *Management Science*, 1962, **9**, 141–153. (e)

Harsanyi, J.C. A simplified bargaining model for the n-person cooperative game. *International Economic Review*, 1963, **4**, 194–220.

Harsanyi, J.C. A general solution for finite non-cooperative games, based on risk-dominance. In L.S. Shapley & A.W. Tucker (Eds.), *Advances in game theory*. Princeton, New Jersey: Princeton Univ. Press, 1964.

Harsanyi, J.C. Bargaining and conflict situations in the light of a new approach to game theory. *American Economic Review*, 1965, **55**, 447–457.

Harsanyi, J.C. A bargaining model for social status in informal groups and formal organizations. *Behavioral Science*, 1966, **11**, 357–369. (a)

Harsanyi, J.C. A general theory of rational behavior in game situations. *Econometrica*, 1966, **34**, 613–634. (b)

Harsanyi, J.C. Some social-science implications of a new approach to game theory. In K. Archibald (Ed.), *Strategic interaction and conflict: Original papers and discussion*. Berkeley, California: Institute of International Studies, 1966. (c)

Harsanyi, J.C. Games with incomplete information played by "Bayesian" players, I–III, Part I. The basic model. *Management Science*, 1968, **14**, 159–182. (a)

Harsanyi, J.C. Games with incomplete information played by "Bayesian" players, I–III, Part

II. The basic probability distribution of the game. *Management Science*, 1968, **14**, 320–334. (b)

Harsanyi, J.C. Games with incomplete information played by "Bayesian" players, I–III, Part III. *Management Science*, 1968, **14**, 486–502. (c)

Hatton, J.M. Reactions of Negroes in a biracial bargaining situation. *Journal of Personality & Social Psychology*, 1967, **7**, 301–306.

Heider, F. *The psychology of interpersonal relations*. New York: Wiley, 1958.

Heilman, M.E. Threats and promises: Reputational consequences and transfer of credibility. *Journal of Experimental Social Psychology*, 1974, **10**, 310–324.

Held, V. On the meaning of trust. *Ethics*, 1968, **78**, 156–159.

Heller, J.R. The effects of racial prejudice, feedback strategy and race on cooperative–competitive behavior. *Dissertation Abstracts*, 1967, **27**, 2507–2508–B.

Hermann, C.F. Validation problems in games and simulations with special reference to models of international politics. *Behavioral Science*, 1967, **12**, 216–231.

Hermann, C.F., Hermann, M.G., & Cantor, R.A. Counterattack or delay: Characteristics influencing decision makers' responses to the simulation of an unidentified attack. *Journal of Conflict Resolution*, 1974, **18**, 75–106.

Hermann, M.G., & Kogan, N. Negotiation in leader and delegate groups. *Journal of Conflict Resolution*, 1968, **12**, 332–344.

Higgs, W.J., & McGrath, J.E. Social motives and decision-making behavior in interpersonal situations. Technical Report No. 4, September 1965, Air Force Office of Scientific Research Report AF 49 (638)–1291, Univ. of Illinois.

Hinde, R.A. (Ed.) *Nonverbal communication*. Cambridge: Cambridge Univ. Press, 1972.

Hinton, B.L., Hamner, W.C., & Pohlen, M.F. The influence of reward magnitude, opening bid and concession rate on profit earned in a managerial negotiation game. *Behavioral Science*, 1974, **19**, 197–203.

Hoffman, A.J., & Karp, R.M. On nonterminating stochastic games. *Management Science*, 1966, **12**, 359–370.

Hoffman, P.J., Festinger, L., & Lawrence, D. Tendencies toward group comparability in competitive bargaining. *Human Relations*, 1954, **7**, 141–159.

Hoffman, T.R. Programmed heuristics and the concept of par in business games. *Behavioral Science*, 1965, **10**, 169–172.

Hoggatt, A.C. An experimental business game. *Behavioral Science*, 1959, **4**, 192–203.

Hoggatt, A.C. Measuring the cooperativeness of behavior in quantity variation duopoly games. *Behavioral Science*, 1967, **12**, 109–121.

Holmes, J.G., Throop, W.F., & Strickland, L.H. The effects of prenegotiation expectations on the distributive bargaining process. *Journal of Experimental Social Psychology*, 1971, **7**, 582–599.

Homans, G.C. *Social behavior: Its elementary forms*. New York: Harcourt, 1961.

Hopkins, R.F. Game theory and generalization in ethics. *Review of Politics*, 1965, **27**, 491–500.

Horai, J., Lindskold, S., Gahagan, J., & Tedeschi, J. The effects of conflict intensity and promisor credibility on a target's behavior. *Psychonomic Science*, 1969, **14**, 73–74.

Horai, J., & Tedeschi, J.T. Effects of credibility and magnitude of punishment on compliance to threats. *Journal of Personality & Social Psychology*, 1969, **12**, 164–169.

Horai, J., Tedeschi, J.T., Gahagan, J., & Lesnick, S. The effects of contingent threats upon target's behavior. *Journal of Social Psychology*, 1969, **78**, 293–294.

Hornstein, H.A. The effects of different magnitudes of threat upon interpersonal bargaining. *Journal of Experimental Social Psychology*, 1965, **1**, 282–293.

Hornstein, H.A., & Deutsch, M. Tendencies to compete and to attack as a function of inspection, incentive, and available alternatives. *Journal of Personality & Social Psychology*, 1967, **5**, 311–318.

Hornstein, H.A., & Johnson, D.W. The effects of process analysis and ties to his group upon the negotiator's attitudes toward the outcomes of negotiations. *Journal of Applied Behavioral Science*, 1966, **2**, 449–463.

Hurst, P.M., Radlow, R., Chubb, N.C., & Bagley, S.K. Drug effects upon choice behavior in mixed motive games. *Behavioral Science*, 1969, **14**, 443–452.

Hutte, H. Decision–taking in a management game. *Human Relations*, 1965, **18**, 5–20.

Iklé, F.C. *How nations negotiate*. New York: Harper and Row, 1964.

Iklé, F.C., & Leites, N. Political negotiation as a process of modifying utilities. *Journal of Conflict Resolution*, 1962, **6**, 19–28.

Isaacs, R. *Differential games*. New York: Wiley, 1965.

Jackson, J.R. On decision theory under competition. *Management Science*, 1968, **15**, 12–32.

Johnson, D.F. Compliance, deterent threats, and the need to maintain face. Paper presented at the meeting of the Eastern Psychological Association, New York April, 1971.

Johnson, D.F., & Tullar, W.L. Style of third party intervention, face-saving and bargaining behavior. *Journal of Experimental Social Psychology*, 1972, **8**, 319–330.

Johnson, D.W. Use of role reversal in intergroup competition. *Journal of Personality & Social Psychology*, 1967, **7**, 135–141.

Johnson, D.W. Communication in conflict situations: A critical review of the research. *International Journal of Group Tensions*, 1973, **3**, in press.

Johnson, D.W. Cooperativeness and social perspective taking. *Journal of Personality & Social Psychology*, 1974, in press.

Johnson, D.W., & Johnson, R.T. Instructional goal structure: Cooperative, competitive, or individualistic. *Review of Educational Research*, 1974, **44**, 213–240.

Johnson, M.P., & Ewens, W. Power relations and affective style as determinants of confidence in impression formation in a game situation. *Journal of Experimental Social Psychology*, 1971, **7**, 98–110.

Jones, B., Steele, M., Gahagan, J., & Tedeschi, J. Matrix values and cooperative behavior in the prisoner's dilemma game. *Journal of Personality & Social Psychology*, 1968, **8**, 148–153.

Jones, S.C., & Vroom, V.H. Division of labor and performance under cooperative and competitive conditions. *Journal of Abnormal & Social Psychology*, 1964, **68**, 313–320.

Joseph, M.L., & Willis, R.H. An experimental analog to two-party bargaining. *Behavioral Science*, 1963, **8**, 117–127.

Jourard, S.M. An exploratory study of body-accessibility. *British Journal of Social & Clinical Psychology*, 1966, **5**, 221–231.

Julian, J.W., Bishop, D.W., & Fiedler, F.E. Quasi-therapeutic effects of intergroup competition. *Journal of Personality & Social Psychology*, 1966, **3**, 321–327.

Kagan, S., & Madsen, M.C. Cooperation and competition of Mexican, Mexican–American, and Anglo–American children of two ages under four instructional sets. *Developmental Psychology*, 1971, **5**, 32–39.

Kagan, S., & Madsen, M.C. Experimental analyses of cooperation and competition of Anglo–American and Mexican children. *Developmental Psychology*, 1972, **6**, 49–59. (a)

Kagan, S., & Madsen, M.C. Rivalry in Anglo–American and Mexican children of two ages. *Journal of Personality & Social Psychology*, 1972, **24**, 214–220. (b)

Kahan, J.P. Effects of level of aspiration in an experimental bargaining situation. *Journal of Personality & Social Psychology*, 1968, **8**, 154–159.

Kahan, J.P., & Goehring, D.J. Responsiveness in two-person zero-sum games. *Behavioral*

Science, 1973, **18,** 27–33.

Kahn, A., Hottes, J., & Davis, W.L. Cooperation and optimal responding in the prisoner's dilemma game: Effects of sex and physical attractiveness. *Journal of Personality & Social Psychology,* 1971, **17,** 267–279.

Kanouse, D.E., & Wiest, W.M. Some factors affecting choice in the prisoner's dilemma. *Journal of Conflict Resolution,* 1967, **11,** 206–213.

Kaplowitz, S.A. An experimental test of a rationalistic theory of deterrence. *Journal of Conflict Resolution,* 1973, **17,** 535–572.

Katonah, G. Review of S. Siegel and L.E. Fouraker, "Experiments in Bilateral Monopoly." *Contemporary Psychology,* 1962, **7,** 272–273.

Kaufman, H., & Becker, G.M. The empirical determination of game-theoretical strategies. *Journal of Experimental Psychology,* 1961, **61,** 462–468.

Kaufman, H., & Lamb, J.C. An empirical test of game theory as a descriptive model *Perceptual & Motor Skills,* 1967, **24,** 951–960.

Kaufmann, H. Similarity and cooperation received as determinants of cooperation rendered. *Psychonomic Science,* 1967, **9,** 73–74.

Kee, H.W. The development, and the effects upon bargaining, of trust and suspicion. *Dissertation Abstracts,* 1970, **30,** 4017–4018–A.

Kee, H.W., & Knox, R.E. Conceptual and methodological considerations in the study of trust and suspicion. *Journal of Conflict Resolution,* 1970, **14,** 357–366.

Keiffer, M.G. The effects of availability and precision of threat on bargaining behavior. *Dissertation Abstracts,* 1969, **30,** 1635–1636–A.

Kelley, H.H. Interaction process and the attainment of maximum joint profit. In S. Messick & A.H. Brayfield (Eds.), *Decision and choice: Contributions of Sidney Siegel.* New York: McGraw–Hill, 1964.

Kelley, H.H. Review of L.E. Fouraker and S. Siegel, "Bargaining behavior." *Contemporary Psychology,* 1965, **10,** 49–50. (a)

Kelley, H.H. Experimental studies of threats in interpersonal negotiations. *Journal of Conflict Resolution,* 1965, **9,** 79–105. (b)

Kelley, H.H. A classroom study of the dilemmas in interpersonal negotiations. In K. Archibald (Ed.), *Strategic interaction and conflict: Original papers and discussion.* Berkeley, California: Institute of International Studies, 1966.

Kelley, H.H., & Arrowood, A.J. Coalitions in the triad: Critique and experiment. *Sociometry,* 1960, **23,** 231–244.

Kelley, H.H., Beckman, L.L., & Fischer, C.S. Negotiating the division of a reward under incomplete information. *Journal of Experimental Social Psychology,* 1967, **3,** 361–398.

Kelley, H.H., Condry, J.C., Jr., Dahlke, A.E., & Hill, A.H. Collective behavior in a simulated panic situation. *Journal of Experimental Social Psychology,* 1965, **1,** 20–54.

Kelley, H.H., & Grzelak, J. Conflict between individual and common interest in an *N*-person relationship. *Journal of Personality & Social Psychology,* 1972, **21,** 190–197.

Kelley, H.H., & Schenitzki, D.P. Bargaining. In C.G. McClintock (Ed.), *Experimental social psychology.* New York: Holt, 1972.

Kelley, H.H., Shure, G.H., Deutsch, M., Faucheux, C., Lanzetta, J.T., Moscovici, S., Nuttin, J.M., Jr., Rabbie, J.M., & Thibaut, J.W. A comparative experimental study of negotiation behavior. *Journal of Personality & Social Psychology,* 1970, **16,** 411–438.

Kelley, H.H., & Stahelski, A.J. Errors in perception of intentions in a mixed-motive game. *Journal of Experimental Social Psychology,* 1970, **6,** 379–400. (a)

Kelley, H.H., & Stahelski, A.J. The inference of intentions from moves in the prisoner's dilemma game. *Journal of Experimental Social Psychology,* 1970, **6,** 401–419. (b)

Kelley, H.H., & Stahelski, A.J. Social interaction basis of cooperators' and competitors' beliefs about others. *Journal of Personality & Social Psychology*, 1970, **16**, 66–91. (c)

Kelley, H.H., & Thibaut, J.W. Group problem solving. In G. Lindzey & E. Aronson (Eds.), *Handbook of social psychology* (2nd ed.), Vol. IV. Reading, Massachusetts: Addison-Wesley, 1969.

Kelley, H.H., Thibaut, J.W., Radloff, R., & Mundy, D. The development of cooperation in the "minimal social situation." *Psychological Monographs*, 1962, **76** (19, Whole No. 538).

Kendon, A. Some functions of gaze-direction in social interaction. *Acta Psychologica*, 1967, **26**, 22–63.

Kennedy, R.F. *Thirteen days*. New York: Norton, 1969.

Kent, G. *The effects of threats*. Columbus, Ohio: Ohio State Univ. Press, 1967.

Kerr, C. Industrial conflict and its resolution. *American Journal of Sociology*, 1954, **60**, 230–245.

Kershenbaum, B.R., & Komorita, S.S. Temptation to defect in the prisoner's dilemma game. *Journal of Personality & Social Psychology*, 1970, **16**, 110–113.

Kimmel, P.R., & Havens, J.W. Game theory vs. mutual identification: Two criteria for assessing marital relationships. *Journal of Marriage & the Family*, 1966, **28**, 460–465.

Klein, E.B., & Solomon, L. Agreement response tendency and behavioral submission in schizophrenics. *Psychological Reports*, 1966, **18**, 499–509.

Kleinke, C.L., & Pohlen, P.D. Affective and emotional responses as a function of other person's gaze and cooperativeness in a two-person game. *Journal of Personality & Social Psychology*, 1971, **17**, 308–313.

Kline, D.K. The effect of bargaining sequence and type of payoff upon coalition structure and stability in the triad. *Dissertation Abstracts*, 1969, **30**, 390–A.

Knapp, W.M., & Podell, J.E. Mental patients, prsioners, and students with simulated partners in a mixed-motive game. *Journal of Conflict Resolution*, 1968, **12**, 235–241.

Knox, R.E., & Douglas, R.L. Trivial incentives, marginal comprehension, and dubious generalizations from prisoner's dilemma studies. *Journal of Personality & Social Psychology*, 1971, **20**, 160–165.

Kogan, N., Lamm, H., & Trommsdorff, G. Negotiation constraints in the risk-taking domain: Effects of being observed by partners of higher or lower status. *Journal of Personality & Social Psychology*, 1972, **23**, 143–156.

Kogan, N., & Wallach, M.A. *Risk taking: A study in cognition and personality*. New York: Holt, 1964.

Komorita, S.S. Cooperative choice in a prisoner's dilemma game. *Journal of Personality & Social Psychology*, 1965, **2**, 741–745.

Komorita, S.S. Concession-making and conflict resolution. *Journal of Conflict Resolution*, 1973, **17**, 745–762.

Komorita, S.S., & Barnes, M. Effects of pressures to reach agreement in bargaining. *Journal of Personality & Social Psychology*, 1969, **13**, 245–252.

Komorita, S.S., & Brenner, A.R. Bargaining and concession making under bilateral monopoly. *Journal of Personality & Social Psychology*, 1968, **9**, 15–20.

Komorita, S.S., & Mechling, J. Betrayal and reconciliation in a two-person game. *Journal of Personality & Social Psychology*, 1967, **6**, 349–353.

Komorita, S.S., Sheposh, J.P., & Braver, S.L. Power, the use of power, and cooperative choice in a two-person game. *Journal of Personality & Social Psychology*, 1968, **8**, 134–142.

Krauss, R.M. Structural and attitudinal factors in interpersonal bargaining. *Journal of Experimental Social Psychology*, 1966, **2**, 42–55.

Krauss, R.M., & Deutsch, M. Communication in interpersonal bargaining. *Journal of Personality & Social Psychology*, 1966, **4**, 572–577.

Kressel, K. Labor mediation: An exploratory survey. Unpublished manuscript, Teachers College, Columbia University, 1971.

Krivohlavý, J. *Interpersonal conflict and experimental games*. Bern, Switzerland: Hans Huber Ver, 1974.

Kubicka, L. The psychological background of adolescents' behavior in a two-person nonzero sum game. *Behavioral Science*, 1968, **13**, 455–466.

Kuhn, H.W. Game theory and models of negotiation. *Journal of Conflict Resolution*, 1962, **6**, 1–4.

Kurke, M.I. Decision determinants in multiple choice games. *Dissertation Abstracts*, 1963, **24**, 405.

Lacey, O.L., & Pate, J.L. An empirical study of game theory. *Psychological Reports*, 1960, **7**, 527–530.

Ladner, R., Jr. Strategic interaction and conflict—negotiating expectations in accounting for actions. *Journal of Conflict Resolution*, 1973, **17**, 175–184.

Lake, D.G. Impression formation, machiavellianism, and interpersonal bargaining. *Dissertation Abstracts*, 1967, **28**, 784–A.

Lamm, H., & Kogan, N. Risk taking in the context of intergroup negotiation. *Journal of Experimental Social Psychology*, 1970, **6**, 351–363.

Lamm, H., & Sauer, C. Discussion-induced shift toward higher demands in negotiation. *European Journal of Social Psychology*, 1974, **4**, 85–88.

Lane, I.M., & Messé, L.A. Equity and the distribution of rewards. *Journal of Personality & Social Psychology*, 1971, **20**, 1–17.

Lane, I.M., & Messé, L.A. Distribution of insufficient, sufficient, and oversufficient rewards: A clarification of equity theory. *Journal of Personality & Social Psychology*, 1972, **21**, 228–233.

Langholm, S. Violent conflict resolution and the loser's reaction. *Journal of Peace Research*, 1965, **2**, 324–347.

Lavalle, I.H. A Bayesian approach to an individual player's choice of bid in competitive sealed auctions. *Management Science*, 1967, **13**, 584–597.

Lave, L.B. An empirical approach to the prisoner's dilemma game. *Quarterly Journal of Economics*, 1962, **76**, 424–436.

Lave, L.B. Factors affecting co-operation in the prisoner's dilemma. *Behavioral Science*, 1965, **10**, 26–38.

Lazarus, R. Review of K.E. Boulding, "Conflict and defense: A general theory," *Contemporary Psychology*, 1963, **8**, 4–5.

Lefcourt, H.M., & Ladwig, G.W. The effect of reference group upon Negroes task persistence in a biracial competitive game. *Journal of Personality & Social Psychology*, 1965, **1**, 668–671.

Leff, H.S. Interpersonal behavior in a non-zero-sum experimental game as a function of cognitive complexity, environmental complexity and predispositional variables. *Dissertation Abstracts*, 1969, **29**, 4103–A.

Leventhal, G.S., Michaels, J.W., & Sanford, C. Inequity and interpersonal conflict: Reward allocation and secrecy about reward as methods of preventing conflict. *Journal of Personality & Social Psychology*, 1972, **23**, 88–102.

Leventhal, G.S., Weiss, T., & Long, G. Equity, reciprocity, and reallocating rewards in the dyad. *Journal of Personality & Social Psychology*, 1969, **13**, 300–305.

Lewicki, R.J. The effects of cooperative and exploitative relationships on subsequent interpersonal relations. *Dissertation Abstracts,* 1970, **30,** 4550–A.

Lewicki, R.J., & Rubin, J.Z. Effects of variations in the informational clarity of promises and threats upon interpersonal bargaining. *Proceedings of the 81st Annual Convention of the American Psychological Association,* 1973, **8,** 137–138.

Lewicki, R.J., & Rubin, J.Z. The effects of motivational orientation and relative power upon the perception of interpersonal influence in a non-zero sum game. Unpublished manuscript, Dartmouth College, Hanover, New Hampshire, 1974.

Lewin, K. *Principles of topological psychology.* New York: McGraw-Hill, 1936.

Lieberman, B. The auction values of uncertain outcomes in win and loss type situations. *Dissertation Abstracts,* 1958, **19,** 1110.

Lieberman, B. Human behavior in a strictly determined 3 × 3 matrix game. *Behavioral Science,* 1960, **5,** 317–322.

Lieberman, B. Experimental studies of conflict in some two and three person games. In J.H. Griswell *et al.* (Eds.), *Mathematical methods in small group processes.* Stanford, California: Stanford Univ. Press, 1962.

Lieberman, B. *i*-Trust: A notion of trust in three-person games and international affairs. *Journal of Conflict Resolution;* 1964, **8,** 271–280.

Lieberman, B. Review of A. Rapoport, "Two-person game theory: The essential ideas." *Contemporary Psychology,* 1967, **12,** 360–361.

Liebert, R.M., Smith, W.P., Hill, J.H., & Keiffer, M. The effects of information and magnitude of initial offer on interpersonal negotiation. *Journal of Experimental Social Psychology,* 1968, **4,** 431-441.

Linker, E., & Ross, B.M. Intergame and intragame analysis of a probabilistic game. *Journal of Genetic Psychology,* 1962, **101,** 113–126.

Lindskold, S.A. Threatening and conciliatory influence attempts as a function of source's perception of own competence in a conflict situation. *Dissertation Abstracts,* 1971, **31,** 4887–4888–A.

Lindskold, S., & Bennett, R. Attributing trust and conciliatory intent from coercive power capability. *Journal of Personality & Social Psychology,* 1973, **28,** 180–186.

Lindskold, S., Bonoma, T., & Tedeschi, J.T. Relative costs and reactions to threats. *Psychonomic Science,* 1969, **15,** 205–207.

Lindskold, S., Culler, P., Gahagan, J., & Tedeschi, J.T. Developmental aspects of reaction to positive inducements. *Developmental Psychology,* 1970, **3,** 277–284.

Lindskold, S., Gahagan, J., & Tedeschi, J.T. The ethical shift in the prisoner's dilemma game. *Psychonomic Science,* 1969, **15,** 303–304.

Lindskold, S., & Tedeschi, J.T. Reward power and attraction in interpersonal conflict. *Psychonomic Science,* 1971, **22,** 211–213.

Lindskold, S., Tedeschi, J.T., Bonoma, T.V., & Schlenker, B.R. Reward power and bilateral communication in conflict resolution. *Psychonomic Science,* 1971, **23,** 415–416.

Littig, L.W. Behavior in certain zero-sum, two-person games. *Journal of Social Psychology,* 1965, **66,** 113–125.

Little, K.B. Personal space. *Journal of Experimental Social Psychology,* 1965, **1,** 237–247.

Liverant, S., & Scodel, A. Internal and external control as determinants of decision making under conditions of risk. *Psychological Reports,* 1960, **7,** 59–67.

Lonergan, B.G., & McClintock, C.G. Effects of group membership on risk-taking behavior. *Psychological Reports,* 1961, **8,** 447–455.

Loomis, J.L. Communication, the development of trust, and cooperative behavior. *Human Relations,* 1959, **12,** 305–315.

Love, R.W. Incentive levels in a mixed motive game. *Dissertation Abstracts,* 1967, **28,** 2338–A.

Lowe, P.M. Some social determinants of two-person non-zero-sum games. Unpublished honors thesis, Harvard Univ., Cambridge, Massachusetts, 1966.

Lucas, W.I. A counterexample in game theory. *Management Science*, 1967, **13**, 767.

Luce, R.D. A note on the article, "Some experimental n-person games." *Annals of Mathematics Studies*, 1959, **40**, 279–285. (a)

Luce, R.D. *Individual choice behavior: A theoretical analysis.* New York: Wiley, 1959. (b)

Luce, R.D., & Raiffa, H. *Games and decisions: Introduction and critical survey.* New York: Wiley, 1957.

Luce, R.D., & Suppes, P. Preference, utility, and subjective probability. In R.D. Luce, R.R. Bush, & E. Galanter (Eds.), *Handbook of mathematical psychology*, Vol. III. New York: Wiley, 1965.

Lupfer, M., Jones, M., Spaulding, L., & Archer, R. Risk-taking in cooperative and competitive dyads. *Journal of Conflict Resolution*, 1971, **15**, 385–392.

Lutzker, D.R. Internationalism as a predictor of cooperative behavior. *Journal of Conflict Resolution*, 1960, **4**, 426–430.

Lutzker, D.R. Sex role, cooperation and competition in a two-person, non-zero sum game. *Journal of Conflict Resolution*, 1961, **5**, 366–368.

Lynch, G.W. Defense preference and cooperation and competition in a game. *Dissertation Abstracts*, 1968, **29**, 1174–B.

Madsen, M.C. Cooperative and competitive motivation of children in three Mexican sub-cultures. *Psychological Reports*, 1967, **20**, 1307–1320.

Madsen, M.C. Developmental and cross-cultural differences in the cooperative and competitive behavior of young children. *Journal of Cross-Cultural Psychology*, 1971, **2**, 365–371.

Madsen, M.C., & Shapira, A. Cooperative and competitive behavior of urban Afro–American, Anglo–American, Mexican–American, and Mexican village children. *Developmental Psychology*, 1970, **3**, 16–20.

Malcolm, D., & Lieberman, B. The behavior of responsive individuals playing a two-person, zero-sum game requiring the use of mixed strategies. *Psychonomic Science*, 1965, **2**, 373–374.

Marlowe, D. Psychological needs and cooperation: Competition in a two-person game. *Psychological Reports*, 1963, **13**, 364.

Marlowe, D., Gergen, K.J., & Doob, A.N. Opponent's personality, expectation of social interaction, and interpersonal bargaining. *Journal of Personality & Social Psychology*, 1966, **3**, 206–213.

Martin, M.W., Jr. Some effects of communication on group behavior in prisoner's dilemma. *Dissertation Abstracts*, 1966, **27**, 231–B.

Martindale, D.A. Territorial dominance behavior in dyadic verbal interactions. *Proceedings of the 79th Annual Convention of the American Psychological Association*, 1971, **6**, 305–306.

Marwell, G., Ratcliff, K., & Schmitt, D.R. Minimizing differences in a maximizing difference game. *Journal of Personality & Social Psychology*, 1969, **12**, 158–163.

Marwell, G., & Schmitt, D.R. Are "trivial" games the most interesting psychologically? *Behavioral Science*, 1968, **13**, 125–128.

Marwell, G., & Schmitt, D.R. Cooperation in a three-person prisoner's dilemma. *Journal of Personality & Social Psychology*, 1972, **21**, 376–383.

Marwell, G., Schmitt, D.R., & Bøyesen, B. Pacifist strategy and cooperation under interpersonal risk. *Journal of Personality & Social Psychology*, 1973, **28**, 12–20.

Marwell, G., Schmitt, D.R., & Shotola, R. Cooperation and interpersonal risk. *Journal of Personality & Social Psychology*, 1971, **18**, 9–32.

Maschler, M. The power of a coalition. *Management Science*, 1962, **10**, 8–29.

Massaro, D.W. A three state Markov model for discrimination learning. *Journal of Mathematical Psychology*, 1969, **6**, 62–80.

Mazur, A. A nonrational approach to theories of conflict and coalitions. *Journal of Conflict Resolution,* 1968, **12**, 196–205.

McBride, G. *A general theory of social organization and behavior.* St. Lucia, Australia: Univ. of Queensland Press, 1964.

McClintock, C.G. Game behavior and social motivation in interpersonal settings. In C.G. McClintock (Ed.), *Experimental social psychology.* New York: Holt, 1972.

McClintock, C.G. Development of social motives in Anglo–American and Mexican–American children. *Journal of Personality & Social Psychology,* 1974, **29**, 348–354.

McClintock, C.G., Gallo, P., & Harrison, A.A. Some effects of variations in other strategy upon game behavior. *Journal of Personality & Social Psychology,* 1965, **1**, 319–325.

McClintock, C.G., Harrison, A.A., Strand, S., & Gallo, P. Internationalism-isolationism, strategy of the other player, and two-person game behavior. *Journal of Abnormal & Social Psychology,* 1963, **67**, 631–636.

McClintock, C.G., & McNeel, S.P. Societal membership, score status and game behavior: A phenomenological analysis. *International Journal of Psychology,* 1966, **1**, 263–272. (a)

McClintock, C.G., & McNeel, S.P. Reward level and game playing behavior. *Journal of Conflict Resolution,* 1966, **10**, 98–102. (b)

McClintock, C.G., & McNeel, S.P. Reward and score feedback as determinants of cooperative and competitive game behavior. *Journal of Personality & Social Psychology,* 1966, **4**, 606–613. (c)

McClintock, C.G., & McNeel, S.P. Cross cultural comparisons of interpersonal motives. *Sociometry,* 1966, **29**, 406–427. (d)

McClintock, C.G., & McNeel, S.P. Prior dyadic experience and monetary reward as determinants of cooperative and competitive game behavior. *Journal of Personality & Social Psychology,* 1967, **5**, 282–294.

McClintock, C.G., & Messick, D. Non-zero-sum games: A conceptual orientation. Paper presented at the meeting of the Western Psychological Association, Honolulu, Hawaii, 1965.

McClintock, C.G., Messick, D.M., Kuhlman, D.M., & Campos, F.T. Motivational bases of choice in three-choice decomposed games. *Journal of Experimental Social Psychology,* 1973, **9**, 572–590.

McClintock, C.G., & Nuttin, J.M., Jr. Development of competitive game behavior in children across two cultures. *Journal of Experimental Social Psychology,* 1969, **5**, 203–218.

McClintock, C.G., Nuttin, J.M., Jr., & McNeel, S.P. Sociometric choice, visual presence, and game-playing behavior. *Behavioral Science,* 1970, **15**, 124–131.

McDaniel, J.W., O'Neal, E., & Fox, E.S. Magnitude of retaliation as a function of the similarity of available responses to those employed by attacker. *Psychonomic Science,* 1971, **22**, 215–217.

McGrath, J. A social psychological approach to the study of negotiation. In R.V. Bowers (Ed.), *Studies on behavior in organizations: A research symposium.* Athens, Georgia: Univ. of Georgia Press, 1966.

McGrath, J.E., & Julian, J.W. Interaction process and task outcome in experimentally-created negotiation groups. *Journal of Psychological Studies,* 1963, **14**, 117–138.

McKeown, C.D., Gahagan, J.P., & Tedeschi, J.T. The effect of prior power strategy on behavior after a shift of power. *Journal of Experimental Research in Personality,* 1967, **2**, 226–233.

McKersie, R.B., Perry, C.R., & Walton, R.E. Intraorganizational bargaining in labor negotiations. *Journal of Conflict Resolution,* 1965, **9**, 463–481.

McNeel, S.P. Training cooperation in the prisoner's dilemma. *Journal of Experimental Social Psychology,* 1973, **9**, 335–348.

McNeel, S.P., McClintock, C.G., & Nuttin, J.M., Jr. Effects of sex role in a two-person mixed-motive game. *Journal of Personality & Social Psychology*, 1972, **24**, 372–380.

Meeker, B.F. An experimental study of cooperation and competition in West Africa. *International Journal of Psychology*, 1970, **5**, 11–19.

Meeker, R.J., & Shure, G.H. Pacifist bargaining tactics: Some "outsider" influences. *Journal of Conflict Resolution*, 1969, **13**, 487–493.

Mehrabian, A. The influence of attitudes from the position, orientation, and distance of a communicator. *Journal of Consulting Psychology*, 1968, **32**, 296–308.

Mehrabian, A. Significance of posture and position in the communication of attitude and status relationships. *Psychological Bulletin*, 1969, **71**, 359–372.

Mehrabian, A., & Diamond, S.G. Effects of furniture arrangement, props, and personality on social interaction. *Journal of Personality & Social Psychology*, 1971, **20**, 18–30.

Messé, L.A. Equity in bilateral bargaining. *Journal of Personality & Social Psychology*, 1971, **17**, 287–291.

Messé, L.A., Aronoff, J., & Wilson, J.P. Motivation as a mediator of the mechanisms underlying role assignments in small groups. *Journal of Personality & Social Psychology*, 1972, **24**, 84–90.

Messé, L., Bolt, M., & Sawyer, J. Nonstructural determinants of cooperation and conflict in the replicated prisoner's dilemma game. *Psychonomic Science*, 1971, **25**, 238–240.

Messé, L.A., Dawson, J.E., & Lane, I.M. Equity as a mediator of the effect of reward level on behavior in the prisoner's dilemma game. *Journal of Personality & Social Psychology*, 1973, **26**, 60–65.

Messick, D.M. Interdependent decision strategies in zero-sum games: A computer controlled study. *Behavioral Science*, 1967, **12**, 33–48.

Messick, D.M., & McClintock, C.G. Measures of homogeneity in two-person, two-choice games. *Behavioral Science*, 1967, **12**, 474–479.

Messick, D.M., & McClintock, C.G. Motivational bases of choice in experimental games. *Journal of Experimental Social Psychology*, 1968, **4**, 1–25.

Messick, D.M., & Rapoport, A. A comparison of two payoff functions on multiple-choice decision behavior. *Journal of Experimental Psychology*, 1965, **69**, 75–83.

Messick, D.M., & Thorngate, W.B. Relative gain maximization in experimental games. *Journal of Experimental Social Psychology*, 1967, **3**, 85–101.

Meux, E.P. Concern for the common good in an *n*-person game. *Journal of Personality & Social Psychology*, 1973, **28**, 414–418.

Michelini, R.L. Effects of prior interaction, contact, strategy, and expectation of meeting on game behavior and sentiment. *Journal of Conflict Resolution*, 1971, **15**, 97–103.

Michener, H.A., & Cohen, E.D. Effects of punishment magnitude in the bilateral threat situation: Evidence for the deterrence hypothesis. *Journal of Personality & Social Psychology*, 1973, **26**, 427–438.

Michener, H.A., Griffith, J., & Palmer, R.L. Threat potential and rule enforceability as sources of normative emergence in a bargaining situation. *Journal of Personality & Social Psychology*, 1971, **20**, 230–239.

Michener, H.A., Lawler, E.J., & Bacharach, S.B. Perception of power in conflict situations. *Journal of Personality & Social Psychology*, 1973, **28**, 155–162.

Michener, H.A., & Lyons, M. Perceived support and upward mobility as determinants of revolutionary coalitional behavior. *Journal of Experimental Social Psychology*, 1972, **8**, 180–195.

Mikula, G. Nationality, performance, and sex as determinants of reward allocation. *Journal of Personality & Social Psychology*, 1974, **29**, 435–440.

Miller, D.R., & Swanson, G.E. *The changing American parent: A study in the Detroit area.* New York: Wiley, 1958.

Miller, G.H., & Pyke, S.W. Sex, matrix variations, and perceived personality effects in mixed-motive games. *Journal of Conflict Resolution*, 1973, **17**, 335–349.

Miller, R.R. No play: A means of conflict resolution. *Journal of Personality & Social Psychology*, 1967, **6**, 150–156.

Mills, T.M. Power relations in three-person groups. *American Sociological Review*, 1953, **18**, 351–357.

Minas, J.S., Scodel, A., Marlowe, D., & Rawson, H. Some descriptive aspects of two-person non-zero-sum games: II. *Journal of Conflict Resolution*, 1960, **4**, 193–197.

Mogy, R.B., & Pruitt, D.G. Effects of a threatener's enforcement costs on threat credibility and compliance. *Journal of Personality & Social Psychology*, 1974, **29**, 173–180.

Morehous, L.G. Two motivations for defection in prisoner's dilemma games. *General Systems*, 1966, **11**, 225–228. (a)

Morehous, L.G. One-play, two-play, five-play, and ten-play runs of prisoner's dilemma. *Journal of Conflict Resolution*, 1966, **10**, 354–362. (b)

Morgan, W.R., & Sawyer, J. Bargaining, expectations, and the preference for equality over equity. *Journal of Personality & Social Psychology*, 1967, **6**, 139–149.

Morin, R.E. Strategies in games with saddle-points. *Psychological Reports*, 1960, **7**, 479–485.

Morrison, B.J., Enzle, M., Henry, T., Dunaway, D., Griffin, M., Kneisel, K., & Gimperling, J. The effect of electrical shock and warning on cooperation in a non-zero-sum game. *Journal of Conflict Resolution*, 1971, **15**, 105–108.

Motivans, J.J. Differential power and conflict: An experimental study of competition. *Dissertation Abstracts*, 1968, **28**, 3781–3782–A.

Mouton, J.S., & Blake, R.R. The influence of competitively vested interests on judgments. *Journal of Conflict Resolution*, 1962, **6**, 149–153.

Mouton, J.S., & Blake, R.R. Influence of partially vested interests on judgment. *Journal of Abnormal & Social Psychology*, 1963, **66**, 276–278.

Muney, B.F., & Deutsch, M. The effects of role-reversal during the discussion of opposing viewpoints. *Journal of Conflict Resolution*, 1968, **12**, 345–356.

Murdoch, P. Development of contractual norms in a dyad. *Journal of Personality & Social Psychology*, 1967, **6**, 206–211.

Murdoch, P. Exploitation–accommodation and social responsibility in a bargaining game. *Journal of Personality*, 1968, **36**, 440–453.

Murphy, J.L. Effects of the threat of losses on duopoly bargaining. *Quarterly Journal of Economics*, 1966, **80**, 296–313.

Myers, A. Team competition, success, and the adjustment of group members. *Journal of Abnormal & Social Psychology*, 1962, **65**, 325–332.

Myers, A.E. Performance factors contributing to the acquisition of a psychological advantage in competition. *Human Relations*, 1966, **19**, 283–295.

Myers, A.E., & Kling, F.R. Experience as an "instructional set" in negotiation. *Journal of Social Psychology*, 1966, **68**, 331–345.

Nardin, T. Communication and the effects of threat in strategic interaction. Paper presented at the Fifth North American Peace Research Conference, Cambridge, Massachusetts, November 1967.

National Education Association. *Management guidelines for school negotiations.* Washington, D.C.: National Education Association and the Bureau of National Affairs, Inc., 1971.

Neisser, H. The strategy of expecting the worst. *Social Research,* 1952, **19,** 346–363.

Nemeth, C. Bargaining and reciprocity. *Psychological Bulletin,* 1970, **74,** 297–308.

Nemeth, C. A critical analysis of research utilizing the prisoner's dilemma paradigm for the study of bargaining. In L. Berkowitz (Ed.), *Advances in experimental social psychology,* Vol. 6. New York: Academic Press, 1972.

Newcomb. T.M. Autistic hostility and social reality. *Human Relations,* 1947, **1,** 69–86.

New York Times. Ridgeway endorses Panmunjom as site for truce parleys. *The New York Times,* Tuesday, October 9, 1951. Pp. 1 and 3.

New York Times. U.S. offers plans to end deadlock in Vietnam talks. *The New York Times,* January 3, 1969. Pp. 1 and 2.

New York Times. Hope is growing in Paris for widened talks soon. *The New York Times,* January 4, 1969. Pp. 1 and 10.

New York Times. A busy New Year's Eve for transit negotiators. *The New York Times,* Thursday, January 1, 1970. Pp. 1 and 14.

New York Times. Both sides firm in L.I.R.R. strike. *The New York Times,* Saturday, December 9, 1972. P. 72.

Nichols, J.S., Jr. The development of cooperation among schizophrenic dyads and non-schizophrenic dyads in the minimal social situation. *Dissertation Abstracts,* 1967, **27,** 4131–B.

Nitz, L.H., & Phillips, J.L. The effects of divisibility of payoff on confederate behavior. *Journal of Conflict Resolution,* 1969, **13,** 381–387.

Noland, S.J., & Catron, D.W. Cooperative behavior among high school students on the prisoner's dilemma game. *Psychological Reports,* 1969, **24,** 711–718.

Novotny, H.R.F. The influence of reinforcement in the prisoner's dilemma game. *Dissertation Abstracts,* 1969, **29,** 3918–3919–B.

Nydegger, R.V. Information processing complexity and gaming behavior: The prisoner's dilemma. *Behavioral Science,* 1974, **19,** 204–210.

O'Brien, G.M. The effects of information accessibility and machiavellianism on interpersonal perception and bargaining behavior. *Dissertation Abstracts,* 1970, **31,** 3041–A.
manuscript, Boston Univ., Boston, Massachusetts, 1962.
Prentice-Hall, 1970.

Ofshe, R. The effectiveness of pacifist strategies: A theoretical approach. *Journal of Conflict Resolution,* 1971, **15,** 261–269.

Ofshe, R., & Ofshe, S.L. Choice behavior in coalition games. *Behavioral Science,* 1970, **15,** 337–349.

Orwant, C.J., & Orwant, J.E. A comparison of interpreted and abstract versions of mixed-motive games. *Journal of Conflict Resolution,* 1970, **14,** 91–97.

Oskamp, S. Effects of programmed initial strategies in a prisoner's dilemma game. *Psychonomic Science,* 1970, **19,** 195–196.

Oskamp, S. Effects of programmed strategies on cooperation in the prisoner's dilemma and other mixed-motive games. *Journal of Conflict Resolution,* 1971, **15,** 225–259.

Oskamp, S. Comparison of sequential and simultaneous responding, matrix, and strategy variables in a prisoner's dilemma game. *Journal of Conflict Resolution,* 1974, **18,** 107–116.

Oskamp, S., & Kleinke, C. Amount of reward in a variable in the prisoner's dilemma game. *Journal of Personality & Social Psychology,* 1970, **16,** 133–140.

Oskamp, S., & Perlman, D. Factors affecting cooperation in a prisoner's dilemma game. *Journal of Conflict Resolution,* 1965, **9,** 359–374.

Oskamp, S., & Perlman, D. Effects of friendship and disliking on cooperation in a mixed-motive game. *Journal of Conflict Resolution,* 1966, **10,** 221–226.

Overstreet, R.E. Social exchange processes in an *n*-person cooperative game. *Dissertation Abstracts*, 1970, **30**, 5068–A.

Overstreet, R.E. Social exchange in a three-person game. *Journal of Conflict Resolution*, 1972, **16**, 109–123.

Owen, G. An elementary proof of the minimax theorem. *Management Science*, 1967, **13**, 765.

Patchen, M. A conceptual framework and some empirical data regarding comparisons of social rewards. *Sociometry*, 1961, **24**, 136–156.

Pate, J.L. Losing games and their recognition. *Psychological Reports*, 1967, **20**, 1031–1035.

Pate, J.L., & Broughton, E. Game-playing behavior as a function of incentive. *Psychological Reports*, 1970, **27**, 36.

Payne, W. Acquisition of strategies in gaming situations. *Perceptual & Motor Skills*, 1965, **20**, 473–479.

Pederson, F.A. Variation of monetary reward and social involvement in a two-person game. *Dissertation Abstracts*, 1961, **21**, 2369–2370.

Pepitone, A. The role of justice in interdependent decision making. *Journal of Experimental Social Psychology*, 1971, **7**, 144–156.

Pepitone, A., Faucheux, C., Moscovici, S., Cesa-Bianchi, M., Magistretti, G., Iacono, G., Asprea, A.M., & Villone, G. The role of self-esteem in competitive choice behavior. *International Journal of Psychology*, 1967, **2**, 147–159.

Pepitone, A., Maderna, E., Caporicci, E., Tiberi, G., Iacono, G., diMajo, M., Perfetto, A., Asprea, G., Villone, G., Fua, G., & Tonucci, F. Justice in choice behavior: A cross-cultural analysis. *International Journal of Psychology*, 1970, **5**, 1–10.

Peters, E. *Strategy and tactics in labor negotiations.* New London, Connecticut: National Foremen's Institute, 1955.

Phelan, J.G., & Richardson, E. Cognitive complexity, strategy of the other player, and two-person game behavior. *Journal of Psychology*, 1969, **71**, 205–215.

Phillips, J.L., Aronoff, J., & Messé, L. Sex and psychological need in triadic bargaining. *Psychonomic Science*, 1971, **22**, 329–331.

Phillips, J.L., & Nitz, L. Social contacts in a three-person "political convention" situation. *Journal of Conflict Resolution*, 1968, **12**, 206–214.

Phipps, T.E., Jr. Resolving "hopeless" conflicts. *Journal of Conflict Resolution*, 1961, **5**, 274–278.

Pilisuk, M. Conciliation and defection in a disarmament game. *Acta Psychologica*, 1964, **23**, 127.

Pilisuk, M., Kiritz, S., & Clampitt, S. Undoing deadlocks of distrust: Hip Berkeley students and the ROTC. *Journal of Conflict Resolution*, 1971, **15**, 81–95.

Pilisuk, M., Potter, P., Rapoport, A., & Winter, J.A. War hawks and peace doves: Alternate resolutions of experimental conflicts. *Journal of Conflict Resolution*, 1965, **9**, 491–508.

Pilisuk, M., & Rapoport, A. Stepwise disarmament and sudden destruction in a two-person game: A research tool. *Journal of Conflict Resolution*, 1964, **8**, 36–49. (a)

Pilisuk, M., & Rapoport, A. A non-zero-sum game model of some disarmament problems. In W. Isard & J. Walpert (Eds.), *Peace Research Society (International) Papers*, 1964, **1**, 57–78. (b)

Pilisuk, M., & Skolnick, P. Inducing trust: A test of the Osgood proposal. *Journal of Personality & Social Psychology*, 1968, **8**, 121–133.

Pilisuk, M., Skolnick, P., & Overstreet, E. Predicting cooperation from the two sexes in a conflict simulation. *Journal of Personality & Social Psychology*, 1968, **10**, 35–43.

Pilisuk, M., Skolnick, P., Thomas, K., & Chapman, R. Boredom vs. cognitive reappraisal in the development of cooperative strategy. *Journal of Conflict Resolution*, 1967, **11**, 110–116.

Pilisuk, M., Winter, J.A., Chapman, R., & Haas, N. Honesty, deceit, and timing in the display of intentions. *Behavioral Science*, 1967, **12**, 205–215.

Podell, J.E., & Knapp, W.M. The effect of mediation on the perceived firmness of the opponent. *Journal of Conflict Resolution*, 1969, **13**, 511–520.

Pollatschek, M.A., & Avi-Itzhak, B. Algorithms for stochastic games with geometrical interpretations. *Management Science*, 1969, **15**, 399–415.

Proshansky, H.M., Ittelson, W.H., & Rivlin, L.G. (Eds.). *Environmental psychology: Man and his physical setting*. New York: Holt, 1970.

Pruitt, D.G. An analysis of responsiveness between nations. *Journal of Conflict Resolution*, 1962, **6**, 5–18.

Pruitt, D.G. Reward structure and cooperation: The decomposed prisoner's dilemma game. *Journal of Personality & Social Psychology*, 1967, **7**, 21–27.

Pruitt, D.G. Reciprocity and credit building in a laboratory dyad. *Journal of Personality & Social Psychology*, 1968, **8**, 143–147.

Pruitt, D.G. Stability and sudden change in interpersonal and international affairs. *Journal of Conflict Resolution*, 1969, **13**, 18–38.

Pruitt, D.G. Motivational processes in the decomposed prisoner's dilemma game. *Journal of Personality & Social Psychology*, 1970, **14**, 227–238.

Pruitt, D.G. Indirect communication and the search for agreement in negotiation. *Journal of Applied Social Psychology*, 1971, **1**, 205–239.

Pruitt, D.G., & Drews, J.L. The effect of time pressure, time elapsed, and the opponent's concession rate on behavior in negotiation. *Journal of Experimental Social Psychology*, 1969, **5**, 43–60.

Pruitt, D.G., & Johnson, D.F. Mediation as an aid to face saving in negotiation. *Journal of Personality & Social Psychology*, 1970, **14**, 239–246.

Psathas, G., & Stryker, S. Bargaining behavior and orientations in coalition formation. *Sociometry*, 1965, **28**, 124–144.

Pylyshyn, Z., Agnew, N., & Illingworth, J. Comparison of individuals and pairs as participants in a mixed-motive game. *Journal of Conflict Resolution*, 1966, **10**, 211–220.

Pyron, B. Choice behavior in game playing situations as a function of amount and probability of reinforcement. *Journal of Experimental Psychology*, 1964, **68**, 420–421.

Quandt, R.E. On the use of game models in theories of international relations. In K. Knorr & S. Verba (Eds.), *The international system: Theoretical essays*. Princeton, New Jersey: Princeton Univ. Press, 1961.

Rabinowitz, L., Kelley, H.H., & Rosenblatt, R.M. Effects of different types of interdependence and response conditions in the minimal social situation. *Journal of Experimental Social Psychology*, 1966, **2**, 169–197.

Radinsky, T.L., & Myers, D.G. The influence of an advantaged third person on collaboration in a prisoner's dilemma game. *Psychonomic Science*, 1968, **13**, 329–330.

Radlow, R. An experimental study of "cooperation" in the prisoner's dilemma game. *Journal of Conflict Resolution*, 1965, **9**, 221–227.

Radlow, R., & Weidner, M.F. Unenforced commitments in "cooperative" and "non-cooperative" non-constant-sum games. *Journal of Conflict Resolution*, 1966, **10**, 497–505.

Radlow, R., Weidner, M.F., & Hurst, P.M. The effect of incentive magnitude and "motivational orientation" upon choice behavior in a two-person nonzero-sum game. *Journal of Social Psychology*, 1968, **74**, 199–208.

Randolph, L. A suggested model of international negotiation. *Journal of Conflict Resolution*, 1966, **10**, 344–353.

Rapoport, Am. A study of human control in a stochastic multistage decision task. *Behavioral Science*, 1966, **11**, 18–32.

Rapoport, Am. Optimal policies for the prisoner's dilemma. *Psychological Review*, 1967, **74**, 136–148.

Rapoport, Am. Choice behavior in a Markovian decision task. *Journal of Mathematical Psychology*, 1968, **5**, 163–181.

Rapoport, Am. Effects of payoff information in multistage mixed-motive games. *Behavioral Science*, 1969, **14**, 205–215.

Rapoport, Am., & Cole, N.S. Experimental studies of interdependent mixed-motive games. *Behavioral Science*, 1968, **13**, 189–204.

Rapoport, Am., Kahan, J.P., & Stein, W.E. Decisions of timing in conflict situations of incomplete information. *Behavioral Science*, 1973, **18**, 272–287.

Rapoport, Am., & Mowshowitz, A. Experimental studies of stochastic models for the prisoner's dilemma. *Behavioral Science*, 1966, **11**, 444–458.

Rapoport, An. Critiques of game theory. *Behavioral Science*, 1959, **4**, 49–66.

Rapoport, An. *Fights, games, and debates.* Ann Arbor, Michigan: Univ. of Michigan Press, 1960.

Rapoport, An. Three modes of conflict. *Management Science*, 1961, **7**, 210–218.

Rapoport, An. The use and misuse of game theory. *Scientific American*, 1962, **207**:6:108–118.

Rapoport, An. Mathematical models of social interaction. In R.D. Luce, R.R. Bush, & E. Galanter (Eds.), *Handbook of mathematical psychology.* Vol. II. New York: Wiley, 1963. (a)

Rapoport, An. Formal games as probing tools for investigating behavior motivated by trust and suspicion. *Journal of Conflict Resolution*, 1963, **7**, 570–579. (b)

Rapoport, An. Critique of strategic thinking. In R. Fisher (Ed.), *International conflict and behavioral science: The Craigville papers.* New York: Basic Books, 1964. (a)

Rapoport, An. Tacit communication in experiments in conflict and cooperation. *International Psychiatric Clinics*, 1964, **1**, 225–244. (b)

Rapoport, An. A stochastic model for the prisoner's dilemma. In J. Gurland (Ed.), *Stochastic models in medicine and biology.* Madison, Wisconsin: Univ. of Wisconsin Press, 1964. (c)

Rapoport, An. *Strategy and conscience.* New York: Harper and Row, 1964. (d)

Rapoport, An. Game theory and intergroup hostility. In M. Berkowitz & P.G. Bock (Eds.), *American national security: A reader in theory and policy.* New York: Free Press, 1965.

Rapoport, An. Experiments in dyadic conflict and cooperation. *Bulletin of the Menninger Clinic*, 1966, **30**, 284–291. (a)

Rapoport, An. Laboratory studies of conflict and cooperation. In J.R. Lawrence (Ed.), *Operational research and the social sciences.* New York: Tavistock Publications, 1966. (b)

Rapoport, An. Strategic and non-strategic approaches to problems of security and peace. In K. Archibald (Ed.), *Strategic interaction and conflict: Original papers and discussion.* Berkeley, California: Institute of International Studies, 1966. (c)

Rapoport, An. *Two-person game theory: The essential ideas.* Ann Arbor, Michigan: Univ. of Michigan Press, 1966. (d)

Rapoport, An. Exploiter, leader, hero, and martyr: The four archetypes of the 2 × 2 game. *Behavioral Science*, 1967, **12**, 81–84. (a)

Rapoport, An. A note on the "index of cooperation" for prisoner's dilemma. *Journal of Conflict Resolution*, 1967, **11**, 100–103. (b)

Rapoport, An. Games which simulate deterrence and disarmament. *Peace Research Reviews*, 1967, **1**, 1–76. (c)

Rapoport, An. Prospects for experimental games. *Journal of Conflict Resolution*, 1968, **12**, 461–470.

Rapoport, An. Conflict resolution in the light of game theory and beyond. In P. Swingle (Ed.), *The structure of conflict*. New York: Academic Press, 1970.

Rapoport, An. *Experimental games and their uses in psychology*. Morristown, New Jersey: General Learning Press, 1973.

Rapoport, An., & Chammah, A.M. Sex differences in factors contributing to the level of cooperation in the prisoner's dilemma game. *Journal of Personality & Social Psychology*, 1965, **2**, 831–838. (a)

Rapoport, An., & Chammah, A.M. *Prisoner's dilemma: A study in conflict and cooperation*. Ann Arbor, Michigan: Univ. of Michigan Press, 1965. (b)

Rapoport, An., & Chammah, A.M. The game of chicken. *American Behavioral Scientist*, 1966, **10**, 10–28.

Rapoport, An., Chammah, A., Dwyer, J., & Gyr, J. Three person non-zero-sum non-negotiable games. *Behavioral Science*, 1962, **7**, 38–58.

Rapoport, An., & Dale, P.S. The "end" and "start" effects in iterated prisoner's dilemma. *Journal of Conflict Resolution*. 1966, **10**, 363–366. (a)

Rapoport, An., & Dale, P. Models for prisoner's dilemma. *Journal of Mathematical Psychology*, 1966, **3**, 269–286. (b)

Rapoport, An., & Guyer, M. A taxonomy of 2 × 2 games. *General Systems*, 1966, **11**, 203–214.

Rapoport, An., & Orwant, C. Experimental games: A review. *Behavioral Science*, 1962, **7**, 1–37.

Rappoport, L.H. Interpersonal conflict in a probabilistic situation. *Dissertation Abstracts*, 1964, **25**, 669.

Rappoport, L.H. Interpersonal conflict in cooperative and uncertain situations. *Journal of Experimental Social Psychology*, 1965, **1**, 323–333.

Rappoport, L. Cognitive conflict as a function of socially-induced cognitive differences. *Journal of Conflict Resolution*, 1969, **13**, 143–148.

Raven, B.H., & Eachus, H.T. Cooperation and competition in means-interdependent triads. *Journal of Abnormal & Social Psychology*, 1963, **67**, 307–316.

Raven, B.H., & Kruglanski, A.W. Conflict and power. In P. Swingle (Ed.), *The structure of conflict*. New York: Academic Press, 1970.

Raven, B.H., & Rubin, J.Z. *People in groups*. New York: Wiley, in press.

Raven, B.H., & Shaw, J.I. Interdependence and group problem-solving in the triad. *Journal of Personality & Social Psychology*, 1970, **14**, 157–165.

Reichardt, R. Three-person games with imperfect coalitions: A sociologically relevant concept in game theory. *General Systems*, 1968, **13**, 189–204.

Rekosh, J.H., & Feigenbaum, K.D. The necessity of mutual trust for cooperative behavior in a two-person game. *Journal of Social Psychology*, 1966, **69**, 149–154.

Restle, F. Review of A. Rapoport, "Fights, games, and debates." *Contemporary Psychology*, 1963, **8**, 1–2.

Richman, J.L. An analysis of the concept of cooperation in the prisoner's dilemma game: Some need structure correlates. *Dissertation Abstracts*, 1971, **31**, 6162–6163–A.

Riker, W.H. *The theory of political coalitions.* New Haven, Connecticut: Yale Univ. Press, 1962.

Riker, W.H. Bargaining in a three-person game. *American Political Science Review,* 1967, **61**, 642–656.

Riker, W.H., & Niemi, R.G. Anonymity and rationality in the essential three-person game. *Human Relations,* 1964, **17**, 131–141.

Robertson, J.G., Jr. Decision making in two-person two-choice zero-sum games under different incentive conditions. *Dissertation Abstracts,* 1961, **22**, 337.

Robinson, C., & Wilson, W. Intergroup attitudes and strategies in non zero sum dilemma games: II. Selective bias in both authoritarians and nonauthoritarians. Unpublished manuscript, Univ. of Hawaii, Honolulu, Hawaii, 1965.

Roby, T.B. Commitment. *Behavioral Science,* 1960, **5**, 253–264.

Roby, T.B. Utility and futurity. *Behavioral Science,* 1962, **7**, 194–210.

Roby, T.B., & Rubin, J.Z. An exploratory study of competitive temporal judgment. *Behavioral Science,* 1973, **18**, 42–51.

Rokeach, M. *The open and closed mind.* New York: Basic Books, 1960.

Roos, L.L., Jr. Toward a theory of cooperation: Experiments using nonzero-sum games. *Journal of Social Psychology,* 1966, **69**, 277–289.

Rosen, S. The comparative roles of informational and material commodities in interpersonal transactions. *Journal of Experimental Social Psychology,* 1966, **2**, 211–226.

Rosenberg, S. Cooperative behavior in dyads as a function of reinforcement parameters. *Journal of Abnormal & Social Psychology,* 1960, **60**, 318–333.

Rosenberg, S. Influence and reward in structured two-person interactions. *Journal of Abnormal & Social Psychology,* 1963, **67**, 379–387.

Rosenberg, S. An experimental test of a stochastic model of intrapersonal conflict in a two-person situation. *Journal of Mathematical Psychology,* 1968, **5**, 281–299.

Rosenberg, S., & Schoeffler, M.S. Stochastic learning models for social competition. *Journal of Mathematical Psychology,* 1965, **2**, 219–241.

Rosenblatt, P.C. Functions of games: An examination of individual difference hypotheses derived from a cross-cultural study. *Journal of Social Psychology,* 1962, **58**, 17–22.

Rotter, J. Generalized expectancies for internal versus external control of reinforcement. *Psychological Monographs,* 1966, **80** (1, Whole No. 609).

Rubin, J.Z. Review of P. Swingle (Ed.), "The structure of conflict." *Contemporary Psychology,* 1971, **16**, 436–437. (a)

Rubin, J.Z. The nature and success of influence attempts in a four-party bargaining relationship. *Journal of Experimental Social Psychology,* 1971, **7**, 17–35. (b)

Rubin, J.Z., & DiMatteo, M.R. Factors affecting the magnitude of subjective utility parameters in a tacit bargaining game. *Journal of Experimental Social Psychology,* 1972, **8**, 412–426.

Rubin, J.Z., Greller, M., & Roby, T.B. Factors affecting the magnitude and proportionality of solutions to problems of coordination. *Perceptual and Motor Skills,* 1974, **39**, 599–618.

Rubin, J.Z., & Lewicki, R.J. A three-factor experimental analysis of promises and threats. *Journal of Applied Social Psychology,* 1973, **3**, 240–257.

Rubin, J.Z., Lewicki, R.J., & Dunn, L. Perception of promisors and threateners. *Proceedings of the 81st Annual Convention of the American Psychological Association,* 1973, **8**, 141–142.

Rubin, J.Z., Steinberg, B.D., & Gerrein, J.R. How to obtain the right of way: An experimental analysis of behavior at intersections. *Perceptual and Motor Skills,* 1974, **39**, 1263–1274.

Sampson, E.E., & Kardush, M. Age, sex, class, and race differences in response to a two-person non-zero-sum game. *Journal of Conflict Resolution*, 1965, **9**, 212–220.

Saraydar, E. An exploration of unresolved problems in bargaining theory. *Dissertation Abstracts*, 1968, **29**, 49–50–A.

Sawyer, J., & Friedell, M.F. The interaction screen: An operational model for experimentation on interpersonal behavior. *Behavioral Science*, 1965, **10**, 446–460.

Sawyer, J., & Guetzkow, H. Bargaining and negotiation in international relations. In H.C. Kelman (Ed.), *International behavior: A social-psychological analysis*. New York: Holt Rinehart, and Winston, 1965.

Sawyer, J., & MacRae, D., Jr. Game theory and cumulative voting in Illinois: 1902–1954. *American Political Science Review*, 1962, **56**, 936–946.

Scarf, H.E. Core of an *n*-person game. *Econometrica*, 1967, **35**, 50–69.

Scheff, T.J. Toward a sociological model of consensus. *American Sociological Review*, 1967, **32**, 32–46. (a)

Scheff, T.J. A theory of social coordination applicable to mixed-motive games. *Sociometry*, 1967, **30**, 215–234. (b)

Schellenberg, J.A. Distributive justice and collaboration in non-zero-sum games. *Journal of Conflict Resolution*, 1964, **8**, 147–150.

Schellenberg, J.A. Dependence and cooperation. *Sociometry*, 1965, **28**, 158–172.

Schelling, T.C. An essay on bargaining. *American Economic Review*, 1956, **46**, 281–306.

Schelling, T.C. Bargaining, communication, and limited war. *Journal of Conflict Resolution*, 1957, **1**, 19–36.

Schelling, T.C. The strategy of conflict: Prospectus for a reorientation of game theory. *Journal of Conflict Resolution*, 1958, **2**, 203–264.

Schelling, T.C. For the abandonment of symmetry in game theory. *Review of Economics and Statistics*, 1959, **41**, 213–224.

Schelling, T.C. *The strategy of conflict*. Cambridge, Massachusetts: Harvard Univ. Press, 1960.

Schelling, T.C. The future of arms control. *Operations Research*, 1961, **9**, 722–731. (a)

Schelling, T.C. Experimental games and bargaining theory. In K. Knorr & S. Verba (Eds.), *The international system: Theoretical essays*. Princeton, New Jersey: Princeton Univ. Press, 1961. (b)

Schelling, T.C. *Arms and influence*. New Haven, Connecticut: Yale Univ. Press, 1966. (a)

Schelling, T.C. Uncertainty, brinksmanship, and the game of "chicken." In K. Archibald (Ed.), *Strategic interaction and conflict: Original papers and discussion*. Berkeley, California: Institute of International Studies, 1966. (b)

Schelling, T.C. Game theory and the study of ethical systems. *Journal of Conflict Resolution*, 1968, **12**, 34–44.

Schenitzki, D.P. Bargaining, group decision making and the attainment of maximum joint outcome. *Dissertation Abstracts*, 1963, **23**, 3528–3529.

Schiavo, R.S., & Kaufman, J. Effects of instructions and sex upon coalition formation in triads. Paper presented at the meeting of the Eastern Psychological Association, Philadelphia, April 1974.

Schlenker, B.R., Bonoma, T., Tedeschi, J.T., & Pivnick, W.P. Compliance to threats as a function of the wording of the threat and the exploitativeness of the threatener. *Sociometry*, 1970, **33**, 394–408.

Schlenker, B.R., Helm, B., & Tedeschi, J.T. The effects of personality and situational variables on behavioral trust. *Journal of Personality & Social Psychology*, 1973, **25**, 419–427.

Schmitt, D.R., & Marwell, G. Reward and punishment as influence techniques for the achievement of cooperation under inequity. *Human Relations*, 1970, **23**, 37–45.

Schmitt, D.R., & Marwell, G. Withdrawal and reward reallocation as responses to inequity. *Journal of Experimental Social Psychology*, 1972, **8**, 207–221.

Schoen, S.J. Individual differences in conflict tolerance and their relationship to decision-making performance. *Dissertation Abstracts*, 1964, **24**, 3440–3441.

Schutzenberger, M.P. Theory of games. In S.H. Steinberg *et al.* (Eds.), *Mathematics and social sciences*. The Hague: Mouton, 1965.

Schwarz, P. *Coalition bargaining*. Ithaca, New York: New York State School of Industrial and Labor Relations, Cornell Univ., 1970.

Scodel, A. Value orientations and preference for a minimax strategy. *Journal of Psychology*, 1961, **52**, 55–61.

Scodel, A. Induced collaboration in some non-zero-sum games. *Journal of Conflict Resolution*, 1962, **6**, 335–340.

Scodel, A., & Minas, J.S. The behavior of prisoners in a "prisoner's dilemma" game. *Journal of Psychology*, 1960, **50**, 133–138.

Scodel, A., Minas, J.S., Ratoosh, P., & Lipetz, M. Some descriptive aspects of two-person, non-zero-sum games: I. *Journal of Conflict Resolution*, 1959, **3**, 114–119.

Scott, M.B., & Lyman, S.M. Paranoia, homosexuality, and game theory. *Journal of Health & Social Behavior*, 1968, **9**, 179–187.

Sermat, V. Cooperative behavior in a mixed-motive game. *Journal of Social Psychology*, 1964, **62**, 217–239.

Sermat, V. The effects of an initial cooperative or competitive treatment upon a subject's response to conditional cooperation. *Behavioral Science*, 1967, **12**, 301–313. (a)

Sermat, V. The possibility of influencing the other's behaviour and cooperation: Chicken versus prisoner's dilemma. *Canadian Journal of Psychology*, 1967, **21**, 204–219. (b)

Sermat, V. Dominance–submissiveness and competition in a mixed-motive game. *British Journal of Social & Clinical Psychology*, 1968, **7**, 35–44.

Sermat, V. Is game behavior related to behavior in other interpersonal situations? *Journal of Personality & Social Psychology*, 1970, **16**, 92–109.

Sermat, V., & Gregovich, R.P. The effect of experimental manipulation on cooperative behavior in a chicken game. *Psychonomic Science*, 1966, **4**, 435–436.

Shapira, A., & Madsen, M.C. Cooperative and competitive behavior of kibbutz and urban children in Israel. *Child Development*, 1969, **40**, 609–617.

Shapley, L.S. Simple games: An outline of the descriptive theory. *Behavioral Science*, 1962, **7**, 59–67.

Shaw, J.I. Situational factors leading to the acquisition of a "psychological advantage" in competitive negotiations. *Dissertation Abstracts*, 1970, **30**, 5069–5070–A.

Shaw, J.I. Situational factors contributing to a psychological advantage in competitive negotiations. *Journal of Personality & Social Psychology*, 1971, **19**, 251–260.

Shears, L.M. Patterns of coalition formation in two games played by male tetrads. *Behavioral Science*, 1967, **12**, 130–137.

Shears, L.M., & Behrens, M.G. Age and sex differences in payoff demands during tetrad game negotiations. *Child Development*, 1969, **40**, 559–568.

Shepard, H.A. Responses to situations of competition and conflict. In R.L. Kahn & E. Boulding (Eds.), *Power and conflict in organizations*. New York: Basic Books, 1964.

Sheposh, J.P. Reactions to moral and hedonic dilemmas in a mixed-motive game. *Dissertation Abstracts*, 1971, **31**, 6163–6164–A.

Sheposh, J.P., & Gallo, P.S., Jr. Asymmetry of payoff structure and cooperative behavior in the prisoner's dilemma game. *Journal of Conflict Resolution*, 1973, **17**, 321–333.

Sherif, M., & Sherif, C.W. *Social psychology*. New York: Harper and Row, 1969.

Sherman, R. Individual attitude toward risk and choice between prisoner's dilemma games. *Journal of Psychology*, 1967, **66**, 291–298.

Sherman, R. Personality and strategic choice. *Journal of Psychology*, 1968, **70**, 191–197.

Shirer, W.L. *Berlin diary: The journal of a foreign correspondent, 1934–1941*. New York: Knopf, 1941.

Shomer, R.W., Davis, A.H., & Kelley, H.H. Threats and the development of coordination: Further studies of the Deutsch and Krauss trucking game. *Journal of Personality & Social Psychology*, 1966, **4**, 119–126.

Shotola, R.W. Cooperation and interpersonal risk. *Dissertation Abstracts*, 1970, **31**, 1375–A.

Shubik, M. *Strategy and market structure*. New York: Wiley, 1959.

Shubik, M. Games, decisions, and industrial organization. *Management Science*, 1960, **6**, 455–475.

Shubik, M. Some experimental non-zero-sum games with lack of information about the rules. *Management Science*, 1962, **8**, 215–234.

Shubik, M. Some reflections on the design of game theoretic models for the study of negotiation and threats. *Journal of Conflict Resolution*, 1963, **7**, 1–12.

Shubik, M. (Ed.) *Game theory and related approaches to social behavior*. New York: Wiley, 1964.

Shubik, M. On the study of disarmament and escalation. *Journal of Conflict Resolution*, 1968, **12**, 83–101. (a)

Shubik, M. Gaming: Costs and facilities. *Management Science*, 1968, **14**, 629–660. (b)

Shubik, M. Game theory, behavior, and the paradox of the prisoner's dilemma: Three solutions. *Journal of Conflict Resolution*, 1970, **14**, 181–193.

Shubik, M. Games of status. *Behavioral Science*, 1971, **16**, 117–129. (a)

Shubik, M. The dollar auction game: A paradox in noncooperative behavior and escalation. *Journal of Conflict Resolution*, 1971, **15**, 109–111. (b)

Shulman, L. A game-model theory of interpersonal strategies. *Social Work*, 1968, **13**(3), 16–22.

Shure, G.H., & Meeker, R.J. A personality/attitude schedule for use in experimental bargaining studies. Report TM–2543, July 1965, System Development Corporation.

Shure, G.H., & Meeker, R.J. Empirical demonstration of normative behavior in the prisoner's dilemma. *Proceedings of the 76th Annual Convention of the American Psychological Association*, 1968, **3**, 61–62.

Shure, G.H., Meeker, R.J., & Hansford, E.A. The effectiveness of pacifist strategies in bargaining games. *Journal of Conflict Resolution*, 1965, **9**, 106–117.

Shure, G.H., Meeker, R.J., Moore, W.H., Jr., & Kelley, H.H. *Computer studies of bargaining behavior: The role of threat in bargaining*. Santa Monica, California: System Development Corporation, SP2916, 1966.

Sibley, S.A., Senn, S.K., & Epanchin, A. Race and sex of adolescents and cooperation in a mixed-motive game. *Psychonomic Science*, 1968, **13**, 123–124.

Sidorsky, R. Predicting the decision behavior of a knowledgeable opponent. *Human Factors*, 1967, **9**, 541–554.

Sidowski, J.B. Reward and punishment in a minimal social situation. *Journal of Experimental Psychology*, 1957, **54**, 318–326.

Sidowski, J.B., & Smith, M. Sex and game instruction variables in a minimal social situation. *Psychological Reports*, 1961, **8**, 393–397.

Sidowski, J.B., Wyckoff, L.B., & Tabory, L. The influence of reinforcement and punishment in a minimal social situation. *Journal of Abnormal & Social Psychology*, 1956, **52**, 115–119.

Siegel, S., & Fouraker, L.E. *Bargaining and group decision making: Experiments in bilateral monopoly.* New York: McGraw-Hill, 1960.

Siegel, S., & Fouraker, L.E. The effect of level of aspiration on the differential payoff in bargaining by bilateral monopolists. In S. Messick & A.H. Brayfield (Eds.), *Decision and choice: Contributions of Sidney Siegel.* New York: McGraw-Hill, 1964.

Siegel, S., & Harnett, D.L. Bargaining behavior: A comparison between mature industrial personnel and college students. *Operations Research*, 1964, **12**, 334–343.

Siegel, S., Siegel, A.E., & Andrews, J.M. *Choice, strategy, and utility.* New York: McGraw-Hill, 1964.

Silver, R.B. Reactions to commitment to relinquish an alternative and power in a bargaining game. *Dissertation Abstracts*, 1969, **30**, 815–816–A.

Singer, E. A bargaining model for disarmament negotiations. *Journal of Conflict Resolution*, 1963, **7**, 21–25.

Singer, E. Type of gain preferred and strategy on a probabilistic decision-task. *American Journal of Psychology*, 1968, **81**, 36–41.

Sisson, R.L., & Ackoff, R.L. Toward a theory of the dynamics of conflict. Paper presented at the meeting of the Peace Research Society Conference, Philadelphia, 1965.

Slack, B.D., & Cook, J.O. Authoritarian behavior in a conflict situation. *Journal of Personality & Social Psychology*, 1973, **25**, 130–136.

Slusher, E.A., Roering, K.J., & Rose, G.L. The effects of commitment to future interaction in single plays of three games. *Behavioral Science*, 1974, **19**, 119–132.

Smelser, W.T. Dominance as a factor in achievement and perception in cooperative problem solving interactions. *Journal of Abnormal & Social Psychology*, 1961, **62**, 535–542.

Smith, G.F., & Murdoch, P. Performance of informed versus noninformed triads and quartets in the "minimal social situation." *Journal of Personality & Social Psychology*, 1970, **15**, 391–396.

Smith, W.P. Some effects of mediated power in three person groups. *Dissertation Abstracts*, 1964, **24**, 3417.

Smith, W.P. Power structure and authoritarianism in the use of power in the triad. *Journal of Personality*, 1967, **35**, 64–90. (a)

Smith, W.P. Reactions to a dyadic power structure. *Psychonomic Science*, 1967, **7**, 373–374. (b)

Smith, W.P. Precision of control and the use of power in the triad. *Human Relations*, 1968, **21**, 295–310. (a)

Smith, W.P. Reward structure and information in the development of cooperation. *Journal of Experimental Social Psychology*, 1968, **4**, 199–223. (b)

Smith, W.P., & Anderson, A.J. Threats, communication and bargaining. Unpublished manuscript. Vanderbilt Univ., Nashville, Tennessee, 1972.

Smith, W.P., & Emmons, T.D. Outcome information and competitiveness in interpersonal bargaining. *Journal of Conflict Resolution*, 1969, **13**, 262–270.

Solomon, La. N. Review of R. Fisher (Ed.), "International conflict and behavioral science." *Contemporary Psychology*, 1965, **10**, 432–433.

Solomon, L. The influence of some types of power relationships and game strategies upon the development of interpersonal trust. *Journal of Abnormal & Social Psychology*, 1960, **61**, 223–230.

Solomon, L. Experimental studies of tacit coordination: A comparison of schizophrenic and normal samples. Unpublished manuscript, Boston Univ., Boston, Massachusetts, 1962.

Solomon, L. The psychological effects of interpersonal threat: The implications of some experimental bargaining studies. Paper presented at the meeting of the Congress of Scientists on Survival, New York City, 1964.

Solomon, L. The influence of varying role requirements and premorbid level of adjustment upon role taking behavior in schizophrenics. Paper presented at the meeting of the Eastern Psychological Association, New York, April, 1966.

Sommer, R. Further studies of small group ecology. *Sociometry*, 1965, **28**, 337–348.

Sommer, R. Small group ecology. *Psychological Bulletin*, 1967, **67**, 145–151.

Sommer, R. *Personal space: The behavioral basis of design.* Englewood Cliffs, New Jersey: Prentice-Hall, 1969.

Soults, D.J. Asymptotic value distributions for matrix games. *Dissertation Abstracts*, 1969, **29**, 3532–B.

Speer, D.C. Marital dysfunctionality and two-person non-zero-sum game behavior: Cumulative monadic measures. *Journal of Personality & Social Psychology*, 1972, **21**, 18–24.

Stagner, R. Review of A. Rapoport, "Strategy and conscience," *Contemporary Psychology*, 1965, **10**, 291–293.

Stahelski, A.J., & Kelley, H.H. Sex and incentive in the prisoner's dilemma game. Unpublished manuscript, Univ. of California, Los Angeles, California, 1969.

Starbuck, W.H. Level of aspiration theory and economic behavior. *Behavioral Science*, 1963, **8**, 128–136.

Starbuck, W.H., & Kobrow, E. The effects of advisors on business game teams. *American Behavioral Scientist*, 1966, **10**, 28–30.

Steele, M.W., Jr. Matrix indexes and behavior in mixed-motive games. *Dissertation Abstracts*, 1967, **28**, 1240–B.

Steele, M.W., & Tedeschi, J.T. Matrix indices and strategy choices in mixed-motive games. *Journal of Conflict Resolution*, 1967, **11**, 198–205.

Stevens, C.M. On the theory of negotiation. *Quarterly Journal of Economics*, 1958, **72**, 77–97.

Stevens, C.M. *Strategy and collective bargaining negotiation.* New York: McGraw-Hill, 1963.

Stevens, O.J. Behavior patterns in power-nonsymmetric simulated conflict models: An experimental investigation. *Dissertation Abstracts*, 1970, **30**, 5527–A.

Stevenson, M.B., & Phillips, J.L. Entrapment in 2 × 2 games with force vulnerable equilibria. *Behavioral Science*, 1972, **17**, 361–370.

Stimpson, D.V., & Bass, B.M. Dyadic behavior of self-, interactive-, and task-oriented subjects in a test situation. *Journal of Abnormal & Social Psychology*, 1964, **68**, 558–562.

Stone, J.J. An experiment in bargaining games. *Econometrica*, 1958, **26**, 286–296.

Streufert, S., Clardy, M.A., Driver, M.J., Karlins, M., Schroder, H.M., & Suedfeld, P. A tactical game for the analysis of complex decision making in individuals and groups. *Psychological Reports*, 1965, **17**, 723–729.

Streufert, S., Kliger, S.C., Castore, C.H., & Driver, M.J. Tactical and negotiations game for analysis of decision integration across decision areas. *Psychological Reports*, 1967, **20**, 155–157.

Streufert, S., Streufert, S.C., & Castore, C.H. Leadership in negotiations and the complexity of conceptual structure. *Journal of Applied Psychology*, 1968, **52**, 218–223.

Strodtbeck, F.L. Husband-wife interaction over revealed differences. *American Sociological Review*, 1951, **16**, 468–473.

Stryker, S. Coalition behavior. In C.G. McClintock (Ed.), *Experimental social psychology.* New York: Holt, 1972.

Stryker, S., & Psathas, G. Research on coalitions in the triad: Findings, problems and strategy. *Sociometry*, 1960, **23**, 217–230.

Summers, D.A. Conflict, compromise, and belief change in a decision-making task. *Journal of Conflict Resolution*, 1968, **12**, 215–221.

Suppes, P.C., & Atkinson, R.C. *Markov learning models for multiperson interactions*. Stanford, California: Stanford Univ. Press, 1960.

Suppes, P., & Carlsmith, J.M. Experimental analysis of a duopoly situation from the standpoint of mathematical learning theory. *International Economic Review*, 1962, 3, 60–78.

Swensson, R.G. Cooperation in the prisoner's dilemma game I: The effects of asymmetric payoff information and explicit communication. *Behavioral Science*, 1967, **12**, 314–322.

Swingle, P.G. The effects of cognitive incompatibility upon the maintenance of cooperative behavior. *Dissertation Abstracts*, 1965, **26**, 2342–2343.

Swingle, P.G. Effects of the emotional relationship between protagonists in a two-person game. *Journal of Personality & Social Psychology*, 1966, 4, 270–279.

Swingle, P.G. The effects of the win-loss difference upon cooperative responding in a "dangerous" game. *Journal of Conflict Resolution*, 1967, **11**, 214–222.

Swingle, P.G. Illusory power in a dangerous game. *Canadian Journal of Psychology*, 1968, **22**, 176–185. (a)

Swingle, P.G. Effects of prior exposure to cooperative or competitive treatment upon subject's responding in the prisoner's dilemma. *Journal of Personality & Social Psychology*, 1968, **10**, 44–52. (b)

Swingle, P.G. Ethnic factors in interpersonal bargaining. *Canadian Journal of Psychology*, 1969, **23**, 136–146.

Swingle, P.G. Exploitative behavior in non-zero-sum games. *Journal of Personality & Social Psychology*, 1970, **16**, 121–132. (a)

Swingle, P.G. Dangerous games. In P. Swingle (Ed.), *The structure of conflict*. New York: Academic Press, 1970. (b)

Swingle, P.G., & Coady, H. Effects of the partner's abrupt strategy change upon subject's responding in the prisoner's dilemma. *Journal of Personality & Social Psychology*, 1967, **5**, 357–363.

Swingle, P.G., & Gillis, J.S. Effects of the emotional relationship between protagonists in the prisoner's dilemma. *Journal of Personality & Social Psychology*, 1968, **8**, 160–165.

Swingle, P.G., & MacLean, B. The effect of illusory power in non-zero-sum games. *Journal of Conflict Resolution*, 1971, **15**, 513–522.

Swingle, P.G., & Santi, A. Communication in non-zero-sum games. *Journal of Personality & Social Psychology*, 1972, **23**, 54–63.

Swinth, R.L. Review of R.E. Walton and R.B. McKersie, "A behavioral theory of labor negotiations: An analysis of a social interaction system." *Contemporary Psychology*, 1967, **12**, 183–184. (a)

Swinth, R.L. The establishment of the trust relationship. *Journal of Conflict Resolution*, 1967, **11**, 335–344. (b)

Swinth, R. Artifacts in the Siegel-Fouraker study of bargaining and group decision making. *Management Science*, 1969, **16**, 85–93.

Swirsky, L.J. Conflict and co-operation on the conflict board: A new mixed-motive game. *Dissertation Abstracts*, 1968, **29**, 656–657–A.

Symonds, G.H. A study of management behavior by use of competitive business games. *Management Science*, 1964, **11**, 135–153.

Symonds, G.H. A study of consumer behavior by use of competitive business games. *Management Science*, 1968, **14**, 473–485.

Tedeschi, J.T. Threats and promises. In P. Swingle (Ed.), *The structure of conflict.* New York: Academic Press, 1970.

Tedeschi, J.T. (Ed.). *The social influence processes.* Chicago, Illinois: Aldine-Atherton, 1972.

Tedeschi, J., Aranoff, D., & Gahagan, J. Discrimination of outcomes in a prisoner's dilemma game. *Psychonomic Science,* 1968, **11**, 301–302. (a)

Tedeschi, J., Aranoff, D., Gahagan, J., & Hiester, D. The partial reinforcement effect and the prisoner's dilemma. *Journal of Social Psychology,* 1968, **75**, 209–215. (b)

Tedeschi, J.T., Bonoma, T.V., & Brown, R.C. A paradigm for the study of coercive power. *Journal of Conflict Resolution,* 1971, **15**, 197–223.

Tedeschi, J.T., Bonoma, T., & Lindskold, S. Threateners' reactions to prior announcement of behavioral compliance or defiance. *Behavioral Science,* 1970, **15**, 171–179. (a)

Tedeschi, J.T., Bonoma, T., & Novinson, N. Behavior of a threatener: Retaliation vs. fixed opportunity costs. *Journal of Conflict Resolution,* 1970, **14**, 69–76. (b)

Tedeschi, J., Burrill, D., & Gahagan, J. Social desirability, manifest anxiety, and social power. *Journal of Social Psychology,* 1969, **77**, 231–239. (a)

Tedeschi, J.T., Gahagan, J.P., Aranoff, D., & Steele, M.W. Realism and optimism in the prisoner's dilemma game. *Journal of Social Psychology,* 1968, **75**, 191–197. (c)

Tedeschi, J.T., Hiester, D., & Gahagan, J.P. Matrix values and the behavior of children in the prisoner's dilemma game. *Child Development,* 1969, **40**, 517–527. (b)

Tedeschi, J.T., Hiester, D.S., & Gahagan, J.P. Trust and the prisoner's dilemma game. *Journal of Social Psychology,* 1969, **79**, 43–50. (c)

Tedeschi, J., Hiester, D., Lesnick, S., & Gahagan, J. Start effect and response bias in the prisoner's dilemma game. *Psychonomic Science,* 1968, **11**, 149–150. (d)

Tedeschi, J., Horai, J., Lindskold, S., & Faley, T. The effects of opportunity costs and target compliance on the behavior of a threatening source. *Journal of Experimental Social Psychology,* 1970, **6**, 205–213. (c)

Tedeschi, J., Lesnick, S., & Gahagan, J. Feedback and "washout" effects in the prisoner's dilemma game. *Journal of Personality & Social Psychology,* 1968, **10**, 31–34. (e)

Tedeschi, J.T., Lindskold, S., Horai, J., & Gahagan, J.P. Social power and the credibility of promises. *Journal of Personality & Social Psychology,* 1969, **13**, 253–261. (d)

Tedeschi, J.T., Powell, J., Lindskold, S., & Gahagan, J.P. The patterning of "honored" promises and sex differences in social conflicts. *Journal of Social Psychology,* 1969, **78**, 297–298. (e)

Tedeschi, J.T., Steele, M.W., Gahagan, J.P., & Aranoff, D. Intentions, predictions, and patterns of strategy choices in a prisoner's dilemma game. *Journal of Social Psychology,* 1968, **75**, 199–207. (f)

Teger, A.I. The effect of early cooperation on the escalation of conflict. *Journal of Experimental Social Psychology,* 1970, **6**, 187–204.

Terhune, K.W. Motives, situation, and interpersonal conflict within prisoner's dilemma. *Journal of Personality & Social Psychology Monograph Supplement,* 1968, **8**, 1–24.

Terhune, K.W. The effects of personality in cooperation and conflict. In P. Swingle (Ed.), *The structure of conflict.* New York: Academic Press, 1970.

Terhune, K.W., & Firestone, J.M. Psychological studies in social interaction and motives (SIAM), Phase 2: Group motives in an international relations game. CAL Report VX-2018-G-2, March 1967, Cornell Aeronautical Laboratory, Buffalo, New York.

Thibaut, J. The development of contractual norms in bargaining: Replication and variation. *Journal of Conflict Resolution,* 1968, **12**, 102–112.

Thibaut, J.W., & Coules, J. The role of communication in the reduction of interpersonal hostility. *Journal of Abnormal & Social Psychology,* 1952, **47**, 770–777.

Thibaut, J., & Faucheux, C. The development of contractual norms in a bargaining situation under two types of stress. *Journal of Experimental Social Psychology,* 1965, **1,** 89–102.

Thibaut, J., & Gruder, C.L. Formation of contractual agreements between parties of unequal power. *Journal of Personality & Social Psychology,* 1969, **11,** 59–65.

Thibaut, J.W., & Kelley, H.H. *The social psychology of groups.* New York: Wiley, 1959.

Thompson, D.D. Attributions of ability from patterns of performance under competitive and cooperative conditions. *Journal of Personality & Social Psychology,* 1972, **23,** 302–308.

Todd, F.J., Hammond, K.R., & Wilkins, M.M. Differential effects of ambiguous and exact feedback on two-person conflict and compromise. *Journal of Conflict Resolution,* 1966, **10,** 88–97.

Tognoli, J.J. Reciprocal behavior in interpersonal information exchange. *Dissertation Abstracts,* 1968, **29,** 1193–1194–B.

Tornatzky, L.G., Jr. The effects of threat, attraction, and balance on interpersonal bargaining. *Dissertation Abstracts,* 1970, **30,** 5527–5528–A.

Tornatzky, L., & Geiwitz, P.J. The effects of threat and attraction on interpersonal bargaining. *Psychonomic Science,* 1968, **13,** 125–126.

Travis, E.J. An investigation of the rational decision making, cooperation, greed, punishment, and withdrawal manifested by schizophrenics in several experimental conflict situations. Unpublished manuscript, Univ. of Michigan, 1965.

Tropper, R. The consequences of investment in the process of conflict. *Journal of Conflict Resolution,* 1972, **16,** 97–98.

Tuchman, B.W. *The guns of August.* New York: Macmillan, 1962.

Tullock, G. Prisoner's dilemma and mutual trust. *Ethics,* 1967, **77,** 229–230.

Turk, T., & Turk, H. Group interaction in a formal setting: The case of the triad. *Sociometry,* 1962, **25,** 48–55.

Tversky, A. Review of A. Rapoport and A.M. Chammah, "Prisoner's dilemma." *Contemporary Psychology,* 1967, **12,** 452–453.

Uejio, C.K., & Wrightsman, L.S. Ethnic-group differences in the relationship of trusting attitudes to cooperative behavior. *Psychological Reports,* 1967, **20,** 563–571.

Uesugi, T.K., & Vinacke, W.E. Strategy in a feminine game. *Sociometry,* 1963, **26,** 75–88.

Ulehla, Z.J. Review of M. Shubik (Ed.), "Game theory and related approaches to social behavior." *Contemporary Psychology,* 1966, **11,** 344.

Umeoka, Y. A 2×2 non-constant-sum game with a coordination problem. *Journal of Conflict Resolution,* 1970, **14,** 99–100.

Van Moeske, P. The truncated-minimax decision criterion. *Psychological Reports,* 1964, **14,** 30.

Vickrey, W. Utility, strategy, and social decision rules. *Quarterly Journal of Economics,* 1960, **74,** 507–535.

Vidmar, N.J. Leadership and role structure in negotiation and other decision-making groups. *Dissertation Abstracts,* 1968, **28,** 3267–3268–A.

Vidmar, N. Effects of representational roles and mediators on negotiation effectiveness. *Journal of Personality & Social Psychology,* 1971, **17,** 48–58.

Vidmar, N., & Hackman, J.R. Interlaboratory generalizability of small groups research: An experimental study. *Journal of Social Psychology,* 1971, **83,** 129–139.

Vidmar, N., & McGrath, J.E. Forces affecting success in negotiation groups. *Behavioral Science,* 1970, **15,** 154–163.

Vinacke, W.E. Sex roles in a three-person game. *Sociometry,* 1959, **22,** 343–360.

Vinacke, W.E. Sex strategies in a competitive game under four incentive conditions. Paper presented at the meeting of the Western Psychological Association, San Jose, California, 1960.

Vinacke, W.E. Intra-group power relations, strategy, and decisions in inter-triad competition. *Sociometry*, 1964, **27**, 25–39.

Vinacke, W.E. Variables in experimental games: Toward a field theory. *Psychological Bulletin*, 1969, **71**, 293–318.

Vinacke, W.E., & Arkoff, A. An experimental study of coalitions in the triad. *American Sociological Review*, 1957, **22**, 406–414.

Vinacke, W.E., Crowell, D.C., Dien, D., & Young, V. The effect of information about strategy on a three person game. *Behavioral Science*, 1966, **11**, 180–189.

Vinacke, W.E., & Gullickson, G.R. Age and sex differences in the formation of coalitions. *Child Development*, 1964, **35**, 1217–1231.

Vinacke, W.E., Lichtman, C.M., & Cherulnik, P.D. Coalition formation under different conditions of play in a three-person competitive game. *Journal of General Psychology*, 1967, **77**, 165–176.

Vinacke, W.E., Mogy, R., Powers, W., Langan, C., & Beck, R. Accommodative strategy and communication in a three-person game. *Journal of Personality & Social Psychology*, 1974, **29**, 509–525.

Vincent, J.E., & Schwerin, E.W. Ratios of force and escalation in a game situation. *Journal of Conflict Resolution*, 1971, **15**, 489–511.

Vincent, J.E., & Tindell, J.O. Alternative cooperative strategies in a bargaining game. *Journal of Conflict Resolution*, 1969, **13**, 494–510.

Vitz, P.C., & Kite, W.R. Factors affecting conflict and negotiation within an alliance. *Journal of Experimental Social Psychology*, 1970, **6**, 233–247.

Voissem, N.H., & Sistrunk, F. Communication schedule and cooperative game behavior. *Journal of Personality & Social Psychology*, 1971, **19**, 160–167.

Von Neumann, J., & Morgenstern, O. *Theory of games and economic behavior*. Princeton, New Jersey: Princeton Univ. Press, 1947.

Wagner, A.B. The use of process analysis in business decision games. *Journal of Applied Behavioral Science*, 1965, **1**, 387–408.

Wahlin, W.S. Machiavellianism and winning or losing mathematical games. *Dissertation Abstracts*, 1967, **28**, 1905–1906–A.

Walker, M.B. Caplow's theory of coalitions in the triad reconsidered. *Journal of Personality & Social Psychology*, 1973, **27**, 409–412.

Wallace, D.G. Group loyalty, communication, and trust in a mixed-motive game. *Dissertation Abstracts*, 1967, **27**, 4569–B.

Wallace, D., & Rothaus, P. Communication, group loyalty, and trust in the PD game. *Journal of Conflict Resolution*, 1969, **13**, 370–380.

Walton, R.E. Leadership strategies for achieving membership consensus during negotiations. *Proceedings of the 18th Annual Meeting of the Industrial Relations Research Association*, December 1965, 1–12.

Walton, R.E. *Interpersonal peacemaking: Confrontations and third-party consultation*. Reading, Massachusetts: Addison-Wesley, 1969.

Walton, R.E., & McKersie, R.B. *A behavioral theory of labor negotiations: An analysis of a social interaction system*. New York: McGraw-Hill, 1965.

Walton, R.E., & McKersie, R.B. Behavioral dilemmas in mixed-motive decision making. *Behavioral Science*, 1966, **11**, 370–384.

Wandell, W.A. Group membership and communication in a prisoner's dilemma setting. *Dissertation Abstracts*, 1968, **28**, 4767–4768–B.

Watson, D., & Bromberg, B. Power, communication, and position satisfaction in task-oriented groups. *Journal of Personality & Social Psychology*, 1965, **2**, 859–864.

Weil, R.L., Jr. The n-person prisoner's dilemma: Some theory and a computer-oriented approach. *Behavioral Science*, 1966, **11**, 227–234.

Wells, R.B. The control of disruptive behavior in a bargaining game. *Dissertation Abstracts*, 1968, **28**, 3268–A.

White, R.K. Misperception and the Vietnam war. *Journal of Social Issues*, 1966, **22**, (Whole No. 3).

White, W.L. Cross-cultural bargaining and game behavior. *Proceedings of the IX Congress of the Inter-American Society of Psychology*, 1964.

Whitworth, R.H., & Lucker, W.G. Effective manipulation of cooperation with college and culturally disadvantaged populations. *Proceedings of the 77th Annual Convention of the American Psychological Association*, 1969, **4**, 305–306.

Wichman, H. Effects of isolation and communication on cooperation in a two-person game. *Journal of Personality & Social Psychology*, 1970, **16**, 114–120.

Wiley, M.G.M. Sex differences in cooperation and competition. *Dissertation Abstracts*, 1969, **29**, 3223–3224–A.

Williams, C.D., Steele, M.W., & Tedeschi, J.T. Motivational correlates of strategy choices in the prisoner's dilemma game. *Journal of Social Psychology*, 1969, **79**, 211–217.

Williams, J.D. *The compleat strategyst: Being a primer on the theory of games of strategy.* New York: McGraw-Hill, 1954.

Willis, R.H. Coalitions in the tetrad. *Sociometry*, 1962, **25**, 358–376.

Willis, R.H. Social influence, information processing, and net conformity in dyads. *Psychological Reports*, 1965, **17**, 147–156.

Willis, R.H., & Hale, J.F. Dyadic interaction as a function of amount of feedback and instructional orientation. *Human Relations*, 1963, **16**, 149–160.

Willis, R.H., & Joseph, M.L. Bargaining behavior: I. "Prominence" as a predictor of the outcome of games of agreement. *Journal of Conflict Resolution*, 1959, **3**, 102–113.

Willis, R.H., & Long, N.J. An experimental simulation of an international truel. *Behavioral Science*, 1967, **12**, 24–33.

Wilson, A.L. An optimal strategy for repeated n-person games. *Behavioral Science*, 1963, **8**, 312–316.

Wilson, K.V., & Bixenstine, V.E. Forms of social control in two-person, two-choice games. *Behavioral Science*, 1962, **7**, 92–102. (a)

Wilson, K.V., & Bixenstine, V.E. Effects of a third choice on behavior in a prisoner's dilemma game. Unpublished manuscript, Kent State Univ., Ohio, 1962. (b)

Wilson, W. Cooperation and the cooperativeness of the other player. *Journal of Conflict Resolution*, 1969, **13**, 110–117.

Wilson, W. Reciprocation and other techniques for inducing cooperation in the prisoner's dilemma game. *Journal of Conflict Resolution*, 1971, **15**, 167–195.

Wilson, W., Chun, H., & Kayatani, M. Projection, attraction, and strategy choices in intergroup competition. *Journal of Personality & Social Psychology*, 1965, **2**, 432–435.

Wilson, W., & Insko, C. Recency effects in face-to-face interaction. *Journal of Personality & Social Psychology*, 1968, **9**, 21–23.

Wilson, W., & Kayatani, M. Intergroup attitudes and strategies in games between opponents of the same or of a different race. *Journal of Personality & Social Psychology*, 1968, **9**, 24–30.

Wilson, W., & Miller, N. Shifts in evaluations of participants following intergroup competition. *Journal of Abnormal & Social Psychology*, 1961, **63**, 428–431.

Wilson, W., & Rickard, H.C. Ingroup versus outgroup choices of strategy made by boys playing a non-zero-sum game. *Psychological Reports*, 1968, **22**, 555–562.

Wilson, W., & Robinson, C. Selective intergroup bias in both authoritarians and non-authoritarians after playing a modified prisoner's dilemma game. *Perceptual and Motor Skills,* 1968, **27**, 1051–1058.

Wilson, W., & Wong, J. Intergroup attitudes towards cooperative vs. competitive opponents in a modified prisoner's dilemma game. *Perceptual and Motor Skills,* 1968, **27**, 1059–1066.

Winter, J.A. Cognitive balance, strategic-balance and discomfort in a competitive situation. *Dissertation Abstracts,* 1964, **25**, 3728–3729.

Wolosin, R.J., Sherman, S.J., & Till, A. Effects of cooperation and competition on responsibility attribution after success and failure. *Journal of Experimental Social Psychology,* 1973, **9**, 220–235.

Wood, D., Pilisuk, M., & Uren, E. The martyr's personality: An experimental investigation. *Journal of Personality & Social Psychology,* 1973, **25**, 177–186.

Worchel, P. Temptation and threat in non-zero-sum games. *Journal of Conflict Resolution,* 1969, **13**, 103–109.

Wrightsman, L.S. Personality and attitudinal correlates of trusting and trustworthy behaviors in a two-person game. *Journal of Personality & Social Psychology,* 1966, **4**, 328–332.

Wrightsman, L.S., Jr., O'Connor, J., & Baker, N.J. (Eds.). *Cooperation and competition: Readings on mixed motive games.* Belmont, California: Brooks/Cole, 1972.

Wyer, R.S. Prediction of behavior in two-person games. *Journal of Personality & Social Psychology,* 1969, **13**, 222–238.

Wyer, R.S., Jr. Effects of outcome matrix and partner's behavior in two-person games. *Journal of Experimental Social Psychology,* 1971, **7**, 190–210.

Wyer, R.S., Jr., & Malinowski, C. Effects of sex and achievement level upon individualism and competitiveness in social interaction. *Journal of Experimental Social Psychology,* 1972, **8**, 303–314.

Wyer, R.S., Jr., & Polen, S.J. Some effects of fate control upon the tendency to benefit an exploitative other. *Journal of Personality & Social Psychology,* 1971, **20**, 44–54.

Yukl, G.A. Effects of situational variables and opponent concessions on a bargainer's perception, aspirations, and concessions. *Journal of Personality & Social Psychology,* 1974, **29**, 227–236.

Zajonc, R.B., & Marin, I.C. Cooperation, competition, and interpersonal attitudes in small groups. *Psychonomic Science,* 1967, **7**, 271–272.

Zellner, A. War and peace: A fantasy in game theory? *Journal of Conflict Resolution,* 1962, **6**, 39–41.

Author Index

Harris, M.G.P., 288, *314*
Harris, R.J., *314*
Harrison, A.A., 188, 237, 238, 270, *314, 322*
Harsanyi, J.C., 131, 132, *314, 315*
Hatton, J.M., 164, 275, *315*
Havens, J.W., *318*
Healy, J.J., 120, *308*
Heider, F., 46, *315*
Heilman, M.E., 285, *315*
Held, V., *315*
Heller, J.R., 163, 270, *315*
Helm, B., 183, 284, *331*
Henry, T., 231, *324*
Hermann, C.F., *315*
Hermann, M.G., 222, *315*
Hiester, D. S., 162, 171, 183, 213, 263, 270, 277, *337*
Higbee, K.L., 169, 173, 284, *303*
Higgs, W.J., 180, 181, *315*
Hill, A.H., *317*
Hill, J.H., 267, *320*
Hill, M., 272, *313*
Hinde, R.A., 97, *315*
Hinton, B.L., 267, *315*
Hoffman, A.J., *315*
Hoffman, P.J., 70, 71, 75, 76, 77, 80, *315*
Hoffman, T.R., *315*
Hoge, P., 242, *310*
Hoggatt, A.C., *315*
Holmes, J.G., 218, *315*
Homans, G.C., 13, 132, 133, *315*
Hopkins, J.R., 242, *310*
Hopkins, R.F., *315*
Horai, J., 171, 172, 186, 213, 215, 270, 284, 286, *303, 311, 315, 337*
Hornik, J., *307*
Hornstein, H.A., 53, 119, 120, 134, 139, 140, 219, 222, 227, 232, 287, *315, 316*
Hottes, J., 172, 173, 174, 277, *317*
Hughes, G.D., 175, 238, *314*
Hurst, P.M., 202, *316, 328*
Hutte, H., *316*
Hylander, L., 230, *303*

I

Iacono, G., 165, 178, 179, 216, 222, *326*
Iklé, F.C., 2, 43, 130, 144, 148, *316*
Illingworth, J., *327*

Insko, C., 169, 272, *340*
Irwin, R., 238, 277, *311*
Isaacs, R., *316*
Ittelson, W.H., 88, *327*

J

Jackson, J.R., *316*
Johnson, D.F., 47, 55, 57, 58, 123, 135, 275, *316, 327*
Johnson, D.W., 53, *316*
Johnson, M.P., 222, *316*
Johnson, R.T., *316*
Jones, B., 213, *316*
Jones, B.R., *305*
Jones, M., *321*
Jones, S.C., 209, *316*
Jonsson, D., *310*
Joseph, M.L., 153, 154, 171, *316, 340*
Jourard, S.M., 90, *316*
Julian, J.W., *316, 322*

K

Kagan, S., 162, 165, 166, *316*
Kahan, J.P., *316, 328*
Kahn, A., 172, 173, 174, 277, *317*
Kanouse, D.E., 169, 202, 242, 248, *317*
Kaplan, K.J., 90, *312*
Kaplowitz, S.A., *317*
Kardush, M., 161, 163, 164, 167, 170, *331*
Karlins, M., *335*
Karp, R.M., *315*
Katonah, G., *317*
Kaufman, J., 171, 204, *331*
Kaufmann, H., 254, 263,
Kayatani, M., 163, 169, *340*
Kee, H.W., 95, 101, *317*
Keiffer, M., 267, *317, 320*
Kelley, H.H., 7, 8, 10, 11, 14, 15, 68, 69, 71, 74, 79, 91, 123, 139, 142, 143, 144, 145, 146, 148, 151, 166, 170, 171, 183, 184, 185, 186, 187, 199, 205, 210, 211, 213, 217, 220, 222, 229, 242, 267, 268, 271, 275, 276, 277, 280, 281, 287, 297, 302, 312, 317, 318, 327, 333, 335, 338

Subject Index